Theoretical and Research Issues in Africana Studies

Edited by James E. Turner

Diasporic Africa Press, Inc

2014 Diasporic Africa Press edition.

ISBN-13: 978-1-937306-23-6
Library of Congress Control Number: 2014938287

Reprinted with the permission of the editor.

Cover image of the African Studies and Research Center building, courtesy of the African Studies and Research Center Library. All rights reserved.

©1984 by the Africana Studies and Research Center, Cornell University. All rights reserved.

CONTENTS

Foreword: Africana Studies and Epistemology, a Discourse in the Sociology of Knowledge   *James E. Turner*   v

Acknowledgments   xxvi

The Artists   xxvii

Introduction   *Jacquelyn L. Haskins*   xxviii

I. From the Maelstrom: Directions in Afro-American History

1. Listen to the Blood: A Preliminary Inquiry into the Meaning of Black History   *Lerone Bennett, Jr.*   1
2. Africana Studies: A Decade of Change, Challenge and Conflict   *John Henrik Clarke*   31

II. The Status of Black Studies: The Second Decade

3. The Status of Black Studies in the Second Decade: The Ideological Imperative   *Tilden LeMelle*   47
4. Intellectual Imperative and Necessity for Black Education   *Shirley N. Weber*   63

III. The Global Significance of African History

5. African Studies and Historical Consciousness   *Lansine Kaba*   77
6. Africa's Contribution: African History in World Context   *I. K. Sundiata*   95

IV. Modernity and Other Directions in Afro-American Literature

7. Modernity and Other Directions in Afro-American Literature: Reflections on Black Literature of the Past Two Decades   *Stephen E. Henderson*   109
8. Afro-American Literature: Its Interpretation and Creation Today in the Light of Historical Considerations   *George E. Kent*   121

V. Theory and Practice: Africana Studies Beyond the Classroom

9. Black Power at Cornell University: Institutions and Identity
   Gayla Cook   143
10. The Nature and Limits of Affirmative Action
    Robert C. Johnson, Jr.   151

VI. Modernity and Other Directions in African and Caribbean Literature

11. The Peopling of a Story: A New View of Characterization in African Literature   *Daniel P. Kunene*   173
12. As a Sounding Brass and a Tinkling Cymbal—Modernist Fallacies and the Responsibility of the Black Writer   *Mike Thelwell*   193

VII. Pan-Africanism and Development in the African World

13. Pan-Africanism, A Contemporary Restatement: Fundamental Goals and Changing Strategies   *W. Ofuatey-Kodjoe*   209
14. Pan-Africanism: From National Liberation to National Reconstruction   *Ronald W. Walters*   233

VIII. Political Economy of the Black World

15. Africanization of Management   *Willard R. Johnson*   257
16. The Political Economy of the Black World—Origins of the Present Crisis   *Bernard Magubane*   281
17. The Political Economy Approach in African Studies
    Nzongola-Ntalaja   301

FOREWORD
Africana Studies and Epistemology:
A Discourse in the Sociology of Knowledge
James E. Turner

> Black Studies begins with the study of Black History . . . because it is relevant, even indispensable to the introduction and development of all the other subject areas. Black history places them in perspective, establishes their origins and development, and thus aids in critical discussion and understanding of them.
> Dr. Maulana Karenga

> We can only understand the present by continually referring to and studying the past; when any one of the intricate phenomena of our daily life puzzles us; when there arise religious problems, political problems, race problems, we must always remember that while their solution lies in the present, their cause and their explanation lie in the past.
> Dr. W. E. B. Du Bois

A decade is actually not much time in the span of history, it is only a short period in the life of a new field of study, and it is inadequate for the full development of a discipline and its complements. But, in another sense, it has been a long ten years, and as might have been expected, along the way there have been many obstacles, serious challenges, and great demands and expectations. However, the achievements during this time have been nothing short of extraordinary.

It was during the summer of 1969 that the Institute of the Black World organized a two-month project for faculty and students to organize a curriculum prototype that would define the conceptual parameters and explain the scholarly method and purpose for what was generally being referred to as *Black Studies*.

The summer workshop was followed by a Black Studies Directors' Seminar on November 7-9 of that same year. The approximately thirty participants came from a cross section of private and public institutions of higher education, and all were involved (under different institutional circumstances) with developing program designs and instructional formats as directors for Black Studies. The significance of this meeting lies in the fact that it was, in a manner of speaking, the founding convention for the field. It was the base for professional association between initial Black Studies educators, a clearinghouse for exchanging critical information, and the launch of

Foreword

our collective endeavor to articulate and operationalize for academic investigation what we meant by the use of the concept *Black Experience*. There was a broad consensus that the field of Africana Studies is a teaching and research enterprise "that is committed to the interpretation and explication of the total phenomenon called the Black Experience." We delineated four basic tasks for the Black Studies scholar: (1) To *defend* (legitimize) against racism and intellectual chauvinism the fundamental right and necessity of Africana Studies, at all levels of American education, for all people, but most especially for African-American people; (2) To *disseminate* (teach and publish) Black Studies social theory and analysis, criticism, and historiography, and to reference the work of pioneering Black scholars; (3) To *generate* (new) knowledge (research) and codify existing information and predicate contemporary study upon the truths formulated by our mentors; (4) To *preserve* the acknowledged value of rare and classical texts in the field (archival and library collections), and maintain the scholarly tradition and rich heritage of African peoples and their descendants.

The reader has undoubtedly noticed at this point that I use "Africana Studies" and "Black Studies" interchangeably. Africana Studies is the more formal and proper terminology, while Black Studies is the more common usage. On this matter I agree with Professor John Henrick Clarke:

> I prefer to use the phrase "Africana Studies" to "Black Studies." Black is an honorable word, and I am glad to see so many people lose their fear of using it, but it has its limitations. Black, or Blackness, tells you how you look without telling you who you are, whereas Africa, or Africana, relates you to land, history, and culture. No people is spiritually and culturally secure until it answers only to a name of its own choosing—a name that instantaneously relates that people to the past, present, and future. As the Caribbean writer Richard B. Moore has said in his book *The Name 'Negro': Its Origin and Evil Use,* "Slaves and dogs are named by their masters. Free men name themselves."[1]

Africana Studies is essentially about renaming self in the world of knowledge and human relations.

The conference organized by the Africana Studies and Research Center at Cornell University was the nexus and logical sequence to the IBW meeting. Some of the key figures from the first meeting were participants at this conference, such as Lerone Bennett, Vincent Harding, William Strickland, Stephen Henderson, and Howard Dotson.

Africana Studies and Epistemology

An introductory essay to a topic as large as the subject of Black Studies will inevitably be selective and representative of the perspective of the writer. However, this book of selected articles is reflective of our continuing intellectual and pedagogical interest in the vitally important task of assessing the progress of the field. The tenth anniversary was certainly a milestone in the life of the Africana Studies and Research Center. It rather naturally occurred to us that this would be a very appropriate occasion to assemble an interdisciplinary group of prominent scholars in Africana Studies, as well as colleagues from other departments and programs from universities across the country, and a selection of some of our best students over the past decade, to exchange ideas about research and teaching experiences. The gathering surpassed our most optimistic expectations and has been widely hailed as the most significant coming together of Africana Studies scholars since the Institute of the Black World meeting.

The development of the Africana Studies and Research Center is quite indicative of the typical pattern generally associated with the concept of the modern Black Studies movement. We trace our origins to the second Black Renaissance of this century during the 1965-75 period, a time of extraordinary intellectual and social ferment and artistic creativity in the African-American community. This period has been generally referred to as the high point of the Black (Arts) Consciousness/Black Power movement. Black students at predominantly white campuses were most often (though not exclusively, as Howard, Jackson State, Fisk, North Carolina A & T, and Atlanta Universities and others were significant) catalysts for promoting the Black Studies proposition at the university and college levels. Black students joined concerned educators and intellectuals in pointing out "the urgent necessity for including the study of African-American experience." Though we refer to a modern stage in Black Studies, we must hasten to point out the fact that, contrary to a broad popularly held belief, Africana Studies is not a recent development. As the author of the preface has explained in a previous monograph, the field has a rich intellectual legacy extending from at least the early nineteenth century, based on the works of such people as Edward Wilmont Blyden, Martin Delaney, Francis Harper, Benjamin Brawley, and Casely Hayford, and from the beginning of this century, with W. E. B. Du Bois, Carter G. Woodson, Leo Hansbury, Arthur

Foreword

Schomburg, Charles S. Johnson, J. A. Rogers, and Ida B. Wells, to name a few. We shall discuss this point further later on in this preface.

There is a unique character to this contemporary stage in the intellectual history of the study of people of African descent. Our social roots (fertilized as they were by the challenges for change of the 1960s) gave rise to an intellectual perspective that proposed that Black Studies would supersede the traditional disciplines by pursuing a holistic structural interpretation in its research and teaching methodology of the Black Experience. Essentially this means a commitment to an interdisciplinary approach in the construction of both social theories and research paradigms of the various dimensions (i.e., social, cultural, political-economic) of African-American societies.

The concept *Africana* is derived from the philosophy of the "African continuum and African consociation," which posits fundamental interconnections in the global Black Experience. Consequently, curriculum is predicated upon a model of Black Studies that begins with the African background and, next, the transformation—slavery—into the African Diaspora, from which the African-American Experience derives textual meaning. The *Black World* is perceived as patterns within a trilateral relationship between Africa, the African Caribbean, and the African Americas with, understandably, primary concentration on African America. Moveover, all segments of the Black world population live under social conditions directly related to the international political economy of advanced industrial capitalism. Africana as a construct is congruent with James Stewart's theory of an "Expansive Model of Black Studies." His paradigm is based on a methodology of Black Studies that transcends and transforms the boundaries of the traditional disciplines into a new *interdiscipline*. An expansive model in Black Studies constitutes an investigative emphasis with an ethnographic orientation. Philosophically its argument is that a more accurate understanding of African-American sociocultural and politico-economic realities is achieved "if the research concerns emanate from their (African-Americans') experience and phenomenological frame of reference."[2] If it is true, and I certainly contend it is, that Anglo-centric (or so-called mainstream) scholarship on the Black Experience is biased towards person-centered variables and *internal* causal contingencies, and attributional schemes with person (group) change implications, then Africana Studies is an "alternative presuppositional perspective"[3] that gives at least as much investigative emphasis to systemic institutional-centered variables and external causal contingencies that impact the life chances and social conditions of Black people. Africana research "which attempts to emanate from the perception and experience of those under study is more apt to illuminate the fact that psychological and behavioral and cultural processes are inextricably linked to their economic-political, social, and situational contexts. Such considerations move the research away from ethnocentric analysis and more toward (systemic) and ethnographic ones,"[4] which is a far more socially useful research on Black people in American society. Stewart's concept *expansive* also assumes a "historical tradition of the linkage between scholarship and activism while simultaneously reflecting the constraints imposed by the contemporary social knowledge and the application of knowledge to promote Black liberation and human dignity."[5]

This is a specifically Black Studies conceptualization of the role for Black intellectuals in terms of their active relationship to the ongoing institutional and organizational process of the African-American community and the oppression and racist inequality that it confronts. An expansive approach to Black Studies assumes that education is based on a philosophy of history. Alkalimat and Bailey, et al., refer to the criticality of a historical focus that elucidates qualitative developments in the dynamic human process; that is the interpretation of history as social analysis, in order to provide an analytical paradigm for the assessment of significant events and quantitative changes in the configuration of society. They posit, particularly in their text *Introduction to Afro-American Studies,* a philosophy of history that associates events with specific time frames, which reflects continuities and discontinuities in the complex of forces that shape the configuration of society. This process is commonly referred to as periodization of the Black Experience. However, to achieve an expansive model in Black Studies the purpose of history must be for higher intellectual exposition than recording and describing the facts of events. Evidentiary statements in historical documentation must give more than a chronicle and should present instead an interpretation that penetrates the social meaning, in human terms, of the important *stages* in the movements of history.

As a methodology, history, in Black Studies, constitutes the foundation for theoretical construction of an analysis of the

Foreword

fundamental relationship between the political economy of societal developments and the racial divisions of labor and privilege, and the common patterns of life chances peculiar to the social conditions of Black people. Basic to the teleology of Africana Studies is the application of knowledge to promote social change. This primary tenet has been the focus of some controversy. The basis of controversy concerning Africana Studies is related directly to an extant perception that Black Studies is at variance with the societal zeitgeist. Though the expansive model subsumes the traditional academic approach, it nonetheless conflicts with the reigning ideological premise that knowledge should be pursued for the sake of knowledge per se. The assumption is that scientific investigation is a value-free process. This argument ignores what some scholars have identified as the "unscientific nature of the scientific enterprise." Research is a social product, and the values and assumptions of the investigator are, more usually than not, congruent with the dominant ideas and prevailing forces that govern the status quo. In the real world virtually all scientific research is geared to one sort of problem or another that changes society progressively. Funded research in the sciences is concentrated, for the most part, on such concerns as military weaponry, food and animal production, reclamation of marine life and water resources, transportation and communication technology, industrial and farm productivity, and medical cures. Knowledge is pursued for enlightenment of social experiences. Art is contemplated more for abstract existential properties. Even the deliberations on aesthetics are not without social purpose. The humanities are all too frequently the bastion of white racism-national/cultural chauvinism, as they serve to perpetuate a basic Euro-centric philosophy of history, language/literature, music/creative production, and sociology of society by essentially omitting and derogating non-European peoples and their projects.

In his discussion of the relationship of Africana Studies to traditional disciplines James Stewart states that "it is important to keep in mind that it [Black Studies] seeks to (a) fill a wide gap in the existing intellectual arena and (b) to resurrect a formal linkage between the academic and social formations. The intellectual task is not then simply to pick or choose among the conceptual and methodological toys of traditional disciplines but to reconceptualize the social fabric and rename the world in a way that obliterates the voids that have inevitably occurred as a result of artificial disciplinary demarcations. It is by renaming the world, that is, by employing linguistic conventions that specifically meet the needs of Black Studies per se, as opposed to imitating the conventions of traditional disciplines, that the power of forgotten voices to speak to the living can be restored. This latter claim implies that *history* has a preeminent hierarchical position in the context of the academic project of Black Studies, with insights from other foci of inquiry serving to clarify patterns of historical continuity and change."[6] Pedagogically and intellectually Africana philosophy seeks to "rename the world" and broaden the knowledge base for all of us through the concept of Afro-centricity in Black Studies.

The Black Studies proposition at the empirical and conceptual levels relates to fundamental methods of acquiring knowledge and organizing curriculum from which we all receive education. In recent years Black educators have criticized with growing intensity the limitations in Anglo-centric assumptions and, particularly, the notion that there are ultimate or absolute truths derived from universal research. The process of accepting new theories in the academic community is not simply a matter of adopting explanations of experimentally verified empirical observations but of accepting competing conceptions of reality and dissimilarities of reference language. Moreover, a scientific theory is more likely to be a conceptually relative entity in the sense that the language of one theory may not be translatable into the language of its predecessor in the same field of research. The major propositions characterizing the mainstream of academic research conclude that empirical laws of social regularity should be the basis of predictions; that social scientists should be disinterested, objective observers of social phenomena and their works (value) free of normative content; that all expressions or normative judgments are reducible to emotive expressions and thus of limited theoretical worth or, at least, open to suspect. However, the major disciplines have a primal tendency to reduce all problems of understanding to technical problems of information gathering and gauging variables.

The dominant fields of knowledge thus surreptitiously support the status quo, because the *normative judgments* germane to its technical procedures, and applications of their findings, are generally ignored and do not face the test of critical examination or empirical verification. Indeed, the normative principles are so ensconced in the conceptual orientation that they are not even recognized as such. For all the contention and support lent by American intellectuals and educators to the possibility of, and need for, value-neutral social theory, the product of the mainstream too often "turns out to be disguised ideology." This is not necessarily a condemnation; the essential point being made here is summed up in the following proposition: If there are grounds for holding that facts of nature are seen through a paradigmatic scheme, in effect there are grounds for believing social facts are not independent of conceptual paradigms used to investigate them. Dr. Lorenzo Morris is particularly poignant on this point: "When social statistics are perceived as meaningful in America, it is because they relate to values in American society. Conversely, when the conditions of Black and White Americans . . . are compared, no social statistic can be completely neutral unless it is also completely meaningless."[7]

The theoreticians of Black Studies use the basic social science concept of the sociology of knowledge to explain the legitimacy of the idea that the position of Black people in the social structure not only offers peculiar insights but also represents a specific meaning about social truth. Furthermore, all knowledge is a perspective on shared experience.

A. Olomenji argues, in a manuscript soon to be published, that one's point of origin, the place from which one looks out at the world, will largely determine what and how one perceives. A collective perception acts as a filter through which all reality is screened and transformed into a practical belief system. The collective perception and belief system define a people's reality, as well as what that reality means. The collective worldview provides a basic framework for viewing what exists in the world, as well as a basic supposition of how the world operates. A belief system reinforces the common assumptions of a collective perception. It is the practical and central reference for all action.

Professor Wade Boykin has pointed out that "there is inherent subjectivity and bias in the research enterprise. . . .One's assumptions are actually so critical in determining the nature of one's research enterprise."[8] We have come to realize with increasing clarity that presupposition effectively modifies perspectives and is the source of a priori bias. Boykin explains that " 'truth' in science is based considerably on a social-cultural-consensual reality."[9] This "consensual reality," vis-à-vis the Black Experience, actually translates into ideational hegemony of Anglo-centric presuppositions and perspective. To be sure, ethnocentrism, prejudice, and ignorance are factors that influence the intellectual tone of many white educators, particularly in terms of their attitudes towards Africana Studies. However, Boykin has made an even more salient observation of common Anglo-centric bias. He postulates what he calls the Law of Personal Presuppositions:

> You will rarely find a researcher-scholar concluding anything in his or her research that is inconsistent, contradictory, or threatening to his or her own self-definition, self-sustenance and value system.[10]

In as much as the raison d'être of Africana Studies, at least partially, is to critically redefine significant aspects of conventional knowledge both in social theory and social values, proponents of Black Studies have had to contend, and continue to do so, with long-standing bias in education, especially in curriculum, that is widespread at virtually all levels and institutions in American academia. Professor Sterling Stuckey, a prominent Black historian at Northwestern University, has commented: "Black people have met with as great injustices from American scholarship as they have from American life. In fact, colleges and universities have long paved the way for confusion and ignorance, arrogance and presumptuousness ... in Black-White relations."[11]

With the beginning of substantial desegregation of public schools and larger numbers of Black young people at predominantly non-Black campuses, the concern for how young Black people were being socialized by their (new) educational environment became a serious "sociology of knowledge" issue throughout Afro-America. Harold Cruse, a Black Studies professor at the University of Michigan and a distinguished social historian and political theorist, offered a poignant comment on this issue: "The further the Negro gets from his historical antecedents in time, the more tenuous become his conceptual ties, the emptier his social connections, the more superficial his visions. His one great and present hope is to know and understand his African-American realities in the United States more profoundly. Failing that, and failing to create a new synthesis in history and the humanities and a new social theory, he will suffer the historical fate of intellectual subterfuge."[12] This very same issue was the focus of Harvard-trained African-American historian Dr. Carter G. Woodson's seminal study, *The Mis-education of the Negro,* thirty-five years earlier.

Woodson observed:

> The "educated Negroes" have the attitude of contempt towards their own people because in their own schools as well as in their mixed schools Negroes are taught to admire the Hebrew, the Greek, the Latin and the Teuton and to despise the African. These "educated" people, however, decry any such thing as race consciousness. . . .They do not like to hear such expressions as "Negro Literature," "Negro Poetry," "African Art," or thinking (B)lack.[13]

This matter of identity and educational socialization—in all its interrelated social and individual aspects—is central to the concerns of Black educators over serious omissions in established knowledge and commission of distortions in the major intellectual enterprises because of exaggerations of Euro-American particularism and its ontological bias. The importance of this point was expressed in the writing of an exceptionally insightful and honest anthropologist, Charles Valentine: "Social issues and political movements have been intertwined with the search for valid knowledge and expressions of the Black experience in the United States ever since early precursors of modern Afro-American Studies."[14] The dean of African-American social science, Dr. St. Clair Drake, social anthropologist and professor emeritus at Stanford University, reports in a significant study recently published in the respected journal *The New York University Education Quarterly,* that since 1974 "Black Studies grew steadily and became entrenched (during) the next five years, though there were some erroneous reports in newspapers and magazines during 1974 that such programs were in decline."[15] In fact, he contends that "the Black Studies field has become institutionalized in the sense that some of its values are being accepted by the educational system."[16] One of these was the concept that "an ideal university community would be multiethnic with ethnicity permitted some institutional expression and with Black Studies being one of the sanctioned forms"[17] as the caste structure in American higher education slowly transforms into an emerging form of pluralism. But there is continuing resistance, based largely upon ideological and theoretical bias, academic nationalism and competitive interests, and some behavior whose motivation can only be explained as racist. In this respect it is important to realize that "at least 250 programs devoted to the study of the Black Experience in the United States exist today. Half of these have been operating since 1970, and of the sixty-four that were granting degrees in 1971, all except four have continued to develop. All give some attention to the implications of an African origin for Black people in the New World, and increasingly a "diaspora" frame of reference focuses some attention upon the Caribbean and Latin America for comparison with the United States."[18]

Sociologist Wilson Record, of Portland State University, conducted a study in 1972 and 1973 of Black Studies on fifty campuses across the country for the purpose of assessing their impact on university procedures for curricular innovation and faculty recruitment. He suggests that the effect of the dynamic development of Black Studies in postsecondary education has effected changes such that "colleges and universities would never be quite the same again."

The establishment of numerous departments of African-American Studies is generally viewed as a recent phenomenon originating in the last ten years. Though it is true that the field of Black Studies is very new in its present developments, its legacy extends to the earliest beginnings of Black intellectual history over two centuries ago. Though one can argue that the concept of Black Studies does predate the twentieth century, its recent emergence as an academic field is much more related to the endeavors of Black intellectuals during the past fifty years. The proper interpretation and inclusion of the historical role, cultural creation, and social circumstance of Black people in America has been of major concern, especially to Black scholars in the humanities and social sciences. The development of African-American Studies in this century can be traced through several stages.

The origins of the modern movement can be traced to the ferment that began between 1918 and 1929. It was during this period that Black scholars actively participated in the mass awakening of the general Black population that was precipitated by the social and cultural renaissance of the era. The second phase of the development of Black Studies was ushered in by the Great Depression and marked by the forced parochialization of many Black concerns. By the mid-1930s the question of Afro-American Studies was almost entirely the domain of Black urban intelligentsia, but it was also during this period that the idea of Black Studies as a separate academic field began to emerge. In 1940 the advent of World War II began a period of dormancy that lasted until roughly 1960. There was a lull that was caused by the war and a gap in the generational shift of Black scholars that was accentuated by the changing of priorities by many postwar academicians. The 1960s witnessed the rejuvenation of the civil rights movement, which provided the atmosphere for the question of Black Studies to become a major innovation in higher education. Campus protests created the subsequent pressure for the recognition and proliferation of Afro-American Studies programs throughout the nation. However, once these programs were established, they were confronted with the essential task of academic construction—of organizing curriculum and developing pedagogical methodology. Essential to this task was the selection of source materials as reference and texts for classroom instruction. The teaching function was to be the foundation for most of the programs. As a "new" field there was the immediate challenge of developing prototypical courses that could serve as beginning models for standardization and cross-reference of courses between the various departments and programs. Each instructor was responsible for developing his or her own individual syllabi. But if the program was to grow and become effectively institutionalized and regularized, there was going to have to be coordination between instructors in a given program in order to achieve a reasonable degree of systematic organization of courses for effective interface and a logical symmetry in intellectual focus. There had to be a meaningful division of academic endeavors that would provide a basis for integrated learning from one course to another in a program.

There are specific functions common to all disciplines, and they are in two dimensions. First, the intellectual parameters of the field must be relatively clearly established with rather apparent theoretical configuration. Second, the ideational and analytical "meanings" of the discipline—that is, what characterizes what *we* do as different, and significantly, from what is done in other disciplines—must be delineated. In sum, a fairly commonly adhered-to definition of the raison d'être of the field must emerge, for example, what is the consequence of "Afro-centric" perspective for the pursuit of truth. This difference must not be different for difference' sake; moreover, it must comprise a *significant* difference in the social construction of knowledge. It should challenge and enrich the learning process and provide a *particular* symbolic ethos of the discipline. This means that Black Studies would (and should) not serve as a secondary appendage or an intellectual afterthought to another established discipline (what would be essentially a modicum of Black content in an erstwhile "Europerspective" subject). This raises the question of whether African-American Studies composes a discipline in its own right and could contribute academically to the development of new knowledge. Other related questions are: Can the field generate new theory? Does Black Studies have a viable intellectual tradition of research investigation and scholarly literature?

There is a great deal of discussion among scholars and educators about what constitutes a discipline. For instance, is a course on Biology and Society, biology or sociology; is Art History, art or history; is History a science or an orientation to factual information within the humanities? What about Social Psychology; is it an academic bastard without sufficient specific identity and legitimate claim to a parent discipline, or is it on the frontier of theory as a consequence of cross-fertilization between and within traditional structures of knowledge? If Political Science is a discipline, what is its cogent theoretical definition and a characteristic explanation/description of its methodology?

The point is, we think, that knowledge is being packaged with new labels and in different arrangements, representing the realities of modern society. Though the initial questions may seem important, they may not be relevant or germane. Nonetheless, these questions about Black Studies as knowledge reveal a complex argument couched in and implied by theoretical development stemming from dominant mainstream criteria concerning adequate theory (empirical interpretive, critical) and converging trends and opinions among the most institutionalized and professionally prestigious academic disciplines concerning self-referential evidence supportive of the Black Studies criteria.

The fact that most of the major arguments in history, social science, anthropology, arts, literature, and the humanities derive from Euro-American particularism in experiences that have been held to be generalizable to the universe reflects a dialectic historicism operative in modern Western theoretical development. Black Studies represents a disillusionment and critique of "certified knowledge," and the historical currents of disillusionment with the mainstream are also a current of progressive contribution towards a more adequate social analysis and public policy. Therefore Black Studies is a "reconstruction discipline," as a synthesis of what its criticisms imply, convergence with theories reviewed, and the philosophic methods of its pedagogical emphasis. If the reconstruction method is, itself, a workable procedure, we have in Black Studies a way of arriving at new theory. Black Studies is a conceptual paradigm that principally tells us, like other academic discourse, what counts as a fact and what problems of explanation exist. It is commonly accepted among social scientists that "what we take to be an action, and even its proper description, is internally related to the interpretations that are intrinsically constitutive of it." But an action, to some extent, can be judged according to the linguistic and conceptual structure through which that action is filtered. A social science bereft of an analysis of the interchange between the subjective and the objective is thus a social science orientation that condones a tendency of "uncritical acceptance of ideological bias" of both a cultural and moral sort. Thus, conclusions about what constitutes a significant contribution to knowledge reveal that a similar filtering process is operative in such evaluation.

This debate, I am sure, will continue to go on and, in my judgment, should go on, because of its intellectual importance and significance in redefining and reformulating issues of theory and methodology. Undoubtedly we can expect continued contentious relations with many non-Black educators and even with neo-conservative Black intellectuals who have gained a sort of prominence as clients of the new-right (and, for that matter, the old right-wing) thrust directed at all institutions of American society—education notwithstanding. I suspect that we will have to come to grips with the reality that ours is not just a protracted contention, but that, as is true in most other arenas of race relations, the difficulties Black Studies scholars will confront, because of the prevailing institutional forces in American education, are endemic. Nonetheless, there has been an impressive degree of 'settling in' that provides a firmer foundation for the next decade. Many of our colleagues who began a decade ago in Africana Studies have been able to achieve relatively permanent, tenured positions at a cross section of colleges and universities in the country.

A recent catalog by Greenwood Press indicates that there are approximately twenty serious academic journals and magazines devoted to Africana Studies. There are better than a half dozen professional associations whose central purpose is the support and advancement of Africana Studies as an academic discipline and the cultivation of scholars. There has been a sound basis in the development of conceptual and theoretical clarity. Though there has been some wane in funding resources for research and a falloff in interest by major publishing houses in recent years, the productivity of scholarship in the field has been steady, evidenced by a discernable increase in the quality and in the quantity of published manuscripts. In spite of the obstacles there have been some major publications in the past few years worthy of note: *The Shaping of Black America,* Lerone Bennett; *The Harder We Run,* William Harris; *Survival and Progress: Afro-American Experience,* Alex Swan; *Black Americans and the Political System,* L. Barker and Jesse Mc Corry; *Langston Hughes: Before and after Harlem,* Faith Berry; *There Is a River,* Vincent Harding; *Black Women Novelists,* Barbara Christian; *The Slave Community,* John Blassingame; *How Europe Underdeveloped Africa,* Walter Rodney; *When and Where We Enter,* Paula Giddens; and the recently published *The Principles of Black Political Economy,* Lloyd Hogan.

This list could be much longer; it is not meant to be exhaustive. My intention is to give a representative sample of the scope and caliber of scholarship characteristic of the field. Perhaps most significant of all has been the publication of two widely used introductory texts in Africana Studies. The two-volume set *Introduction to Afro-American Studies,* an edited collection by Peoples College, and the more recent, first single-authored text, *Introduction to Black Studies,* by Maulana Karenga, have made critical contributions to the standardization of the Black Studies curriculum. These introductory texts are vitally important to conveying a coherent definition and common identity to the discipline. Ultimately, the consolidation of Africana Studies will be predicated upon a foundation of an integrated, standardized curriculum.

While we have good reasons to enjoy a reasonable sense of satisfaction at this stage, the path ahead will not necessarily be unobstructed. The conservative mood in the country is impacting educational policy. Dr. Faustine Jones, of Howard University, has identified definite patterns of erosion in commitment to inclusion of formally neglected and oppressed national *minority* groups in the educational system. With the election of the Reagan administration there have emerged neoconservative political action groups that are targeting public sources of information and public education for political assault as part of their version of a "holy" war to safeguard the "soul" of the republic from what they perceived to be unwelcome ideas. Prominent among these self-initiated guardians of society are organizations like the Committee for a Free World, which began in 1981 and issued the following statement: "We are persuaded that the struggle for freedom may in the end be won not on the battlefields but in books, newspapers, broadcasts, classrooms, and in all public institutions."[19]

Their rallying cry is for an ideological war to control America's mind. We can expect that such political chicanery will enduce encounters, at the institutional level, that will challenge us to stand firm on the ground we have achieved thus far. It is precisely because of this kind of raging conservatism, which is being mobilized as a retrogressive social movement, that Africana Studies is all the more essential to the preservation of the modest gains made by African-Americans over the last decade. There will very likely be those who will ask, with the transformations of society toward greater technological concentration in the scientific and computer age of the 1980s and 1990s, is Black Studies feasible or necessary. Stewart has pointed out in this regard that "the current socialization of students prior to entry into higher education is undeniably generating a careerist mentality. This trend has its counterpart among Black Studies faculty, many of whom face continuing subtle and overt harassment by non-Black Studies colleagues. Many of the first faculty in the field are gradually de-emphasizing involvement in community activities as they have succumbed to (or have been seduced by) the orthodox norms of academic traditionalism in their pursuit of careerist aspirations for legitimacy and acceptability for purposes of job stability and security. Younger faculty have not been quite as engaged by commitment to community outreach and the wedding of intellectual and social activism on behalf of the liberation of the Black community.

This phenomenon is denying Black Studies both a critical bridge to the potential beneficiaries of applied scholarship, that is, the external community, and a source of power to facilitate the continuation of innovative projects in the face of renewed opposition. Dr. Robert C. Johnson, writing on "Why Colleges and Students Need Black Studies" in the *Chronicle of Higher Education,* states that academically and vocationally Black Studies are important for a variety or reasons. Some of his reasons are as follows: one-third of all children born in the country are Black, Hispanic, Asian, American Indian, etc.; 25 percent of the population consists of racial ethnic groups; many regions (particularly urban centers) and institutions (that is, urban public schools) are rapidly approaching a Black and Hispanic majority; and the vast majority of the people in this world are racial ethnic groups of non-Anglo linkage. He concludes that "for the most part, the majority of the students in American institutions of higher education are being grossly underprepared to function in a multiethnic, multiracial, multicultural world."[20] Dr. Eleanor Traylor indicates a similar point when she states: "Moreover, in a country as culturally plural as the United States, we enjoy the large opportunity to educate our children multi-culturally and multi-linguistically. And because of the nature of our world today, nothing is more desirable than multi-literate citizens whose respect for one another transforms old enmities or superstitions threatening the very existence of the planet itself."[21]

The research department of the New York Urban League recently conducted a tri-state study of New York, Pennsylvania, and New Jersey to ascertain the kind of mentor relationships Black students have in graduate schools. Their findings revealed that for most of these students there was no significant mentor relationship to encourage and guide them in their study. This is due, in part, to too few Black faculty in American higher education. In the *Chronicle of Higher Education* Charles Farrell reports that "virtually no gains are being made in increasing minority representation in the faculties and administrations of predominantly white colleges, according to many educators familiar with academic recruiting."[22]

This observation is supported by a special investigative study of the shortage of Black professors by the *Wall Street Journal.* The *Journal* found: "In few industries today are Blacks as scarce as in higher education. In predominantly white schools, Blacks usually make up only about 1 percent of the tenured and non-tenured faculty. Princeton University has only 9 Black faculty out of a total staff of 581. The University of Michigan has 20 out of a total of 684—and that's the

Foreword

highest percentage of Blacks in the Big 10."[23] The University of Pennsylvania had 31 Black faculty in 1972 and it has 31 Black faculty in 1984. The situation is getting worse because the potential pool is getting smaller. For the past five years the number of Blacks applying to arts and sciences graduate schools has steadily declined. Between 1975 and 1980 Harvard, Yale, and Princeton each produced a total of 10 or fewer Black undergraduates who went on to earn their doctorates; Howard University produced 275. Institutions such as Morehouse College in Atlanta have been far more successful than most white institutions in encouraging Black students to go on to graduate school. Black colleges educate only about a quarter of the Black undergraduates, but over half the Blacks with new Ph.D.'s got their undergraduate education there.

The vice-provost and dean of graduate studies at Stanford University, Gerald Lieberman, says, "Part of the problem is a national climate of indifference and even suspicion toward affirmative action. Many colleges seem to have developed a 'plateau mentality' that does nothing more than maintain present ratios of minorities and whites."[24] An associate director of the American Council on Education's office of minority affairs, Sarah Melendez, says, "It is very clear that there is an underrepresentation of minorities on faculties and administrations."[25]

The future prospects are not good, as there is little, if any, expectation of improvement. The prognosis is that the situation will get worse as minority faculty are terminated by denial of tenure and through the syndrome of "last hired, first fired" during programs of retrenchment and fiscal austerity. Currently the proportion of Black faculty in American higher education is 4.0 percent. Lorenzo Morris points out, "The data on the status of Blacks from 1975 through 1977, however, show that progress in all areas of higher education has slowed down and in areas like professional education, it has come to a standstill."[26] In a special report, "Participation of Black Students in Higher Education. A Statistical Profile from 1970-71 to 1980-81," prepared by the National Center for Educational Statistics and released November 1983 by the U.S. Department of Education, the following summaries were offered:

During the first half of the 1970s:

The large increase in Black enrollment coincided with the

expansion in both federal legislation and federal policies aimed at reducing barriers to higher education for minorities and low-income students.

By 1975 the percentage of Black high school graduates who enrolled in college was the same as that for whites (although high school graduation rates were still lower for Blacks than whites).

Black enrollment at the postbaccalaureate level did not experience an equivalent upsurge. In fact, by 1976 there was a smaller proportion of Blacks in graduate and first professional schools than there had been in the early 1970s.

During the last half of the 1970s:

Black participation in higher education stabilized in most areas.

The number of Blacks who enrolled in college remained about the same, in spite of the fact that the number of Black youth eligible for college increased by almost 20 percent.

The number and proportion of degrees awarded to Blacks remained about the same at the bachelor's, doctor's, and first professional levels, while there were substantial declines at the master's level.

The number of Blacks receiving master's degrees declined 16 percent, four times greater than the decline for non-Blacks.

Doctoral degrees awarded to Black students for the years 1976, 1979, and 1981 were 3.6, 3.9, and 3.9 respectively. Though the data are not firm for the past three years, there is evidence that indicates trends of decline in Black student enrollment in both undergraduate and graduate schools. Professors Laurie Hatch and Kent Mommsen, from their study of racial gaps in education, report that "from this analysis two major points emerge. The substantial and widening racial gap in American higher education is accounted for primarily by remaining inequities among males."[27] The pattern seems to be significantly related to the Reagan administration's cutbacks and changes in federal aid to higher education, particularly the government's support for need-based financial assistance to students and guaranteed low-interest loans. The shift has been especially severe among indigenous Black males.

These trends appear to have some rather direct implications for the progress of Black Studies, in the long term if not immediately. Fewer African-American faculty would mean that there is a lessened

Foreword

likelihood that students will have mentors who will introduce them to Africana Studies and encourage them to seriously consider academic careers in the field. There will also be a diminishing potential source of new colleagues necessary to further the field. Relatively fewer Black students in American higher education will reduce the natural constituency and bridge of support for the field. How these problems are resolved or transcended will impact as much, critically, upon the future of Africana Studies as will the ongoing discourse on questions related to ontology and epistemology.

1. John H. Clarke, "Africana Studies: A Decade of Change, Challenge, and Conflict" (paper presented at the conference "Consolidating Africana Studies: Bonding African Linkages" on the occasion of the tenth anniversary of the Africana Studies and Research Center, Cornell University, September 26-28, 1980), p. 1.
2. A. Wade Boykin, "Black Psychology and the Research Process" (unpublished manuscript), p. 14.
3. Ibid., p. 15.
4. Ibid., p. 16.
5. James B. Stewart, *Toward Operationalization of an "Expansive" Model of Black Studies* (Atlanta, Institute of the Black World, 1983), p. 1.
6. Ibid., p. 5.
7. Lorenzo Morris, *Elusive Equality* (Washington, D.C., Howard University Press, 1980), p. 18.
8. Boykin, op. cit., p. 1.
9. Ibid., p. 8.
10. Ibid., p. 7.
11. Sterling Stuckey, comments made during a lecture at a symposium on Black Studies at the Institute of the Black World, Atlanta, 1970.
12. Harold Cruse, comments from a paper presented at a conference sponsored by the University of Michigan on African American Studies, Ann Arbor, April, 1978.
13. Carter G. Woodson, *Mis-education of the Negro,* (Washington, D.C., The Associated Publishers, 1969), p. 7.
14. Charles Valentine, *Afro-American Studies: An Intellectual Tradition* (New York, Bobbs Merrill Reprint Series, 1980), p. 9.
15. St. Clair Drake, "Black Studies in Higher Education," *New York University Education Quarterly* 21, no. 3: p. 2.
16. Ibid., p. 4.
17. Ibid., p. 5.
18. Ibid., p. 12.
19. Richard Goldstein, "The War for America's Mind," *The Village Voice,* 8 June 1982, p. 1.

20. Robert Johnson, "Why Colleges and Students Need Black Studies,'" *Chronicle of Higher Education,* 17 November 1980, p. 24.
21. Eleanor Traylor, letter to the director of the National Endowment for the Humanities, Washington, D.C., July 1984.
22. Charles Farrell, "Minorities Seen Making No Gains in Campus Jobs," *Chronicle of Higher Education,* 13 June 1984, p. 1.
23. Anne MacKay-Smith, "Large Shortage of Black Professors in Higher Education Grows Worse," *Wall Street Journal,* 10 July 1984, p. 2.
24. Farrell, loc. cit.
25. Ibid.
26. Morris, op. cit., p. 18.
27. Laurie R. Hatch and Kent Mommsen, "The Widening Racial Gap in American Higher Education," *Journal of Black Studies* 14, no. 4 (June 1984): p. 470.

ACKNOWLEDGMENTS

We wish to express our appreciation to the following participants in the conference, who were an outstanding group of serious and dedicated Black educators. They have in their own right made seminal contributions to the field and to our people's long tradition of struggle to command the critical dimensions of our self-definition and the salient theoretical concepts in the analysis of our history, culture, and social condition and its structural implications for the political economy of the Black experience: Sister Toni Cade Bambara; Mr. Lerone Bennett, Jr.; Dr. Johnella E. Butler; Dr. John Henrik Clarke; Ms. Gayla Cook; Minister Louis Farrakhan; Mr. Hoyt Fuller; Prof. Ewart Guinier; Dr. Vincent Harding; Dr. Robert L. Harris, Jr.; Dr. Stephen E. Henderson; Ms. Makila James; Mr. Robert Johnson, Jr., Esq.; Prof. Willard R. Johnson; Prof. Lansine Kaba; Mr. George E. Kent; Mr. Kamau B. Kokayi; Prof. Daniel P. Kunene; Mr. George Lamming; Dr. Tilden J. LeMelle; Prof. Bernard Magubane; Dr. Manning Marable; Prof. J. Congress Mbata; Dr. Andre N. McLaughlin; Ms. Janis L. McManus; Ms. Delores M. Mortimer; Dr. William E. Nelson, Jr.; Prof. Nzongola-Ntalaja; Dr. W. Ofuatey-Kodjoe; Prof. William W. Sales, Jr.; Mr. Frank P. Scruggs II, Esq.; Dr. Ibrahim K. Sundiata; Prof. Michael Thelwell; Dr. Bettye C. Thomas; Dr. Eleanor W. Traylor; Prof. Ivan Van Sertima; Dr. Ronald Walters; Dr. Shirley N. Weber; Prof. Sylvia Wynter.

We are deeply appreciative of John Ackerman's assistance with the editing and proofreading of the manuscript.

Additional thanks and praise to Robbi Ewell, the video technician, for his excellent work in taping and recording the conference proceedings.

Special thanks to the secretarial staff, without whose help the efficient organization of the conference could not have been accomplished: Ms. Beverly IshRenick, Mrs. Ida Early, Mrs. Daisy Rowe, Mrs. Rashida Sawyer.

THE ARTISTS

David P. Bradford was born in Chicago in 1937. He has studied at the School of the Art Institute of Chicago; the Otis Art Institute in Los Angeles; Lincoln University, Jefferson City, Missouri (B.S. 1963); and the University of California at Berkeley (M.A. 1970). He has been a free-lance illustrator and designer for advertising, books, and magazines. In 1968 and 1970 he completed murals in Oakland, California.

Phillip L. Mason was born in St. Louis, Missouri, in 1939. He holds the B.F.A., M.F.A., and Ph.D. degrees. He has taught at many colleges and universities, and his work has been featured in several news articles and textbooks. His art has been shown all over the United States and abroad and hangs in various public and private collections, including Johns Hopkins University, the University of Notre Dame, the DuSable Museum of African-American History, and the National Collection, Republic of Guyana, South America.

Bertrand Phillips is a painter and photographer. He received his B.F.A. degree from the School of the Art Institute of Chicago and his M.F.A. from Northwestern University. He is currently teaching painting and drawing at the School of the Art Institute of Chicago. He exhibits nationally, and his works are found in the permanent collections of the Illinois State Museum, the University of Chicago, Columbia College in Chicago, the Erie Art Center in Erie, Pennsylvania, the DuSable Museum of African-American History in Chicago, Governors State University, and others. He continues to derive inspiration from Black culture, and his most recent paintings are visualizations of Jazz, Blues, and dance.

INTRODUCTION
Jacquelyn L. Haskins

Black Studies as a field of scholarship did not begin with the student turmoil of the late sixties. Men and women have, for many years, studied and written about African-American history, literature, and art. A small number of scholars have, for a long time, engaged in critiques of American society from the perspectives of Black Americans. An important fact about these early scholarly endeavors is that they occurred almost entirely at Black colleges and universities or outside of the higher education setting altogether. When the late Carter G. Woodson, a pioneer in African-American history, observed that the whole system of education in America conspires to teach Black people to despise themselves, he was referring to the characteristic of the white-dominated education system that almost wholly excluded consideration of Blacks in the history, culture, and economic life of America and, to the extent it did so, recognized African-Americans only in peripheral and negative ways. Thus what Black people were in America was defined by what white people thought them to be. The surge of interest among Black students in Black Studies on white campuses stemmed, in no small part, from the drive in the wider Black community for Black people to define their own existence.

Neither this latter impetus nor the campus turmoils that were its outward manifestations can undermine the legitimate history of Black Studies nor alter the plain fact of their long neglect at predominantly white institutions.

In April 1969, one hundred Black students occupied Willard Straight Hall, the student-union building at Cornell University, and emerged after thirty-six hours carrying rifles, shotguns, bandoliers, and homemade spears. It was the most stunning moment of a tumultuous spring on the nation's campuses. Unprecedented numbers of Black students agitated for a new "relevancy" in the form of Black Studies programs, alarming many professors, administrators, alumni, and students. The thought was that the Black Studies movement was simply a fit that was taking place among a troubled minority and that it would run its course.

In response to this idea the Africana Studies and Research Center was founded in April 1969 to demonstrate that the purpose of education in any society is to provide skills and tools and a body of

Introduction

knowledge necessary to ensure the progress of that society. Two factors had emerged from the ongoing educational system of the country, both of which convinced Black people of the necessity for greater recasting and reorientation of their programs. The first factor was that higher education in America had consistently remained the domain of white America, and it was only later that a strong challenge was issued to change its status, function, and direction in the country. The other factor was the almost invariable estrangement of college-trained Blacks from their communities—the very communities that stood most in need of the knowledge and skills that the more fortunate of their youth had been able to acquire.

Basic to the concept of Black Studies in general, and the Africana Studies and Research Center in particular, has been the recognition that the responsibility of the Black educator is not only to pioneer and develop Black Studies as an educational field but also to produce intellectually disciplined, creative, insightful social analysts and to lay the background for technically competent professionals. The center is an international center for Black Studies with a strong emphasis on research, broadly conceived, and effective and innovative teaching.

From the outset the Africana Studies and Research Center sought, as did its counterparts on other campuses, to define the field of Black Studies. The educational principle was a unified approach to learning rather than the conventional discipline-bound approach. The center realized that the designing and construction of its field could be a task of many years.

The center opened with 160 students enrolled in ten courses, offered by six members of the faculty. Soon after the center was established, it offered the undergraduate major and the master's degree. Now about 700 students a year enroll in the center's many courses, taught by nine faculty members.

The first students to obtain the master's degree at the center did so in 1973. Of the students that have been awarded the degree since then, many went on to doctoral degree programs and are now teaching; others went to law school; and many others went directly into employment as affirmative action officers, social research analysts, and members of university administrations.

In September 1980, the Africana Center held a conference that provided experts in the field with a rare opportunity to collectively look at the theoretical and methodological questions raised by

Introduction

changing times. Participants also discussed achievements, failures, and other concerns regarding the current state of Black Studies in the United States.

We have collected some of the papers from the conference to publish in book form. It is our hope that this book will furnish information that will help build a foundation by providing material from scholars so that Black people may reexamine, investigate, define, and be the authorities on scholarship about themselves.

I

From the Maelstrom:
Directions in Afro-American History

The Organizer, Bertrand Phillips

CHAPTER 1

Listen to the Blood: A Preliminary Inquiry into the Meaning of Black History

Lerone Bennett, Jr.

> Considered in the light of its fundamental dimensions, all periods of history appear as manifestations of a single drama—without our knowing whether it has an ending. Because we are in the world, we are *condemned to meaning,* and we cannot do or say anything without it acquiring a name in history.[1] —Maurice Merleau-Ponty

On the last page of his seminal book, *The Gift of Black Folk,* W. E. B. DuBois penned a postscript of ten lines. This is what he wrote:

> Listen to the Winds, O God the Reader, that wail across the whip-cords stretched taut on broken human hearts; listen to the Bones, the bare bleached bones of slaves, that line the lanes of Seven Seas and beat eternal tomtoms in the forests of the laboring deep; listen to the Blood, the cold thick blood that spills its filth across the fields and flowers of the Free; listen to the Souls that wing and thrill and weep and scream and sob and sing above it all. What shall these things mean, O God the Reader?

DuBois answered his own question. He said:

> You know. You know.[2]

In these lines, and in the challenge accompanying them, DuBois brings us face to face with the central—I almost said the only—question of African-American history. Without artifice or evasion, he puts the question straight:

What is the meaning of the Black odyssey in this land?

Why are we here instead of there?

Has our suffering and our humiliation and our joy served some great, though hidden, purpose? Or did the slaves and the sharecroppers and the martyrs and victims bleed and dream and die in vain?

Lerone Bennett, Jr. is Senior Editor of Ebony Magazine, Chicago, Illinois

Brutal questions, *dangerous* questions.

To ask them in this way is enough to take your breath away. Which is one reason modern historians seldom if ever ask them—in sharp contrast with the pioneer Black historians, who seldom if ever asked anything else.[3] There are, of course, other reasons for the general silence on these questions. First, and perhaps foremost, many, perhaps most, Black historians have been influenced—some would say intimidated—by what Robert L. Harris, Jr., calls "the gatekeepers" of American history, who have generally taken the view that *thinking about history* is both dangerous and useless.[4] And it is worth emphasizing here that this attitude is rooted in factors deeper than race. When Charles Beard ventured into the realm of philosophy, the gatekeepers of the American historical power structure were appalled, and today they say as little as possible about that phase of his career. It is to be observed also that when Beard felt the need for more light and air, he had to go outside the boundaries of America. That situation has not changed, as I discovered fifteen years ago when I started thinking about meaning and history. And it is my belief, for what it is worth, that if Black historiography wants to widen its boundaries, it will have to go to school with Raymond Aron, Maurice Merleau-Ponty, C. L. R. James, Jean Paul Sartre, E. P. Thompson and, of course, the Black masses.[5]

There is another reason for the general silence on meaning in Black history. Black historians—and I include myself in this general analysis—have been so hemmed in by their own history, by the struggle to give meaning to their own struggle as historians and historical beings, that they have had little inclination for speculative thinking that might in the end rob their own history of meaning. Over and above this, Black historians have been so involved in a desperate struggle to create Black history, and to institutionalize it, that they have had understandably little time for the thinking game.

One is obliged to say here, in passing, that we will never be able to repay the pioneer Black historians for the brilliant and selfless struggle they waged on that level. Because of Carter G. Woodson, Benjamin Quarles, Charles Wesley, Dorothy Porter, John Hope Franklin, and others, we are today within striking distance of that intellectual emancipation without which all other emancipations are meaningless. Because of these men and women, the foundation of Black history is secure. And our task today is to build on that foundation, following the furrow of W. E. B. DuBois, who was perhaps the greatest philosopher of Black history. The question of meaning haunted DuBois, and he tells us in his postscript, quoted above, that it ought to haunt you.

Listen, he said, addressing *you* personally.

Listen to the Bones of Martin and Malcolm and the anonymous millions who lie unmourned and unhonored in unmarked graves.

Listen to the screams and groans of the 73,000 nights of slavery.

Listen to the Niagara of Blood gushing from the wounds of institutional racism and greed and pride.

Listen!

What shall these things mean?

That's the question, the *only* question. *That* question worried DuBois so much that he walked up to God one day—in a poem—and demanded an answer:

> Doth not this justice of hell stink in thy nostrils, O God? How long shall the mounting flood of innocent blood roar in Thine ears and pound in our hearts for vengeance?

DuBois went on to charge God with dereliction of duty, or worse.

> Bewildered we are and passion-tossed, mad with the madness of a mobbed and mocked and murdered people, straining at the armposts of Thy Throne, we raise our shackled hands and charge Thee, God, by the bones of our stolen fathers, by the tears of our dead mothers, by the very blood of Thy crucified Christ: What meaneth this? Tell us the plan; give us the sign![6]

Meaning: the history of African-Americans is, among other things, the history of a quest for meaning. This paper is a preliminary inquiry—I stress the word preliminary—into the implications of that quest for Black history and Black historians. It will be my thesis that Black history is a process permeated with meaning and charged with demands for concepts that release that meaning. I intend to maintain further that Black historians are condemned to meaning, and that it is their task to gain a greater theoretical understanding of the fundamental meaning-structures of Black history in order to free themselves and their history for the meaning mandated by that history.

The task that I have set for myself is obviously a tall order, and I want to emphasize here, at the beginning, that this attempt is provisional, and that I undertake it with reluctance. I have been grappling with these questions for at least fifteen years—to tell the truth, I have been grappling with them since the day I was born Black in Mississippi—and I have been hoping for at least that long that other

This is the plan of the paper, but it is impossible to carry out that plan without dealing first with the theoretical implications of meaning in history.

Time, Space, and Black History[7]

Let me begin this theoretical discussion by saying that I do not intend to get bogged down in an endless discussion about the meaning of meaning. I assume here, as Karl Popper assumed, that most people know with "sufficient clarity" what they mean when they talk about the meaning of history or the meaning of a person's life.[8] It is in this sense that I raise the question of the meaning of Black history.

Now there are only four or five broad answers to that question.[9] The first is that Black history is ruled by Jehovah or Allah, who moves in mysterious ways His wonders to perform. The second is that Black history is chaos or one damned thing after another. The third is that Black history is a part of nature and revolves endlessly in cycles—birth, growth, and death; progression and retrogression; the first Reconstruction and the second Reconstruction. The fourth answer is that Black history is a moment in a larger whole that is moving in some direction upward—"We are climbing Jacob's ladder"—to an ideal order of the kind articulated by either Karl Marx or Herbert Spencer or the makers of the Declaration of Independence. The fifth, which is really a variation of the fourth, is that Black history is powered by the internal logic of the challenges inherent in that history and that Black people have, by virtue of that history, a mission to democratize either America or the world. It is possible, of course, to put a number of ideas into these different vessels. One can say, for example, that history is a matter of biology/race or economics/class or politics/nationhood.

There are other possible answers to the question, but almost all of them fall under one of these broad headings. For example—and here we are treading on dangerous grounds—the assertions, often found in nationalist literature, that African-American history is a historical abortion and that the African-American adventure is doomed to failure, or worse, are in reality assertions of chaos. To take this approach is to say, without explicitly reflecting on the implications, that African-American history is meaningless and that the only answer to it is to get out of it.

We have before us then five possible answers to the question of the meaning of Black history. For the purposes of this discussion, we can reduce the number to four by eliminating the nihilistic view. This has nothing at all to do with my subjective views or dispositions. It has everything to do with the nature of history and the historical vocation. The hypothesis of chaos takes the a priori view that there is no order or meaning in Black history. There is nothing wrong in taking an a priori position. The problem here, as Beard and others have pointed out, is that it is impossible to write history if you believe there is no order in history.

As for the other four hypotheses, we are not concerned at the moment with their truth or falsity. What we are concerned to do here is outline possible answers and investigate the choices that they impose on the historian. For with so many possible answers, how is the historian to choose a possible meaning for his historical life and his historical vocation? And since there are no "facts" anywhere that prove the truth or the falsity of any one of these propositions, is it necessary or meaningful or useful for the historian to make a choice?

Let me answer these questions by quoting at some length from Charles Beard's presidential address to the American Historical Association. I chose this particular quotation for two reasons. First, Charles Beard was an *established* historian. Second, he said these words in 1933 to the establishment of the American historical power structure. This is what he said:

> The historian who writes history . . . consciously or unconsciously performs an act of faith, as to order and movement, for certainty as to order and movement is denied to him by knowledge of the actuality with which he is concerned. . . . His faith is at bottom a conviction that something true can be known about the movement of history and his conviction is a subjective decision, not a purely objective discovery.[10]

Beard went on to say that the historian is condemned by the very structure of history to a choice of meaning. He is condemned to meaning, Beard said, because his selection and arrangement of facts is controlled by the frame of reference in his mind. "This frame of reference includes things deemed necessary, things deemed possible, and things deemed desirable. It may be large, informed by deep knowledge, and illuminated by wide experience; or it may be small, uninformed, and unilluminated. It may be a grand conception of history or a mere aggregation of confusions. But it is there in the mind inexorably."[11]

Beard concluded that it was the duty of the historian to "examine his own frame of reference, clarify it, enlarge it by acquiring knowledge of greater areas of thought and events and give it consistency of structure by a deliberate conjecture respecting the nature or direction of the vast movements of ideas and interests called world history. This operation will cause discomfort to individual historians but all, according to the vows of their office, are under obligation to perform it."[12]

The point that emerges most clearly from this statement is that the question of meaning is grounded in the structure of time and history. People talk sometimes as though history were a discipline focused entirely on the past. But history is an ambiguous phenomenon, because historical time, lived time, is "a structured unity of a lived *no longer* and a lived *not yet* in the explosion of a project that gathers the *now* and the *no longer* and the *not yet* into a lived synthesis."[13] And, as John Dewey has said, "changes become history, or acquire temporal significance, only when they are interpreted in terms of a direction *from* something *to* something." Dewey added—and this is the main point—"There is no history except in terms of movement toward some outcome, something taken as an issue."[14] There is no history, in other words, except in terms of meaning.

The Committee on Historiography of the Social Science Research Council reached the same conclusion by a different route, pointing out that "the 'meaning' of any historical fact is what it does, how it continues to behave and operate, what consequences follow from it." From this standpoint, we understand what comes before by what comes afterward, and our principle for understanding what is "basic" in history is some "dynamic element," some "tendency" moving toward the future.[15]

And how does the historian determine what is "basic" in history?

The historian determines that, the report said, by choosing "as his principle of selection 'the real pattern of events,' what is 'being realized,' what is 'working itself out.' " How does he choose this principle of selection? The Committee said that "the historian's choice of a principle of selection necessarily involves a certain order of allegiance, an act of faith in one kind of future rather than another."[16] But—and this is the crucial point for our analysis—this act of faith cannot be a mere leap into fantasy. For if our reading of history is not to be capricious or arbitrary, it must be grounded on the real movement of history. It must, in other words, "have an 'objective' emphasis or focus in something to be done, something [the historian] sees forced on men. The history of what is basic *for that problem*—of the conditions that generated it, the resources men had to draw upon, how they dealt with it—will then be perfectly 'objective,' in a sense in which no mere recording of arbitrarily selected 'facts' could ever be."[17]

These considerations are of crucial importance for our analysis. They remind us that historical meaning is not a meaning imposed on history; rather it is a meaning embedded in history. And if we think about it for a moment, we will realize that it could not be otherwise. For if history did not in general terms display a certain direction; if, in other words, things did not *court* our freedom and offer us meaning, anything could happen at any time in history, and I could make myself a White Man or an African or a West Indian by a simple act of will. The fact that I cannot do this, the fact that I am obliged by my historical situation to yield to history the meaning history has given me, means, at least on a first level of approximation, that historical beings—and historians are historical beings—make meaning because they *are* meaning.

To summarize then, I have maintained that there are four or five possible meanings in Black history and that the Black historian is obliged, by his vocation, by the structure of time, by the meaning of events themselves, to choose a meaning that will define him and his history. I have also maintained, between the lines, that so-called scientific historiography is an illusion created out of whole cloth by defenders of the status quo who were defending, consciously or unconsciously, meanings that benefitted them and the status quo. No one understood this point better than Beard, who criticized the philosophical presuppositions of Leopold von Ranke, the godfather of "scientific" historiography, and pointed out that "Ranke, a German conservative, writing after the storm and stress of the French Revolution, was weary of history written for, or permeated by, the purposes of revolutionary propaganda. He wanted peace.... Written history that was cold, factual and apparently undisturbed by the passions of the time served best the cause of those who did not want to be disturbed."[18] The point here—and we should be clear on this point—is that *the purpose of a quiet history is to keep things quiet*.

Let there be no misunderstanding of my meaning. I am not arguing here for bias. I am saying that since bias—a point of view, a frame of reference—is inevitable, the only way we can control it is to become aware of it. Louis Gottschalk made the same point in his evaluation of historical writing, saying that "the writer who thinks he has no philosophy of history or who believes he is detached is self-deceived, unless he is more than human, and therefore more likely to deceive others than if he were deliberately lying."[19]

It should also be said that I am not questioning the priority of documents or the need for fairness in the use of documents. Rather, my point is that documents only answer adequate theoretical questions, and that the *idea a particular document gives you on Black people in history depends on the idea that you have of Black people, and of history*.

"God is on Our Side"

With an understanding of the theoretical principles involved, we are now in a position to explore the meanings Black people have given to their meaning. And the first point to be made under this heading is that the overwhelming majority of Blacks, at least until recent times, opted for the providential view that God controlled history and the universe.

He's got the whole world in His hands.[20]

This view runs like a black thread through the whole fabric of our history and it must, no matter what our philosophy, give us pause and warning. The men and women who created that philosophy of history could see the face of God nowhere in Mississippi and Alabama and Louisiana and yet they dared to dream that He was everywhere. Everything they could see—the chains, the ropes, the walls, the signs—told them the world was absurd and capricious to its core, and yet they dared, out of a terrible and eloquent hope, to bet on that which they could not see, saying to themselves, to their children, to the wind, to the sky, that something—call it God, call it Mind, call it Spirit—that something bigger and stronger than the White man was at work in history.

That dream—that vision, that philosophy of history—was based on two different dreams. The first said, in so many words, that the Black odyssey would be fulfilled on the Last Day in a place beyond history. The second dream dreamed of a fulfillment down here by a God who fought the battles of men and women in history.

Didn't my Lord deliver Daniel,
And why not every man?[21]

Two dreams, two visions, within the same dream.

And we must be very careful in appraising them, for the evidence indicates that most Black people believed both versions at the same time. When I was a child in Mississippi, I often heard otherworldly Blacks rejoice over the misfortunes of Whites—misfortunes that were explained by the almost universal phrase, "God don't like ugly." An additional and perhaps even more important point in this connection is that large numbers of very religious Blacks also believed that history moved at the behest of other forces—charms, curses, and so forth. This kind of belief means, as I have said elsewhere, that the "slave's God was not the White man's God. Nor was his devil the White man's devil."[22] Zora Neale Hurston very wisely observed that "the devil is not the terror that he is in European folklore. He is a powerful trickster who often competes successfully with God."[23] Another commentator who caught the meaning Black people gave to God was ethnologist Paul Radin, who said: "The antebellum Negro was not converted to God; he converted God to himself."[24] This is a profound point, and it warns us against the danger of assuming that the Black providential view is the same as the White providential view.

This is neither the time nor the place—and I am not the person—to give a detailed history of the Black maneuver in the world of the spirit; we can only note here, in passing, that the providential view of a God-controlled history led to some interesting views on the meaning he had assigned Black people in his unfolding plan. On the one hand, there was the rather sophisticated view of Alexander Crummell who said, in so many words, that Black people were a race God had preserved to do something with.[25] On the other hand, there were the views of other influential Blacks, who said God had transported Blacks to America to prepare them for a mission of "grace" and salvation in Africa.[26] This was almost certainly a minority view. As a matter of fact, it appears from the record that most Blacks did not rise to the level of formulating precise expressions of God's plan for Blacks. The general view, it seems, was that there was a plan but that it was a hidden plan—beyond the understanding of man. We meet this view in the great, Job-like utterance of Nathaniel Paul, who demanded an answer from God in 1827 and then backed down, astonished by his own audacity. Here are his words:

> Tell me, ye mighty waters, why did ye sustain the ponderous load of misery? O speak, ye winds, and say why it was that ye executed your office to waft them onward to the still more dismal state. . . . And, oh thou immaculate God, be not angry with us, while we come into this thy sanctuary, and make the bold inquiry in this thy holy temple, why it was that thou didst look on with the calm indifference of an unconcerned spectator, when thy holy law was violated. . . . Hark! while he answers from on high: hear his proclaiming from the skies—Be still, and know that I am God! . . . I do my will and pleasure in the heavens above, and in the earth beneath; it is my sovereign prerogative to bring good out of evil and cause the wrath of man to praise me.[27]

Nathaniel Paul walked to the edge of the abyss and pulled back. Other men and women, bolder perhaps, certainly more desperate, crossed the line. These men and women belonged to a minority party, a party we might say, speaking metaphorically, of Saturday night—a party that scoffed at pretty words and pretty dreams, a party that said, with blood, that life was absurd and that a God who would consign Blacks to such a living hell was either a madman or an idiot. The doctrine of this party was eat, drink, make love, and take all you can, wherever you can, however you can, from whomever you can, for the fast black train of death is coming.

> Same train carry my mother,
> Same train, same train.[28]

This party had deep roots in the slave quarters. Sterling Brown tells us that "irreverent parodies of religious songs . . . passed current in the quarters," where otherworldness was mocked and "Bible stories, especially the creation, the fall of Man and the flood were spoofed. 'Reign, Master Jesus, reign' became 'Rain, Mosser, rain hard! Rain flour and lard and a big hoghead, Down in my back-yard.' "[29]

The party of the nihilists or proto-nihilists grew in strength after the overthrow of Reconstruction and the establishment of new forms of slavery. In that period, and afterward, some Blacks spoke the language of existential absurdity:

> Our father, who is in heaven,
> White man owe me eleven and pay me seven,
> Thy kingdom come, thy will be done,
> And if I hadn't took that, I wouldn't had none.[30]

The adherents of this party were and are, in general, apolitical types—hustlers, con men, drifters. But the party has attracted some activists. It is strange, however, that neither the political nor the apolitical wings of the party has created a systematic philosophy of nothingness or absurdity. Lawrence D. Reddick made this point, among others, in an important essay, "No Kafka in the South." "Many a sensitive Negro in the South—and without doubt in other places, too—must have felt or dreamed that he was a cockroach . . . or that he is daily called upon to face trial on charges that are never stated, by an accuser he can never confront . . . or that as he pursues some ever-receding hilltop, a vast invisible leprosy eats away life, his life."[31] Many Blacks must have felt these things, in the old days, and in our days, but, as Reddick said, the Black South—and I would add the Black North—has not produced a Kafka or—I would add—a Sartre. That fact is very strange, and for the purpose of this discussion, meaningful.

In the light of this general background, there would seem to be little reason to question the thesis that most Blacks—at least until recent times—supported the providential view of a God-controlled Black history. One piece of evidence in support of this assertion is the almost universal approval of the Black National Anthem—"Lift Every Voice And Sing." You know the words:

> *God of our weary years, God of our silent tears,*
> *Thou who has brought us this far on the way,*
> *Thou who hast by thy might, led us into the light,*
> *Keep us forever in the path, we pray.*[32]

It is only fair to note that the coauthor of this anthem—James Weldon Johnson—is on record as saying that he never believed the philosophy of this song and that it was his personal view "that the universe is purposeless [and] that man, instead of being in the special care of a Divine Providence, is dependent upon fortuity and his own wits for survival in the midst of blind and insensate forces." Curiously enough, Johnson added that history is nevertheless "charged with meaning" and that human beings need at the very least "the idea of God."[33]

Whatever the meaning of Johnson's personal quest for meaning, it is established beyond doubt that the meaning he gave "Lift Every Voice And Sing" became the central, almost official, Black view of Black history. This view gained strength in the sixties with the triumph of the Freedom movement and the popularity of "We Shall Overcome," which stated explicitly that God is on our side and that the Black cause will triumph one day all over the world.

> *The whole wide world around*
> *The whole wide world around,*
> *The whole wide world around some day.*[34]

There are cynics who will tell you they never believed that foolishness. But I was there, and I tell you truly that there were few, if any, disbelievers in the foxholes of Selma and the trenches of Mississippi. But the situation was more complicated behind the battle lines. I recall a night in Chicago, at a rally on the West Side, when that song literally had men and women weeping in the aisles. Some of us, on that faraway night, made long and undoubtedly dull speeches on the inevitability of the historical process. The last speaker of the night was Nahaz Rogers, one of the most talented agitators of the sixties. Rogers began his speech with a blunt statement that also brought the house down. "People," he said, "are running around here saying that God is on our side. If God is on our side, we are in more trouble than I thought we were." The fact that this audience responded so enthusiastically to both sides of the argument probably means that this audience, and probably most Black people, believed and believe both things at the same time.

To this analysis, we must add another ingredient: the sensational and continuing success of Martin Luther King's "I Have a Dream" speech, which said that the universe is governed by a moral law and that there will be a time of fulfillment and meaning either on the Last Day, or on some day before it, when "the rough places will be made plain, and the crooked places will be made straight."[35] This speech's success would seem to indicate that the providential view is still alive and well in Black America. But it is impossible to overlook statistical facts—the growing army of drug addicts, Black-on-Black crime, and so on—which seem to indicate that the opposing party has moved, for perhaps the first time, into a position that poses a serious challenge to the providential view. There is also some evidence to indicate that the collapse of the Freedom movement and the institutionalization of an age of almost permanent economic depression have led to a massive failure of historical nerve in Black America, and that a feeling is growing that History and the White man are too much for us.

Climbing Jacob's Ladder

Against this larger background, we can turn now to the responses of Black historians. And we should not be surprised to learn that Black historians have generally followed Black orthodoxy. As is well known, George Washington Williams, who wrote the first comprehensive history of Black America, said on the last page of his work that "in the interpretation of *History* the plans of God must be discerned. *'For a thousand years in Thy sight are but as yesterday when it is passed, and as a watch in the night.'* "[36] The same note was struck in the histories of William T. Alexander and Edward A. Johnson.[37] It is perhaps relevant in this general connection that Williams and many of the first supporters of Black history were ministers with a devout commitment to the dramatic Christian conception of history. As late as 1921, Benjamin Brawley, another minister, concluded his history by saying that "above the law of the state—above all law of man—is the law of God."[38]

With the founding of the Association for the Study of Negro Life and History and the institutionalization of the study of Black history, the providential view receded into the background and was replaced in almost all Black histories by what Lawrence Reddick called a vague sense of "liberalism" and "progress."[39] There is some evidence to indicate that Carter G. Woodson, the founder of the Association, had, in the words of Benjamin E. Mays, "a slight disbelief in an all-seeing Providence."[40] Mays inferred this from Woodson's comments on the world view of rural Blacks:

> They laugh at those who doubt the existence of an all-seeing Providence and question the divinity of His Son. The Lord has delivered these Negroes from too many trials and tribulations for them to doubt His power or His interest in mankind. God is not held responsible for the Negroes' being carried away captive to be the slaves of white men; but he is given credit for delivering them from bondage. God has nothing to do with their long persecution and the intolerable conditions under which they have to live, but great praise should be given Him for permitting them to exist under the circumstances.[41]

From the tone of this and other passages in Woodson's writings, it is possible to infer that he believed that the meaning of Black history was in the hands of Black people and that God—if he existed—helped Black people who helped themselves. It is possible to infer this, but it is not possible to assert it, for—astonishingly—there has been little or no systematic examination of the philosophy of history of the father of Negro history.

In his brilliant address to the twenty-first annual meeting of the Association, Lawrence Reddick said that "it is remarked that the history of Negro historiography falls into two divisions, *before* Woodson and *after* Woodson. In this later span, remarkable improvement has been made in method and scholarship. But when it comes to the fundamental frame of reference, that is, the final interpretation, the philosophy, even this division may not be necessary."[42] It would seem that on the level of meaning, on the level of "the final interpretation," very little has changed in Black historiography since publication of Reddick's address. And it is my view, based on a study of general histories written by Black historians, that Black historiography, my own works included, is still organized around a "Jacob's Ladder" reading, that it posits linear progress toward a largely undefined goal.

We can see this tendency clearly if we look for a moment at representative responses of modern Black historians. Perhaps the best place to start is in the 1940s with Richard Wright's "folk history," *12 Million Black Voices*. Writing in 1941, Wright saw Black history as a process of "cataclysmic" social change in an abbreviated time span.

> We have tramped down a road three hundred years long. We have been shunted to and fro by cataclysmic social changes.
> We are a folk born of cultural devastation, slavery, physical suffering, unrequited longing, abrupt emancipation, migration, disillusionment, bewilderment, joblessness, and insecurity—all enacted within a *short* space of historical time![43]

Wright added:

> Standing now at the apex of the twentieth century, we look back over the road we have traveled and compare it with the road over which the white folks have traveled, and we see that three hundred years in the history of our lives are equivalent to two thousand years in the history of the lives of the whites![44]

What was the meaning of the road and the journey?

> We black folk, our history and our present being, are a mirror of all the manifold experiences of America. What we want, what we represent, what we endure is what America *is*.[45]

In his pathfinding general history, John Hope Franklin said Blacks had "a special function" in American and world history. Black Americans, he wrote, "had become an integral part of Western culture and civilization, and their fate was inextricably connected with it. The rejections that they had suffered doubtless wounded them considerably, but such treatment gave them a perspective and an objectivity that others had greater difficulty in obtaining." He concluded: If America's role was to lead the world toward peace and international understanding, Negro Americans had a special function to perform in carrying forward the struggle for freedom at home, for the sake of America's role, and abroad, for the sake of the survival of the world.[46]

The doctrine of challenge was also articulated in J. Saunders Redding's history, published in 1950. He quoted, with approval, the 1947 Report of the President's Committee on Civil Rights and added:

> When, later, the report was made the basis of a national civil rights program, Negroes knew that whatever came, the direction of inexorable and unforgiving history was set, as indeed—though in doubt and terror and pain and blood (which may not cease till the millennium)—it had been all along, toward the fulfillment of democracy and the total equality of all men.[47]

History moved in the same general direction for Benjamin Quarles, who said in his 1964 history that the Black American was "a watchman on the wall"—a watchman who had played a major role "in enlarging the meaning of freedom and in giving it new expressions."[48] He added, "The story of the Negro in the United States is a combination of the tragic and the heroic, of denial and affirmation. But most of all, it is the record of a tidal force in American life."[49] At another point in the same work, Dr. Quarles said:

> Negro history not only furnishes a preface to racial understanding; it unfolds a dramatic story, if indeed not an epic one, studded with interesting and arresting personalities, white and colored. Moreover, the role of the Negro in this country has been rich in meaning; Frederika Bremer saw it as symbolic, reminding Americans in 1849 that "the romance of your history is the fate of the Negro."[50]

The same general vision informed C. Eric Lincoln's history, which was published in 1967. He interpreted Black history as "a pilgrimage" into "the mainstream of American culture and life." That pilgrimage, he said, "is not over. We have not seen the end of the anguish and the bitterness, the hardships and disappointments which have characterized so much of the social history of America. But the end is near. The very fact that there has been such a pilgrimage—a fateful and persistent journey by a highly visible minority across the historical and social domain of a powerful majority, from slavery to freedom to responsible participation in every phase of the life of the prevailing society—is itself a monument to the persistence and forbearance of the American people."[51]

As this brief survey indicates, almost all modern Black histories are organized around two germ cells—the concept of the debt and the doctrine of challenge. I believe, in opposition to some of my colleagues, that both concepts contain the seeds of possible meaning. This is particularly true of the doctrine of challenge. The problem I have with the traditional approach to this doctrine is that it is almost always focused on the challenge that Black history presents to American civilization. A more viable approach, in my view, is that Black history is first and foremost a challenge to Black people.

Beyond all that, I would say that neither "challenge" nor "contributionism" is a philosophy in and of itself. The same thing can be said about the new generation of Black historians who have organized themselves around the idea of "the critical stance." I am in total agreement with men and women who say that Black historians are obliged, by their vocation, to take a critical stance toward the whole of American history. But a critical stance is a mood, not a philosophy. And the task before us now is the task of organizing isolated concepts and moods and frames of reference into a systematic philosophy of meaning and significance. That I would say is our *second* task. Our *first* task is the task of banishing forever from Black historiography the ahistorical concept of New Negroes and New Blacks. There are no new Blacks. New Blacks are simply old Blacks standing on the shoulders of their fathers.

Nothing attests to this view more forcefully than the career of W. E. B. DuBois, who is an exception to almost anything you can say about Black historians. As we have noted, DuBois grappled with the question of meaning until the day of his death. And Vincent Harding is almost certainly correct when he identifies DuBois with a philosophy of "Black Messianism" which conceived of "Africa's rejected children" as the vanguard of a vast crusade to save the human race.[52] But, as we have said, DuBois is an exception to everything, including W. E. B. DuBois. And there are other elements in the DuBois synthesis which resist easy conceptualization. For one thing, he repeatedly used the word God—either as a myth or as a shorthand symbol for History or the Ultimate Cause. And in one of the most extraordinary utterances of his life he suggested—the same idea was suggested in another form by Howard Thurman[53]—that God needs man in order to save Himself.

> Prayest Thou, Lord, and to me?
> *Thou* needest me?
> Thou *needest* me?
> Thou needest *me*?
> Poor, wounded soul!
> Of This I never dreamed. I thought—
> *Courage God,*
> *I come.*[54]

Since DuBois's death, Black historians have generally avoided systematic explorations into the question of meaning. But the questions he raised still haunt Black historians and Black historiography. And it is worth emphasizing that a number of Black thinkers, most notably Samuel DuBois Cook, Vincent Harding, and Earl E. Thorpe, have continued to build on the foundations he raised.[55] The collapse of the Freedom movement and the challenge of the conservative backlash have underlined the urgency of this quest—a quest that is a matter of moment to all Blacks. For all men and women have philosophies of history; and their practical philosophies, *the philosophies they live,* determine, in large part, what they do and what they think of themselves and of their historical group.

By all this we must understand that the history men and women make is a function of the meaning they give history. For it is from their practical philosophies, from the frames of reference they use to judge events and leaders and movements, that they get their level of hope and challenge. The indomitable tenacity of spirit of our forefathers and foremothers was based, in part, on a sense of unfolding meaning and purpose. They endured, they found the courage to live, and the courage to struggle, and the courage to die, in the meaning they gave history. We may quarrel, from our vantage points, with the meaning they gave *their* blood, but we cannot rise to the level of their historical passion if we do not make explicit in our own minds what we think *our* blood means and where we think our history is going.

For all these reasons, and for others as well, we are condemned to the task of trying to make sense out of our history. It is our task, as Beard said, to examine our own frames of reference and to give them consistency of structure "by a deliberate conjecture respecting the nature or direction of the vast movements of ideas and interests called world history."[56] That task is being pursued on the level of theology, on the level of *ultimate* meaning, by a number of brilliant Black theologians, including Gayraud S. Wilmore and James Cone.[57] And I believe the future of Black history, and the future of Black people *in* history, depends on a similar quest on the level of history. And from my perspective, that quest must unfold within the context of five propositions.

The Inside Outsiders

I. Black history is history and must be interpreted historically against the unfolding stream of world history. This is easier said than done, for history is a heartbreakingly difficult and dangerous enterprise, and it is neither safe nor wise to deal with it on its own level without the aid of either philosophy, theology, or hard drink. Hegel said in the introduction to his *Philosophy of History* that history is a slaughter bench on which the dreams and ideals of peoples have been repeatedly sacrificed. We didn't need Hegel to tell us that, for we are witnesses of a history of blood and suffering. And we know, or at least we should know, that history is hard, history is unforgiving, and a book is not its goal.

But there is another dimension of history, for if history is a gravedigger, it is also a midwife. And if we take the risk of situating ourselves on the level of history, and history alone, then our only hope in history is the mastering of history. On the concrete level of historical interpretation this means that we are invited to take the leap from our sector of history into history by considering Black history as a moment, a crucial moment, in history, defined here as the ongoing, continuing, never-ending flow of mankind to itself. But in order to make such a leap we must first see ourselves, and all Blacks, as historical and social actors confronted by overwhelming and incontrovertible forces, facing one of the greatest historical challenges of all times, with the odds 100 to 1 against us, and all the high ground in the hands of our adversaries.

II. The second proposition is that Black history is real. That's a simple point, but simple points must be made. For most people—perhaps most historians—don't believe that history is real. They think it is a story in a book or a career or a monograph in a scholarly journal But history, read right, is a much more fateful encounter than that. Read right, history—and Black history is history—is the ground of our being. For we are not historical because we historicize; rather we historicize because we are historical in the very depths of our being, because history is in us and around us, because history to us is what water is to the fish. History, in other words, envelops us, situates us, defines us, and names us. It prestructures our lives in general, throwing us down here instead of there, with this color instead of that color, with this task instead of that task. And from this standpoint, it means something real to be born Black in the United States of America. It does not mean, as so many people say, that we have a certain history. We do not have that history; that history has us. More precisely, we are that history. And there is nothing we can do in history that will ever free us of that history.

There is meaning, historical meaning, in that fact, and we cannot, no matter what we do, escape the meaning history gave us and the meaning that history demands of us. There is meaning in the fact that we were born in a certain place with real and inescapable relations to particular historical conflicts that we did not start but that we cannot avoid by virtue of the fact that we were born *there, then,* and *with*. . . . And we understand ourselves and our history when we understand that we are not only responsible for what we have done but also for what our group has done, when we understand that history requires us to answer not only for our own lives but also for the lives of the men and women who share our historical destiny.

There is another point that bears on this subject, and it has to do with the fact that history is a determining force that sets real limits to the social strivings of men. It is history that creates the paths and the tools and the contexts that lead to or away from certain goals. It is history that creates the conditions that make some things possible and other things impossible. It follows from this that men and women cannot do anything they want to in history. They are always limited by objective historical conditions. Within this real but limited Limit, they are free to make their own history. But the only history they can make *in that situation,* as so many people, including C. L. R. James, have said, is the history that *history*—the relation of forces and the orchestration of effective public demand as embodied in dominant currents and trends—makes it possible for them to make.

All this has bearing on our interpretation of Black history. For these considerations enable us to understand that the voluntarist fallacy—so widespread in Black historical interpretations—is a snare and delusion which leads us away from history. Precisely similar reasons argue against historical interpretations based on the whims and caprices of personalities and leaders. These interpretations do not advance our understanding of history; for leaders—even a Booker T. Washington, even a Martin Luther King, Jr.—are functions of specific historical situations, and they, too, are limited by prevailing historical conditions—by the available instruments, the ratio of forces, the level of consciousness, and the balance of group interests. Not only that, leaders are products of history, and to understand them—and history—one must interpret the personalities by the history, and not the history by the personalities. The important point is that history is not a personality contest but a life-and-death struggle between groups who, at various points in their trajectory, throw up individuals who can tell us, if we know how to question them, the level of consciousness of the people who support them or at least tolerate them. And from this perspective, every historical movement has the leaders and cadres that it deserves—that is to say, the only leaders and cadres that were possible or available under those historical circumstances at that level of consciousness.

This is a crucial nuance, which reminds us once again that it is impossible to understand historical actors without an understanding of historical Limits. But this notion of Limits requires a very delicate delineation if it is not to be used as an excuse for inaction. The problem here is to steer a steady course of analysis and action between the Scylla of Black conservatives and moderates, who tend to see Limits everywhere, and the Charybdis of Black nationalists and radicals, who tend to see possibilities everywhere. If we hope and intend to redeem the pledges of our fathers and mothers, and if there is still time, we must create a new paradigm of action and analysis that integrates these unprofitable alternatives into a higher synthesis. This synthesis, in turn, must be based on a hard and continuous confrontation with the question of what is objectively possible in particular historical situations. This question must be posed anew for every situation, for what was objectively possible in 1960 may not be objectively possible today, and certainly was not objectively possible in 1890. And in our attempt to answer this question, we must never forget that the possibilities of historical action are enormously extended in times of crisis and that there are magic moments— Montgomery, Watts, the Sit-Ins—when almost anything is possible. Beyond all that, it is necessary to remember that the impossible in history is established not by analysis but by action, and that the impossible is sometimes a synonym for the untried.

Having said all that, we must immediately add that history has decided that some things *are* impossible for Blacks in America. It is not possible, for example, for Blacks to take over and *hold* the United States government or the government of any state or city. Nor is it possible for Blacks to create an independent Black state in America or to take over a section of a city and establish an independent economy. Will someone say that the only reason these things are impossible is because they haven't been tried? But they have been tried—by White men with large armies—and the question was settled once and for all at Appomattox.

Equally strong reasons argue against the possibility of transporting the Black people of America to Africa. Without going into the question whether Blacks want to emigrate, it can be said that there are not enough boats, planes, or planks in the world to transport 26 million people anywhere, and there is no country in the world willing or able to receive 26 million people. We are here then, and here we almost certainly will remain. "This," to quote DuBois again, "the American black man knows: his fight here is a fight to the finish. Either he dies or wins. If he wins it will be by no subterfuge or evasion of amalgamation. He will enter modern civilization here in America as a black man on terms of perfect and unlimited equality with any white man, or he will enter not at all. Either extermination root and branch, or absolute equality. There can be no compromise. This is the last great battle of the West."[58]

This line of reasoning is hard, but it leads in the direction we want to go. For history is real and it has real exigencies that must be understood before they can be transcended. Black history is an invitation to an understanding of both the exigencies and the possibilities of their transcendence. For it is the exigencies that define the possibilities and the possibilities that define the exigencies, which are not absolute limits on our freedom but the preconditions of our freedom. For our purposes, the meaning of Blackness is precisely the necessity of freely re-acting (with pride, humiliation, joy, sorrow) to the coefficient of Blackness in the world. Black history is an invitation to an understanding of both the necessity and the freedom. It is an invitation to our inheritance as sons and daughters of a people history couldn't destroy, a people who never ceased to resist and hope, a people who mastered—in the fields of slavery and the streets of Montgomery and Watts—the philosophical maxim that freedom is necessity confronted, understood, and transcended.

III. The third proposition is that Black history is a totality in the process of becoming. It is the sum total of the micro- and macro-projects of *all* Black people. It is the movement or lack of movement of that totality as determined by the pressure or lack of pressure of millions of acting and nonacting individuals. (And from this point of view, nonaction is action.) And the historical significance of any particular moment, the apathy of this individual, the action of that individual, the proposal of this group or the call to action of that group—the significance of these particular projects is determined and *judged* by their impact or lack of impact on the movement or lack of movement of the totality.

Now this proposition has several dangerous implications. For it means, first of all, that *the history of Black people is the history of Black people*—and not the history of any particular sector or group. It is not the history of nationalists, integrationists, Marxists, or capitalists—it is rather the history of nationalists, integrationists, Marxists, capitalists, *and* the overwhelming majority of Black people, who are none of these things, and perhaps all of them.

Another dangerous implication is that individual leaders get their meaning from their relationship, or lack of relationship, to the movement of the Black totality. There is, in fine, a dialectical relationship between the people and their leaders. For in the final analysis, Black history is made not by isolated leaders and representatives but by the movement of the totality which creates contexts—in response to the movement of the White totality—which make it possible for certain individuals with certain skills and temperaments to come to the fore.

This dialectic applies not only to individual leaders but also to individual historians, for the historian is historical and has an obligation to the history he writes and the history he inhabits. And within that ensemble of ideas, we ought to put it down as a maxim that anyone—Black or White—who deals with Black history without dealing with himself in that history has understood neither himself nor the history. For as Maurice Merleau-Ponty has said, "Historical knowledge is a coexistence with the meaning of a people and not the solitary reflections of a historian."[59]

IV. Black history is a real moment in the history of two larger and contradictory histories—the history of the American people, an entity in the Western world, and the history of Africans and other peoples of color, who are by definition outsiders in the Western world. Black history is therefore a history with a double simultaneous reference and a double simultaneous contradiction. *It is a history of the inside outsiders.* And it must be interpreted, in my view, both in terms of its particularity and its universality. Two fifty-dollar words, which mean simply that our history is linked to, dependent upon, and a reflection of the worldwide struggles of Africans and peoples of color. But it is a universal struggle unfolding in a particular context at a particular time under determinate conditions.

V. Black people have a mission, a world-historical mission, by virtue of their historical situation. This mission is not imposed. It is not abstract. It is not subjective. It is one with their situation, which cannot be comprehended without reference to the meaning that is inherent in the situation.

This proposition brings us squarely to a point that has never been explored adequately, to my knowledge, on the philosophical level. And that point is that *the Black people* of America did not come to America. Let me say that again in a different way: *African-Americans did not come to America.* Who came to America? Millions of Africans from different national and linguistic groups. They came, these Africans, as individuals, but they came from the same historical space and they shared certain cultural and philosophical presuppositions. And when these *individuals* stepped off the ship, they stepped into a new historical space with three or four historical imperatives that were addressed to them personally. The first imperative was survival. And the second, growing out of the first, was the creation of a people, a social group or, if you please, a nation. And the record shows that our African fathers and mothers met that challenge. In the unpromising setting of the Slave Rows of America, and in the free Black communities of Philadelphia and Boston and New York, our founding fathers and mothers remade themselves as they remade America, creating a new synthesis, in part African, in part European, in part X. And the creation of that synthesis, and the creation of the foundations of America, were two of the greatest flights in the history of the human spirit. If our ancestors had done nothing else, they would have a claim on us and history. But, astonishingly, they did do something else. There was another challenge in their situation, the challenge of freedom, and in order to give meaning to that meaning, African-Americans were forced by their circumstances to struggle for a deepening of the meaning of freedom in America. We know what that struggle has meant, and what it *is*, and if we want to get a historical perspective on our situation, we need only imagine what historians would say if the slaves, the external proletariat (to appropriate Arnold Toynbee's phrase) of Rome had changed the Roman Empire as much as African-Americans have changed the most powerful empire in the history of the world.[60] That struggle is by no means over. The struggles of slavery and the Civil War and the Reconstruction and the sixties were stages on the road to an unfulfilled meaning that lies before us like our own shadows projected on a wall.

This formulation will no doubt disturb those Blacks who have taken the position that they are tired of saving America and other people. But that response, which is certainly understandable on the emotional level, is the wrong answer to the wrong question. History doesn't ask us to save America; what it asks us to do is to save ourselves—if we can. But—and this is the key point—history in its wisdom, or its malevolence, has put us, as it has put so many other peoples, in a situation where in order to save ourselves we have to perform a world-historical task that will not only help us but will also help others. But all this is intolerably abstract. The only thing I am saying here is that we have been placed at the bottom of a crucial social formation at the center stage of world history. And if we rise from our space in our own name and interest, we will throw upward and outward all the strata that have been resting on our backs. That was the meaning of the Black maneuver in the Civil War. It was the meaning of the Black maneuver in the sixties, and it is the meaning of the Black situation today. For we find ourselves once again in the eye of one of history's greatest storms. That storm brought us out of Africa and scattered us pell-mell over the Western Hemisphere. And now, after only five hundred years—a mere second in the history of the world—that storm, the great storm of European expansion and conquest, is receding before the massed might of the colored peoples of the world, who are struggling to reclaim themselves and their lands and their visions. As Americans, as *African*-Americans, as inside outsiders, we have a central and contradictory relation to that struggle, which is one of the greatest events in the history of mankind. To put the matter bluntly and simply, we occupy crucial ground in a crucial country that is going to play a crucial role in determining the outcome of that struggle and the future of mankind. And from this perspective, Ralph Ellison was correct when he said, in another connection, that "the end is in the beginning, and lies far ahead."[61]

And so, at long last, we are in a position to look DuBois's question full in the face. He asked—Remember?—what shall our suffering and triumphs and trials mean? My answer to that question is that the meaning of our history, like the meaning of history, is in process, and that it is up to us to create the meaning that we already are by deepening the furrows of a meaning that has been given to us. There is nothing deep or mystical about this. We have all seen relay races on TV in which several men run *one* race by covering a certain amount of territory and then passing the baton on to another runner who repeats the same process. This same dynamic is at work on a deeper and more desperate level in the rhythm of the generations. For peoples, races, and nations advance on the shoulders of succeeding generations. One generation runs as fast as it can and then passes the baton on to another generation, which runs as fast as it can and then passes the baton on, *ad infinitum*.

It is easy to see from all this that each generation is dependent not only on the generations immediately preceding and following, but on all the generations that will run the race. And thus we are responsible, totally responsible, not only for ourselves but for the whole of the Black experience. For it is only through us that the dreams of the past can be fulfilled. It is only through us that the first slave can reach the finish line. It is only through us that Martin Luther King, Jr., can reach the peak of the mountaintop and the slaves can finally say, "Free at last! Free at last!"

What does it all mean?

It is up to us to decide what it means by what we say, by what we write, by what we do. It is up to you, it is up to me, it is up to us, working together, to make sure that the slaves and the sharecroppers and the martyrs and victims did not bleed and dream and die in vain.

There is no meaning for the Black living or the Black dead or the Black unborn outside the great Black chain of that hope.

Notes

1. Maurice Merleau-Ponty, *Phenomenology of Perception* (New York, 1962), p. xix.
2. W. E. B. DuBois, *The Gift of Black Folk* (Boston, 1924), p. 341.
3. Earl E. Thorpe does not necessarily share my point of view, but his critique of *Black Historians* (New York, 1971), contains valuable insights.
4. Robert L. Harris, Jr., "Coming of Age: The Transformation of Afro-American Historiography," mimeographed (Africana Studies and Research Center, Cornell University), p. 5.
5. Raymond Aron, *Introduction to the Philosophy of History* (Boston, 1961); C. L. R. James, *The Black Jacobins* (New York, 1963); Maurice Merleau-Ponty, *Signs* (Evanston, 1964), *Sense and Non-Sense* (Evanston, 1964), *The Primacy of Perception* (Evanston, 1964); Jean-Paul Sartre, *Being and Nothingness* (New York, 1956), *Search for a Method* (New York, 1963), *Critique of Dialectical Reason* (London, 1976), *Situations* (New York, 1965); E. P. Thompson, *The Making of the English Working Class* (New York, 1966). See also Paul Ricoeur, *History and Truth* (Evanston, 1965).
6. W. E. B. DuBois, *Darkwater* (New York, 1920), p. 25.
7. See Lerone Bennett, Jr., "Of Time, Space and Revolution," in *The Challenge of Blackness* (Chicago, 1972).
8. Karl Popper, "Has History Any Meaning?" in *The Philosophy of History in Our Time*, Hans Meyerhoff, ed. (New York, 1959), p. 304.
9. I have followed here and adapted for my purposes a schema suggested by Charles A. Beard's presidential address to the American Historical Association, "Written History as an Act of Faith," *American Historical Review* 39, no. 2 (January, 1934): 219-229. I did not intend here to exhaust all the possibilities; I simply wanted to show the broad possibilities and limitations. See also Karl Löwith, *Meaning in History* (Chicago, 1949), and Marc Bloch, *The Historian's Craft* (New York, 1953).

10. Beard, "Written History," p. 226.
11. Ibid., p. 227.
12. Ibid., p. 228.
13. Lerone Bennett, Jr., *The Shaping of Black America* (Chicago, 1975), pp. 114-115.
14. John Dewey, "Historical Judgments," in *Philosophy of History*, pp. 170-171.
15. Committee on Historiography, *Theory and Practice in Historical Study*, Social Science Research Council (New York, 1946), p. 20.
16. Ibid., p. 21.
17. Ibid., pp. 22-23.
18. Beard, "Written History," p. 221.
19. Louis Gottschalk, *Understanding History* (New York, 1964), p. 9.
20. *Golden Encyclopedia of Folk Music* (New York, 1973), pp. 180-181.
21. James Weldon Johnson and J. Rosamond Johnson, *The Books of American Negro Spirituals* (New York, 1944) 1: 148.
22. Bennett, *Shaping of Black America*, p. 162.
23. Zora Neale Hurston, *Mules and Men* (Philadelphia, 1935), p. 306.
24. Paul Radin, "Status, Phantasy, and the Christian Dogma," in God Struck Me Dead: Religious Conversion Experiences and Autobiographies of Negro Ex-Slaves, A. P. Watson, Paul Radin, and Charles S. Johnson, eds., unpublished manuscript (Nashville, 1945) quoted in Lawrence Levine, *Black Culture and Black Consciousness* (New York, 1977), p. 33.
25. Arthur Huff Fauset, *Sojourner Truth* (Chapel Hill, 1938), p. 176.
26. Benjamin E. Mays, *The Negro's God* (Boston, 1938), p. 61. See also Otey M. Scruggs, "We the Children of Africa in This Land: Alexander Crummell," in *Africa and the Afro-American Experience*, Lorraine A. Williams, ed. (Washington, 1977), pp. 77-95.
27. Carter G. Woodson, *Negro Orators and Their Orations* (Washington, 1925), p. 69.
28. Johnson and Johnson, *American Negro Spirituals*, 2: 60.
29. Sterling A. Brown, "Negro Folk Expressions," *Phylon* 14 (first quarter, 1954): 50.
30. Ibid., p. 52.
31. Lawrence D. Reddick, "No Kafka in the South," *Phylon* 11 (fourth quarter, 1950): 380-383.
32. Langston Hughes and Arna Bontemps, eds., *The Poetry of The Negro* (New York, 1970), p. 32.
33. James Weldon Johnson, *Along This Way* (New York, 1933), p. 413.
34. Guy and Candie Carawn, eds., *We Shall Overcome* (New York, 1963), p. 11.
35. Doris E. Saunders, ed., *The Day They Marched* (Chicago, 1963), pp. 81-85.
36. George W. Williams, *History of the Negro Race in America* (New York, 1883), p. 552.
37. William T. Alexander, *History of the Colored Race in America* (Kansas

City, 1888); Edward A. Johnson, *A Short History of the Negro Race in America* (Chicago, 1891).
38. Benjamin Brawley, *A Social History of the American Negro* (New York, 1921), p. 389.
39. Lawrence D. Reddick, "A New Interpretation for Negro History," *Journal of Negro History* 22 (January 1937): 21.
40. Mays, *Negro's God*, pp. 211-212.
41. Ibid., p. 212.
42. Reddick, "A New Interpretation," p. 21.
43. Richard Wright, *12 Million Black Voices: A Folk History of the Negro in the United States* (New York, 1941), p. 142.
44. Ibid., p. 145.
45. Ibid., p. 146.
46. John Hope Franklin, *From Slavery to Freedom* (New York, 1980), p. 505.
47. J. Saunders Redding, *They Came in Chains* (Philadelphia, 1950), p. 303.
48. Benjamin Quarles, *The Negro in the Making of America* (New York, 1964), pp. 264-265.
49. Ibid., p. 9.
50. Ibid., p. 8.
51. C. Eric Lincoln, *The Negro Pilgrimage in America* (New York, 1967), p. 158.
52. Vincent Harding, "W. E. B. DuBois and the Black Messianic Vision," *Freedomways* (first quarter, 1969), pp. 44-58.
53. Mays, *Negro's God*, p. 175.
54. DuBois, *Darkwater*, p. 252.
55. Samuel DuBois Cook, "A Tragic Conception of Negro History," *Journal of Negro History* 45 (October 1960); Vincent Harding, "The Gift of Blackness," *Christian Century,* February 1968, "Beyond Chaos: Black History and the Search for a New Land," in *Amistad* I (New York, 1970); Earl E. Thorpe, "Philosophy of History: Sources, Truths, and Limitations," *Quarterly Review of Higher Education Among Negroes* 25 (July 1957), *The Uses of Black History* (Raleigh, 1980).
56. Beard, "Written History," p. 228.
57. James H. Cone, *Black Theology and Black Power* (New York, 1969), *A Black Theology of Liberation* (Philadelphia, 1970); Gayraud S. Wilmore, *Black Theology and Black Radicalism* (New York, 1972).
58. W. E. B. DuBois, *Black Reconstruction* (New York, 1935), p. 703.
59. Merleau-Ponty, "Phenomenology and the Sciences of Man," *Primacy of Perception,* p. 92.
60. Arnold J. Toynbee's discussion of internal and external proletariats in vol. 5 of his *Study of History* is suggestive, but he fails, in my view, to make a proper distinction between the two categories. The internal proletariat, he said, is composed of "three distinct elements: disinherited and uprooted members of the society's own body social; partially disinherited members of alien civilizations and primitive [?] societies

that had been conquered and exploited without being torn up by the roots; and doubly disinherited conscripts from these subject populations who were not only uprooted but were also enslaved and deported in order to be worked to death on distant populations." There is, in my view, a fundamental difference between the first category and the *internal* external proletariats of the second and third categories.

61. Ralph Ellison, *Invisible Man* (New York, 1947), p. 5.

CHAPTER 2

Africana Studies: A Decade of Change, Challenge and Conflict

John Henrik Clarke

Nearly a generation ago, in "The Negro Writer and His Relationship to His Roots," the speech that opened the first conference of Black American Writers to be held in this country, Saunders Redding said:

> I do not feel in the least controversial or argumentative about the announced subject. Indeed I have touched upon it so often in one way or another that I long ago exhausted my store of arguments, and if I now revert to a kind of expressionistic way of talking, my excuse for it is patent.[1]

The subject of my paper was already old, with me, before this decade, and before the Black Studies explosion. The serious study of the plight of African people all over the world, in all ages, conditions, and geographical settings, has been the main part of my life's work. It is the all-consuming passion of my existence. It is something I do, just as breathing is something I do.

In his speech, Professor Redding said that his was the kind of subject which, if he talked directly on it for more than twenty minutes, he would have to talk at least a year. He assured his audience that he would not talk directly on the subject and, of course, that he would not talk a year; that his treatment would be more suggestive than exhaustive. The rereading of his paper has influenced my approach to Africana Studies. I prefer the phrase "Africana Studies" to "Black Studies." Black is an honorable word and I am glad to see so many people lose their fear of using it, but it has its limitations. Black, or Blackness, tells you how you look without telling you who you are, whereas Africa, or Africana, relates you to land, history, and culture. No people are spiritually and culturally secure until it answers only to a name of its own choosing, a name that instantaneously relates that people to the past, present, and future. As the Caribbean writer Richard B. Moore has said in his book *The Name "Negro": Its Origin*

Dr. John Henrik Clarke is a Professor in the Department of Black and Puerto Rican Studies at Hunter College (CUNY) New York, New York

and Evil Use, "Slaves and dogs are named by their masters. Free men name themselves."[2] In his book, Moore also expresses something that is increasingly rare in the present academic climate—a conviction based on research and reason. "Human relations," he writes, "can not be peaceful, satisfactory, and happy until placed on the basis of mutual self-respect. The proper name for people, has thus become, in this period of crucial change and rapid reformation on a world scale, a vital factor in determining basic attitudes involving how, and even whether, people will continue to live together on this shrinking planet."

One of the many crises in what is called Black Studies is a crisis in semantics. What exactly do we mean by Black Studies?[3]

I have called Black Studies a dilemma at the crossroads of history. This dilemma has long historical roots and we cannot understand it if we regard it as only a current event. Indeed, the dilemma dates from the rise of Europe in the fifteenth century. Looking back, we see that entire peoples have to be read out of the respectful commentary of history in order to justify the slave trade and the colonial system that followed.[4] Europeans and white people, in general, benefitted from this distortion of world history, and it is clear that they know more about history than they are prepared to admit. They had to know a great deal in order to distort history so effectively, and then use this distortion as an element of world control. They knew that history is a two-edged sword that can be used both as an instrument of liberation and as a weapon of enslavement. And I might add, they knew then and they know now that history, like a gun, is neutral—it will serve anyone who uses it effectively.

To understand, then, what brought this dilemma into being, we return, at least briefly, to the fifteenth and sixteenth centuries, the period of the second rise of Europe. All the world was changed to accommodate this event, which was followed by the European conquest of most of mankind. This conquest was achieved by the astute use of two political instruments—the Bible and the gun. In addition to colonizing the world, the Europeans colonized information about the world—the writing of world history. They were so successful that today not a single book with the title "World History" is an honest history of the world and all of its people. World history lost its broad definition and became a rationale for European conquest and control, and a means for the glorification of European people at the expense of other people and nations whose civilizations were old before Europe was born.

The first European attack was on African culture. The next move was to deny that this culture ever existed. A look at African culture, especially in West Africa, will show what Africana Studies Programs are about, or should be about.[5]

There is now a need for a global approach to Africana Studies, one that embraces the Africans in Africa, in North and South America, and in the Caribbean Islands, as well as the millions of Africans in Asia and the Pacific Islands who are just discovering that they are African people. Because history is both topical and ancient, and cannot be separated, there is no way to talk about Africana Studies without looking again at the roots of world history and the interplay among the histories of various peoples. The Black historian, who knows his people's history and its relationship to the history of the world, should start with the bold assertions that Africa is the basis of world history, and that African people are the mothers and fathers of mankind. Black scholars, the world over, must be courageous enough to make this assertion and prepare themselves to prove it academically.

This is the basis of the Black scholar's dilemma and the root of the crisis over definition and direction. The special role that history assigns to the scholar eludes most of us: the role is simple, therefore it is complex. In most societies the scholar is not required to labor in the fields, to draw the water, or to bring wood for the fires. Then what is the scholar required to do? What is his or her special mission? The scholar is the clock watcher of history and the keeper of the compass that must be used to locate his or her people on the map of human geography: where they have been and what they have been, where they are and what they are. Most important, the scholar should be able to prophesy where his people still must go and what they still must be.

The scholar should be able to find the special clock that tells his people their historical, cultural, and political time of day. Part of our tragedy is that we have been, figuratively speaking, telling time by our oppressor's clock. By his clock it could be midnight in December because he is losing control of the world. Because we are reemerging, with hope flowing before us like a river, it is a morning in spring on our special historical clock.

If we look honestly at the Black writer in crisis, we must see that

Black writers collectively are an integral part of all those Black people who have been in a continuous crisis ever since their forced exile from Africa to what was later called the New World. It is logical that a people who live in continuous crisis should produce a literature of crisis and this, in essence, is what Black literature has been from the beginning and what it remains today. There is no place that Black writers can hide from this crisis; they take it with them wherever they go. Indeed, they are bound to it most profoundly even on those sad occasions when some of them try to pretend that they have escaped it. In spite of these pretenders who think that they are writers first and Black people second, most Black writers feel their responsibility to Black people.[6]

More than any other writers in the world, Black writers live in the midst of their material and cannot escape from it. Estranged in the Western world, where even after five hundred years of exile from Africa their people are neither guests nor citizens, their life is a repeated contradiction; and so is the literature about their life. It is a literature that is simultaneously negative and positive. It is negative because it is a literature about alienation; it is positive because it is a literature about heroic struggle and survival in spite of alienation.

Black writers are, concurrently, the most fortunate and the most unfortunate writers of this age. They are fortunate because the most important thing that is happening in this age is happening to their people. They are unfortunate because, in most cases, they do not understand the nature and historical importance of this happening. The reverberation of their people's struggle has pushed the oppressor's originality, if indeed he ever had any, to the limits of its logic, has worn its source out, and has forced him to lose control of the world. Part of the crisis of Black writers is to explain this world to themselves and to their people—a task that cannot be accomplished without a historical frame of reference.

This is an extraordinary situation so let us use our imagination to create an extraordinary way of looking at it. Let us take this crisis out of the framework of history and sociology for the moment and instead regard it as a drama with many dimensions and with long historical roots. The drama is not pure: part comedy and part tragedy, it is sometimes also a satire and there are even elements of farce. It is a mystery play about the greatest crime ever contrived by the mind of man. The recurring theme of this drama is rape—the rape of a continent and its people. This rape set in motion an act of protracted genocide that lasted for five hundred years and that has not completely exhausted itself today. The aftermath of this crime is the basis of the Black world drama and the crisis that no Black writer can avoid.

With this said we can now, figuratively, put the players on stage. In the unfolding of this great human drama that we call the "Black Crisis," the characters play every role from saint to buffoon. The first scene in the play is pleasant, and there is nothing that suggests future developments. Some sailors have arrived along the coast of West Africa. The year is 1438. With their customary hospitality to strangers, the Africans have invited the sailors to dinner—a scene that will be repeated many times before it is turned into a tragedy. The Africans do not know the temperament of these strangers, nor do they sense the ambition and intent that are hidden behind their smiles. The sailors have come from a thawed-out icebox in northern Asia called Europe. The people from this violent land have begun to search for new gold, labor, and a new supply of food. They find all of these items in Africa and they do not buy or bargain for them—they take them. In the second scene of our play's first act, the dinner is over and the guests are looking around the house of their hosts. They like many of the things that they see, including the wife of the host. Suddenly all expressions change. The guests take out guns, rape the wife of the host, and enslave both of them (and I do not mean figuratively). Thus the long night begins. The curtain falls on the first act of a play that, in many ways, is still on the road.

My basic point is that all Black writers in the West, and most of them in Africa, have been reacting to the consequences of this play. As guests in the homes of non-European people, the Europeans turned on their hosts and forced them away from their homes to labor in the far reaches of the world, mainly in North and South America, the Caribbean Islands, and in the United States. The dilemma and the crisis in Black writing is how to interpret this event and its far-reaching, tragic aftermath. These consequences are the primary content of the literary heritage of Black writers—the materials from which they can never escape. Out of these materials came the slave narratives, the spirituals, and the blues.

I am talking about something that is both historical and topical, which helps to explain why we can understand the present by looking through the lenses of the past. We need both vantage points in order to understand the present disputes over the ideas of nationalism and Pan-Africanism. We Blacks have had these arguments before, much to our sorrow. As a people, each time we forget that our Blackness (or Africanity) is our rallying cry, our window on the world, and the basis of our first allegiance, we find ourselves in serious trouble. To explain this fact I must make an admission that breaks my heart as well as yours. Throughout history we have been a politically naive people. We have never made a good alliance with another people, least of all with white people. I do not mean that we have never made alliances with other people, only that they have not been in our favor. In the future we should enter into only those alliances that we can control.[7]

Africans are the only people who permit other people to live in their home, meaning their country, for hundreds of years without declaring allegiance to their house. We have nearly always invited our future conquerors to dinner. This misplaced humanity and hospitality to strangers is at once the strongest and the weakest aspect of an African way of life. It is the strongest because it is the basis of African humanity; it is the weakest because all too many strangers have come into Africa and taken advantage of the African's generosity. People who think they can trust every stranger who enters their home are politically naive. This is an aspect of the African world situation which we have not studied or fully acknowledged as a problem, and it will remain as long as we ignore its ancient roots. When what we call Black Studies matures, we will take a global view of African people and understand how they relate to other peoples. This will be the culmination of a long intellectual struggle that started in the first half of the century.

Early in the twentieth century there emerged Black scholars who began to analyze and interpret the history and struggles of African people from an international point of view. They saw how African history related to world history, and they, more than their predecessors, were successful in locating their people on the map of human geography. A new African awareness developed with the concept of Pan-Africanism.

This atmosphere nurtured new men and movements, who gave Black scholarship the real text of its existence: DuBois's book of essays, *The Souls of Black Folks,* published in 1903. This was a different kind of scholarship, more explanatory than argumentative. In 1905, DuBois helped to bring the Niagara Movement into being. In 1909, the ideas of this movement helped to create the National Association for the Advancement of Colored People (NAACP).

The need to analyze and interpret the place of African people in world history grew more critical during the first two decades of this century. In his own way, Carter G. Woodson answered that need. After serving many years as a teacher in public schools, Woodson became convinced that the role played by his people in American history and in the history of other cultures was being either ignored or misrepresented. In 1915 he founded the Association for the Study of Negro Life and History to conduct research into "the history of the Negroes all over the world." The next year he began publication of the *Journal of Negro History,* which has never missed an issue.

A chronicle of Woodson's far-reaching activities must include: the organization in 1921 of the Associated Publisher, Inc. to "make possible the publication and circulation of valuable books on the Negro not acceptable to most publishers"; the establishment of Negro History Week in 1926; the initial subsidizing of research in Black history; and the writing of many articles and books on Afro-American and American life and history.[10]

Woodson believed that there was no such thing as "Negro history," insisting that what was called Negro history was only a missing segment of world history. He devoted the greater portion of his life to restoring this segment. He also realized that once this segment was integrated into school textbooks and taught with respect and understanding, there would no longer be a need for a Negro History Week.

Woodson also argued that history cannot be restricted by the limits of race, nation, or people. Roman history is Greek as well as Roman; both the Greek and the Roman are Egyptian because the entire Mediterranean was civilized from Egypt; and Egypt in turn borrowed from other parts of Africa, especially Ethiopia, and from the Orient. Africa came into the Mediterranean world mainly through Greece, which had been under African influence; and then Africa was cut off from the melting pot by the turmoil among the Europeans and the religious conquests incidental to the rise of Islam. Prior to these events, Africa had developed an indigenous history and civilization. It reentered the general picture of history through the penetration of

North Africa, West Africa, and the Sudan by the Arabs, but subsequently was subjected to the ravages of the European and American slave traders. The imperialist colonizers and missionaries finally entered the scene and prevailed until the recent reemergence of independent African nations.

In sum, we can say that scholars such as DuBois and Woodson created the theoretical basis for the "Black Power" and "Black Studies" explosion, and for a reconsideration of the concept of Pan-Africanism.[11]

Up to the end of the nineteenth century, with a few exceptions, American literature was still an imitation of European literature. American literature, coming from white writers in the genuine American way, is principally a literature of the twentieth century. Before this time there was very little that was imaginative in American literature except the slave narrative and the slave autobiography, which was an improvement on the slave narrative.

During the same decades that DuBois and Woodson were laying the foundations of the future Black Studies Movement, education was a recurring theme in Black writing. In most cases the educated Black man was the pillar of the Black community. A generation later, some Black writers would see, in retrospect, how miseducated a large number of Blacks were, for they had been trained to fit into a society that had rejected them. This, in part, was the basis of the fight between Booker T. Washington and W.E.B. DuBois. A few Black scholars believed that the Afro-Americans had no African heritage to reclaim. W.E.B. DuBois and his followers opposed this view. At the start of the twentieth century, then, Afro-Americans found that two schools of thought competed for their attention in their search for new directions: the school of Booker T. Washington and the school of W.E.B. DuBois.[9]

Black Americans had entered the twentieth century searching for new directions politically, culturally and institutionally. The Black woman was very much a part of this search. Booker T. Washington's Atlanta Cotton Exposition Address (1895) had set in motion a great debate among Black people about their direction and their place in the developing American social order. As new men and movements were emerging, some men, principally Bishop Henry McNeal Turner, questioned whether Black people had any future in America. The Black woman answered this question in the affirmative by pouring massive energy into building new institutions, primarily schools.[12]

This nineteenth- and early twentieth-century reaction to oppression by the Black American intellectual community was part of the search for direction, definition, and status in the world community. At the center of this search stood W.E.B. DuBois.[13]

After being introduced to the international significance of Africa at the First Pan-African Congress in London in 1900, DuBois remained committed to the unification of Africa for the rest of his life. At the Second Pan-African Congress in Paris in 1919 (sometimes referred to as the First Congress), DuBois emerged as the movement's world leader, the capacity in which he appealed to the League of Nations and other international organizations on behalf of African people.

In his essay "My Mission," published in *Crisis Magazine* in April 1919, DuBois said: "I went to Paris during the time of the Peace Conference because the destinies of mankind for a hundred years to come were being settled by the big four, because they had the power through their armed forces, capital and propaganda machines to do so." He went on to say that thirty-two nations, people, and races had permanent headquarters in Paris. He felt it imperative for African people to make their presence known in Paris at this time.

The Second Pan-African Congress adopted eleven resolutions and submitted them to the Peace Conference then meeting at Versailles. The first two resolutions applied only to Africans, calling for a Code of Laws for the international protection of Africans and for the establishment of a permanent bureau to oversee the application of that code to their political, social, and economic welfare. The remaining resolutions applied to Africans and people of African descent living in countries outside the African continent. The question of the slave trade had been raised by the British at the Congress of Vienna and the specific question of the Belgian Congo, had been raised on the international level, but the Second Congress marked the first time that the Blacks themselves had raised the international issue of the Black condition.

Referring to this congress, DuBois has said:

> "I went [to Paris] with the idea of calling a "Pan African Congress" and trying to impress upon the members of the Peace Congress meeting at Versailles the importance of Africa in the future world. I was without credentials or influence, but the idea took on. I tried to get a conference

with President Wilson, but only got as far as Colonel House, who was sympathetic but non-commital."

The Pan-African Congress of 1921 made resolutions similar to those of the 1919 congress, but was more specific in the proposals that it presented to the new League of Nations. It called for the establishment, under the League, of an international institution for the study of African problems and asked that an international section to protect African labor be set up under jurisdiction of the Labor Bureau of the League.

After the Pan-African Congress of 1921, DuBois went to Geneva where he met with the head of the Mandates Commission and talked with Albert Thomas, head of the International Labor Organization. Through the Haitian representative to the League, the Pan-African Congress submitted a petition that asked that a "man of African descent" be appointed to the Mandates Commission as soon as a vacancy occurred. The petition also asked the League to devote some of its attention to the plight of the millions of Black people living in countries outside Africa who were being discriminated against. An interesting landmark in the development of Black political thought, this petition has far-reaching implications for international politics both because it asserts that the race problem is international and because it maintains that an international organization has a responsibility to concern itself with that problem within particular nations. The petition also asserts the ultimate aim of self-government for all people.

The petition thus illustrates my point that W.E.B. DuBois was never a narrow partisan. For most of his public life, extending over two generations, he had an international view of the problems of his people. He was a nationalist, a Pan-Africanist, and a socialist, and he saw no contradiction between these three positions; his love of his own people gave him an appreciation of all people. He was one of the pioneers in calling for a reinterpretation of the history of Africa and of African people throughout the world. A generation before the proliferation of Black Studies Programs in the United States, he said:

> Afro-American History cannot be honestly taught without some reference to its African background and the Black American's search for the meaning of that background and its relationship to their present-day lives.
>
> The Africans who came to the United States as slaves started their

attempts to reclaim their lost African heritage soon after they arrived in this country. They were searching for the lost identity that the slave system had developed. Concurrent with the Black man's search for an identity in America has been his search for an identity in the world, which means, in essence, his identity as a human being with a history, before and after slavery, that can command respect.

The elder statesman among Afro-Americans, DuBois addressed himself to the broader aspects of this situation on the celebration of the Second Anniversary of the Asian-African (Bandung) Conference and the rebirth of Ghana of April 30, 1957, when he said:

> From the fifteenth through the seventeenth centuries, the Africans imported to America regarded themselves as temporary settlers destined to return eventually to Africa. Their increasing revolts against the slave system, which culminated in the eighteenth century, showed a feeling of close kinship to the motherland and even well into the nineteenth century they called their organizations "African," as witness the "African Unions" of New York and Newport, and the African churches of Philadelphia and New York. In the West Indies and South America there was even closer indication of feelings of kinship with Africa and the East.

DuBois affirmed this statement in practice during the last years of his life. In the fall of 1961, he and his wife, Shirley Graham DuBois, took up residence in Ghana at the invitation of the late Kwame Nkrumah, then president of Ghana. He had gone to Ghana mainly to work on the *Encyclopedia Africana,* a massive project that he had conceived as early as 1909. Soon after arriving in Ghana, he and his wife became Ghanaian citizens, a choice consistent with their Pan-Africanist commitment. He had helped to organize and participated in all of the Pan-African Congresses that occurred in his lifetime.

DuBois died in Accra, Ghana, on 27 August, 1963 at the age of ninety-five, on the eve of the historic March on Washington. On 9 September, the Board of Directors of the NAACP passed a resolution mourning his death and calling him "a pioneer in the struggle for human rights." The members of the Board noted that DuBois was:

> the prime inspirer, philosopher and father of the Negro Protest Movement, a founder of the NAACP, an impassioned and eloquent spokesman for equal rights, a fierce and uncompromising foe of colonialism and promoter of the Pan-African Congress, and the most eminent scholar and historian of the Black race in America and Africa. . . .
>
> His literary, historical and sociological contributions were so vast and all-inclusive that no serious research in the African field can be done without reference to the work of Dr. W.E.B. DuBois.

All the events that I have reviewed constitute a long preface to the change, challenge, and conflict in Africana Studies over the last decade. Beyond the search for definition and direction is the search for an ideology. Africana Studies without an ideology is a recitation of days, places, personalities, and events. A people search for their past in order to understand the present and reshape the future. The search referred to here is a recurring theme in the history of African people, in particular, and of all people in general. Because our memories are short and we have not creatively converted history into an instrument of our liberation, most of us do not know that there was no ideology in our world until we created one. Therefore, our search for an ideology is a search for our lost values. We are trying to restore what the slave trade and colonialism took away. Ours is a search for a positive ideology, an ideology of liberation—an ideology that asks and answers the question: How will our people stay on this earth?

Yet at this critical moment in our history, Black intellectuals, young and old, are engaged in an ideological battle that is a sad waste of time. They are trying to resolve the proposition, "to be or not to be a socialist," despite the fact that everyone who has done any serious thinking lately realizes that some form of socialism is our only viable political alternative. Men and women of vision and intelligence, with a knowledge of history, no longer debate this point. My argument is with the new motley crew calling themselves "socialists," which they are not. In most cases they are political copouts, looking for another white slavemaster; failing that, they will accept a yellow master from China or a mulatto master from Cuba. They will do anything except be their own masters.

These self-proclaimed "theoreticians" act as though Black people have no ideological contributions to make to their own salvation, yet, had they done their homework they would know that the concept of socialism was old among African people before Karl Marx and even Europe—was born. If the matter were left to them, they would lead us—like whores and hungry dogs—in search of the political ideological leavings of a dying people. For our salvation we should draw on the intellectual heritage of the whole world—beginning with our own intellectual heritage. If our people are cold, we should invade hell and borrow fire from the devil, but we should not become the devil's disciple. We should properly read the signs of history and remember: What we do for ourselves depends on what we know of ourselves and what we accept about ourselves.[14]

This is what the struggle in Africana Studies over the last decade has been about. This is what our revolt against white scholars in Montreal, Canada, in 1969 was about. All too many of us who were at Montreal, and who were also founding members of the African Heritage Studies Association (AHSA), seem to have forgotten the challenge we flung before white scholarship at Montreal, a challenge that we also agreed to accept for ourselves. We dreamed some big dreams that day and we promised to make them into realities. Just for the record, let's hear some of them again, taken from the "Aims and Objectives of AHSA":

INTRODUCTION:

The African Heritage Studies Association (AHSA) is an association of scholars of African descent, dedicated to the preservation, interpretation and academic presentation of the historical and cultural heritage of African peoples both on the ancestral soil of Africa and in diaspora in the Americas and throughout the world.

AIMS AND OBJECTIVES:

Education

1. (a) Reconstruction of African history and cultural studies along Afrocentric lines while effecting an intellectual union among Black scholars the world over.
   (b) Acting as a clearing house of information in the establishment and evaluation of a more realistic African Program.
   (c) Presenting papers at seminars and symposia where any aspect of the life and culture of the African peoples are discussed.
   (d) Relating, interpreting and disseminating African materials for Black education at all levels and in the community at large.

International

2. (a) To reach African countries in order to facilitate greater communication and interaction between Africans and Africans in the Americas.
   (b) To assume leadership in the orientation of African students in the U.S. and orientation of Afro-Americans in Africa (established contacts).
   (c) To establish an Information Committee on African and American relations whose function it will be to research and disseminate to the membership information on all aspects of American relations with respect to African peoples.

Domestic

3. (a) To relate to those organizations that are predominantly involved in and influence the education of Black people.
   (b) To solicit their influence and affluence in the promotion of Black Studies and in the execution of AHSA programs and projects.
   (c) To arouse social consciousness and awareness of these groups.
   (d) To encourage their financial contribution to Black schools with programs involving the study of African peoples.

Black Students and Scholars

4. (a) To encourage and support students who wish to major in the study of African peoples.
   (b) To encourage Black students to relate to the study of the heritage of African people, and to acquire the ranges of skills for the production and development of African peoples.
   (c) To encourage attendance and participation including the reading of papers at meetings dealing with the study of African life and history so that the American perspective is represented.
   (d) To ask all Black students and scholars to rally around AHSA to build it up as a sturdy organization for the reconstruction of our history and culture.

Black Communities

5. (a) To seek to aid Black scholars who need financial support for their community projects or academic research.
   (b) To edit a newsletter or journal through which AHSA activities will be known.

In Montreal we called for an Afrocentric approach to the history of African people. In the last decade most of the books written from an Afrocentric point of view have been written by African and Afro-American writers who did not belong to our group. In closing I would like to call attention to the importance of this approach to our history.

Notes

1. Saunders Redding, "The Negro Writer and His Relationship to His Roots," in *The American Negro Writer and His Roots: Selected Papers from The First Conference of Negro Writers, March 1959,* (New York, 1960), The American Society of African Culture, pp. 1-8.

2. Richard B. Moore, "The Name "Negro": Its Origin and Evil Use," (New York, 1960), Afroamerican publishers, Inc. Also Raphael P. Powell, "Human Side of a People and The Right Name," (New York, 1927). The

Philemon Co. Reprinted by University Microfilms, Ann Arbor, Michigan, 1969.

3. "Black Studies, A Dilemma at The Crossroads." By John H. Clarke, Lecture prepared for the Afro-American Studies Program, Simmons College, Boston, Mass., 5 April 1978.
4. "Black History and The Future." Lecture by John H. Clarke, prepared for Department of Afro-American Studies, Howard University, Washington, D.C., 18 February 1976.
5. "The Black American Writer in Crisis." By John H. Clarke, Lecture prepared for The National Conference of Afro-American Writers, Howard University, Washington, D.C., 8-10 November 1974.
6. "Black-White Alliances: A Historical Perspective." By John H. Clarke. Institute for Positive Education. Chicago, Illinois, 1972.
7. A Adu Boahen, in The Horizon History of Africans of Africa (New York: 1971), pp. 304-351. American Heritage Publishing Co. In the same book see also, John H. Clarke, "Africa: Time of Trouble," pp. 352-399.
8. W.E.B. DuBois, *The Souls of Black Folk,* (Greenwich, Conn.: 1961) Crest Books, Fawcett Publications, pp. 42-53.
9. John H. Clarke, "The Black Woman in Education: A Figure in World History," *Black Collegian Magazine,* vol. 5, no. 2 (1974): p. 40. Also see, Dorothy Porter, "Early Negro Writers 1760-1837." (Boston, 1937), Beacon Press, p. 3.
10. John H. Clarke, "Education in The Making of the Black Urban Ghetto," in *Black Manifesto For Education,* James Haskins (New York: William Morrow and Co. Inc., 1973), pp. 16-40.
11. Sadie Iola Daniel, *"Women Builders"* (Washington, D.C., 1969), Associated Publishers, pp. 79-167.
12. "Pan-Africanism and The Liberation of Southern Africa: A Tribute to W.E.B. DuBois." Edited by John H. Clarke, for the United Nations Centre Against Apartheid. Published by the African Heritage Studies Association. New York, 1978. See Introduction.
13. "The Black American's Search For An Ideology." By John H. Clarke. Lecture prepared for the Eighth Conference of the Center for African and African-American Studies, Atlanta, Ga., 4-6 December 1975.

II

The Status of Black Studies: The Second Decade

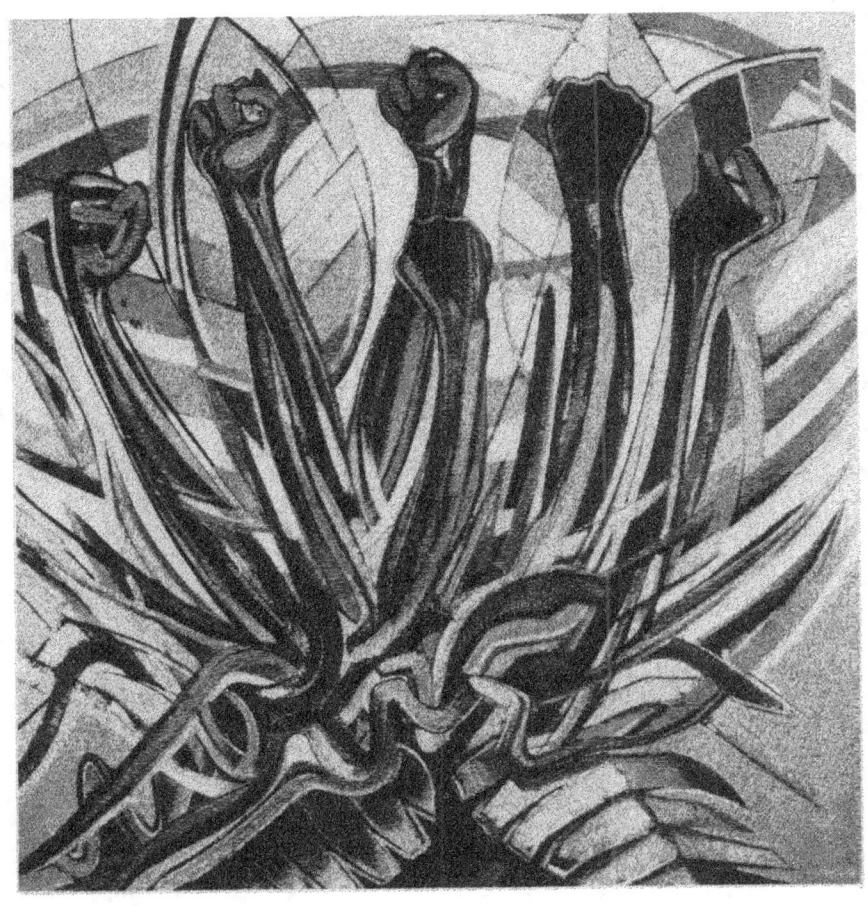

Natural Growth, Bertrand Phillips

CHAPTER 3

The Status of Black Studies in the Second Decade: The Ideological Imperative

Tilden LeMelle

In its second decade the status of Black Studies will be a function largely of the kinds of answers its faculty and students give to two as yet unresolved questions that confronted Black Studies in the first decade. Indeed, though the answers may change according to the changing realities that the Black world must address, the questions will always remain the same:

1. Why Black Studies? What are the historical and academic imperatives for Black Studies?

2. Black Studies for what? What is the educational mission of Black Studies?

The answer to the first question has been, is, and will remain the same for a long time to come. The historical imperative for Black Studies is now a matter of record, and the academic imperative will remain until the socialization function of Black Studies has transformed the psyche of the United States—Black and non-Black—to the point that the legitimacy of Blackness is as fully institutionalized as the legitimacy of whiteness is today. That point lies beyond the lifetime of every member of this conference.

The historical and academic imperatives of Black Studies are founded in the following historical logic:

1. Traditional education afforded Black Americans in the United States has been largely dysfunctional. It has been designed and has served primarily to meet the needs of a white dominant, racially stratified society. Thus, it has not only neglected and disregarded the needs and interests of the Black American but has aimed to socialize the Black man to anti-Black values and has aimed to tool the Black man only to the degree it was necessary for the Black man to serve the needs and interests of the dominant white community. In a word, education has served to maintain and secure the dominant/subordinate relationships between white and Black in the United States.

Dr. Tilden J. LeMelle is Acting Provost of Hunter College (CUNY) New York, New York

2. This dysfunctionalism is largely a product of the almost total and systematic exclusion from the various academic disciplines—especially the humanities and social sciences—of the Black experience as a legitimate subject matter.
3. When the Black experience has been included as part of the academic curriculum, it has been studied from the dominant white point of view.
4. Since the Black experience is an inherent and integral part of the total American experience, it must be included as an integral and essential part of the total educational process.
5. Finally, since Blacks cannot now entrust whites with what whites failed to do or did poorly in the past, the establishment and development of the Black curriculum must be in the hands of and under the control of Blacks.

To most participants in this conference, this statement of the historical and academic imperatives of Black Studies may seem a statement of the obvious, but it has not always been perceived as such. Moreover, there remain many for whom these historical and academic imperatives are not obvious or for whom they must be ignored or subsumed under some ideological prerogatives. These latter are the ideologues—the political religionists—who view ideology as an end in itself rather than as a means to an end. Blinded by this teleological approach, they fail to recognize that in a white dominant, racially stratified society such as the United States, Black Studies is per se political and, accordingly, constitutes its own justification. Consequently, they look for an ideological justification that imposes a priori directions and limitations on matters of curriculum and methodological development.

The danger that the continuing irresolution of the first question poses for Black Studies in the next decade is the same that has plagued traditional education for American Blacks for the last century and that currently plagues education for Blacks in the newly independent African states on the continent and in the Caribbean. That danger is the development of countervailing ideologies and philosophies of education that will make Black Studies a mere servant of their ends—a situation that would ultimately render Black Studies irrelevant to the educational needs and interests of Blacks. It was, of course, the irrelevancy of much of traditional education that contributed, at least in part, to the demand for Black Studies in the first place. The reduction of Black Studies to irrelevancy would be a travesty of the highest order.

The countervailing ideologies that have traditionally plagued education for American Blacks and that now pose a threat to Black Studies as well can be reduced to two categories Black assimilationist ideologies and Black self-determinationist ideologies.

The Black assimilationist ideologies are those that historically have informed the traditional education of American Blacks at both the Black and the predominantly white colleges. These ideologies are born of the ambivalence that white America has had about American Blacks and that those Blacks have had about themselves—ambivalence about the Black man's place in the United States, ambivalence about the educability of Black people, and, therefore, ambivalence about the realistic function of education for Blacks and their relationship to U.S. society in general and to the Black community in particular.

This environment of uncertainty has naturally had an impact on the educational process in all aspects of Black education: Could the American Black be educated? Was he to be educated for total participation in American life or only for participation in the Black community? What kind of education should he have? These were some of the questions that those concerned with education for Blacks had to answer. A philosophy of education depended on the answers and an ideology for educational development demanded precise answers.

Whether the American Black was educable was answered by the fact that, when given the opportunity, Blacks successfully completed the best curricula U.S. education had to offer. Despite their achievement, however, and notwithstanding the fact that they were considered inferior in all other respects, Black educational achievers were looked upon either as the exceptions that proved the rule or as people who owed their success to the "white" blood of their slavemaster progenitors or to their associations with "superior" whites.

Lest some of us think that the foregoing are the racist assumptions of a bygone era, we should be reminded that the Jensens and the Shockleys are of our own day and are bent on "proving scientifically" that Blacks are less capable of educational achievement than whites. Moreover, since the *Brown v. Board of Education* decision of 1954, the basic premise of school desegregation has been that Blacks can achieve quality education only through "integration" with whites. Not only do racist whites accept this premise and fight it through antibusing tactics, but such Black organizations as the NAACP also believe it and support it through their insistence that school "integration" is the only means for achieving quality education for Blacks, regardless of whether such integration achieves this end or not. Furthermore, the attitude, often expressed by many inner city Black youth, that Blacks who achieve in school are trying "to be white" is a further, unconscious expression of the belief in the superior educability of whites. The doubters, Black and white, persist today despite all evidence to the contrary.

American Blacks have not yet resolved the questions about the academic rationale of education for Blacks philosophically and ideologically, but factually and historically these questions were resolved by the reality of the American Blacks' dual existence in a racially stratified American society. Education for Black citizens has reflected the irresolution and ambiguity of the Black/white conflict, and answers to the question about the content of education for Black citizens have reflected the same duality. As a result, education for American Blacks has not developed its potential in relation either to white dominant American or to subordinate Black America. The old ambivalence remains the millstone it has always been and the rhetoric goes on, now threatening even Black Studies. Such ambivalence derives from the utter futility of assimilationist rationalizations in a fundamentally anti-Black society.

Black Assimilationist Ideologies and Black Studies

The Black assimilationist ideologies are Black Accommodationism, Black Reconciliationism, Black Liberal Idealism, and Black Marxism-Leninism. These ideologies are essentially "other" oriented and, accordingly, they are anti-Black. In a racially stratified society (racist) such as the United States, where there is only one legitimate point of reference in terms of race (i.e., white), any Black who is "other" oriented is fundamentally anti-self—anti-Black.[2]

The "other"-orientation of these Black ideologies is manifested in:

1. The expressed need to be accepted by the "other," as illustrated by:
    (a) Positing change in the relationships with the "other" by making accommodations to the will of the "other" (Accommodationism).

(b) Positing change in the relationships with the "other" by appealing to the *good will and moral sense* of the "other" (Liberal Idealism).
2. The need to be associated with the "other," as illustrated by:
   (a) Positing the reconciliation of differences in Black/white relationships solely in accordance with the rules established by the "other" (Reconciliationism).
   (b) Positing change in the relationships with the "other" through the formation of coalitions with some members of the "other" on the basis of a misconceived notion of class which disregards "race" as if it did not exist (Marxism-Leninism).

Each of the Black assimilationist ideologies gives rise to a philosophy of education which defines its goals primarily from a non-Black context.

The Ideology of Black Accommodationism

Among American Blacks, the best-known exponent of Black Accommodationism was Booker T. Washington, who clearly enunciated that ideology in his Atlanta Exposition Speech:[3]

> The Negro in the South has it within his power if he *properly* utilizes the forces at hand, to make of himself such a valuable factor in the life of the South that he will not have to seek privileges, they will be freely *conferred* upon him.[4]

In other words, Washington advised the Black man to serve his white betters in a way that would demonstrate his ability to achieve the levels of responsibility and respectability deemed acceptable by the white community, in return for which he would be deemed worthy of the rights and privileges enjoyed by the responsible and respectable white man. In pursuit of his policy of conciliation and accommodation, Washington formulated an educational program that called for the vocational training of Black men—in essence an attempt to fulfill the basic role inherited from slavery and assigned to the Black American by the post-slavery white community. More important, the black education that Washington envisaged nurtured attitudes of resignation to and compliance with the Black man's status in a racist society. It tended to legitimize only those aspirations which did not disturb the status quo and, in limiting what he *ought* to achieve, in reality imposed arbitrary limits on what the Black man *could* achieve. Contrary to the stated goals of Black self-development, this program tailored Black education to the needs and aspirations of the white community, thereby thwarting meaningful development in the Black community. Fortunately for Black education and the Black community as a whole, Washington's philosophy did not prevail. It was countervailed by the ideology of reconciliationism.

The Ideology of Black Reconciliationism

The ideology of Black Reconciliationism, which unlike accommodationism does not avoid conflict, seeks compromise through confrontation—confrontation within the established rules of the game. This ideology was best articulated by W. E. B. DuBois in his dissertation, *Talented Tenth*. Here DuBois writes that

> the Negro race, like all races, is going to be saved by its exceptional men. The problem of education, then, among Negroes must first deal with the Talented Tenth; it is the problem of developing the Best of this race that they may guide the Mass away from the contamination and death of the Worst, in their own and other races.[5]

It is interesting to note DuBois' allusion to the type of leader Black education should produce—a leader like the *Best* in other races. He continues:

> Indeed the demand for college-bred men by a school like Tuskegee, ought to make Mr. Booker T. Washington the firmest friend of higher training. Here he has as helpers the son of a Negro senator, trained in Greek and the humanities, and graduated at Harvard; the son of a Negro congressman and lawyer, trained in Latin and mathematics, and graduated at Oberlin; he has as his wife a woman who read Virgil and Homer in the same classroom with me; he has a college chaplain, a classical graduate of Atlanta University; as teacher of science, a graduate of Fisk; as teacher of history, a graduate of Smith. . . .[6]

This passage clearly expresses the type of Black leadership to be produced by this kind of Black education: the select Harvard and Smith graduate of the day, easily quoting from the Latin Virgil and the Greek Homer, fashionable and proper, using the correct fork at banquets and quoting the latest witticism from Europe. These were the people who would *speak* to the plantation Black and to the domestic worker—undoubtedly in the idiom of Virgil and Homer.

Aside from his unrealistically elitist orientation, the assimilationist-reconciliationist assumes that the culture—the values—of the "other" are superior and, hence, he shapes Black education to produce Blacks who define the "good" in terms of those values and define their goals in terms of the interests of the assumedly superior "other." Clearly, in a racially stratified (racist) society, to pursue the goals of the "other" is to act in a way that is inherently anti-self.

The Ideology of Black Liberal Idealism

Black Liberal Idealism has been best espoused in recent times by Martin Luther King, Jr. It is the philosophy of the "last true believers" in the values and ideals of the normative theory of American liberal democracy. It is the expression of an undying faith both in the assumption of man's basic goodness and in the conviction that goodness will eventually triumph over the evils of American society.

The political and economic realities of U.S. society force liberal idealism to remain an ideal as an ideology for Black educational development. The vested interest in the present brokerage and group orientation of U.S. politics and the quid pro quo of the economic marketplace preclude the concrete realization of liberal idealism in any U.S. social institutions, thus making it impossible to conceive of this ideology as the basis for the renewal of education for U.S. Blacks. As expressed in the dictum "Education for Democracy," this ideology has even been rejected by many young whites.

The real danger in Black liberal idealism is that despite its irrelevancy to progressive change and development in U.S. Black/white relations, both groups may accept it because it is emotionally and psychologically satisfying. It holds out to Blacks the traditional assimilationist hope of "Black and white together," whereas it provides whites with a cathartic assuagement of conscience which allows them to think of themselves as "nice guys." The disengagement of white liberals from the Civil Rights Movement once they were confronted with Black self-assertion is evidence of the futility of liberal idealism as an ideology for Black educational development.

Like Black Accommodationism and Reconciliationism, Black Liberal Idealism channels Blacks toward dependency on the "other" as the guarantor of their rights and the legitimizer of their interests and aspirations. That "other" is the same liberal who screamed racism-in-reverse and condemned Black self-assertion as Black separatism, and for whose anti-Black behavior the term "white backlash" was created.

The Ideology of Black Marxism-Leninism

Black Marxism-Leninism deludes itself in disregarding the racial factor and instead defining its plans for Black education solely on a misconceived class basis. At the same time, its exponents erroneously equate class with income level, defining middle and upper income Blacks as a "Black middle and upper class"—a definition fully consonant with the self-delusions of many such Blacks. These Black Marxist-Leninists view low-income whites as "working class," and, in an attempt to actualize the rhetoric of "working classes of the world unite," they seek coalitions with the white working class—precisely the group that has perennially been the overseer keeping U.S. Blacks in their place. That American Blacks neither individually nor collectively control the regulation of society (political power) or the production and distribution of wealth (economic power) escapes the Black Marxist-Leninists. That the pension funds and collective wealth of white labor vie with and join with white corporate and financial institutions to control political and economic decisions in the United States also escapes them. Moreover, they seem unaware that middle and upper incomes for Blacks indicate only an ability to consume (often conspicuously) and that this consumption in turn strengthens the hands of those who regulate society and control the production and distribution of its wealth. Accordingly, the Black Marxist-Leninist—often in the middle and upper income brackets and a conspicuous consumer—spurns fellow Blacks in his pursuit of an alien ideology that tells him to make coalitions and alliances with the "other."

These same ideologues label African communalism "primitive" and "unscientific," deriding it as a source of socialist inspiration. Their, "scientific" rhetoric blinds them to the fact that race and class are coterminous in a white dominant, racially stratified society, and that the race/class controversy is therefore irrelevant. The Black Marxist-Leninist believes that education for Blacks should develop values that transcend race, incorporating the values and interests of those members of the "other" who are most often the immediate instruments of the oppression of Blacks. Noble though those seemingly nonracial ideals are, they are as unrealistic as the assumptions that provided a rationale for Washington's accommodationism and as racist as the assumptions that underlay the paternalism of the French *colons* and the white liberalism of the 1960s.

The Ideologies of Black Self-Determination

At best, Black assimilationist ideologies lead to activities that provide an opportunity to change only the *conditions* of American Black existence while retaining their *position* as the underclass. In a reaction to that realization and to the futility of the assimilationist ideologies of the Civil Rights Movement, the ideologies of Black Self-Determination came to fruition in the mid-1960s. These were the ideologies that led Black students and faculty on predominantly white college campuses to demand the establishment of Black Studies programs.

The Black self-determinationist ideologies can be categorized under the more general heading of Black Nationalism. Like the assimilationist ideologies, Black Nationalism in the U.S. was not a phenomenon unique to the 1960s. Black slave revolts, the Garvey Movement, some aspects of the Harlem Renaissance, Carter G. Woodson's Black History Movement, and so on, are all manifestations of a Black Nationalism in the United States. Furthermore, it should be noted that the confusion that often surrounds the false dichotomy between Black Nationalism and Pan-Africanism derives from the attempt to make a real distinction between the domestic and the international focus of Black Nationalism. Borrowing the limited European definition of nationalism as a phenomenon of the modern nation-state, some of us impose that definition on Black realities, thereby distorting our perception of them. If Black Nationalism means anything, it means identification with the interests and aspirations of Black people wherever they may be, regardless of state boundaries.

In analyzing the history of Black Nationalism in the United States, we can draw a useful distinction between Psychological Nationalism and Separatist Nationalism. The former distinguishes clearly between the self and the other and identifies self-interest as *distinct* though not necessarily always separate from the interest of the other. Thus, it does not inherently seek physical separation or social distance from the other, but rests satisfied with its own worth and posits self-directed interests and goals. Separatist Nationalism, on the contrary, while positing self-directed interests and goals, seeks physical separation and social distance from the other. Psychological Black

Nationalism is the ideology that informed the demands and efforts leading to the creation of Black Studies programs and departments on predominantly white college campuses, whereas Black Separatist Nationalism is best reflected in the establishment of the independent Black institutions of the early 1970s.

The Ideological Threats to Black Studies

Outside Black Studies programs and curricula, the Black Nationalist ideology has had little impact on education for U.S. Blacks. Traditional education for Blacks has generally continued in the assimilationist mode, the persistence of which is one of the threats to Black Studies in the next decade.

The Assimilationist Ideologies

All the assimilationist Black ideologies pose threats to Black Studies, but that from the Black Marxist-Leninists is less easily perceived and therefore the most serious.

First of all, Black Marxism-Leninism, like Black Liberal Idealism, is Black only in the sense that ideologues socially defined as Black subscribe to it. As pointed out earlier, this ideology is fundamentally "other" oriented. Its "other" orientation lies not so much in the alien nature of its source as in its attempt to define Black reality solely in terms of the "other." By equating the status of Blacks with that of an undefined white working class, the Black Marxist blithely dismisses the role of race in a society that he simultaneously and facilely labels as racist—a society that has defined itself as racists through its history, laws, traditions, and institutions. The Black Marxist-Leninists further ignore the historical fact that their would-be ally—the white "working class"—has been just as discriminatory toward the Black working class as toward the so-called Black bourgeoisie. How then does one analyze the relationship of American Blacks to the American labor movement? How does one account for the cycles of displacement of Black labor by European immigrants? For the recent *Webber* case? How can we explain the South African-type wage differential that until recently existed between Black and white worker in the United States? Or the expulsion of the Black Knights of Labor by the all-white AFL in an attempt to reserve employment for European immigrants? Are these realities to be explained by a "scientific" class analysis just because Karl Marx says so? Are our students to be so naive as to look forward to the embrace of the white working class or the white proletariat because Marx says so?

A second danger of Black Marxism-Leninism is the seductiveness of its militant anticapitalist rhetoric, which can engender an easy identification on the part of Blacks. Because the white capitalist has in fact been the oppressor of Blacks, such identification is understandable. It is, however, based on a very superficial analysis. Leftist hostility to white capitalism is easily misconstrued as a pro-Black sentiment. The illogic of this misunderstanding, however, is no different from that which for generations led Blacks in the American South to misconstrue the conflict between the industrial North and the agrarian South as a sign that they should seek refuge in the de facto segregated North. That illogic, coupled with the fact that the white working class whom the Black Marxist-Leninists identify as the natural ally of American Blacks is in fact a partner in capitalism, defies the class analysis. One cannot, at the same time, be both capitalist and noncapitalist; the terms are mutually exclusive. How does Black Studies reconcile this contradiction? Do Blacks have no alternative but to choose between "good" capitalists and "bad" capitalists?

The emotionally satisfying militant rhetoric and the unquestioning acceptance of the political religion of Black Marxism-Leninism are, indeed, serious problems for Black Studies in the decade ahead. The danger is a subtle one that, unless addressed head on, can transform Black Studies into a platform for the dissemination of an alien ideology that contradicts the realities of the Black experience. Black Studies has no need to develop a separate class analysis. In racially stratified systems such as the United States and the current international system, race and class are coterminous—one and the same thing. In contrast to the situation for whites, there is no Black middle class, for class, or a group's position in society, is a function of its political and economic power. A group's political position is a function of its ability to control the decisions that regulate the society. Its economic position is a function of its ability to control decisions governing the production, distribution, and consumption of the society's wealth. Income, which is often used as the indicator of class, is only an indicator of the ability to consume. In the United States, a white dominant, racially stratified system, the mobility factor is governed by race, and white incomes are therefore usually also an indicator of the ability both to control directly the decisions that regulate society as well as those that direct the production, distribution, and consumption of wealth. The mobility factor prevents middle- and upper-income Blacks from gaining access to the levers of political and economic power. As such, Black incomes are indexes of the ability to consume, not to control, except as expressed in a negative sense when Blacks have the will to withhold their consumption—the selective boycotting by the Civil Rights Movement being one example. When Blacks do exercise their ability to consume, they thereby *increase* the ability of the decision makers to control the production and distribution of wealth. Based on government-defined levels of income, there are Blacks who indeed can be categorized as middle and upper income. Since these definitions are based on levels of white income, however, those same Blacks can be defined out of a particular income level, as the white level changes. Black middle income cannot be equated with middle class.

The Marxist-Leninist analysis may have some validity when applied to the Black community itself. Given the declining importance of color among Blacks, that community is indeed stratified primarily along class lines. But those class lines cannot be defined by government-established income levels, nor do they reflect any real political and economic power on the part of Blacks within the Black community. Instead they are based more on differences among Blacks in terms of their ability to consume. Some Blacks have interpreted this ability to consume at a level higher than other Blacks as a real class difference, whereas it is more a reflection of the house servant's condescension to the field hand than an indication of any real political and economic power. It represents a change in the *condition* in which the higher consuming Black exists and not a change in his *position* or *class* in the society. Since any differences having a common denominator can be classified, one might talk about classes of consumers, but this is a notion quite different from the concept of class as defined by Marx and purportedly applied by the Black Marxist-Leninists.

The Self-Determinationist Ideologies

The Black self-determinationist ideologies are also something of a threat to Black Studies in the next decade. They are self-assertive and purport to base their self-assertion on an evaluation of the realities of the Black world, but there is a thin line between being pro-Black and anti-white. The understandable anger and frustration of Blacks as a racially subordinate group both in the United States and throughout the international system makes it easy to confuse anti-white with pro-Black sentiments—but it is an unnecessary and dangerous confusion.

To set out to be anti-white in a white dominant, racially stratified system is unnecessary because in such a system to espouse any group except the whites (or to favor anything other than what they define as legitimate) is in effect to be anti-white. That is, since white is the only legitimate point of reference—all the protestations about racial pluralism notwithstanding—the very existence of Black Studies is a statement that the dominant group perceives as hostile—as anti-white. This was the reason that Black Studies Programs were often labeled as racist-in-reverse, separatist, un-American, and so on, by both whites and assimilationist Blacks. To be pro-Black, however, is not the same as defining Black as the only legitimate point of reference. To label a pro-Black stance "racism-in-reverse" is the epitome of racism, for such a label implies the legitimacy of white exclusivity. Racism is based on the assumption of the a priori exclusivity of one race. Accordingly, an anti-white stance is irrelevant and unnecessary to the mission of Black Studies, and Black Studies faculty should be ever vigilant that curricula and students do not confuse the program's proper subject matter.

In addition to being unnecessary, anti-white posturing is essentially "other" oriented. In contrast to a pro-Black position, an anti-white posture retains a white point of reference, negative though that reference may be. It is a further indication of the task that still awaits Black Studies—the task of breaking the emanative ties that have bound Blacks psychologically to the dominant group.

Thus, despite their role in reorienting Blacks to a positive sense of self-identity and providing a realistic rationale for Black Studies, the self-determinationist ideologies can all too easily be corrupted. The danger increases as Black Studies staff and students lose sight of the functional role of ideology and make ideology an end in itself.

Many tasks await Black Studies. For some relatively well-established programs, the revisionist or reconstructive critique of the past is an important part of their curricula. For them there is an opportunity to begin moving toward the development of what we might call the constructive curriculum. That is, there is a need to construct new concepts and theories about human behavior, social institutions, and social systems. One can argue that the revisionist critique by Black Studies shows not only the need for the development of a new social science and a new humanities, but also demonstrates that Black Studies is the only hope for such a development. Even white scholars are conceding that Euro-American "coventional schooling has failed to prepare people for the complexity of global issues and is thereby contributing to further deterioration of the human condition."[7]

Yet, there are some Black Studies programs that are still grappling with the problems of survival—problems created in some instances by the struggle over countervailing ideologies. These programs play into the hands of those who would encourage them to destroy Black Studies, and thus make the task of those who oppose Black Studies easier.

For all Black Studies programs, success or failure in developing curricula, recruiting competent and dedicated staff, and attracting studious and inquiring students—that is, in developing programs that realistically answer our second question, "Black Studies for what?"—will depend to a large degree on the resolution of the ideological struggles within Black Studies. A successful philosophy of education depends on a unified base of ideological support. Without the clear resolution of the ideological problem, the African proverb will become a reality: If a person does not know where he is going, any road can take him there!

Notes

1. Tilden J. LeMelle, "Black Studies for What?" *Black Prism*, vol. 2 (Winter 1972), pp. 5-6.
2. For a detailed analysis of Black ideologies affecting education for American Blacks, see Tilden J. LeMelle and Wilbert J. LeMelle, *The Black College*, chap. 3, ("An Ideology for Black Educational Development") (New York: Praeger, 1969), pp. 38-53.
3. The Cotton States and International Exposition in Atlanta, Georgia, September 1895.
4. Booker T. Washington, *The Future of the American Negro*. (Boston: Small, Maynard and Co., 1899), pp. 201-244 (italics in original).

5. W. E. B. DuBois, "The Talented Tenth," in Booker T. Washington et al, *The Negro Problem: A Series of Articles by Representative Negroes Today* (New York: James Pott & Company, 1963), pp. 33-75 *passim*.
6. Ibid.
7. "Colleges Still Living in Yesteryear, Futurists Charge," *The Chronicle of Higher Education*, 28 July 1980, p. 3.

CHAPTER 4

Intellectual Imperative and Necessity for Black Education

Shirley N. Weber

The conditions that in the 1970s have produced a shortage of revenue, a decline in activism, and an increase in conservatism make the 1980s a very critical period in the life and growth of Black educational units. For when the win and loss columns of the 1960s are tabulated, it becomes abundantly clear that the only tangible remains of that struggle are the Black Studies programs on various college campuses. Those who have been entrusted with the development and safekeeping of those units therefore have a tremendous responsibility, not just to their professional careers, but to the young Blacks throughout the nation who jeopardized their lives and careers for Black education (Black Studies).

Over the past five years, there have been numerous attacks on Black Studies. Some believe that after a decade, the system is ready to assimilate these units into the American melting pot and thereby eliminate them as discrete identities. Others who never accepted Black Studies as a legitimate discipline merely believe the fad is over and it is time to move on to other concerns. Fortunately, there are still those, including this author, who believe that Black education is a necessary endeavor of value to both Blacks and non-Blacks. This paper addresses the intellectual imperative and necessity for Black education which will exist as long as Black people are Black. As a prelude to this topic, we must discuss education in general and its relationship to Black education, after which some factors essential to the development and retention of Black educational units through the 1980s are offered.

The process of education has always been of extreme importance in African society. The methods of educating the child are interwoven in the community structures, and the time and content of instruction

---

Dr. Shirley N. Weber is Chairperson, Afro-American Studies Department, San Diego State University, San Diego, California

are prescribed in a systematic manner. It therefore comes as no surprise that among both the continental Africans and Africans displaced to the Americas, those who have been denied access to and control over the educational systems that affect their lives have continually struggled for "quality and equitable" education. Education currently symbolizes progress and success and, because oppressors have always understood its power, they have sought to manipulate, control, and oppress either through a policy of "no education" or by creating institutions that deliver "poor education."[1]

When we examine the African-American's experience, we find that upon emancipation, Blacks developed an overriding concern for education and the establishment of educational facilities. In response to this concern, Black elected officials placed education high on their list of priorities. They proved successful in establishing free education, and schools were set up with aid from the government, Quakers, and white philanthropists. In structure and content, however, these Negro schools were inferior carbon copies of white institutions. Their emphasis was primarily vocational—an emphasis that was not threatening to the dominant white culture. This emphasis led to a conflict between Black educators committed to vocational training and those who favored elite education. Nevertheless, Negro colleges that were not oriented toward vocational training were also carbon copies of white institutions and made no attempt to focus on education as a tool for the masses. As E. Franklin Frazier states in *Black Bourgeoisie,*

> Instead of trying to promote a distinctive set of habits and values in their students, they were by almost any standard, purveyors of super-American, ultra-bourgeois prejudices and aspirations. Far from fighting to preserve a separate subculture, as other ethnic colleges did, the Negro colleges were militantly opposed to almost everything which made Negroes different from whites, on the grounds that it was "lower class."[2]

Nevertheless, some Black scholars did advocate the need to include Black research and the study of the Black in general in university curricula. W. E. B. DuBois was one of the advocates of Black research and curriculum, but his impact on the total system of education was minimal.[3]

An examination of the general African-American experience and of statistics regarding Black success in the educational system shows that the system has failed to produce for Black children the same results it has for others. According to Charles H. Curl:

> The truth of the matter is that education has not worked significantly to make for Blacks a reality of the American dream; education does not insure commensurable jobs and economic power. What education for the Negro has been is an attempt figuratively to transfer him fom Black to white. And the most tangible result it has produced is to make him dissatisfied.[4]

The last decade has witnessed a preoccupation with attempts to implement the mandates of *Brown* v. *Board of Education* of 1954. Once again, the efforts of Blacks have aimed to attain the "same" education as whites. At some point, before we implement new programs, emphases, and so on, however, we must both pose and answer the question: What is education for?

There are serious doubts whether Blacks have ever clearly understood the real purpose and potential of education in America. Like so much of America's propaganda, the "scholarly" arguments of objectivity, purity, and scholarship have always confused the issue of education for the masses, consequently blurring its real effects and potential. It must be clearly understood that *all* education is politically motivated. It serves either to liberate or to oppress—there is no middle ground. And, while there are some "facts" in scholarly endeavors, the most significant aspect of scholarly work is the interpretation that the scholar places on the "relevant" facts. This interpretation is determined by the individual scholar's perception and training; more crudely put, the outstanding feature of scholarly interpretation is its subjectivity.

In *Introduction to the Philosophy of Education,* George Kneller states, "To educate men wisely we must know what we educate them to become. To know this it is necessary to ask what men live for—to ask, that is, what can be the purpose of life and what sort of life it should be."[5] The primary goal of American education has always been to maintain the current social and political system. The desired end product is a citizenry loyal to American ideas. And, given the fact that slavery was an integral part of that system, American education could never, in reality, do for Black America what it purports to accomplish for white America. The exclusion of African and African-American accomplishments and contributions to U. S. and world history is a deliberate attempt to reduce Black life to a mere footnote about slavery, thereby increasing Blacks' loyalty to the concepts of white supremacy.

The desire of Blacks to develop schools that parallel white schools in form and content illustrates their belief in and commitment to the current structure and values of American society, which are basically oppressive. An education that produces persons capable of wrestling with the issues of oppression and poverty has not been the overriding concern of Black America. Instead, education has been allowed to remain one of the oppressive tools of the society. William McClindon concludes,

> Education has been viewed for some time by many observers from assorted placements as falling apart throughout the American nation. In many ways this is seen as similar to the disintegrating of American imperialism. In considering the conventional roles of American education and its institutionalized discrimination, exploitation, rejections and particularization, blacks in many sectors of life come to the conclusion that educators occupied one of two positions: they were either oppressors or liberators . . . all education is unequivocally political and black education can ill afford not to be so.[6]

When we talk about Black education, one hopes that we are discussing a very distinct type of education which produces particular results. It is not white education in Black face; it is not the mere recounting of Black facts. Instead, Black education implies that the material is researched and taught from a different perspective or framework—a Black perspective. Black education seeks to produce the liberated scholar whose particular commitment is to the race and ultimately to the world. On this subject, Nathan Hare states:

> A Black education which is not revolutionary in the current day is both irrelevant and useless. To remain impartial in the educational arena is to allow the current partiality of whiteness to fester. Black education must be based on ideological and pedagogical blackness. . . . On the positive plane, Afro-American education must activate and energize the black intelligentsia toward giving greater direction to the people of the black nation.[7]

Given the revolutionary potential of Black education, it is not surprising that the media has deluged the public with propaganda designed to discredit and destroy Black Studies departments, which represent the first real forms of Black education in white institutions. The "concern" for "quality education" claimed by administrators when making recommendations for the destruction of Black educational units is suspect given their lack of concern for educating Black youth—an attitude evidenced by poor instructors, poor facilities, and poor results in Black public schools. It is apparent that this "concern" is in fact a backhanded tribute to the success many Black units have enjoyed in educating Black youth politically.

When one understands the political nature of education and the devastating effects of miseducation, the urgent necessity for Black education becomes abundantly clear, as does the inescapable responsibility Black educators have regarding Black liberaton. Specifically, the intellectual imperative and necessity for Black education are: (1) to develop a new discipline that presents accurate information, conclusions, and solutions regarding Black life; (2) to generate a new value system that promotes positive self-concepts; and (3) to create a level of competence and commitment in individuals to wrestle with the problems of Black life from an alternative perspective.

First, Black education is a new discipline that requires a "new" body of knowledge. If all of the African experiences are researched and explained by white nationalist scholars, the results will be the same as they have been for hundreds of years. This sort of education cannot produce our desired result: a liberated Black person. The Black perspective seeks to add a new dimension to already existing facts and discovers new, forgotten, or ignored information. For example, Marcus Garvey was portrayed for years as a flamboyant egotist who swayed the "ignorant" masses by his garb and his "empty" displays of eloquence. The "scholars" who made this argument, however, completely ignored the fact that only about 10 percent of all Garveyites ever saw Garvey in person, a circumstance that invalidates their position. Fortunately, research by such individuals as Emory Tolbert and Tony Martin takes a different perspective in its attempt to resurrect the legend of Marcus Garvey and his national and international involvements.

This Black perspective demands new frameworks for examining Black life, which eventually will provide some direction and impetus for future actions and change. In this connection, Molefi Asante's recent book, *Afrocentricity—The Theory of Social Change,* suggests an alternative approach. Asante's basic premise is that a framework binds the research to a value system and thereby dictates the researcher's conclusions. Since frameworks are culturally determined, they are usually inadequate to the scholarly investigation of cultures other than those that produced them. For example, Aristotle's concepts of rhetorical analysis have proved incapable of measuring the dynamic aspects of Black communications and its role in the Black community. In analyzing Black communication, it is more accurate to utilize the philosophy of Nommo (the power of the word) and its relationship to Muntu (man) as two interacting forces in Black life. Scholars who have not utilized this framework have often arrived at either meaningless conclusions (Dr. Smith is a good speaker because he averages 5.3 letters per word in his speeches) or detrimental conclusions (Black audiences need only empty rhetoric to arouse them emotionally). Those who have used this framework have been able to recreate the richness and vitality of an important aspect of African tradition in African-American life. Similarly, if the political scientist accepts the basic framework that one's benefits from a system depend upon and equal one's input, then he or she concludes that the Blacks' lack of equity is the consequence of their not having worked hard enough within the system—a conclusion that exonerates the system and indicts its victims.

In a recent seminar, historians were discussing the frameworks they use in teaching Black history. One instructor said his framework was that of "love." His contention was that no matter what happened to Blacks during slavery, they always maintained a loving attitude. Although this framework may not appear to be negative, it in effect castrates Blacks and makes those who were not "loving" appear abnormal. In contrast to this framework, the other historians used a framework of "resistance." They highlighted the various activities of Blacks that constituted examples of their resistance to oppression: revolts, runaways, spirituals, slothfulness, and so on. Obviously, the latter framework creates a new perspective on the African-American. All people work vigorously to be free, for to do less is to be less than human; by numbering Black people among those who struggle for their freedom, this framework restores their humanity.

Black education is a discipline which requires alternative methods of analysis. Whether they be Afrocentric, ethnocentric, or unnamed, these methods must diverge from the Europocentric analysis that uses European standards to judge African-based concepts. The failure to make this change creates a Black intellectual void in scholarship, leading us to develop courses and materials that ape those of other disciplines (with a few Black heroes thrown in) and that could therefore be taught by anyone from another academic unit.

Second, Black education is necessary to create and maintain a new value system, the basis of a new Black pride and excellence. If most of Black life is reduced to a single reference in a history lecture on slavery, then surely the Black ego is in grave need of being uplifted and clearly, Black education is one of the appropriate vehicles for effecting this change. Too often white educators and Negro traditionalists are either appalled that an academic unit can concern itself with matters of ego and self-concept, or they argue that such a unit is merely a student conseling service with no place in academic circles. Their reaction stems from their ignorance not only of Black education, but of education in general. The salute to the flag, singing of "America the Beautiful," hero worship of the rioters and looters at the Boston Tea Party, and so on, are all examples of attempts to build a positive self-concept and pride in young white men and women. Current educational propaganda has been so effective in disguising European ego-building programs under the mask of scholarship that Blacks often see attempts to improve the Black self-concept as negative and racist. We must hope, then, that Black education makes Blacks feel good about being Black. Furthermore, studies have shown that there is a direct correlation between achievement and self-concept. Those who are high achievers generally have higher self-concepts than those who are not.[8] While research on Black college students enrolled in Black Studies departments reveals some discrepancy in the results, the researchers maintain their position that Black Studies will improve self-concept and increase academic success. The discrepancy found in college students results from not knowing how to account for the impact of eighteen years of weak self-concepts and poor academic training, obstacles that one course is unlikely to overcome. This situation is a strong argument in favor of having Black education extend beyond the college level. The movement of the 1960s did not have an impact beyond the college level, as a result of which students arriving on college campuses in the 1980s will have little or no knowledge of our past struggles or of the general Black experience in America. It is to be hoped that in the current decade, Black education will manifest itself in primary and secondary educational institutions as well.

Third, Black education is necessary to create the level of competence and commitment essential to the liberation of the masses.

Competence refers to education that is practical, useful, and of excellent quality. While it is acknowledged that education was originally designed for the leisure class, this has not been the case to any large extent with Black education. Blacks have gone to college to "get a better job"—to change their economic as well as social status. And, with the influx of the working class into colleges and universities, degree programs that lead toward employment are booming while those in the liberal arts are declining. Black education is thus challenged to equip students with a dual emphasis—the liberal arts practically applied—programs that teach art, music, literature, and history, as well as community design, and so on.

Additionally, Black education must be designed to develop committed young men and women. Historically, Blacks have been educated for the sole purpose of leaving the past behind and escaping into the predominant white culture. In education of this sort, the commitment has been to self and not to the masses; the credentialed Black, rather than being trained in a commitment to the masses, is taught how to form a new elite that plays by the rules of white society. Haki Madhubti observes that as a result of white education and socialization the vast majority of Blacks have not betrayed white America, concluding that it is therefore reasonable to assume that if Blacks were educated in Black educational systems from birth to adulthood, they would not betray Black people.[9] Black education is paramount in the struggle to increase the manpower needed to effectuate change in the status of Blacks.

In order to be able to meet effectively the challenges that have called forth Black education, a viable structure is necessary. It is no easy task to develop a Black educational unit. The current programs of Black Studies are struggling to maintain quality, relevant education within the confines of traditional white institutions. Some Black educators believe that the restrictions and structures of traditional white universities make it impossible for Black Studies to attain these goals. Furthermore, they argue that, given the history and conservatism of Negro colleges, it is ridiculous to think that white authorities will certify and support a genuine Black education. Even for those who argue that a university supported by many different groups is obligated to provide a structure that supports the research and teaching of the Black experience, however, the actual development of such units remains a daunting challenge.

The first challenge is to develop a sound philosophy of operation. Most Black Studies programs came into existence with a set of "demands"—usually for Black courses, Black instructors, Black students, and university funding and support. Because those who made the demands were students and not educators, they seldom articulated a philosophical basis for the program. Once established, most programs began to offer courses, usually history, literature, and music, which addressed the question of the African-American's contributions to these disciplines. Faculty were hired, and departments or programs were launched. Sometimes, faculty were hired and then courses that met the faculty's expertise were introduced. Either way, the curricula of the early Black Studies departments were often hodgepodges that lacked continuity and structure. Many faculty were permitted—under the guise of academic freedom and integrity—to offer all types of courses without any scrutiny from their colleagues. And when some groups clamored for a philosophy—for guiding operational principles—others screamed that such guidelines were too oppressive and restrictive.

I argue that a philosophy of Black education, while it does restrict, also gives direction and purpose to program development. Every philosophy of Black education must address itself to liberation through the process of education.

Once a sound and workable philosophy is developed, a curriculum that implements that philosophy can be introduced. While the emphasis of many programs is strictly African-American, a curriculum cannot restrict itself to that focus if it is to be liberating. Ever since the African's arrival in the Americas, society has used all its methods of propaganda in an attempt to sever his ties with Africa. If this goal could be accomplished, then the African-American would have no past other than that of slavery. He would know nothing of his ancestors and therefore have little appreciation for the Africanness that lies within him. In this logic, any traits peculiar to the African-American would of necessity be viewed as a consequence of his slave experience; by definition, then, those traits that mark the African-American's individuality should be eradicated. An example of this negative perspective is found in Gordon Green's article "Negro Dialect, The Last Barrier to Integration."[10] Green argues that Black English is nothing but the residue of slavery and should therefore be eliminated so that Blacks will no longer be "separated" from the melting pot of U.S. society. It is unfortunate that this educator did not examine Black English beyond the slave experience because, had he done so, he would have had a clear and accurate perspective of Black English, possibly even an appreciation for it. Black curriculum must first reflect the entirety of the Black past in order to appreciate and assess the present.

Additionally, the curriculum of Black education must be oriented to solutions. It is not enough to know the problem; what is important is the ability to solve it. Whether the subject is art, literature, sociology, or psychology, the solutions to the problems of racism, degradation, and dehumanization should be the guiding factors in its study. Finally, the curriculum must be rigorous, demanding, stimulating, and logically structured to produce competent and committed scholars. Fortunately, the National Council of Black Studies Curriculum Committee is providing some guidance in the area of curriculum development to give the discipline some core consistency nationwide.

As with any educational unit, it is the human factor that makes the program successful. Without competent and committed faculty, a good philosophy and an excellently written curriculum are almost a waste of human effort and time. The faculty must be competent. This is probably one of the most difficult criteria to assess in a Black unit, primarily because so many Black scholars have not been trained in Black Studies. Some administrators believe that any Black who possesses a Ph.D. is competent to teach Black Studies. Criteria in addition to, as well as in lieu of, the Ph.D. will have to be devised in an attempt to recruit competent instructors. The unfortunate aspect of the struggle for competent faculty is that most Black units have given up on identifying nontraditional criteria, and have succumbed to accepting *only* Ph.D.'s on their faculties.

In addition, the faculty must be committed—committed to the development of the discipline and the liberation of Black people in particular. In *From Poverty to Dignity,* Hampden Turner contends that the problem with the black agencies that were established after the revolts of the sixties was that they were demanded by the committed individuals but then administered by the competent individuals (defined as degree-holding persons) who had not participated in, or who had even criticized, the revolts. As a result, these agencies were short-lived and the results of their work were temporary. Turner resolves that any Black unit dies quickly if it is led by a competent but uncommitted staff. The selection criteria for faculty should therefore consider both their demonstrated ability to research and teach Black Studies and their commitment to utilize their teaching, writing, and other involvements to further the liberation of students and the Black community in general.

Finally, the Black educational unit must be structurally viable. The arguments that it can enjoy "autonomy" within a white or Negro university or school are ludicrous. If Black education is to exist, it must have a sound structure that allows it to impact on every aspect of the system of which it is a part. Units that offer no tenure and do not have adequate representation on the institution's major decision-making bodies must rely on either the continued protest and fervor of students or the good will of the administration. And given the level of student apathy and the lack of institutional commitment to Black people, it is unwise to have a program that does not feed into the decision-making units. Departments that are structurally sound are more difficult to eliminate and will probably weather the storms of university retrenchment and fiscal shakeups in the 1980s.

In conclusion, the intellectual imperative and necessity for Black education are directly linked to the movement to liberate the masses from Europocentric analysis and human degradation. To be able to produce alternative conclusions and research that combat the Western perspective of Black people is a significant challenge. Black educators are now responsible for the completion of the work begun by student demands in the 1960s. The challenge of Black education for the 1980s can be met only by competent and committed scholars who thoroughly understand the potential and power of Black education.

Notes

1. Paulo Freire, *Pedogogy of the Oppressed* (New York: Seabury Press, 1968).
2. E. Franklin Frazier, *Black Bourgeoisie* (New York: MacMillan, 1957), p. 84.
3. W. E. B. DuBois, "The Study of the Negro Problem" *Annal of The American Academy of Political and Social Science,* 11 (January 1968): 14, 17.
4. Charles H. Curl, "Black Studies: Form and Content," *CLA Journal,* 13, (September 1969): 3.

5. George F. Kneller, *Introduction to the Philosophy of Education* (New York: Wiley and Son, 1964), p. 1.
6. William H. McClendon, "Black Studies: Education for Liberation," *Black Scholar*, 6 (September 1974): 15.
7. Nathan Hare, "What Should Be the Role of Afro-American Education in the Undergraduate Curriculum?" *Liberal Education*, 55 (March 1969): 42-50.
8. Philip Carey and Donald Allen, "Black Studies: Expectation and Impact on Self Esteem and Academic Performance," *Social Science Quarterly*, 57 (March 1977): 811-820.
9. Haki Madhubuti, *Enemies: The Clash of Races* (Chicago: Third World Press, 1978), pp. 117-118.
10. Gordon C. Green, "Negro Dialect, The Last Barrier to Integration," *Journal of Negro Education*, 32 (Winter 1963): 81-83.

Bibliography

Adams, Russell L. "Black Studies Perspectives." *Journal of Negro Education*, 46 (Spring 1977): 99-117.

Akar, J. J. "An African's View of Black Studies with International Dimensions." *CLA Journal*, 14 (September 1970): 7-17.

Allen, Robert L. "Politics of the Attack on Black Studies." *Black Scholar*, 6 (September 1974): 2-7.

Bailey, Ron. "Black Studies in Historical Perspective." *Journal of Social Issues*, 29 (1973): 97-108.

"Black Education: The Future of Black Studies" (Symposium). *Black Scholar*, 6 (September 1974): 2-42.

Blassingame, James W. "Black Studies: An Intellectual Crisis." *American Scholar*, 38 (Autumn 1969): 548-561.

Carey, Paul and D. Allen. "Black Studies: Expectation and Impact on Self-Esteem and Academic Performance." *Social Science Quarterly*, 57 (March 1977): 811-820.

Crouchett, L. "Early Black Studies Movements." *Journal of Black Studies*, 2 (December 1977): 89-92.

Cummings, Robert. "African and Afro-American Studies Centers: Towards a Cooperative Relatonship." *Journal of Black Studies*, 9 (March 1979): 291-310.

Fuller, Hoyt. "On Black Studies and the Critics." *Black World*, 23 (May 1974): 49-50.

Hare, Nathan. "Battle for Black Studies." *Black Scholar*, 3 (May 1972): 32-47.

Harris, William and Darrell Millman. *Perspectives on Black Studies*. (Washington, D.C.: University Press of America, 1977).

Madhubuti, Haki. *Enemies: The Clash of Races*. (Chicago: Third World Press, 1978).

McClendon, William H. "Black Studies: Education for Liberation." *Black Scholar*, 6 (September 1974): 15-25.

McGinnis, James. "Towards A New Beginning: Crisis and Contradiction in Black Studies." *Black World,* 22 (March 1973): 27-35.

Robinson, A. L. et al. *Black Studies in the University.* (New Haven: Yale University Press, 1969).

Rosser, James R and E. T. Copeland. "Reflections: Black Studies—Black Education." *Journal of Black Studies,* 3 (March 1973): 287-295.

Walker, Samuel J. "Black Studies: Phase Two." *American Scholar,* 42 (Autumn 1972): 604-615.

Wells, E. E. "Black Studies: An Educational Dilemma." *Negro History Bulletin,* 36 (February 1973): 29-33.

III

The Global Significance of African History

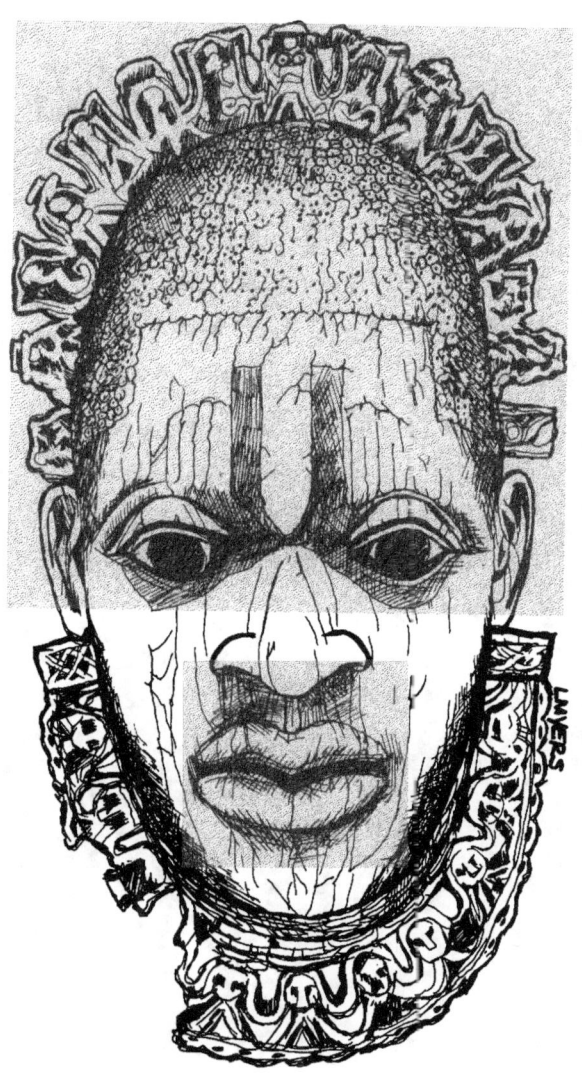

African mask from the
Bini of Nigeria,
sixteenth century

CHAPTER 5

African Studies and Historical Consciousness

Lansine Kaba

Africa is still perceived in the West with prejudice and narrow-mindedness, despite the impressive accomplishments by Africanist scholars during the last three decades. Some recent examples of such views include the reactions against *Roots* and the coverage of the uprisings in Zaire and Zimbabwe. Lewis H. Lapham of *Harper's*, in an editorial blitz against Andrew Young for supporting majority rule in Southern Africa and against Alex Haley for suggesting the existence of an African civilization, wrote:

> During the early years of African independence . . . as a newspaper correspondent assigned to the [U.N.] General Assembly, I was obliged to write down whatever I was told. The newly arrived [African] delegates spoke about the evils of colonialism (evils that I also could name and condemn), but then they went on to conjure forth the phantom civilization of Prest John and the Queen of Sheba. Their eloquence forced me to go to libraries in search of proofs. . . . Although I could find little evidence for civilizations of any kind, I could read extensively about the slave trade, cannibalism, tribal wars, wood carving, raffia weaving, and the steady state of Stone Age cultures that had survived for possibly as long as 250,000 years.[1]

Lapham's diatribe went on to accuse Africans of enslaving their own friends, wives, and children. The author tried to ease the consciences of his white readers by stating that "the Western European nations sickened of slavery in a far briefer period than did the Greeks, the Romans, the Arabs, or the Africans." Lapham had probably done some research. But clearly, he looked in the wrong places and with preconceived ideas! Not surprisingly, therefore, he noted only those works that substantiated his preconceptions.

Larry Heinzerling of the Associated Press, and most United States daily papers that published his "analysis" of the invasion of Zaire in May 1978, exhibited other kinds of misrepresentations and biases. In the most alarming tone, they claimed that "Whites are hunted," that

---

Lansine Kaba is a Professor in the History Department at the University of Minnesota, Minneapolis, Minnesota

Africa "suffers from the effects of the vacuum left when the European colonial powers withdrew, and that the key element in all this remains tribalism."[2] Obviously, this statement contains several misconceptions. It also implies that the "vacuum" created by decolonization left uneducated "tribesmen" incapable of governing themselves to revert back to old ways. Heinzerling ignores the reality of contemporary Africa, overlooking the dominant economic and political conditions and the disruptive consequences of neocolonial exploitation.

The preceding examples indicate how the old myths that Africa and Africans are "primitive" and "savage" have not yet vanished. These misconceptions have retained, in Basil Davidson's words, a kind of underground existence, have settled like a layer of dust on the minds of large numbers of otherwise thoughtful people, and are constantly being swirled about.[3] The question whether Africans ever reached the stage of historical consciousness, therefore, is a crucial issue. A positive answer to this question will enhance our understanding of racism and exploitation and our commitment to African liberation. The main issue is one of emancipation from political, cultural, and economic domination, and hence of control over one's own history and future. Such understanding has a definite ideological implication.

This paper considers these issues in terms of the aims of African Studies programs, for any academically strong and politically responsible program works to equip its students with the knowledge and the tools needed to deal with precisely these issues and to develop a more positive image of Africa. Although it may be redundant to preach to the converted, I think that certain words of wisdom bear repeating. Thus, my paper will define historical consciousness in general, and discuss the reasons why and how its existence in Africa was first denied and then acknowledged. As a historiographical exercise, it will illuminate some African writers' contributions to the field of African history, and hence the connection between scholarship and politics. I hope that this discussion will provide groundwork for a better understanding of the predicaments of Africa in today's world. Accordingly, I hope that it will again demonstrate that African studies have a global significance.

Consciousness as Knowledge and Social Reality

The consciousness that we are proceeding toward the future is one of the main characteristics of human life. As living beings we are aware of a specific quality of time and tend to use it for our purposes. To be is to be conscious of time and space with all the implications of this awareness. Given the gregarious nature of human beings, it follows that societies are also affected by the same dynamic drive to achieve their goals in a progressive manner. All great societies and civilizations attempt to deal with this challenge, and hence, are necessarily concerned with consciousness in a historical perspective.

It seems, however, that the degree of historical consciousness cannot be the same for all groups or individuals. Its forms depend on broad societal and intersocietal relationships. The political domination of one country or group by another, the presence of uneven exchange relationships between economic zones, and the existence of an unequal distribution of wealth within a society—all these factors greatly affect the nature of historical consciousness. Implicitly, one is not born with any particular form of consciousness. Rather, it results from a combination of factors, material as well as social.

As living units, individuals and societies obey the general laws of motion, causality, and necessity. Consciousness is an element of their relations to themselves, to others, and to the outside world. It is, in part, what some philosophers have called "immanence," "inwardness," or "interiority"; that is, the quality of remaining and operating within oneself.[4] This quality is one of the starting points of most human experiences and activities, including thoughts, feelings, and creativity. At this level, consciousness refers to an acute awareness of both one's existence in the universe and one's separation from it. Clearly, this process cannot be limited to "interiorization," because to exist implies a necessary coexistence with others. It contrasts a conscious subject with an external reality that is one object of the awareness. Consciousness is a way of dealing with others and the world and thus is a source of knowledge, which requires reasoning capacity.

The preceding remarks assume little dichotomy between reason and consciousness. Although reason appears to be the primary tool of the objective study of the exernal world and consciousness is the "gate to the knowledge of oneself," their goals nevertheless remain almost analogous: they aim at comprehending oneself and the universe. The two processes are complementary. In a broad sense, consciousness can be viewed as a process of thought which may relate itself to its own self, to another, or to the outside, thereby indicating one's existence in the world in general and in a society in particular.

Within this context, historical consciousness represents the highest level of consciousness because of the historical essence of human beings as both the products and authors of history. All human actions occur in a historical process, and societies evolve historically. Social systems are never completely still. They are in a constant process of change, moving either forward or backward. This view implies that history consists of dynamic periods rather than undifferentiated and static units, and suggests that every society must be analyzed in its own historical context.

Despite the very valuable contribution to the scientific study of Africa made by two generations of Western scholars and their African adepts, many of these works are marred by an unnecessary claim of objectivity, by the assumption that scholarship is value-free. Furthermore, consciously or unconsciously, some of these scholars have transposed foreign ideas and structures into the African realm, thereby denaturing it. For example, the intrusion of foreign models of thought and theories has raised serious questions in the areas of African slavery, production system, religion, and women. To understand a society dynamically, however, one must make an effort to analyze its foundations, the causes of its growth, and the internal and external contradictions that may lead to its decline: Africanists have yet to apply this method consistently.

Historical consciousness must be at the root of a methodology based on the idea that change is necessary in historical analysis. It is above all a consciousness of motion. It deals with a sense of historicity rather than an encyclopedic knowledge of facts. It asserts the historical nature of every society, regardless of its material conditions, establishes causation between two stages of development, and helps to formulate objective approaches to problems confronting societies. Therefore, its political implications are manifest; and scholarship has an implicit function.

The differences existing within a society make it necessary for each of its groups to develop a particular historical consciousness reflecting its own conditions and needs. For example, the consciousness of a ruling class deals mainly with how to reinforce and perpetuate its domination and legitimize its position, whereas disadvantaged groups want to eliminate inequality and promote a just system. Similarly, the historical consciousness of the colonized or oppressed opposes that of the colonizers and oppressors. Nkrumah, Fanon, Cabral, Biko, and Malcolm X could not have the same historical consciousness as Churchill, DeGaulle, Salazar, Vorster, and Richard Nixon. In other words, people having antagonistic interests cannot be expected to develop identical views of history. Therefore, historical consciousness tends to have a class character, each group having its own needs and ideology. As new conditions emerge, they call for new visions and new levels of consciousness. A significant change in the socio-economic context would affect other aspects of social life, including thoughts and world views.

Scholarship is, by definition, engaged in the propagation of a particular form of consciousness. This situation is especially true of African studies, a multidisciplinary field dominated by non-African scholars and derived in part from two opposite sources, namely the political needs of the colonial administrations and the demands of newly emergent African nationalism after 1945. According to an author's attitudes, this scholarship is either apologetic or critical of colonial rule, and hence opposed or sympathetic to African peoples' aspirations. These factors should enable us to view historical consciousness as the active force at work in a positive affirmation of people's identity, worth, and contribution to world civilization. Consciousness as a source of knowledge and an ideology implies an affinity between the subject and object of history. The notion of affinity raises the question whether and under which conditions a scholar can objectively study a foreign society and write a dispassionate account of its history. A balance can be found between objectivity and subjectivity. The task is not impossible, but it is difficult because of the strong tendency, despite good intentions, to exhibit ethnocentrism.

African Historical Consciousness and European Expansion

Despite the thought that humans are *par essence* historically minded, classical Western scholarship once questioned the historicity of African societies. The question was whether those who, in Aimé Césaire's words, "neither invented gunpowder and compass nor tamed steam and electricity"⁵ could reach historical consciousness. Hegel stated that Africa

> is a land of childhood, removed from the light of self-conscious history and wrapped in the dark mantle of night. . . . In Africa, history is in fact out of the question. Life there consists of a succession of contingent happenings and surprises. No aim or state exists whose development can be followed. . . . The characteristic feature of the Negroes is that their consciousness has not yet reached an awareness of any substantial objectivity—for example, of God or the law—in which the will of man could participate and in which he could become aware of his own being.⁶

Hegel cannot be considered a racist or a bigot, although racist scholars could use some of his ideas. Despite the rise of intellectualized racist ideology in the nineteenth century, and despite the importance of race-thinking and racial prejudice in modern Western thought, I do not think that this quotation implies a rationalized attempt to explain what was considered "the natural inferiority of the black race." Hegel mentioned "Africans' backwardness" in a geographical context but unlike some other European scholars, he did not relate it to biological deficiencies associated with the frontal lobes, the cortex, the genes, or the small size of the brain.

Hegel had one of the most encyclopedic minds of his generation, and his logic and thought have exerted a decisive influence on the evolution of philosophy. He firmly believed that universal motion and contradiction were essential aspects of human thought. His *Philosophy of History* is a major attempt to prove that thought is essential to humanity. The work shows that "the only thought which philosophy brings with it to the contemplation of History is the conception of Reason."⁷ Describing reason as the "Sovereign of the world," Hegel viewed history as a necessarily rational process characteristic of humankind. Africa, however, was not included in his notion of humanity. Hegel denied rationality, intelligibility, and history to African peoples. This denial is a serious contradiction in a system that claimed to be universal and logical.

Hegel was undoubtedly ignorant of African history. The Black scholars of Timbuktu, as is well known, dealt with all aspects of knowledge, including theology and history.⁸ No one would hold a grudge against Hegel for his lack of information, however, for, from the point of view of the Europeans of the 1820s, there was no major history worth studying beyond that of the West and the Mediterranean. The main problem lies in the tendency of most European writers to make eloquent self-congratulatory generalizations and to assert arguable opinions as if they were rigorous scientific truths. This dogmatic ethnocentrism, if it is to be satisfactorily understood, must be seen in relation to the class interests of the bourgeoisie as it extended its hold over the world economy. Philosophers and other scholars tended to legitimize this process of global domination by ignoring or minimizing other peoples' achievements and cultures. African peoples and civilization thus fell prey to Western expansion and became victims of Western intellectualism.

Since Hegel's time, generations of Western intellectuals have further elaborated on the absence of history and civilization in Africa. Frenchmen, such as Jules Romain and J. Gourou, and British writers, such as F. B. Jevons, J. C. Carothers, H. Trevor-Roper, and B. Malinowski, to name only a few, have all suggested reasons for the backwardness of African societies. In a strong spirit of self-glorification, they have also related the African historical awakening to the contact with the "superior" European civilization. African history, then, was viewed as an extension of the Western historical experience, a product of Europe's expansion and enlightenment. Implicitly, Hegel's authority was lent to such views. Despite Claude Lévi-Strauss's argument that history is not superior to myth,[9] Black Africa has been disparaged as the land of mythical thought inferior to historical consciousness, a world consisting of an amorphous mass of uncivilized societies known as "tribes," and hence not worthy of serious historical attention.

To refute methodically such biases calls for some historical recollection. I think that this is a major purpose of a serious and responsible Africanist scholarship, regardless of the origin of the investigators. Europe and Africa had no direct contacts before the Atlantic navigation of the fifteenth century, prior to which there could be little cultural arrogance on the part of the Europeans. For example, references to Blacks in a letter from the French theologian Abélard to his beloved Héloise in the 1130s contained no derogatory remarks about Africans despite his belief in the moral superiority of Catholicism. Even after the first years of direct contact between Europe and Africa, these images changed very little. Eanes de Azurara, Valentim Fernandes, Ca de Mosto, and other chroniclers of the navigation on the Guinea Coast did not "claim to be the harbingers of a superior order."[10] The Portuguese respected the kings of Mali, Benin, and Congo to the point that they envisioned diplomatic exchange with them.[11]

Thus, the hypocrisy, in Césaire's words, is of recent origin. It goes back to the discovery of America and the need to exploit its vast resources after the decimation of the Indians. The subsequent rise of the slave trade and its existence as the single most important pattern of relations between Africa and Europe for three full centuries drastically altered the nature of the contact, the dynamics of African societies, and the attitudes of the Europeans.[12] Obviously, the growing bourgeoisie could not condone slavery and at the same time accept Africans as intelligent and equal. Montesquieu made some pertinent comments about this issue in his *Lettre sur l'esclavage des Noirs*. It is well known that any system of exploitation and oppression must promote an ideology legitimizing its practices.

As a result, the derogatory image associated with the African peoples originated in the need to legitimize morally an obnoxious trade system created by and for Europe's expanding economy.[13] This fact explains why there was no significant knowledge about African civilization in the seventeenth and eighteenth centuries, despite the scientific atmosphere of the Enlightenment. The myth of Africa's stagnation led to a systematic indifference to her positive achievements. The works of Arab scholars and Christian writers who mentioned the strength and splendor of African states and institutions in the fifteenth century were abandoned to oblivion.

Consequently, the myth of Africa's darkness reflected the Westerners' ignorance of the African past rather than Africa's lack of historical consciousness. Although the trans-Atlantic slave trade had declined by the 1820s when Hegel was writing the lecture that became his *Philosophy of History,* this myth had reached even larger proportions, and newer self-serving ideas were emerging. Subsequently, as slavery became an obstacle against the establishment of "legitimate" trade and the penetration of European influence to "civilize Africans," it was abolished. The abolition, however, was for the benefit of those who had promoted it in the first place.

Accordingly, despite the repeated claims of impartiality made by many writers, scholarship is neither totally objective nor neutral. The orientation of historiography, whether implicit or explicit, reflects economic and other interests and personal predispositions. This condition applies to the writings of Hegel and other Western scholars who followed him, and whose names have been associated with the myth that African societies lack historical consciousness. Their works contributed both to the justification of commercial, political, and missionary activities in Africa and also to the colonial powers' self-glorifying claims, in particular their theories of the "civilizing mission" and the "white man's burden," notions so central to colonial ideology.

With the establishment of colonial rule in the late 1890s and early 1900s, the political implication and role of social sciences became even bolder, and served as part of the broad methodical plan of domination and acculturation. African history was reduced to the history of conquest and colonization. Within this context, ethnology, which later became anthropology, dominated the field of African studies. This discipline, unlike history or sociology, originated in the colonizers' need to understand and control the colonized rather than in any consideration of the broad philosophical questions about society. Thus, anthropology was essentially the academic discipline that served European expansion and colonialism.[14]

At the same time, however, no one can ignore anthropology's other implications. At the time when most Europeans considered African values as savage or at best as exotic curiosities, anthropologists attempted to study and appreciate their functions and rationale. They tried to explain scientifically their political institutions and the religious, social, and aesthetic values. In the context of their time, such efforts were positive and significant. For too long, however, anthropologists held a timeless view of African societies. They ignored history, and generally rejected a historical interpretation of the traditions and institutions under study. Africa was depicted as being unaffected by the law of dynamic progression, and change was seen only in terms of the impact of the superior Western civilization upon blurred masses.[15] Such synchronic observations suited well the self-serving ideology of colonialism. The collusion between this sort of scholarship and the colonial doctrine culminated in the rise of the "tribal" image of African societies among Westerners and was the origin of the conservative aspect of anthropology.

Despite the vagueness of the concept of "tribe" in its present usage, it generally refers to a type of society and to a stage of social evolution very different from, and inferior to, the Western ones. "Tribalism," according to the Western concept, clearly denotes primitiveness and backwardness, a view obviously consistent with the colonial doctrine. Elliot Skinner's pertinent idea that "many of the so-called 'tribal' groups were creations of the colonial period"[16] provides a special insight into precolonial and colonial politics.

It is possible to argue that there were no "tribes" before colonization, and that African states transcended "tribalism." Although ethnic groups spoke different languages and sometimes practiced different religions, some kind of cooperation and value-congruency bound them together. For example, ancient Ghana and Mali, Muenemutapa and Ashanti, to name only a few, included various ethnic and linguistic groups, despite their particular local origins. The process of historical development overcame narrow regionalism, and thereby reinforced unity. In other words, "tribal" ideology is *par essence* foreign to Africa. Hence, African societies in terms of "tribalism" may not be fully aware of the implications of this terminology.

Whatever the case may be, the words "tribe" and "tribalism" are derogatory when they apply exclusively to non-Western groups and values. Most writers who view Africa from a "tribal" perspective will not use the same terms in a Western context analogous to the African one. For example, "tribalism" has yet to be applied to the analysis of the Irish crisis or the Basque and Brittany questions or to the study of the problem of national integration in Belgium. Obviously, the concepts of "tribe" and "tribalism" cannot be applied cross-culturally, a circumstance that reveals that they are questionable, if not derogatory and improper.

Historical Consciousness and Political Change

With the rise of nationalism after the Second World War, there began a real effort to investigate from an African perspective both Africa's past and the theories underlying African social and cultural institutions. This endeavor sought to refute the prevailing assumption that Blacks had no history and created no civilization. The writings of pioneering African scholars, in particular of Cheick Anta Diop, Boubou Hama, and A. Hampate Ba from the former French West Africa, J. F. A. Ajayi and K. O. Dike from Nigeria, E. W. Blyden, W. E. B. DuBois, Carter G. Woodson, L. Hansberry, Claude McKay, Langston Hughes, Aimé Césaire, and Léon Dalmas from the Americas, testify to a strong and vibrant scholarship and artistry.[17] They also express the emotions of the African world in Africa as well as in the diaspora, and denote a sense of urgent struggle with the West, placing their primary stress on a common identity among all the peoples of African descent despite their differences. As a scholarship rejecting the complex of inferiority and asserting Black achievement and pride, these works had significant revolutionary and liberalizing implications. They have reinforced our belief in the necessary and intimate association between Afro-American and African studies. Above all, they always remind us of the need to be vigilant and cautious: a positive Africanist scholarship must question the premises of the so-called objective works. In other words, African studies may be viewed as a struggle of liberation in the academic field. As such they ought to stress the unity of the African civilization rather than its diversity. Only such a direction can conform to the view that African studies have a global significance.

The rise of African history as a full-fledged field of study has been associated with the historical foundations of African unity and the worth of Africa's past achievement. Such pan-African consciousness dismisses "tribal" ideology. As "a reflection of Africa's recovery and reawakening,"[18] it involves strong philosophical and political commitment to the struggle for true independence and development instead of neocolonial dependence. At the core of this positive consciousness lie four main principles that reclaim Black cultural and historical values and have direct political implications.

First, African societies are historical groups obeying the universal laws of progress and following rational processes. As such, they are dynamic and can both respond to internal or external challenge and control it. As a corollary, they can absorb new values and adapt to new conditions in an orderly fashion. They can engage in meaningful forms of contact and exchange with other societies without losing their sense of identity and pride. This dynamic process demands the right and the freedom to determine the path of one's historical progression. Since these attributes are incompatible with colonial rule, this consciousness calls for a strong anticolonialist thought and action, and opposition to neocolonialism.

Second, such thoughts must transcend the individualistic interpretation of history. African historical consciousness asserts that peoples, as groups committed to particular goals, make history, and that individuals succeed only when their actions become part of a collective effort. This assertion is demonstrated in the cases of Sundiata of ancient Mali, Samori of Guinea, Chaka of South Africa, Cabral of contemporary Guinea-Bissau, Dr. Martin Luther King and Malcolm X of the United States, and Walter Rodney of Guyana— all of whom led their societies to great achievements and symbolized political values of the highest order.

Third, this consciousness categorically rejects the myth widely spread by racists and colonialists that Africa is a backward continent of "tribes" which has contributed nothing to universal civilization. To refute this belief it must be noted: (1) that Africans tamed the continent from which, according to available scholarly information, humankind originated;[19] (2) that, despite the predispositions of most Western historians and art historians, Pharaonic Egypt—one of the, highest points in world history—was neither Semitic nor Caucasian, but African, and hence African civilization affected the growth of science and philosophy in the Mediterranean world;[20] (3) that the civilizations of Timbuktu and the Swahili city-states in the fifteenth and sixteenth centuries achieved a brilliant level in the humanities and philosophy at the time when the Renaissance was beginning in Europe;[21] and (4) that African music and African arts have made the greatest contributions to the cultural heritage of humanity in this century because of their liberating and refreshing effects on Western traditions.[22] The awareness of this achievement is a major weapon against acculturation and inferiority complexes. Césaire wrote:

> I have always thought that the Black man was searching for his identity. And it has seemed to me that if we want to establish this identity, then we must have a concrete consciousness of what we are—that is, of the first fact of our lives: that we are Black; that we . . . have a history, a history that contains certain cultural elements of great value; and that *Negroes** were not born yesterday, because there have been beautiful and important Black civilizations. At the time we began to write, people could write a history of world civilizaton without devoting a single chapter to Africa, as if Africa had made no contributions to the world. Therefore, we affirmed that we were *Negroes* and that we were proud of it, and that we thought that Africa was not some sort of blank page in the history of humanity; in sum, we asserted that our *Negro* heritage was worthy of respect, and that this heritage was not relegated to the past, that its values . . . could still make an important contribution to the world.[23]

This positive consciousness is based in part on the notion that no society is inherently superior or inferior, despite the differences in technological and economic levels. It rejects European cultural chauvinism and arrogance and the racist interpretation of world culture and history. The matrix of history does not reside in biological or psychological factors but rather in people's capacities to respond to both external and internal challenges, to resist exploitation and oppression, and to control their destinies. At this level, historical consciousness turns into a potent ideology at the service of the people's struggle. This situation is what has occurred among Africans.

Since 1945, African peoples have seriously asserted their culture, and have expanded their nationalist movements, actions that imply a positive Black consciousness and pride, a belief in the historical unity of all the peoples of African descent, and a commitment to the African peoples' struggle against colonialism and racism. To a large extent, whether it remained positive or became exploitative,[24] a strong relationship existed between this emerging nationalism and the need for rigorous African studies. In fact, one activist anticolonialist African scholarship devoted to a positive interpretation of Africa's past emerged under the leadership of several writers who later on assumed major political responsibilities. The scholarship of Aimé Césaire of the Antilles, Cheikh Anta Diop of Senegal, Boubou Hama of Niger, Fodéba Keita of Guinea, Kwame Nkrumah of Ghana, Dike and Ajayi of Nigeria, and Jomo Kenyatta of Kenya, to name only a few, does not contradict in any way the anticolonialist positions that they adopted in the 1950s. Their political engagement made their writing pertinent, while their erudition heightened their political actions. This example of symbiosis between theory and praxis has contributed to decolonization and liberation.

The first generation of Africanist historians encouraged archaeological research and a methodical use of oral traditions. These efforts have resulted in a greater understanding of the history of many societies. A substantial effort has also been made to reinterpret the writing of ancient historians about Egypt, the Muslim travel accounts about the kingdoms of the Sudan,[25] and the memoirs of the fifteenth-century Christian navigators about the coastal states. Africans are reclaiming their history. In the process, the Black African origins of the Pharaonic civilization and of the impressive Muenemutapa ruins have been established. The prosperity and the high level of political organization in Ghana, Mali, and Songhay have been asserted. The scholarship of the Sudanese scholars and the humanism of Timbuktu in the fifteenth and sixteenth centuries have eloquently refuted the myth that "African consciousness has not reached an awareness of... God, the State, or the law." The leaders of the African resistance against colonialism are no longer viewed as "bloodthirsty tyrants" but rather as the heroes of nationalism.[26] African art has been recognized as a heritage of humanity. To deny African history or to overlook Africa's contribution to world civilization has become a testimony to ignorance and bigotry.

*I italicize this word to show that the word "nègre" in French is as derogatory as its English counterpart "nigger." Césaire used it as a defiant mechanism.

Conclusion: A Different Emphasis

As I have suggested, history can be both a methodical scholarly endeavor and an ideological force. It is the interaction of these two dimensions of historical consciousness which has led to the establishment of African studies centers and the acceptance of African history as a legitimate branch of history.

In the exercise of reconstructing the history of Africa, however, some nationalist-conscious African historians, seeking to affirm national cohesion, have tended to portray the cultures of precolonial African states as harmonious and classless. In such works, the present stratifications in African societies are characterized as remnants of the colonial legacy. Since the first years of independence, however, it has become evident that the history of African peoples cannot be presented as conflict-free, however grandiose such an achievement might have been. For example, most African societies experienced "domestic slavery" and other forms of oppression and exploitation, although their intensity should not be exaggerated. It is necessary, therefore, to analyze the full range of African social organizations and the processes of their internal differentiation. The role of the commoners, for example, cannot be ignored for the sake of asserting an imaginary national cohesion. Thus, class analysis, with its emphasis on the material bases of history and the social formations corresponding to these material conditions but freed of its metaphysics, may help us to reach a more complex understanding of Africa's past.

Furthermore, this approach is more consistent with the analysis of the constraints that external relations have placed on African states in both the precolonial and post-independence eras. Since the 1960s, most writers have noticed a growing Third World dependence on the industrialized world, and a worsening of underdevelopment in Africa in particular. Neocolonialism, a more subtle and pervasive form of domination, has replaced the old colonial system in Africa. Therefore, the continent is confronted with the prospect of growth without economic development, of political independence without economic prosperity and national security. Within this neocolonialist context, a new historical consciousness has emerged—one that is critical of both the capitalist world's control of the African economy and the African political elite's connivance with this process.[27] This consciousness operates on two main premises: (1) that underdevelopment must be studied historically because a society's capacity to shape its destiny is partly determined by its past and existing conditions; and (2) that an analytical critique of Africa's uneven relations with the outside world may heighten African peoples' consciousness and subsequently lead to a radical social change that will ensure true liberation and development. Class analysis and revolutionary consciousness have come to dominate historical thought in African studies.

Notes

1. Lewis H. Lapham, "The Black Man's Burden," *Harper's,* June 1977, p. 16.
2. Larry Heinzerling, "Attack on Zaire Reflects Poverty and Tribal Divisions in Africa," *Minneapolis Tribune* (AP), 21 May 1978.
3. Basil Davidson, *African Genius* (Boston: Little, Brown, 1969), p. 25.
4. For instance, see Jean-Paul Sartre, S. Kierkegaard, or Henri Bergson: Sartre, *Existentialism and Human Emotions* (New York: Philos. Lib., 1947); Kierkegaard, *Philosophical Fragments,* 2nd ed. (Princeton: Princeton University Press, 1962); Bergson *Les deux sources de la morale et de la religion* (Paris: P.U.F., 1969 ed.).
5. Aimé Césaire, *Return to My Native Land* (Paris: Présence Africaine, 1968), p. 1.
6. Georg Wilhelm Friedrich Hegel, *Lectures on the Philosophy of History,* trans. H. B. Niblet (London: Cambridge University Press, 1975), pp. 174-176.
7. Ibid., p. 9.

8. See Sékéné-Mody Cissoko, *Tombouctou et l'empire Songhay* (Dakar: N. E. A., 1975).

9. Claude Lévi-Strauss, *La pensée sauvage* (Paris: Plon, 1962), pp. 5-27.

10. Aimé Césaire, *Discourse on Colonialism*, trans. Joan Pinkham (New York: Monthly Review Press, 1972), p. 11.

11. For an overview of early Portuguese contact with Africa, see Th. Monad, R. Mauny, and G. Duval, eds., *De la première découverte de la Guinée*, récit par Diogo Gomes (Bissau, 1959); Pacheco Pereira, *Esmeraldo de situ orbis*, trans. R. Manny (Bissau, 1957); Georges Balandier, *Daily Life in the Kingdom of the Congo in the 16th Century*, trans. H. Weaver (New York: Pantheon, 1968); Gomes Eanes de Zurara, *Chronique de Guinée*, trans. L. Bourdon (Dakar: IFAN, 1960).

12. For a discussion of some of these issues, see Walter Rodney, *How Europe Underdeveloped Africa* (Washington, D.C.: Howard University Press, 1974), and Jean Suret-Canale, *Afrique noire* (Paris: Editions Sociales, 1961).

13. For a discussion of the myth about the Blacks in America, see George M. Fredrickson, *The Black Image in the White Mind, 1817-1914* (New York: Harper, 1972).

14. This tendency was quite apparent in the functionalist school, whose main theoretician was Bronislaw Malinowski.

15. See Bronislaw Malinowski, *The Dynamics of Culture Change: An Inquiry into Race Relations in Africa* (New Haven: Yale University Press, 1945).

16. Elliot P. Skinner, "Group Dynamics in the Politics of Changing Societies: The Problem of Tribal Politics in Africa," in June Helm, ed., *Essays on the Problem of Tribe* (American Ethnological Society, 1968).

17. To stress this view, it would be most useful to offer more courses or seminars on the historiography of African peoples and authors.

18. Kwame Nkrumah, "Address to the Opening of the First International Congress of Africanists," in L. Brown and M. Crowder, eds., *The Proceedings of the First International Congress of Africanists* (Evanston: Northwestern University Press, 1960), p. 10.

19. See L. S. B. Leakey, "Man's African Origin," *Annals of the New York Academy of Sciences* 96 (1962): 495-503.

20. See Cheikh Anta Diop, *Antériorité des civilisations nègres: Mythe ou vérité historique* (Paris: Presence Africaine, 1967).

21. See Sékéné-Mody Cissoko, *Tombouctou et l'empire songhay*, and Félix DuBois, *Timbuktu the Mysterious* (1898) (to be read with caution).

22. See W. Fagg and E. Elisofon, *The Sculpture of Africa* (New York: Praeger, 1958), or Frank Willet, *African Art* (New York: Praeger, 1967).

23. Aimé Césaire, "An Interview with Aimé Césaire," *Discourse on Colonialism*, p. 76.

24. There is no doubt that many people have profited from African studies. Some of them have abandoned it because of political and other reasons.

25. Sudan refers to the "Land of the Blacks" in general. In the context of this discussion, I am speaking of the Western Sudan, which extends roughly from the Chad Lake to the Atlantic.

26. For example, see Yves Person, *Samori: une révolution dyula*, 3 vols. (Dakar: IFAN, 1968, 1975); Michael Crowder, ed., *West African Resistance* (Evanston: Northwestern University Press, 1971); T. O. Ranger, "Connexions Between Primary Resistance Movements and Modern Mass Nationalism in East and Central Africa," *Journal of African History* 9 (1968):437-453, 631-642.

27. Examples of this literature include: Frantz Fanon, *The Wretched of the Earth* (New York: Grove Press, 1969); K. Nkrumah, *Neo-colonialism* (1969); E. A. Brett, *Underdevelopment and Colonialism in East Africa* (New York: NOK, 1977); Samir Amin, "Underdevelopment and Dependence," *The Journal of Modern African Studies* 10, 4 (1972); Walter Rodney, *How Europe Underdeveloped Africa*; I. Wallerstein and P. Gutkind, eds., *The Political Economy of Contemporary Africa* (New York: Monthly Review, 1976); Basil Davidson, *Can Africa Survive?* (Boston: Little, Brown, n.d.).

CHAPTER 6

Africa's Contribution: African History in World Context

I. K. Sundiata

What are the highlights of Africa's contribution to the progress of the world? This is a question which has long bedeviled historians inside and outside Africa. A concomitant of the European economic and political exploitation of Africa was the denial or devaluation of Africa's past. Not only was it argued tht Africa had made no contributions to the progress of the world, but it was also asserted that the continent below the Sahara had no history to speak of. Africa above the Sahara had a history, but it was maintained that this history was only a footnote to the history of another region, the so-called Middle East.

Today, though African Studies (including African history) have been present in major American universities for more than thirty years, the African contribution to world progress remains undefined. Although the study of African history has burgeoned in the past several decades, it has shied away from an examination of the broader role of Africa in world history and contented itself with microstudies of discrete societies and migrations. According to many Western social scientists, African history is not to be understood as the history of the entire continent, for any society that is technologically sophisticated and/or literate is characterized as anomalous and beyond the pale of "African" history. Working from a paradigm of what an African society should be, the social scientist seeks to fit the whole of African history onto the Procustean bed of his assumptions. Although more cleverly formulated than in earlier racist statements about the "Dark Continent," the basic assumption is the same: Africa, the home of the Black peoples of this world, stands outside the great human process of the growth and interchange of ideas and technologies. As we shall see, such a view does violence to the facts, it is

---

Dr. Ibrahim K. Sundiata is a Professor in the History Department at the University of Illinois at Chicago Circle in Chicago, Illinois

the reflection of biases that arose from centuries of contact between Africa and the West, centuries of slaving and economic imperialism.

Some writers have even contended that to raise the question of Africa's contribution is an altogether specious undertaking. In the early 1970s, the Black sociologist Orlando Patterson attacked what he chose to call "contributionism" as doing "violence to the facts" and being "ideologically bankrupt, and . . . methodologically and theoretically deficient." Patterson argued that those who attempted to evaluate the African role in the progress of humanity were using the false canons of historiography. According to him, African history must confine itself to small, preliterate groups and their "unspectacular techniques of survival." Patterson strongly asserted (and perhaps a great number of his confreres agreed with him) that:

> More recent adherents of this view [contributionism] either play down the American contributions (which is not to say that they do not recognize the achievement of blacks in American music and art) or, more aggressively, by adopting a "sinking ship" view of America, consider all discussions of contributions to it either irrelevant or insignificant.

> Instead, they head for the civilization big-time: to Carthage and Egypt and Nubia and the rest of the "great" civilizations of ancient North Africa and the ancient Near East. The role of the black historian is to get the black man back into the wonderful "birth of civilization" story, to prove that white history has been a big lie, that the black man lived not only in preliterate tribal societies, but was right there in all the major events of world history. The grand versions of the contributionist thesis I shall call the three P's approach—black history as the rediscovery of princes, pyramids, and pageantry . . . . A sad state of affairs indeed.[1]

There is, whether academia wants to recognize it or not, a growing dichotomy in African history—the academic and the popular. Popular writers, writing from a commitment to ethnic integrity, produce a history far different from that published by university-bred academicians. The latter often excise Egypt, Nubia, and so on from their histories and concentrate on the preliterate cultures of sub-Saharan Africa. Many are increasingly concerned with small communities that have had relatively little contact with outside cultures. We might call this tendency "anthropologism." Anthropologism views African history as patronizingly *sui generis.* Perhaps because of their early connection with ethnology and anthropology, academic African historians confine their investigations to small-scale and preliterate societies, viewing other developments as unrepresentative or anomalous. It has been noted that

> for some sixty years, from about the 1880s onwards, professional historians had little or no contact with the African past. Its study was but little advanced by workers in other disciplines.... Moreover, perhaps because African studies were so largely concerned with nonliterate societies, there was a tendency to regard them as a junior or poor relations of oriental studies.... The newer generation of anthropologists who went into the African field from the 1920s onwards were at first little concerned with the past of the societies they were exploring.[2]

Although African history has emerged as a full-blown discipline, it retains many of the biases of another discipline. The anthropological approach applies a double standard to African history, thus creating an essentially false history. An anthropological approach to African history would be justified only if all history were written with the same bias. The basic concerns of world history would have to be revised to focus on "the poor and oppressed and their quiet, unspectacular techniques of survival." No doubt the Africanist who leans toward an exclusive study of the small-scale and preliterate would be rather puzzled if his university made the study of medieval Letts and Livonians as important as that of Capetian France.

One issue cannot be avoided: many of the "contributionists" are Black and many of the "anthropologists" are not. The exclusion from African history of certain North African societies (which some writers continue to call "Caucasoid") raises difficulties. The tacit assumption that "Black" means "preliterate tribal societies" skews historical reality. The assertion that North African peoples are beyond the ken of African history because they are not "genuine Negroes" is, in light of American racial taxonomy, more than specious. Many "contributionists" point out that from a North American standpoint, all of Africa is Black. It does violence to history, to label a man one thing in Egyptian Memphis and another in Tennessee.

Africa, nay-sayers both Black and white notwithstanding, is where mankind originated and where that very "civilization" denied to Africa in fact evolved. Egypt, which is said to be the fount of "Western" civilization, lay at the crossroads of Asia and Africa and was both a unique society in the African context and a uniquely African one. Writing, mathematics, and astronomy all made their appearance in Egypt by the fifth millennium B.C. The argument that these developments were unique to Egypt does not invalidate the point that they are African developments. Furthermore, other African societies were to witness many of the same developments by the end of the first millennium A.D.

The peoples of sub-Saharan Africa acquired knowledge of iron metallurgy at an early date (in the main by the opening of the present era). Recent discoveries in Ghana suggest that West Africans had mastered iron smelting techniques by early in the second millennium A.D., well in advance of Europe. In the so-called European Dark Ages it must also be remembered that the majority of Europe's gold came from West Africa, a point of no little significance when we consider the later commercial expansion of late-medieval banking systems in Europe.

The agricultural role of Africans in the Americas is easily recognized. Not so readily recognized is the African contribution to the world's stock of food crops. Plants indigenous to and first domesticated in West Africa may include sorghum, Guinea yams, okra, calabash, watermelon, tamarind, cotton, and sesame, along with varieties of cereal grains, peas, beans, and potatoes.

The anthropologist G. P. Murdock has, over much criticism, championed the theory that agriculture itself had an independent origin (c. 5000 B.C.) in West Africa, not too long after its beginnings in Western Asia (c. 8000 B.C.):

> We should expect the particular people who first advanced from a hunting and gathering economy to an agricultural one to have multiplied in number and to have expanded geographically at the expense of their more backward neighbors, with the result that the group of languages which they spoke should have spread over an unusually wide expanse of territory.... Our criteria are fully satisfied ... in the Western Sudan by the far-flung Nigritic stock and particularly by its Mande subfamily, which centers on the upper Niger River. Not only do the speakers of Mande exhibit [Black] agriculture in its fullest and most developed form, but their distribution demonstrates that they have spread in all directions at the expense of their immediate neighbors."[3]

In the Diaspora, African learning and technology also had important influences, some of them little recognized. In the rice fields of South Carolina, West African techniques and technologies provided the basis for an entire economy. In all of the Americas, African agricultural techniques and ingenuity aided in the expansion and development of a myriad of colonial agricultural systems. In certain areas, such as northeastern Brazil, African people, specifically the Hausas, brought with them a higher level of literacy than that of the white settler society that surrounded them. Even the most conservative of historians have been forced to admit the African contribution to the whole structure of life in the Americas:

> Even the field hands who labored in the plantations were far from being unskilled. They came from societies with a culture considerably more elaborate than that of, say, the Indian aborigines in Brazil or North America. Being skilled farmers, the African slaves were better adjusted to the needs of tropical agriculture than the Indians. They also supplied the New World with all manner of specialized skills. Brazilians, for instance, obtained from Africa . . . technicians for their mines, experienced herdsmen for their ranches, and also members of more specialized professions including cloth and soap merchants, schoolmasters, and even priests or men learned in the Koranic traditions.[4]

The contribution of Africa and Africans to the arts and language has long been recognized. Africa has molded the musical traditions of the Western Hemisphere. Without the influence and contribution of Africa, it would be safe to say that the musical and linguistic expression of all regions of the Americas would not be what it is today. The feeling and pattern of African music is found throughout the New World and is, perhaps, Africa's most noticeable gift to the Old.

Whatever the arguments about the "African Personality," "Negritude," or "Soul," it must be admitted that migrants from Africa have injected the whole of the Americas with patterns of behavior and world views that vary from those of the dominant white colonizers. As investigations in many parts of North and South America show, despite the virulent racism of whites in the Americas and in Africa, Africanism has influenced the culture of the oppressors to a remarkable degree. From the appropriation of Black religious music by white Bible Belt evangelists in the United States, to the diffusion of African-based rites in Brazil and santeria in the Caribbean, it is obvious that Africans captured the minds and spirits of their oppressors:

> An account either of the folk literature or more sophisticated literary works produced by Afro-American writers in English, French, Spanish, or Portuguese would fill many volumes. So would an account of black influence on the European languages spoken in the New World. Such a

survey would have to range all the way from the creation of independent French and English *patois* in the West Indies to the infiltration of the individual words into English, terms like "tote" (to carry) or "juke" as in "juke box." The musical quality, the tonality, the cadence of American Negro speech is reflected in southern white dialects. The African influence on southern American English was apparently of greater significance than the Bantu impact on Afrikaans in South Africa."[5]

The African contribution goes far beyond the level of culture, however. Indeed, as Peter Hammond has pointed out:

> The ancestors of present-day Afro-Americans contributed more to the New World than jazz, spirituals, chicken gumbo, and Br'er Rabbit. For four centuries they contributed, without pay, their labor, and often their lives, to the economic development of nearly every American nation . . . [that is,] not only to development of the plantation economies of the tropics and subtropics and to the shipping fortunes of New England, but to the accumulation of capital derived from the profits of slave labor that significantly helped finance the industrialization of much of Western Europe and all of North America."[6]

The African continent was not engaged in a symbiotic relationship with Europe and America. Africa's contribution, in terms of an outflow of manpower and skill during the period of the slave trade, weakened Africa and immeasurably aided the development of the societies that were most active in their propagation of the idea of Black inferiority.

A corollary of African enslavement outside Africa has been the African contribution to the idea of liberty and revolutionary struggle. This struggle began in Africa with the anti-slaving protest of such men as Affonso of Kongo, Agaja of Dahomey, and the ruler of Futa Toro. It also found expression in the frequent revolt of slaves bound for the Americas in the Middle Passage. Africans have contributed much to the idea and practice of liberation—an idea that persists down to the present time. Black liberation, the neglected theme in the triumvirate of eighteenth-century revolutions, has been a paradigm for many subsequent Third World revolutions. Far more than the revolt of the North American establishment in 1776, the Haitian Revolution demonstrated the potential of colonial peoples to throw off the shackles of white dominance and gross economic exploitation. Far more than the rhetorical egalitarianism of the French Revolution of 1789, the Haitian Revolution, whatever its later shortcomings, demonstrated the possibility of colonial peoples everywhere to take their destiny into their own hands. Blacks in Africa and in the Diaspora have given a continuing revolutionary example to the peoples of the world. The liberal abolitionism of nineteenth-century Britain was fueled by the knowledge that Blacks desired their freedom from the economic straitjacket of slavery. The liberal thinkers of Europe and later the Marxist thinkers of Europe and America could not help but see, however dimly, that the revolt of Africa and the Diaspora was the one revolt that might go well beyond the restructuring of the status quo and move toward a truly radical reorganization of economic relations.

In short, Blacks' greatest contribution to the world is the concept of liberation. A curious example of the triangular trade of the eighteenth century has been the grudging realization in the West of the idea of Black liberation. The white Euro-American world has made repeated attempts to stifle or ignore this development, but the movement for African liberation goes on apace. The African example runs through the successful liberation of Angola, Mozambique, and Zimbabwe to the eventual liberation of South Africa. The African example cannot help but inform the consciousness of the entire world.

One of the techniques of colonial domination is the destruction of a people's past. We must look at how this technique has been used in the case of the African on both the African continent and in the Diaspora. The most blatant technique has been the expunging of Africa from the historical record. Racists have ignored much of the evidence of African historical development and have juggled evidence. Even when the evidence was overwhelming, racists and colonial writers have set up paradigms of what is called African and then proceeded to exclude societies that do not fit the model. In the early twentieth century, the British Egyptologist Sir Flinders Petry went to great pains to argue the non-African origins of Egyptian society, only to be grudgingly forced back to the position that the ancient Egyptians were of a "coarse" Afro-Asiatic stock. Evidence of the African basis of Egyptian societies was suppressed and a plethora of pseudoscientific explanations were introduced for example, the Hamitic hypothesis.

The negation of the unity of Africa was attacked through a series of arbitrary divisions between Africa's people: Muslim and non-Muslim, literate and nonliterate, Caucasoid and Negroid. "High African civilizations" were separated from the record of what were considered the truly African societies. As mentioned, outstanding African contributions in the realms of technology and social organization were dismissed as being unrepresentative of African development. The claim that Africa had never contributed anything to the civilization of the world was bolstered by the artificial gerrymandering of the African continent: North Africa was divided from sub-Saharan Africa, Muslim Africa from non-Muslim Africa, Africans in the Diaspora from non-Diaspora Africans, and literate Africans from nonliterate or preliterate Africans. Outsiders fragmented the larger pattern of African development into a series of units; they decided what was African and what was not. This approach persists and accounts for the lack of a clear overview of what African history means as Black history. Indeed, in some situations the very emphasis on the study of the minutiae of African history has supported the assertion that the continent itself has little or no cultural unity and that whatever "culture" does exist in Africa is the product of outside stimuli. The Hamitic hypothesis, today largely in desuetude, has subtly been given second life through the distinction drawn between "Black Africa" and the rest of the continent—a distinction that is said to represent a basic division between societies that do not possess the rudiments of "civilization" and those that do.

The problem of manipulation of African history is further compounded by the legacy of colonial miseducation. It has become a cliché to note that French colonial education in Senegal slighted African history and sought to teach young Senegalese the glorious past of their ancestors, the Gauls. The same process obtained in the British colonies, where in the first half of the twentieth century, such Africans as Sir Kitoyi Ajasa of Nigeria could extol the benefits of the Pax Britannica and condemn the teaching of African history as a futile exercise. Today, colonial miseducation is still present, although it is far less strident than in the pre-independence period. One commentator has noted that cultural imperialism is still rife among the African intellectual elite:

> Some African intellectuals, especially those educated in Britain, resist changes in curriculum or in the pattern of courses because they confuse such changes with a lowering of standards. They are accordingly suspicious of any divergence from the British pattern. Some of them are particularly allergic to proposals for incorporating African studies into

the curriculum. This is, they say, the first step toward disarming us intellectually; to substitute Arabic and African languages for the classics; to teach English to Africans as Chinese is taught to Englishmen, not as Englishmen learn English at Cambridge; to neglect Tudor history in favor of the history of Africa; to regard oral tradition as legitimate material for scholarship; to take seriously the political institutions of a Yoruba town; to reflect on the indigenous ethical systems of animists and Muslims as well as on Christian ethics."[7]

In commenting on the continuing "brainwashing" of Africans in African universities, a West African scholar has noted that in spite of the "liberalization" of African higher education since independence, foreign models continue to predominate, with white American models in certain situations taking over from British ones. The problem is thus perpetuated:

The institutions continue to train a class of persons African in blood, black in color, but white Anglo-American in tastes, in opinions, in morals and in intellect; they are doing little or nothing to produce what they ought, above all, to be producing—a class of persons African in tastes, in opinions, in morals, in intellect, and uncompromisingly nationalist in temperament. That is their fundamental problem."[8]

European racism produced an image of the "Dark Continent" and then bequeathed this image to Blacks in Africa and in the Diaspora. Today, twenty years after the upsurge of Black consciousness, the problem is still with us. As W. E. B. DuBois noted in the early 1930s, in an article entitled "Pan-Africa and New Racial Philosophy," the Black world receives its image of the various parts of Africa and the Diaspora through the white media.[9]

Although many would argue that the images of the past have been somewhat softened, the truth is that the distortion and abuse of the African past continues. Blacks in the Diaspora continue to be presented with an image of Africa as the "Dark Continent." There are continued attempts to cut Blacks in the Diaspora off from their continental past. Films and other media continue to destroy a true picture of Africa just as surely as the racists and slavers of the past century attempted to deny that the continent even had a past.

If we were asked to define the responsibilities of modern Black scholars in correcting the distortion caused by colonial imposition, the first and most important point would be to allow Africans to develop their own *national* histories. African history must ultimately be written by Africans in response to their own perceived interests.

The subject matter and concerns of African history must ultimately flow from African history's own internal dynamic. Some non-African historians have attempted to write an Afrocentric view of aspects of African history, often with dire results. African history must ultimately be written by Africans in response to their own perceived interests.

In looking for the African past, we can use history as something more than a record of the dead events of the past. History can aid in an attempt to determine the strengths and weaknesses of African society before the advent of the slave trade. African history does not begin with colonialism, and neither does the history of the Diaspora begin with the landing of African men and women in the Western Hemisphere. A West African writer cautions against seeing the past as a model for modern Africa. At the same time, he notes that the pre-slaving period may offer significant insights into statecraft. These insights may help modern Africa avoid some of the pitfalls of its post-independence experiments with Western parliamentarianism:

> The culture-scape upon which a renascent Africa was to be erected was a heap of social debris from nearly five centuries of disintegration, slaving, conquest and colonization: debris accumulating ever since the sixteenth century, when autonomous African development was interrupted as the holocaust of western European expansion overwhelmed Africa. In any serious attempt at African renaissance it would be necessary to dig through that debris, down to the cultural trajectory. Whereas the attainments of the twentieth-century West could provide a reference point for defining some of what we have speedily to accomplish, sixteenth-century Africa, that twilight era between Africa's autonomous past and her Dark Ages of satellization to Europe, is a reference point for measuring how much cultural ground Africa lost during the ensuing centuries.... Whereas the twentieth-century West helps to define our future goals, sixteenth-century Africa helps to clarify what tasks of social repair we should speedily undertake.[10]

Africans had systems of law long before the advent of European colonialism. They also had checks and balances against the arbitrary use and abuse of power. Could not the African past provide traditional techniques and values that would check what many see as a drift toward arbitrary rule in Africa? One of Africa's greatest contributions to the world may lie in the resuscitation of neo-traditional checks and balances based on institutions grounded in the past (like the Oyo Mesi Council of Oyo). These institutions may go a long way toward binding the elite politics bequeathed from the colonial era together with the thought and perceptions of the great masses of African peoples.

The various approaches to the study of African history must be put into their proper pedagogical framework. Emphasis on state formation and large-scale political formation should precede the more detailed analysis of smaller units. It is important to know history's purpose. There is nothing intrinsically wrong with giving students an introduction to societies that may conform to current notions of greatness. Indeed, the greater danger lies in constructing artificial and patronizing canons of excellence and labeling them African. The last person to attempt interpretation of the traditional African world view is the American university academician.

Finally, to argue that Afro-Americans in particular should confine themselves to studying only the culture of their West African ancestors is ludicrous in the extreme. In presenting African history as a background to Afro-American history, it is important to stress the Guinea coast and its contributions. There is little reason to exclude African history on a continental scale, however. The interrelatedness and cultural crosscurrents of a continent provide a backdrop to the national histories of the groups from which immigrants have come.

The need in African (and Afro-American) history is for a new synthesis, one that goes well beyond African history. All history must increasingly concern itself with what has been, until recently, the great majority of mankind: the nonliterate rural masses. At the same time, however, we must avoid patronizing—isolating African history and seeing nothing else. We must equally avoid the creation of a past that never existed.

Notes

1. Orlando Patterson, "Rethinking Black History," *Africa Report*, 17, 9: 30.
2. J. D. Fage, "History," *The Arican World*, ed. Robert A. Lystad (New York: Frederick A. Praeger, 1965), pp. 42-43.
3. G. P. Murdock, *Africa* (New York: McGraw Hill, 1959), pp. 66-67.
4. Lewis H. Gann and Peter Duignan, *Africa and the World* (San Francisco: Chandler Publishing, 1972), p. 332.
5. Ibid., p. 337.
6. Peter B. Hammond, "West Africa and the Afro-Americans," *The African Experience*, ed. John N. Paden and Edward W. Soja (Evanston: Northwestern University Press, 1970), p. 209.

7. Sir Eric Ashby, *Universities: British, Indian, African* (Cambridge, Mass.: Harvard University Press, 1966), pp. 211-212.
8. Chinweizu, *The West and the Rest of Us* (New York: Random House, 1975), p. 335.
9. W. E. B. DuBois, "Pan-Africa and New Racial Philosophy," *The Crisis*, XL (November 1933): 247-262.
10. Chinweizu, p. 188.

IV
Modernity and Other Directions in Afro-American Literature

Any Moment Now We Shall Disappear Leaving Only Space to Mark the Place Where We Have Been, Phillip L. Mason

CHAPTER 7

Modernity and Other Directions in Afro-American Literature: Reflections on Black Literature of the Past Two Decades

Stephen E. Henderson

Our task—an examination of Black literature of the past two decades—is complex and challenging. Part of this complexity stems from the literature itself, part from the times that produced it, part from our proximity to it, and part from the nature of its reception. Notwithstanding these problems—and they are difficult, some probably insoluble—we are all aware not only of the considerable quantity of that literature, but also of its peculiar vitality and, more recently, its neglect.

The topic of this panel, "Modernity and Other Directions in Afro-American Literature," contains several terms that merit attention. The first is "modernity," by which the framers of the conference signify the "immediate present" of the writers and their work. The second is "other directions," which implies movement in a discernible pattern or path toward a consciously or unconsciously assumed goal. Thus, the topic assumes a pattern, however complex or obscure, in Afro-American literature, and a movement (or complex of movements) toward those goals. In other words, we ask ourselves, where has Black literature been heading over the past twenty years? Where is it headed presently?

Such questions beg other questions, of course, and in order to avoid this fallacy, as much as possible with my limited knowledge, let me say that it is foolhardy, wasteful, and misleading to speak about the "direction" of Black literature without attempting to establish some bearings, some sense of logical and historical location. As readers, consumers, students, and, ideally, as co-creators of literature, we quickly perceive our limitations. We must have organizing principles

---

Dr. Stephen E. Henderson is the Director of the Institute for the Arts and Humanities at Howard University, Washington, D.C.

and categories to work with; but we are so close to the literature that such organization is difficult and deceptive; categories coalesce and assume unwieldy size or fragment themselves in bewildering numbers. We are left, therefore, with a set of problems, which may be addressed in systematic fashion, and a set of perceptions and impressions. They are, perhaps, two sides of the same coin. The *problems,* as they appear to me, are situations that require the assistance of scholarship. They are: (1) problems of incomplete knowledge, (2) problems of discontinuous knowledge, and (3) problems of distorted knowledge or misinterpretation.

These problems may occur in any period of Black literature, or of any literature, but whenever they occur they quite obviously are affected by other considerations, some of which are mentioned at the beginning of this paper—the nature of the literature itself, the times that produced it, its reception, and our proximity to it. To repeat, these problems are challenges to the scholar and critic. As we shall see later, the creative writer has another set of problems, some of which are related to these and some of which are peculiarly the artist's, in this case, the Black writer's.

At any rate, both the scholar/critic and the creative writer are involved, consciously or not, in this matter of "direction." The latter may want to do his or her "own thing"—make a personal statement—which, from the scholar's perspective, may turn out to be an expression of a "typical direction"—an impulse, style, or ideology typical of a given period. It should not be difficult, then, to see how "incomplete knowledge" of what others are doing, or of a given subject/theme, may result in conflicting evaluations and perspectives. An example of this problem is the poems on the Black matriarch which were so popular in the 1960s, despite excellent earlier treatments of the theme by Owen Dodson, Sterling Brown, and others. Thus, in a poem to his grandmother, Don L. Lee is certainly making a personal statement, at the same time that he is also making a statement "typical" of the 1960s, exploring a typical topic of Afro-American poetry.

To elaborate somewhat, problems of incomplete knowledge complicate our understanding of persons, canons, and periods. The period of Afro-American literature which seems to have attracted the greatest scholarly interest is the 1920s and 1930s, variously called the Harlem Renaissance, The Negro Renaissance, or the New Negro

Movement. Writers who have attracted the greatest attention are Langston Hughes and Jean Toomer. More recently, some attention has focused on Sterling Brown, who pointedly denies the existence of a "Harlem Renaissance," and Zora Neale Hurston. The next generation, which matured in the 1940s, included such writers as Gwendolyn Brooks, Robert Hayden, Margaret Walker, Ralph Ellison, and especially Richard Wright, and is now gradually attracting attention. For the 1950s the interest has largely centered on James Baldwin.

In the meantime, the Black writers of the 1960s and early 1970s, who created some of the most moving and challenging literature of their time, have scarcely received any critical or scholarly attention at all. Their work often has not even been reviewed, and even when it has been, the result is often cursory or superficial. We cannot evaluate their work, of course, if we do not know about it. We certainly cannot project extensions from it if we neither know it nor take it seriously. But even honest, well-intentioned efforts run headlong into the problem of incomplete knowledge, which in the case of recent and contemporary writers is formidable. Many of the writers who came into prominence in this period are still fairly young—in their middle thirties or early forties—and have not completed their canon, so to speak, although we have no way of ascertaining this, since a writer's canon may be closed long before the end of his or her life. Moreover, a writer's published work may represent only a small fraction of the "canon." Fortunately, there have been some salutary moves to correct this situation, prominent among them being Random House's publication of the works of Henry Dumas, under the editorship of Eugene Redmond. Other prominent examples are the *Selected Plays and Prose of Amiri Baraka/LeRoi Jones* and *The Selected Poetry of Amiri Baraka/LeRoi Jones*, which represent a kind of interim report on his impressive talent.

But there are many other writers—so numerous, in fact, that they are easily overlooked, especially if they published only a few works or were not "widely anthologized," as the cliché goes. How is one, then, to organize all of this information? How is one to find it in the first place? I think that one should begin with the traditional methods of research, employing the most sophisticated and efficient means currently available. Indeed, the beginnings of that work are emerging, examples of which include: Eugene Redmond's *Drumvoices: The*

Mission of Afro-American Poetry (Anchor Press/Doubleday, 1976); A Johnson and R. Johnson, *Propaganda and Aesthetics: The Literary Politics of Afro-American Magazines in the 20th Century* (The Univ. of Massachusetts Press, 1979); Barbara Christian, *Black Women Novelists: The Development of a Tradition, 1892-1976* (Greenwood, 1980); Janet L. Sims, *The Progress of Afro-American Women: A Selected Bibliography and Resource Guide* (Greenwood, 1980).

These studies can and should take many forms, from the bibliographical to the interpretative. Those cited above are merely examples of the kind of spadework that remains to be done. This work is chiefly that of the professional scholar; and since the task is so enormous and its achievement so important, the role of institutions like the Africana Studies and Research Center is crucial, although all of us can play our part, however modest, in addressing the "built-in" problem of incomplete knowledge.

The writers themselves have a special obligation to the resolution of this problem—an obligation that they can fulfill as they see fit. However, they should first organize and preserve their literary legacy of notes, manuscripts (both published and unpublished), memorabilia, their autobiographies, and so on, and make these materials available to a Black institution as a bequest, either in stages or in toto. Atlanta University, for example, has some manuscript poems of Gwendolyn Brooks from her early work. The writers can also help us by publishing collections of their topical work, such as Ishmael Reed's *Shrovetide in Old New Orleans* (Doubleday, 1978), or their autobiographies, such as Addison Gayle's, *Wayward Child* (Anchor/Doubleday, 1977), and Julius Lester's *All Is Well* (Morrow, 1976). In addition to autobiographies, interviews are vital sources of information. Despite such efforts, the problem of incomplete knowledge will always be with us, of course, since there is no consensus of what "complete knowledge" should be, or even whether it is attainable. Nevertheless, we obviously need a base of information about our literature and our culture, especially during this period, upon which we can erect the political and aesthetic structures necessary for our future well being.

Discontinuous knowledge is to incomplete knowledge what "coherence" is to "unity" in the older rhetoric. A composition, we were told, must have a beginning, a middle, and an end—unity. It must have all of its parts, and those parts must also relate harmoniously and flow logically from one level to the next—coherence. We are conditioned to seek patterns of unity and coherence in other aspects of our lives, but in literature the problems of discontinous knowledge are the purview of the specialist, who assembles smaller bodies of information into significant conceptual wholes in such a manner that individual anecdotes and memoirs eventually enable us to speak of a socially shared experience such as a "Dasein Group," an "Umbra Group," a "Harlem Writers' Guild," or a "Harlem Renaissance."

E. Ethelbert Miller, Theodore Hudson, John O'Neal, Ishmael Reed, Tom Dent, Barbara Smith, Eugene Redmond, and others have produced or are producing critical histories of "Black Literary Communities," to use Miller's evocative term. This kind of endeavor is absolutely essential to an understanding of Black literary accomplishment during the past two decades, and one may venture to say that an analysis of these histories may have important lessons for us, from a programmatic viewpoint, as we try to assess the recent past and prepare for the future. Briefly, Black literary communities are primarily and most obviously *regional* and may center around an individual or around an institution such as a museum, a workshop, or a university. Examples include the Studio Museum of Harlem, the Harlem Writers' Guild, the Institute of Positive Education, Reed and Johnson Publishing Company, Karamu House, and the Ascension Poetry Series. The regional emphasis quickly shades into the intellectual and the ideological, however, especially where a publication is involved; examples being the Institute of Positive Education and *Black Books Bulletin,* OBAC (Organization of Black African Culture) and *Black World,* the Howard Poets and *Dasein,* and so on.

Complicating matters are the relationships between the various communities, characterized by some of the same behavior patterns that exist between elements in the larger, nonliterary communities. Two of these relationships are:

Regionalism and/or Parochialism. There are some positive aspects of the former, as, for example, in the contemporary Southern Movement, embodied in *Callaloo.* There are negative aspects also, as manifested in the urban versus rural syndrome characteristic of some writing of the sixties, which looked down upon or ignored the Southern heritage. A contradictory aspect of this syndrome was the idealization of things Southern.

Migration of Writers Between Communities, Formation of New Ones. Some indication of the importance of this phenomenon can be seen in the movement to California of such significant New York writers as Ishamel Reed, David Henderson, Joe Johnson, and Alice Walker. Of further interest is the fact that Walker is originally a Southerner with strong cultural ties, who is rapidly maturing as a politically sensitive spokesperson; Reed, Henderson, and Johnson were part of the *Umbra* group. They have all done important work, of course, in their new context, but it is clear that their migration was, in effect, a cultural transplantation. Such developments invite the scholar to analyze the earlier work of these writers, comparing it with the more recent and determining, if possible, whether the change of environment had anything to do with the evolution of the new work.

Two other *Umbra* writers who can be mentioned are Tom Dent and Askia M. Touré, the former Roland Snellings. Since returning to New Orleans, Dent has become a major force in the Black Southern literary cultural movement and is a founder of *Callaloo*, along with native Mississippian Jerry Ward and native Alabamian Charles Rowell. Touré spent a brief period in Atlanta before returning to the East, where he is politically active in Philadelphia and New York.

To return briefly to the South, one must note the presence in Atlanta of two major figures, both recent immigrants—Toni Cade Bambara, who is here today and who has recently published her first novel, *The Salt Eaters,* which unlike her previous work is set in the South—in Georgia, in fact. Also a part of the Atlanta community is another conference participant, Hoyt W. Fuller, editor of *First World.* Although he is not a Southerner and *First World* is an "international journal of Black thought," Fuller was born in Atlanta and is now also a catalyst in the Atlanta community. And in both intellectual and institutional terms Atlanta is the chief focal point, meeting point, of the "Black Southern cultural movement."

These examples certainly do not exhaust the notion of Black literary communities or the effect that the migration of writers has upon them. One hopes, indeed, that an examination of these "communities" in their historical perspective will be assumed by students of the literature and certainly by the writers themselves.

Before we leave the topic, however, we should mention a special kind of "migration"—that of the Caribbean or African writer who spends extended periods of time in the United States, or actually takes

U.S. citizenship, and produces work in the adopted country. This is one of the most fascinating cases for the student of the literature. One cannot easily forget the special voice of Willie Kgositsile, for example, or the early Michael Thelwell, who tells us himself that Chinua Achebe influenced the writing of *The Harder They Come*. In an interview Thelwell has promised to write a novel on the Civil Rights Movement. The perspective should open vistas. One also should mention Dennis Brutus, Wilson Harris, George Lamming, Sylvia Wynter, Joan Cambridge Mayfield, Ayi Kwei Armah, Ivan Van Sertima, Leroy Clarke, Edward Brathwaite, and others who stretch their hands toward us from across the sea—Gideon Mutiso from Kenya, among them, and young scholars like Mariame Sy of Senegal. Here is the fusion, the melting, the spiritual bonding; here is the seedbed of the new literature; here is the new dimension. Here is the new culture.

The new culture must be struggled for, or its evolution will be determined by the forces that shape the rest of society. The critic/scholar's orientation provides him/her with the system and the vocabulary to describe the struggle, but on the most basic level, we already understand it since it undergirds the developments of the past two decades, and, though muted, it clearly suffuses the present. But struggle is complex. It is both internecine and external. It manifests itself in conflicts between individuals and organizations and among individuals within organizations. It shows itself in rivalries between organizations and the use of their publications as ideological forums. Internecine strife seems endemic to human struggle, political or otherwise. Black writers have no monopoly on it.

But at the same time, Black writers do have an obligation, or if the word offends, an opportunity. At the Institute of the Black World, we saw the involvement of the Black artist and intellectual as "the struggle to define the struggle," and Lerone Bennett once made the observation that "It is finally not so important that we love one another but that we confront one another." And so the struggle continues, both outside the group and within it.

With struggle there is drive; without it, there is drift. And in our attempt to make sense, to find pattern and direction in this literature of the recent past and the present, we must realize that we are now dealing with another category of problems, *problems of distorted knowledge and/or misinterpretation*. The confrontation with this problem is the endless struggle, an essential outgrowth of the first two sets of problems. There is nothing more to say here except that in the final analysis what is needed goes beyond scholarly accuracy, philosophical insight, ideological correctness, or intellectual clarity—what is needed is courage.

This lack of courage may even be perceived as another pervasive set of problems—a kind of endemic self-doubt, a moral apathy, a cultural entropy. But we leave it here. If we are serious about our presence here, in our concern for our literature and our artists, about our future in the 1980s and beyond, then we play out the role that best suits us.

There are challenges on all levels and there are heroic possibilities for all—for the writer, for the editor, for the reader in any of his/her various roles. We begin with the editors of the past two decades who made the movement possible, and with individuals who published their own work in mimeograph form: Carolyn Rodgers and others, single heroic figures such as Dudley Randall, and still others with their own brand of heroism—Hoyt Fuller, Ishmael Reed, and Joe Johnson, to name but a few. The campus publications, on Black campuses and white. These were movements toward struggle, and finally toward a tentative unity, as the struggle moved on. Today a handful of Black editors of differing perspectives still exert major influence on our literature—Toni Morrison comes to mind naturally, Marie Brown, Phil Petrie, Kalamu Ya Salaam, Hoyt Fuller, Haki Madhubuti. They are essential, as long as they confront us and themselves. They will play a major role in signaling directions that the literature will take. If they do not confront us, we must confront them.

For the writers themselves, there are hard choices and heavy challenges. They too must confront their individual selves and their communities and their previous work. They must decide, if they haven't already, their relationship to the community—the how's, the why's—they must also consider (and many, I assume, have already considered this) their relationship to their own work. They must confront the work of others. I see their situation as a set of three challenges: (1) the challenge of the folk base; (2) the challenge of "tradition"; (3) the challenge of the modern world.

Reactions to these challenges may be conscious and deliberate or they may be unconscious. A writer, to begin with, has the prerogative of consciously ignoring the challenges. Such a writer, however, is not likely to consider himself or herself a "Black" writer. I speak of those who have no such reservation. But even these "Black" writers may not consciously see the challenges that I have listed. That fact does not make them any less Black, especially if they write about "their immediate present." But if the literature is to grow and develop, then we must be conscious of the challenges of the culture—the cultural imperatives. The challenge that was most enthusiastically embraced in the past two decades was that of the folk base. Indeed, the folk resource has attracted our writers almost from the very beginning of our American stay. I have merely to mention a few names: Edwin Campbell, Paul Laurence Dunbar, James Weldon Johnson, W. E. B. DuBois, Langston Hughes, Robert Hayden, Sterling Brown, Margaret Walker, Zora Neale Hurston, Richard Wright, Gwendolyn Brooks, James Baldwin, Ralph Ellison. From the past two decades: Amiri Baraka, Henry Dumas, Verta Mae Grosvenor, James Forman, Ahmos Zu-Bolton, Rikki Lights, Larry Neal, the *Dasein* Group, the *Umbra* Group, Sarah Fabio, Julia Fields, Jayne Cortez, Jodi Braxton, Ethelbert Miller, Toni Morrison, Thulani Davis, the *Callaloo* writers, and others.

This involvement notwithstanding, the challenge of the folk base is enormous. Glimmerings of new models appear in such works as *The Salt Eaters,* in the lovely and neglected poetry of Julia Fields (her poem "Mr. Tut," for example); in the New Hoo-Doo syndrome of Ishmael Reed and others; in Henry Dumas' work, both poetry and prose—in "Shall the Circle Be Unbroken?" These works, and indeed the challenges of the folk base, go beyond the picturesque and the nostalgic to explore pre-Western lifestyles and modes of thought. The folk base is amenable to as many different approaches—ideological and aesthetic—as the writer has the courage and the imagination to apply.

By "tradition" I mean the larger patterns of literary production which affect the writer, in this case the Black American writer. The writing of the past twenty years reveals that Black writers are well read not only in their own tradition, but also in that of others: the Euro-American tradition, the European, and in particular, the so-called Third World writers, who range from Mao Tse-tung, to Frantz Fanon, Nicolas Guillén, Wole Soyinka, and Leon Damas.

Even the work of the 1960s was clearly and explicitly affected by this worldwide production. Closer to home, one could easily discover, for example, the influence of an e.e. cummings, that "American master" of whom Sonia Sanchez even wrote a delicious parody. Sonia and other poets also wrote haikus, tantras, and other formal works based on Eastern models.

Essentially, then, the movement was away from "Western forms," a movement in an important "direction" which occasionally produced some startling and original work. Some of us tried to describe the work and suggested ways to appreciate its originality. Those efforts, though partly successful, have met a mixed reception that ranges from dismissal, based on simplistic misreading or ideological difference, to alternative analysis, resulting from a reassessment of the data presently available.

Still, the movement away from Western forms has not really ended, if only for the fact that so-called Western forms themselves are harder to define in the modern world. Indeed, it is precisely a lack of tradition which characterizes the modern world and modern aesthetics. As a result, the "immediate present" by which the framers of this conference designate "modernity" is also a fundamental element in the concept of "Modernism," which in literary history signifies the work of such diverse writers as Gertrude Stein, James Joyce, T. S. Eliot and others, and seeks, in effect, to find a kind of permanence in art, in ritual, and in myth. It has been succeeded by other styles and fashions, not only in literature and the other arts, but also in the accompanying scholarship and criticism.

I do not pretend to any mastery of this knowledge; indeed, I am not sure that it can be mastered. Nevertheless, one key to grasping the problem lies within Afro-American culture itself. We have produced a cultural paradigm in Black art, especially in Black music, which enables one to focus the discontinuities and disjunctures of the modern world. I have spoken about that paradigm at some length on other occasions. Now, I shall merely quote Larry Neal and say, "the answer is in our music." Our music, at its best, has always addressed the problem of continuity and change, fragmentation and reintegration. The music is analytical and probing and unafraid. It is engaged and involved. It is problem solving—in a technical as well as an emotional sense. The music is not afraid of new philosophies or new technologies or old philosophies and technologies, for it deals with time filtered through the pulses of African sensibility. So no ideological hang-up should prevent Black poets from writing "sound poems," especially with the models of Bob Kaufmann, Ella Fitzgerald, Louis Armstrong, and the moaning of the Baptist preacher. The answer is in the culture. We must *study* the culture, not take it for granted.

There is an encouraging recent development in our literature which I shall mention in closing. It is perhaps the most important development since the 1960s. I speak of the prominence, the achievement, and the promise of Black women writers. I have already named a few of them. They have always played a significant role, and certainly made major contributions to the literature of the sixties and seventies; however, the new prominence demonstrates that the bearers of the culture and its essential creators have also accepted the challenge of the modern world—the challenge of disunity and fragmentation. We shall all be the stronger for their primal vision.

"Turn the face of history to your face," says the poet June Jordan in a poem dedicated to her mother. That, after all, is the only important direction.

CHAPTER 8

Afro-American Literature: Its Interpretation and Creation Today in Light of Historical Considerations

George E. Kent

The flurry of activity which marks the development of Afro-American literature over the past two decades can be properly evaluated only when we have distinguished clearly between quantitative and qualitative changes in its basic situation. William Wells Brown, W. E. B. DuBois, Claude McKay, Langston Hughes, Zora Neale Hurston, Charles W. Chesnutt, Walter White, Anne Spencer, Melvin Tolson, Chester Himes, Richard Wright, James Baldwin, Haki Madhubuti, and Imamu Baraka have each been discussed in one or more books. Others have been the subjects of considerable analysis in quarterlies or in sections of books. During the 1970s, a new history of the Black novel and the first comprehensive treatment of Black poetry appeared, while other provocative works attempted to lay a new basis for the interpretation of Black poetry and drama. One comprehensive anthology appeared, along with more specialized ones, and an elaborate bibliography of Black literature and resources for its interpretation was published. In addition the period saw some stabilization in a number of Afro-American Studies programs, the appearance of a few new quarterlies, and numerous conferences where literary matters were discussed with increasing seriousness. Nationalist ideologies, by giving coherence to viewpoints or a pattern against which others could react, helped writers and critics to make additional discoveries about reality and literature and the Black situation in America. And though its numbers were usually exaggerated, a black audience gradually arose, a much-needed authenticating audience—in other words, an audience that could give psychological support rather than ambushing the writer suddenly,

---

*Deceased—Mr. George E. Kent, English Department, University of Chicago, Chicago, Illinois

questioning whether or not he had *proved* he or she was human.

Such developments thus have created a much more encouraging set of circumstances for the Black writer. One no longer encounters those conferences (or individual contacts) at which one is asked to prove that Black literature is worthy of study, to name the two or three people *really* worth reading, or to present all that is needed to teach the literature at a two-day institute. Today, no one runs up to you to plead for an outline of your course in Black literature to send to his cousin in some large city where no one has ever heard of any black authors other than Paul Laurence Dunbar and, perhaps, Langston Hughes, but where he has now been assigned to teach *the* course in Black literature. The three black students in the government-funded summer course for newly integrated schools no longer meet you quietly after class to say how glad they are that this course was given, since they came through Northern schools where Blacks were hardly mentioned in any course.

The growing attention accorded to Black literature over the last two decades has also necessitated an increased understanding of some aspects of African, West Indian, and South American literature. As a result, there is a more widespread sense of the elements of Black literature and life which are shared by various societies, as well as a clearer sense of those elements that are particular to individual societies. More than ever, one is likely to be aware of the linguistic dynamics of the rituals by which the Calibans of the colonized areas freed themselves from definitions imposed by the Prosperos.

None of the foregoing is meant to imply that we have arrived at consensus on the interpretation of Afro-American literature or at a sufficient level of representation and innovation in our creative writings. In my opening paragraph I deliberately mentioned instruments that are on the fringe of interpretation, doing so in order to suggest that "interpretation" arises not merely from the comments of critics, but from the sum of those means through which literature moves from author to reader and elicits the reader's appreciation. I call this totality of means an "intermediary system," and hope that I can leave it to individual readers to name all its parts. In industrialized countries, literature, once the direct expression of a communal response to existence, attains the status of a product, and in so doing acquires this elaborate means for its domestication in the minds of its readers—the intermediary system. In order to accommodate the elaborate sifting of a body of literature by various minds (an act that is essential if there is to be even a temporary consensus), the intermediary system must be adequately developed and somewhat efficient. Thus, one can see immediately the roles played by the schools, colleges, universities, media, publishing instruments, and various scholarly endeavors. Of not the least importance in this system is the interaction between routine ways of interpretation and radical (meaning simply, at the roots) organs of innovation.

These radical organs often comprise creative writers and those writers and critics committed to the so-called little magazines. The Black literature of the 1960s and 1970s, and eventually of earlier periods, thus had the advantage of bold formulations by such creative writer-critics as Zora Neale Hurston, James Weldon Johnston, Sterling A. Brown, Richard Wright, James Baldwin, Ralph Ellison, and LeRoi Jones (later Imamu Baraka). Such writers had often had the opportunity to work out theories in the smaller magazines, which were radical either in their approach to literature or to politics or to both. Academic critics need infusions from the theories of creative writers so that they won't quote Aristotle or Northrop Frye forever. Such academic critics perform an excellent service by developing means by which a literature is domesticated for the schools and, to some extent, for the community. For example, Alain Locke's anthology of Black Renaissance writings, *The New Negro,* was a triumph for the 1920s; Sterling A. Brown, Arthur P. Davis, and Ulysses Lee's anthology *The Negro Caravan* was the triumph for the 1940s (Brown, of course, is also a creative writer); Richard Barksdale and Keneth Kinnamon's anthology *Black Writers of America* was a triumph of the 1970s. Generally speaking, however, academic critics prove most vulnerable to other academic critics, and thus their domination of the interpretation of Afro-American literature can be a danger sign (though the creative writer-critics also have their own vulnerabilities).

Questions regarding the adequacy of our intermediary system are a test that helps us to avoid an inaccurate estimation of where we are, and thus, they prevent us from again becoming the easy victims of self-congratulation. We can look almost casually at our intermediary system and see that, both historically and at present, we are victimized by the small amount of labor available for the system. The academic source of such efforts has always been funded, but our history as teachers before the 1960s shows that the inordinate weight of our teaching and general school or college duties did not leave us much time or energy to devote to the intermediary system. Since the 1960s these burdens have not been reduced uniformly throughout the colleges. Thus, while in some institutions the debate rages as to what constitutes a true literary history, we find that we have not yet created an overall history of Black literature of any sort. As a result, we each must assemble some version of literary history from the partial histories that exist for particular genres and periods and from our individual reading. Understanding the present and creating a consensus about it are not easy tasks when our methods for doing so remain inadequately developed. Since we have not fully analyzed the critical formulations created between the turn of the century and the present, and since we have no well-informed history of these formulations, we usually don't know when we are making real progress in the creation of our intermediary system and when we are simply getting caught in old traps.

Many of the old formulations were taken from the literary establishment and couched in terms of overly simple oppositions: protest versus literature, sociology versus literature, Negro writer writing about Negroes versus writer writing about the human condition and thereby transcending race (usually conceived as the "narrow and parochial" concerns of Black experience) and becoming involved in the human condition. Such oppositions were rarely described with precision. A rather popular formula that often pops up in academic journals is the notion that we had a literature of protests until Richard Wright, its chief exemplar, brought it to a climax. Then James Baldwin, Ralph Ellison, and others arrived to begin the creation of a literature of the human condition. Presently, our reaction against the overcommitment to ideology which characterized much of the criticism of the 1960s makes us vulnerable to simply embracing the old dicta in revised forms: "literary journalism" (for protest), "the autonomy of literature" (for excluding concern with politics), "the mind as a theater for contradictory alternatives" (for evasion of social reality). When one tries to discuss literature as literature, one finds that contemporary criticism has robbed us of a vocabulary that could also include discussion of social and racial tension. Regarding criticism as an autotelic activity, the critic becomes preoccupied with the proliferation of terms that issue from the academic theorists. In the process, the critic risks submerging himself in a specialized and self-multiplying vocabulary that contradicts the important mission of delivering the literature to an authenticating black audience. Thus, the intermediary system can become subverted.

If the system and its condition can tell us more accurately where we stand regarding interpretation, perhaps historical investigation of the questions that confronted the literature in the past and study of the responses by earlier critics can define our situation with even greater precision. Writers emerging from self-conscious nineteenth-century Black communities confronted two questions that Black writers have, consciously or unconsciously, faced ever since. First, what future, if any, is there for Blacks in the United States? Writers might answer the question positively, negatively, or qualifiedly, but it would be impossible for them to write without suggesting an answer. Obviously, their answers reflect the ways in which we image ourselves. An agonized and ambiguous answer appeared in David Walker's *Appeal* during 1829 and 1830—one that included images of taut rebelliousness, degradation, confusion, delusion, scornful pride, and exemplary intelligence. The slave narratives, with their commitment to democracy and Christianity, tended to express faith in an American future, although the insistence of some narrators that they remain in Canada qualified this faith. In his novel *Blake,* the nineteenth-century nationalist Martin R. Delany implied a negative answer in his images of the self-possessed man drawing upon both common sense and Black cultural patterns for his revolutionary work. W. E. B. DuBois reflected the pressure of the question in formulating his well-known concept of double-consciousness and in applying it to the artist. As we shall see, the question still influences current critics' sense of modernism.

The second of these still-pressing questions is: What strategy is to be adopted regarding the dependence of Black literature on what Harold Cruse has called a "white liberal critical consensus"? It will be recalled that this consensus has adopted various stances toward Black literature: the benevolent paternalism that provided writing and publishing opportunities for Phillis Wheatley; the religious radicalism of the antislavery movement out of which Frederick Douglass, among others, emerged; the disillusionment and quest for new values and freedom which characterized the advanced literati of the Roaring Twenties, with their support for the New Negro Renaissance; the radical Left of the 1930s and its important role in the emergence of a writer such as Richard Wright; and so on. I need not review here the fact that the support of the white liberal critical consensus has had both a positive and a negative impact. We shall see that this consensus influenced criticism and creative writing, and that a major goal of the radical literary movement of the 1960s was to emancipate the literature from its dependence upon the activity of the white liberal critical consensus. And it can be anticipated that the issue of outside control could provide a test for the degree of independence now exercised by our modernism.

Working within the framework provided by these questions, we can gain perspective on the quality of our modernism, first by looking broadly at the historical development of our critical and creative efforts and then by assessing our present situation. During the nineteenth century and well into the twentieth, our criticism was primarily a eulogistic roll call of writers and artists whose existence illustrated the race's capacity for achievement as defined by American civilization. The files of the NAACP for the 1920s, for example, reveal the acceptance of this principle by such cosmopolitan men as James Weldon Johnson and Walter White. In a letter to W. E. B. DuBois, White defended Carl Van Vechten's *Nigger Heaven* from DuBois's attack with the argument that the novel advanced interracial understanding by acquainting whites with black types of whose existence they had been unaware.

In its varied critical approaches, however, the New Negro Renaissance was optimistic about the future of Blacks in America. It saw itself as defining authentic Black creativity and recording its contributions to American culture, and aggressively collaborated with the white consensus in publishing and critical ventures. Besides compiling and editing the famous anthology *The New Negro,* Alain Locke theorized that if Blacks were to present an authentic image they must exploit their residual African temperament, their folk tradition, and their peculiar history in America. In a series of books he strove to articulate the whole of Black culture, although he had a theoretical concept and not the practical writer's workshop grasp of the utility of folk forms which would reach greater sophistication in the hands of Hughes, Wright, Ellison, and others. James Weldon Johnson and Thomas Talley published anthologies of folk materials and advanced the level of criticism in their introductory comments. Johnson also produced a landmark anthology of poetry which included influential critical commentary and theory. Though there were dissenting political and cultural voices from black socialists and Marcus Garvey, the Renaissance remained steadfast in its attempt to set the Black cultural house in order and to deliver the richness of the Black racial temperament to the rest of America.

The New Negro Renaissance clearly placed its greatest emphasis on race definitions and tensions. The 1930s saw several critics continuing the work of the Renaissance, but also witnessed the emergence of writers on the left such as Richard Wright, who would create images that revealed a tension between the claims of race and those of class. Important book-length criticism appeared in Benjamin Griffith Brawley's *Early Negro American Writers* (1935) and *The Negro Genius* (1937); in Sterling A. Brown's *The Negro in American Fiction* (1937) and *Negro Poetry and Drama* (1937); and in J. Saunders Redding's *To Make A Poet Black* (1939). Critical explorations of folk forms and traditions also received a further boost in the 1930s. Sterling A. Brown made an important contribution as editor of *Negro Affairs,* and the Federal Writers' Project (1936-1939) affected the production of folk histories and helped prepare Brown to write seminal analyses of folk forms. Other important contributions were made by Zora Neale Hurston, including her essay "Characteristics of Negro Expression" in Nancy Cunard's *Negro Anthology* (1934), the folk materials in *Mules and Men* (1934), and the travel book *Tell My Horse* (1938), covering experiences in Jamaica and Haiti and by Richard Wright, in his essay "Blueprint for Negro Writing," *New Challenge I* (1937).

With the publication of these works, the foundation and the general pattern of Black criticism was largely complete, though it would continue to increase in quantity, serviceability, and reach until the 1960s. The white liberal consensus was of impact and service from two directions: left-leaning liberalism and the radicalism of the American Communist party. One senses the impact of the left generally in the wide-ranging sympathies of a Sterling A. Brown. But it is Wright's "Blueprint," a manifesto combining folk nationalism and tradition, Marxism, and literary modernism, which marked an emancipation from the old abolitionist sensibility. This sensibility was marked by the principles of the Enlightenment Christianity, and moral suasion. Wright's Marxism aligned him, instead, with the myth of the international class struggle and freed him from the persisting abolitionist myths and from those of the white American middle class, whose versions of democracy had been imposed upon most earlier Black creative writers. Eventually, however, he did not feel liberated by the Party but constrained to the point of revolt. According to the testimony in his papers (deposited at Yale), the Party had offered the young writer new ways of seeing, freedom from the oppressions and distortions of the instruments of popular culture, and an international audience, but in the early 1930s it became an instrument of constraint.

At any rate, Wright's education in Marxism constituted the most important ideological revolt prior to the radical movement of the 1960s. His education as a writer was highly stimulated by his genius put to school in the classroom of the modern masters. As is well known, Black literature would be different after *Uncle Tom's Children, Native Son,* and *Black Boy,* and the impact of his criticism (particularly *White Man, Listen* [1957]) would be felt well into the 1960s.

The crowning academic contribution to the development of black criticism was the anthology *Negro Caravan* (1941), edited by Sterling A. Brown, Arthur P. Davis, and Ulysses Lee. It provided fine selections drawn from eight genres as well as incisive introductions. Other academic contributions appeared in quarterlies and in a few book-length works that began as dissertations. J. Saunders Redding became nationally recognized as a black critic not only in academia but also by publishing companies and such cultural organs as the *New York Times,* the *American Scholar,* and the *Saturday Review of Literature.* Besides articles, he wrote books of cultural and historical significance. But in the generalized liberal optimism of the post–World War II world, Ralph Ellison, James Baldwin, and LeRoi Jones would bring a much bolder set of new concepts and vigor to the criticism.

Despite the critics' real contributions, there were shortcomings that would leave a legacy of problems. Ever since the Renaissance, Black critics had seen themselves as aiding white understanding of Black literature and thus helping to close the gulf between the white subsidizing audience and the small black one. Indeed, from the 1930s on, they repeatedly proclaimed a new readiness on the part of whites to accept Black writers simply as writers. In fact, however, the white liberal critical consensus was providing contradictory prescriptions of what it expected from the Black writer. On the one hand it expected protest, as evidenced by remarks that author X gave a compelling sense of what it means to be a Negro. On the other hand, it admonished the Black writer that the path to the universal was through a transcending of racial considerations, and some comments seemed to suggest that black materials were, at best, unpromising. Thus, Langston Hughes reported that editors and publishers considered Negro material to be exotic and claimed that their magazines could use only so many Negro stories per year or that their house had already filled its quota of one Negro novel for the fall list. Hughes went on to say:

> The market for Negro writers, then, is definitely limited as long as we write about ourselves. And the more truthfully we write about ourselves, the more limited our market becomes. Those novels about Negroes that sell best, by Negroes or whites, those novels that make the best-seller lists and receive the leading prizes, are almost always books that touch very lightly upon the facts of Negro life . . . make our black ghettoes . . . seem very happy places . . . our plantations . . . idyllic in their pastoral loveliness.[1]

In the winter 1950 issue of *Phylon*, devoted to discussions of the state of Black literature, numerous critics announced that the gap between audiences had been closed and emphasized a need for universalism. Lloyd W. Brown of *Masses and Mainstream* believed that these critics were telling the Black writer to abandon race protest and the tensions inherent in race materials. Brown devoted two articles in *Masses* to his counterattack upon their position. This uneasiness, even incoherence, on the question of audience persisted right up to the 1960s, along with statements certifying that the problem had been resolved—a view evident in Ralph Ellison's 1955 interview on *Invisible Man,* Herbert Hill's *Anger and Beyond* (1966), and *The American Negro Writer and His Roots* (1959). Thus, by the time of John Oliver Killen's 1967 Fisk Conference, a whole new agenda had emerged regarding audience and writing and politics. There seemed to be a Black audience that was prepared to listen, not just to the race-proud things (as assumed by earlier critics), but also to talk about the depths of their condition and the roles a Black writer should assume in light of that condition.

Although the intermediary system had developed as I have described it, it could not develop very far because the interest expressed by the audience was too meager. Regarding the old question—What future, if any, is there for Blacks in America?—the easy optimism born of the Supreme Court decision against school segregation proved misleading. It concealed the facts that integration could be strung out for a couple of hundred years, that the price of the little integration occurring was often the loss of Black identity, that automation and cybernation were geared to making most Blacks an economic irrelevancy, and that racism was so institutionalized in America that it made liberal whites irrelevant and ineffectual as agents of genuine social change. Only a few individuals realized that the white liberal consensus, simply by remaining in its own orbit and acting from its cultural compulsives (Cruse's phrase), could continue to contribute both sympathy and confusion to the creative sensibilities of Blacks. Blacks had done some indispensable conceptualizing about Western culture and its destructiveness, a considerable articulation of what it was doing to manness, but most did not follow up completely the implications of their discoveries. As a result, they failed to recognize that Western culture had habits of mind which consigned most of mankind to what Frantz Fanon called "bloodless genocide." The facing of such implications formed the agenda of the 1960s and early 1970s—an agenda that called for clear recognitions, articulations, and action.

In the area of art the situation called for a complete reorientation of the artist's relationship to the community and its resources and a deemphasis upon art as product—devices in its Black intermediary system must make art as communal as possible. Critical activity now required a grasp of the folkloric, the cultural patterns, and the intellectual fund available from Black traditions. On a simple, sometimes simplistic, level the critic was to evaluate the genuineness of an art that now emerged from a Black consciousness that had overcome its frictional and neutralizing doubleness. He was to assess its power for liberation, distinguishing "liberation" from "revelation" and "protest," the terms that belonged to the Black consciousness of the period before the 1960s. On a more complex level, critical activity should identify the communal resources—or simply earlier communal art—that could be used in the present, and assess the degree to which deep definition of a people has been achieved. The criticism of the 1970s related to politics in its advocacy of Black consciousness, rebellion, or some version of revolution, singly or in combination. These statements of what criticism should concern itself with implied what the concerns of the literary artist should be, as well.

In all of these developments, we note that there has been a considerable freeing up of energy. In response to the question whether Blacks have a future in the United States, the answer was now simply and precisely: No, unless and until we become the kind of people who cannot be done in. To the question about black dependence on the white liberal consensus, the answer was simply and precisely: Its representatives are no longer useful unless they are John Browns. Look to Africa and the East!

Given the historical framework outlined above, what are the continuities and innovations in literature on which we should place critical emphasis in order to extract greater meaning for certain purposes? What are the neglected themes and forms?

First, one should note that there has been both a positive and a negative reaction to the literary movement of the 1960s and 1970s because the movement completed was only a demolition phase (destroying earlier gods) and was dissipated by the strategies of the American government before it could complete its creative phase—the phase in which it would have corrected its excesses and oversimplifications. Thus in criticism, there has been a reaction against the confinement primarily to the ideological and the thematic which characterized the period. (It might be noted that pre-1960s criticism was also largely thematic.) In general, there is also restiveness regarding the tendency to use arbitrary ideas that define the boundaries of Black culture and establish parameters beyond which one is considered a traitor to the culture. In creative writing, there is restiveness regarding restriction of themes, resources, and definitions of what constitutes Black—all of which characterized the literary movement of the 1960s and 1970s. Since our focus is on continuities and important innovations, however, we will deal primarily with the positive responses to the literature of this period.

Black poetry received criticism mainly in the magazines until the appearances of Don L. Lee's *Dynamite Voices* (1971). Lee used music and other devices as essentials of the new black poetry.

> polyrhythm—uneven, short and explosive lines
> intensity—deep, yet simple; spiritual, yet physical
> irony—humor, signifying/the dozens

> sarcasm—the new comedy
> direction—positive movement, teaching, nation-building, concrete subject matter—reflection of a collective and personal life style
> musicality—the unique use of vowels and consonants with the developed rap, demanding that the poetry be read out loud.[2]

The whole, of course, should add up to Black consciousness.

The most important influences on poetry criticism are probably Stephen Henderson's *Understanding the New Black Poetry* (1973) and the general critical emphasis upon the resources available from folk poetry. Sherley Anne Williams shows Henderson's influence in her essay "The Blues Roots of Contemporary Afro-American Poetry" (in Dexter Fisher and Robert B. Stepto, ed., *Afro-American Literature: The Reconstruction of Instruction* [1979]). Henderson analyzed the direct introduction of Black speech and Black music as essential ingredients in the new poetry as well as some of the old. Williams comments:

> Most critics pay lip service to the idea that Afro-American music, speech, and life-styles influence the form and structure of Afro-American writing. Thus Stephen Henderson's discussion, in *Understanding the New Black Poetry* (1973), of some of the techniques of Afro-American speech and singing that have been carried over virtually unchanged into Afro-American poetry is rare in its concrete descriptions of these devices. This paper builds on his work, concentrating on the transformations that result when the blues of Afro-American oral tradition interfaces with the "poetry" of European literary tradition.[3]

Specifically, Williams, whose own sensibility is quite agile and ranging, uses terms and certain applications of terms provided by Henderson to analyze blues tendencies and the transformations of blues patterns in the poetry of Langston Hughes and Lucille Clifton. Using her close knowledge of Black music of various kinds, she convincingly demonstrates the significance of music as a referent in the new poetry.

There exist several groundbreaking studies of poetry or of cultural forms related to poetry that manifest certain continuities with earlier traditions. These works include: Bernard Bell, *The Folk Roots of Contemporary Afro-American Poetry* (1974), Blyden Jackson and Louis D. Rubin, Jr., *Black Poetry in America* (1974), John Lovell, *Black Song: The Forge and the Flame, the Story of How the Afro-*

American Spiritual Was Hammered Out (1972), LeRoi Jones, *Blues People* (1963) and *Black Music* (1967), and Eugene B. Redmond, *Drum Voices* (1976)—a critical history of Black poetry. This list suggests continuities in cultural studies to such pre-1960s critics as W. E. B. DuBois (spirituals), James Weldon Johnson (spirituals), Thomas Talley (secular folk lyrics), Langston Hughes (blues), Sterling A. Brown, (seminal studies of all folk forms), Richard Wright (folk forms and formal poetry), and Ralph Ellison (folk forms). And we could add to the elements of continuity in criticism and the collection of folk materials by citing such names as Gladys Frye and Daryl Dance.

It is difficult to say how far we have advanced over earlier critical principles. But it is clear that the work on folk and cultural forms is now more oriented toward the needs of a black audience and that a greater frankness and raciness is preserved than heretofore. Another important step results from the extensive work by specialists on folk forms, which has relieved critics and creative writers from having to become their own experts. A sufficient quantity of studies are now available to advance both criticism and creative writing. Given this situation, it is all the more notable that a growing number of literary critics evince such a total grasp of Black culture. Indeed, Houston A. Baker's most recent book, *The Journey Back: Issues in Black Literature and Criticism* (1980), insists upon a complex grasp of Black culture as a prerequisite for the job of critic—who in Baker's view is essentially an anthropologist of literature.

Our critical attention to poetry itself also reveals continuities. Blyden Jackson is himself a continuity since he has been a critic of Black literature longer than most people. A goodly fund of earlier critical conceptions and perceptions had Sterling A. Brown as its source, and his influence remains strong today, particularly given our concern with language and folk forms. Brown was also concerned with modernism in poetry in general.

Having said the preceding about continuities in the criticism of folk forms and poetry, however, I would have to say tentatively—while awaiting correction from the specialists—that, as in our approach to other genres, we are now all dressed up to go, but have not yet gone a far piece. Despite a stronger commitment to individual poems and authors than was customary before the 1960s we seem to be arrested in our progress by the following: the sheer quantity of good poetry accumulated over the last twenty years; the necessary absorption of some of our best minds in theory, which reduces the time for so-called practical criticism; the relatively small number of poetry critics and the commitment of a disproportionate amount of energy to thematic approaches. I am also made apprehensive by my impression that academia is now almost the sole source of our criticism, a situation which may draw too many of us back under the aegis of a white liberal critical consensus from which we emancipated ourselves in the 1970s. I should like to be clear that criticism is, on the one hand, a negotiation with whatever ideas are abroad in the field. On the other hand, a neglected area of literature would not, I think, want its priorities set or the energies of its critics dissipated in directions not pertinent to its most demanding needs. The job of Black critics, I think is still closely bound up with the simple task of domesticating the literature with an authenticating audience that can imbue it with health. The dangers to which a Black criticism is exposed in academia are at least twofold, including the dangers stemming from academia's tendency to favor approaches to literature which divert it the furthest from daily life and—relatedly—those dangers that stem from academia's tendency to proliferate vocabularies in which specialists talk to specialists and not to a general audience. American literature is generally protected from the most destructive of academia's tendencies by the numerous organs that afford varying levels of vocabulary while remaining serious and able to address complex issues. I think we have held our ground well thus far, despite the blow that resulted from the loss of the semipopular magazines *Black World* and the slow pace at which we develop new quarterlies. But, as we grow more distant from the fierce independence sprouted by the radical period, we may be increasingly threatened by narrowness of communication.

I turn now to some comments on criticism of narrative, some developments in fiction, and the question of the strategic placement of criticism and attention to neglected themes and forms. Much of what I have said regarding criticism and poetry applies to other genres, and I shall try to avoid unnecessary repetition.

Criticism of fiction has been more plentiful and probably more varied than criticism of poetry. Such quarterlies as *Callaloo* and *CLA Journal* have devoted special issues to Richard Wright, Langston Hughes, James Baldwin, and Ernest Gaines. *Black American Literature*

Forum has also provided special issues devoted to particular writers, and the now discontinued *Black World* provided special focus on particular writers and periods. In her study of the hero in "neo-black" literature, Sherley Anne Williams gave much attention to fiction and other genres and entitled her work *Give Birth to Brightness* (1972). In *From the Dark Tower* (1974) Arthur P. Davis dealt with Black literature across the board but refused to deal with radical developments in literature, and his work remains informative rather than searching as a result. In a long article entitled "Novels of the New Black Renaissance (1960-1977): A Thematic Survey" (*CLA Journal*, June 1978), Davis deals briefly with some radical works. His conservatism appears to be more of an emotional recoil than an intellectual or artistic assessment of works in this field.

Addison Gayle's *The Way of the New World* (1975) commits itself entirely to the novel and represents the first comprehensive survey by a black critic in many years, and the first challenging one since Robert Bone's *The Negro Novel in America* (1958, 1965) In his judgments of the novelists, he is frequently hard ridden by his rigorous ideology, but *The Way of the New World* is particularly interesting for the care with which Gayle deals with the early fiction, his assemblage of a set of intellectual principles for ideological dealings from nineteenth-and twentieth-century Black thinkers, and for his application of the Black aesthetic approaches that had been formulated in his earlier books. At the same time, his ideological rigor does leave Gayle vulnerable to some of the strictures that appear in Deborah M. Austin's searching review essay (*Obsidian* [Winter 1977]), the basic point of which is that he deals insufficiently with novels as works of art.

In a sense, Gayle's work is more representative of innovation than of continuity. If one looks at American literature in times of crisis (World War II, for example), one does find literature turning in the direction of defense and attack. But in Black criticism Gayle's closest kinship to the past is to the passionate militancy of the early J. Saunders Redding, best expressed in *To Make a Poet Black* (1939). Otherwise one must turn to W. E. B. DuBois or to the nonliterary thoughts of a person such as Martin R. Delany in order to establish a pattern of continuity for Gayle's work.

Two works, ostensibly involved with fiction, are in fact as much involved with theories which go beyond a simple examination of fiction. Robert B. Stepto's *From Behind the Veil: A Study of Afro-*

American Narrative (1979), and Houston A. Baker's *The Journey Back* (1980). Both works are an extension of the cultural approaches developed before the 1960s and intensified during the last twenty years. Stepto examines Black narratives for a dialectical pattern of challenge and response pattern. Thus he finds peculiar dialectical relationships between such works as *Up from Slavery* and *The Souls of Black Folk,* on one hand, and *The Autobiography of an Ex-Coloured Man,* on the other; between Richard Wright's *Black Boy* and Frederick Douglass's *Narrative;* and between Ralph Ellison's *Invisible Man* and both *The Souls* and the Douglass *Narrative.* As I pointed out earlier, Houston A. Baker's approach to fiction demands what he calls an anthropology of art—a complete cultural context in which we can see how different fields of meaning present the story of the Black adventure.

Baker's explanation of his quest provides a basis for understanding some developments in criticism since the period of the Black Arts Movement, although his posture is distinct from that adopted by some of the younger academic critics. He speaks of encountering students and scholars today who deem "much of the work produced under the aegis of black nationalism . . . [to be] the sound and fury of a troubled past." Such persons feel that "the present is an age of theory; the conversation has moved to another plane." Baker's response both identifies these people and points to some of the dangers involved in their views:

> I find such assertions unsettling, since they come from men and women situated at institutions that, fifteen years ago, would not have dreamed of admitting many of those who spoke for our rights and defended our dignity during the sixties and seventies. I ask myself if there is always to be a protective insularity surrounding colleges and universities. To see life steadily and to see it whole is not an easy matter; the academy frequently seems ready to close debate before the task has even begun.[4]

Baker goes on to say that it is time to move beyond the prescriptions of nationalism, though he evinces a desire to "carry over the best that has been thought and said at earlier stages of the argument." Baker, of course, is by now a seasoned critic, one who puts his earlier experiences to positive use.

Most innovations seem to have as their source an elaborate knowledge of the theorizing that is now the obsession of the universities. In terms of continuity, however, all serious Black criticism can draw on the rich theoretical and cultural criticism that has been building up steadily since the Harlem Renaissance. By such an approach, the critic can avoid diversion from crucial but less fashionable areas.

Still, it is difficult to identify those aspects of Black literature on which our critical attention can most usefully be focused. Our intermediary system comprises so few persons (and so few organs), relatively speaking, that to divert our energies from one area to another is simply to create yet another area of neglect. For example, although we have extremely competent short fiction, criticism has neglected it, woefully. Individual writers, poetry, and autobiography are also neglected, and though the novel has fared better, it too needs much more attention.

So, instead of suggesting genres or individuals for attention, I should like to advance a principle: the major object of the criticism should be to deliver the literature to an authenticating audience—a black audience, to be precise. The realization of this principle might perform a greater service to the literature because it draws on talents that are probably more abundant than those required for theorizing. This approach would place strategic emphasis upon a criticism that would increase the general mastery of devices required in the act of reading, witnessing, and appreciating texts. One might draw an analogy to a ball game, in which one's enjoyment increases as one understands the organization of the team, the roles of individual members, and the dynamic interplay among them. In short, I am proposing an emphasis on the strategic use of the approaches that characterize a *practical* criticism. Theoretical activity should also involve us in more thinking regarding the relationships between art and politics. I agree that the approaches of the 1960s and early 1970s would now be simplistic and misleading in their overall drift. A criticism closely tied to a revolutionary praxis would find little to nourish it in our daily life; a criticism that pounded away at nationhood would be regarded as cliché-bound. On the other hand, I think it is clear that groups who have become viable in America have brought or developed a strong *people-hood*, a strong sense of their definitions, a strong capacity to absorb from the past. That achievement is likely to remain an important objective and to precede revolution or nationhood.

I close with a brief comment regarding our fiction. Black fiction as a whole is marked by a high level of competence and the capacity to deliver stories through a wide range of fictional resources. With apparent ease the writers make strategic and temporary alliances with a variety of forms: the tale, the older resources of story telling, cinema, painting, folk song, comic strip, autobiography, and other devices. Modes are often abruptly changed and mixed: comedy dissolves to tragedy or pathos, realism to fantasy or expressionism. Critics too often see this skill and flexibility as a conscious transcending of Richard Wright's realism and naturalism, though in fact one can easily trace a history of nonrealistic devices in the line of Black writers extending from Charles Chesnutt's *The Conjure Woman*. Wright himself managed symbol, myth, and ritual with great skill and insisted upon a writer's being conscious of what he wished to do and of the available resources for doing it.

The novels of black males have been dominated by the theme of asserting, retaining, or recovering a virility that is usually threatened in a racist society. During the 1960s especially, the theme was frequently expressed as some sort of reach for revolution, by such novelists as John Oliver Killens, Sam Greenlee, John A. Williams, and others. Several writers explored the issue through street settings and characters, the strongest of these probably being Nathan Heard. Ishmael Reed ranged through folklore motifs or heroes who could easily be seen as folk figures carrying the essential powers of the race, and thus useful for his satiric purposes. There was a tendency to move away from the depiction of a male so agonized that the denouement of the novel frequently brought him to destruction or neutrality. On the other hand, the compulsion to show the Black man as a revolutionary or as superior in some other way to the total scheme of oppression was often lost in romanticism, sentimentalism, and masochism. Ernest Gaines is among those producing the most persuasive images of manhood, womanhood, and community, since he deals with his characters through community-formed rituals in which his people have had to constitute their manness and their womanness from the materials available in day-to-day life.

Among such younger novelists as Raymond Andrews (*Appalachee Red* [1978]) and Wesley Brown (*Tragic Magic* [1978]), the themes of community and manhood (or selfhood in Brown's case) seem responsive to the techniques used. Andrews's range involves the folkloric bad man or simple John Henry type, a type with a highly developed, Malcolm X-like Black consciousness and copious resources, and a still more intellectual type that seems geared to the freedom of the community. Brown's primary focus is upon the single character who has been forced to struggle for genuine selfhood through the maze of the radical and liberal worlds in the context of the modern city. Such novels imply that we are on our way to a broader conception of maleness and, perhaps, that we are moving away from figures that quickly can run to stereotype.

Women writers seem concerned with recovering their image from the secondary and often distorted roles imposed by male writers. Their theme is essentially identity, whether in historic or contemporary roles, and it may or may not be pursued with overtones of hostility. In her most recent anthology of women's short fiction by women, *Midnight Birds* (1980), Mary Helen Washington refers to such themes as rejection of victimization, reconciliation with other women, redefinitions of man-woman love which challenge the ways in which women have been involved with men, confrontations with the racism of white women, and identity. Continuity is acknowledged by references to the works of pre-1960s black women writers: Nella Larsen, Zora Neale Hurston, Ann Petry, and Gwendolyn Brooks. The innovations of such younger writers as Alice Walker, Toni Morrison, Gayl Jones, Toni Cade Bambara, and others is their refusal to pursue definitions of womanhood through the traditional roles that society has prescribed. Such roles (wife, mother) are held at a distance while the nature of identity is analyzed. In recent years this kind of questioning has produced most of the fiction that affords the reader the excitement of being in the territory where discoveries are being made.

This broad suggestion of current themes may also say something about themes that are being neglected. At this point, both men and women writers seem to be on the threshold of a breakthrough to a greater variety of concerns. Although there are references to history, historical themes are, for the most part, conspicuous by their absence. Despite the present-day censure on simple realism, there seems to be room for any number of simple stories of the past which would provide a clearer and deeper definition of a people. The sheer power of parts of Alex Haley's *Roots* is highly suggestive, although I hasten to add that I am not advocating the repetition of his formula. The slave narratives have not been sufficiently mined for their suggestions of vital and deep responses to existence. The contemporary form of the slave narrative is the prison narrative, and this literature, which expresses the tragic confrontations of today's youth with imprisonment, has as yet been little explored. The representation of newer levels of racial conflict and sympathetic explorations of the ironies of contemporary leadership are promising areas whose pursuit would give our fiction an important public dimension. Similarly, in the name of the development of a greater peoplehood, we need to treat those instances in which Blacks relate positively to one another—and even enjoy being together.

The confrontation with modernism will thus involve a fuller utilization of the strength and insight that Blacks have gained from our striving in the last two decades.

Notes

1. Langston Hughes, "Fighting Words," in *The Negro Caravan: Writings by American Negroes,* selected and edited by Sterling A. Brown, Arthur P. Davis, and Ulysses Lee (1941; Rept. New York: Arno Press and the *New York Times*), p. 11.
2. Don L. Lee, *Dynamite Voices* (Detroit: The Broadside Press, 1971), p. 35.
3. Sherley Anne Williams, "The Blues Roots of Contemporary Afro-American Poetry," in *Afro-American Literature: The Reconstruction of Instruction,* ed. Dexter Fisher and Robert B. Stepto (New York: The Modern Language Association of America, 1979), pp. 72-73.
4. Houston A. Baker, Jr., *The Journey Back: Issues in Black Literature and Criticism* (Chicago: University of Chicago Press, 1980), pp. xi-xii.

V

Theory and Practice: Africana Studies beyond the Classroom

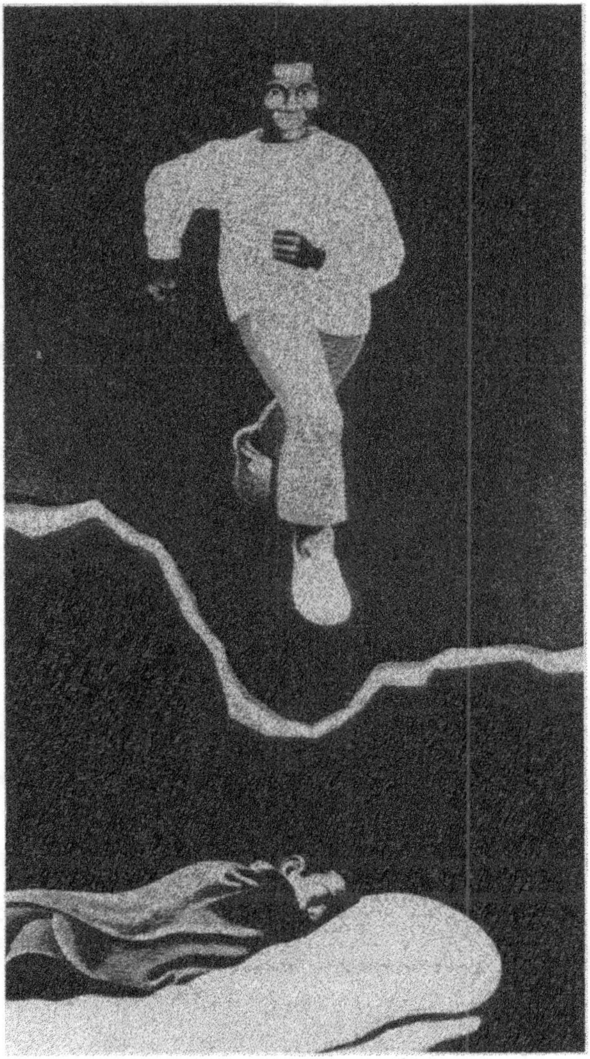

The Dream, Phillip L. Mason

CHAPTER 9

Black Power at Cornell University: Institutions and Identity

Gayla Cook

We were all very tired that first night in Willard Straight Hall—but it was hard to sleep. Especially for Skip. Because he had a gun and he wanted to be very, very sure of what it meant: to have it and to have to use it. The night before in that spring of 1969 everyone who had come to the meeting of Black students had been kept overnight in our meeting house, in preparation for the takeover of the student union building the next morning. We wanted to be sure there were no security leaks.

Dawn had found us marching across campus to the Straight. Any campus security guards who saw us along the way were too dumbstruck to do anything, as were the parents lodging at the Straight for Parents' Weekend, whom we unceremoniously ejected. Later in the siege we would discuss our demands with the powers that were. We wanted a Black Studies Program, more Black faculty, more Black students. The signs of the times had penetrated to the ivory tower in the isolated, wooded serenity of Cayuga valley. We wanted to confront the racism of the University—and of the society at large.

So when the dawn broke that second morning, Skip was already awake, his rifle across his knees. Skip's major was philosophy. He wanted to be completely aware and conscious of what he was doing and why. The situation would become increasingly tense, unpredictable, and violent. Black Power had come to Cornell.

I will readily say that I loved my stay at Cornell and that my education has heavily influenced the course of my life. I must hasten to add, however, that my experience resulted from the configuration of people and events; Cornell was the setting because we were there, not because Cornell wanted it that way.

Ms. Gayla Cook is the Director of the Women and African Development Program at the African American Institute in New York City

There were sixty-seven Black people, I believe, in my freshman class in 1967, out of a total of 679 Arts and Sciences students, and few Blacks beyond that number in the total freshman class of more than three thousand. At least that was more than the year before, when there had been thirteen. Not until I came to Cornell did I absorb the full meaning of being "a minority," and that growing and deepening realization was a dominant impression throughout those four years.

I was a colored girl from Cleveland. I grew up there during the segregated times, when we Blacks and whites went to school together, before even the poor whites fled the inner city, leaving their neighborhoods to us Blacks. But in those segregated times, in the working-class neighborhoods where I grew up, we were all more or less equal. I never knew that I was "a minority" then, or that I was one of the "disadvantaged." After all, in our neighborhood, and at Sears & Roebuck where I worked during high school, there were Poles and Italians and Czechs and Jews and Greeks and Puerto Ricans, whereas we Black folks were one big group—all Black.

But at Cornell I soon found out that I was in a distinct and disadvantaged group. It was not so much that our situation there told us what we were; it told us what we were not. We were not rich. We did not come from the families that had power and influence. Many of our classmates did, however, and they were comfortable in playing their role at an Ivy League institution: the best and the brightest who would go on to fulfill their destinies. Their privileged position set up a direct contradiction with those of us who came from the segment of society which was powerless. I had come to Cornell because of the physical beauty of the wooded, small town setting, however, and only later would I appreciate the advantage of having been educated at a prestigious institution. The confrontation was inevitable, but unanticipated.

Certain memories stand out; memories such as the sociology class. Those on welfare were the losers in our society, and maybe that was something that we could not change, maybe some people are just losers and that's something that we needed to examine. So said the white sociology professor. Certainly he did not know he was setting the stage for conflict because he had probably never before had a student in his class who had grown up on welfare, who had been traumatized by the welfare system, and who was now sitting here in the hallowed halls of Cornell being told that his was the heritage of a loser.

Then I remember the time that Stephanie and Skip and Tom and I were all sitting at the County Clerk's office downtown. Skip and I were there to serve as witnesses to Tom and Stephanie's separation decree. They had gotten married, Stephanie had had the baby, everything was a mess, and now they were separating. We were all about nineteen years old, and I know that I at least was baffled by the whole affair—wondering what the hell we were doing there. At that time there were no older (Black) people we could identify with, confide in, or ask advice of. There were no Black people older than us at Cornell.

And then there are the things you don't understand until much, much later. We twelve little Black girls in Wari Co-op (a residence we won from one of our rounds of confrontation with the University which later ironically became the subject of legal desegregation suits) with our lovers, quarrels, jealousies, and anxieties, getting high to rap far into the night about the foibles of brothers and why we were lonely. And not knowing enough to help each other, so that only years later did we understand that the changes that the one sister—a brilliant but erratic girl—was going through were actually a nervous breakdown.

We students were a microcosm of American society, but our extremes in terms of family background and psychological and social history accentuated the larger society's contradictions in ways that many of us—Black and white—had not been aware of before. When we struggled for an Africana Studies and Research Center, it was an instinctive battle to preserve our identity and to know who we were. The center was a very important component of my education. In my mind that experience includes the events leading up to its creation, in which my energies were largely absorbed for a period, as well as other events that happened and people who came to Cornell, because of the center's existence

Because of it, we were no longer isolated. The poets and writers came: Don L. Lee, Baraka, Mike Thelwell, Shirley Graham DuBois, Sonia Sanchez, Julian Mayfield. There were the scholars: J. Congress Mbata, Rukudzo Murapa, James Turner, John Henrik Clarke, Gloria Joseph, Harry Edwards. There were the thinkers and doers: Cleve Sellers, Chico Nesblitt, Minister Louis Farrakhan. Some fit in all categories, and some were a total experience, defying description: Chestyn Everett.

It was indeed a blessing to know and learn from so much talent, knowledge, and experience. The courses and experiences provided by the center in turn provided a context and critical complement to the rest of Cornell. Certainly, to be a truly educated person, as I would later tell my own students, is to analyze, to challenge oneself to comprehend fully the things that we know and experience. The environment provided by the center was instrumental in providing us with this intellectual and emotional capacity. So when I worked — among my many part-time jobs at Cornell — at the Synchrotron Laboratory, where scientists were involved in atomic energy research, I could contemplate the relationship of institutions and power in societal terms.

Likewise did we seek to comprehend events that were at once simple and complex: apartheid, Vietnam, the death of Malcolm.

Through the center and ancillary activities, we were engaged in a learning experience. We were participants and cooperators, not merely interlopers. In that sense, our experience may have been a unique one that Black students coming later would not completely duplicate. The process of what happened in those years, and our involvement in it, was just as important as what came out of those struggles. The personal conflicts, our distrust of each other, the way the liberals and conservatives of the University lined up on the issues — all provided instruction on how people and institutions behave and relate. But the very nature of building an institution within an institution dictated that there would continue to be confrontations and new challenges and experiences that would engage later students. History has borne this out.

I have been lucky in my life's work. After Cornell I went on to teach, to make films, to work on community and economic development problems in Black communities here and in Africa. I have certainly been more fortunate than my father and mother and many other Black people. I have had options. I have done things that I wanted to do. And when teaching became too debilitating, and when I couldn't make the films that I wanted to make, then I did something else that I wanted to do until I could do those things in the way that I wanted to.

I have been most fortunate, also, in having worked in and with

Black institutions and Black people. The Africana Studies and Research Center was the beginning of my experience with new and evolving Black institutions. My identity had been shaped somewhat by some other Black institutions—the Black church and the family—but the center was even instrumental in my recognition of those influences. And in many ways, it was long after leaving Cornell that I came to appreciate that experience and the importance of the center, as well as the nature of institutions. Because it is those institutions, along with others, such as the Black universities, the Booker T. Washington Foundation, and the agriculture teams—started by Cornell Black students coming together from the Diaspora which make up the moral and intellectual center that becomes our frame of reference for who we are.

Needless to say, institutions providing other frames of reference abound, making the creation of our own institutions essential to keep things in perspective and balance. Institutions are powerful forces in the society—that is why there was an inherent contradiction in creating the Africana Center as an institution within an institution. But we must know that we need our own institutions, and we must build them. Nobody is going to let you join their club and call the shots—you've got to build your own club. Witness the Third Press, the Institute of the Black World, *Black World* magazine, Makerere University, and the liberation movements in South Africa. And witness the forces that come together to work against their existence.

These are among the reasons that the Africana Studies and Research Center is important to me. It is one of the forces that has made me who I am and it influences what I do. As a woman, mother, wife, daughter, worker, and member of the Black race, its influence is among those helping me make my life choices. Even as one evolves and grows, those influences are your roots. After I had left Cornell, I went through the stage where one who was properly revolutionary wouldn't dream of working for the "Man" (meaning whites, especially big business) to a more difficult stage of making choices based on weighing of values, knowledge, and experience. And even as you make those choices, a flash in your mind's eye reminds you of something you haven't thought about in years.

I see Chestyn Everett thoughtfully selecting the quotation to caption the picture that showed the first site of the Africana Center going up in flames: "To act is to be committed, and to be committed is to be in danger."

I see Shirley Graham DuBois' eyes twinkling as she gave us insights into her husband, W. E. B. DuBois, who had foretold the present-day unfolding of world events.

And I see Julian Mayfield, intensely explaining the African concept of self as revealed in African literature, recreating the political history of the times to make us understand the relationship of Booker T. Washington and W. E. B. DuBois and why each was a powerful man, telling us about meeting Malcolm X who questioned the group of self-exiled Black intellectuals who professed to having no spiritual beliefs.

Yes, these visions flash into my mind's eye and I keep on gettin' up, feelin' strong, and knowing who I am.

VOICES OF THE PAST SPEAK TO THE PRESENT

Reveal, Ancient of Days, the Present in the Past and prophesy the End in the Beginning. For this is a beautiful world; this is a wonderful America, which the founding fathers dreamed until their sons drowned it in the blood of slavery and devoured it in greed. Our children must rebuild it. Let then the Dreams of the Dead rebuke the Blind who think that what is will be forever... Teach us, Forever Dead, there is no Dream but Deed, there is no Deed but Memory.

—W.E.B. Du Bois

CHAPTER 10

The Nature and Limits of Affirmative Action

Robert C. Johnson, Jr., Esq.

Introduction

The concept of affirmative action is gaining greater legitimacy among American employers. Although many institutions continue to experience considerable difficulty in defining the term precisely, most agree that its general purpose is to allow for greater utilization of minorities, women, Vietnam veterans, and the handicapped. Prior to *Bakke,* the American public equated affirmative action with preferential treatment for Blacks, which many felt ran against the grain of the American tradition of meritocracy and the commitment to individual rights. The recent decisions by the United States Supreme Court, most notably *Bakke* and *Weber,* however, have significantly enhanced the stature of the concept and consequently forced employers at least to pay lip service to its implementation.

This chapter does not examine the extent to which affirmative action has been implemented as required by federal/state laws and regulations. Considerable research has already revealed that most employers carry out their recruitment activities, particularly for Blacks, in a nonaffirmative manner and that Blacks remain the last hired and the first fired, notwithstanding the pervasive legislation requiring affirmative action. Rather, this chapter examines the historical evolution of affirmative action and the role it has played in shaping fundamental civil and political rights in American society. Seen in this context, affirmative action is a continuing legacy of the African-American struggle for full political, social, and economic justice—a legacy that has significantly enhanced the political and social fabric of American society. In short, this paper explores the interrelationship between affirmative action and the development of political/social values in America.

Mr. Robert Johnson, Jr., Esq. works in the Affirmative Action Office at the University of Massachusetts/Boston in Dorchester, Massachusetts

Legacy of Slavery

Historically, African-Americans have engaged in affirmative action to secure basic human rights in the face of European capitalism and racism. Concomitant with the development of capitalism, characterized primarily by the private ownership of production, was the degradation of both African and European labor. This period of labor exploitation, especially prevalent in the seventeenth and eighteenth centuries, ushered in an era of European development at the expense of human toil and misery.

An inordinate amount of this burden fell upon African people. According to W. E. B. DuBois, the African slave trade served as catalyst for the development and expansion of capitalism.[1] In the fourteenth century Europe emerged from the "Dark Ages" with a newly discovered sense of nationalism and a desire to expand its geographical boundaries into the larger and richer nonwhite world. This expansion was initially manifested by the Portuguese exploration for shorter maritime routes to the East, which unexpectedly resulted in European contact with the African continent in 1415. Shortly thereafter, in 1441, the first cargo of slaves and gold was brought to Lisbon.[2] From then until 1571, when the French landed on the continent, the Portuguese maintained a monopoly of the lucrative slave and gold trade, which accrued a 50 percent to 800 percent return on investments.[3]

The economic success of Portugal encouraged other European nations to invest in the exploitation of African minerals and peoples. Queen Elizabeth of England commissioned Sir John Hawkins to coordinate the first English venture into Africa. Like most others, this British venture was financed by members of the English ruling class, including the British crown through the Royal African Company. Pressure by British merchants led in 1750 to the establishment of free trade, which immediately stimulated a boom. DuBois comments on this free trade:

> In the first nine years of this "free trade," Britain alone shipped 160,950 Negroes to the sugar plantations. In 1760, 146 ships sailed from British ports to Africa with a capacity of 36,000 slaves. In 1771 there were 190 ships and 47,000 slaves. The British colonies between 1680 and 1786 imported over two million slaves.[4]

The suffering inflicted upon Africans, particularly in the "middle passage," was a reflection of the inhumane attitudes toward the black race which were emerging. A report in the House of Commons described the condition of the Blacks on the ships:

> The Negroes were chained to each other hand and foot, and stored so close that they were not allowed above a foot and a half for each in breadth. Thus rammed together like herrings in a barrel, they contracted putrid and fatal disorders; so that they who came to inspect them in a morning had occasionally to pick dead slaves out of their rows, and to unchain their carcasses from the bodies of their wretched fellow-sufferers to whom they had been fastened.[5]

Institutionalized Racism

From this process of dehumanization and economic exploitation sprang the development of Europe and America, the corollary of which was the evolution of the racist ideology that supplied philosophical justification for the social and economic privilege of the western elite. Racism facilitated the economic exploitation of African people by denying the essential humanity of the race. As a result, the popular slogan—"A Negro is not a man"—represented an acceptable characterization of Blacks in the nineteenth century.[6]

According to DuBois, this debasement of the African race created a paradox in the intellectual and institutional fabric of early America—a paradox best typified by the contradictory thinking on questions of liberty and slavery. At the Constitutional Convention of 1787, for example, the very question of whether Africans should be considered human beings or property was debated.[7] George Washington, founding president and slaveholder, attended the discussions on slavery but did not speak out in opposition to the widely supported proposals to classify Africans as property. In the final analysis, the economic realities of the plantation system outweighed any consideration of the slaves' humanity. Consequently, when America ratified its first constitution, this paradox of liberty and slavery had not yet been resolved: the African was seen as three-fifths of a man.[8]

Inevitably, the legal ideals of justice and equality became compromised by racism. Hence, the use of American law as the social instrument that justified the dehumanization and exploitation of African peoples received widespread judicial sanction. The decision of *Dred Scott* v. *Sanford,* 600 U.S. 393 (1857), made institutional racism the supreme law of the land, as the highest United States tribunal defined Africans as "articles of commerce," "beings of an inferior order and altogether unfit to associate with the white race."

Struggle For Humanity

Affirmative action had to assume a more aggressive posture, for African people found themselves faced with a pervasive racism whose basic goal was the complete dehumanization and genocide of African people. This situation in turn meant that the struggles waged by African people against racism and economic exploitation had to take on both violent and nonviolent characteristics. Individuals such as Frederick Douglass, Phillis Wheatley, and John Brown Russwurm sought freedom through nonviolent agitation, while Nat Turner, Denmark Vesey, and others chose the path of violent revolt.

Regardless of its means, however, the goal of affirmative action—to secure full human rights and the political and social benefits that naturally flow from such rights—was uncompromising. This militancy was best represented in the writings of David Walker, a Boston free Black. In *An Appeal,* Walker wrote:

> We must and shall be free I say, in spite of you. You may do your best to keep us in wretchedness and misery, to enrich you and your children; but God will deliver us from under you. And wo, wo will be to you if we have to obtain our freedom by fighting. Throw away your fears and prejudices then, and enlighten us and treat us like men, and we will like you more than we do now hate you.[9]

Affirmative Legal Action

This affirmative action on the part of African peoples precipitated affirmative legal action, designed to secure for blacks those human rights which had historically been reserved for white citizens. The issuance of the Emancipation Proclamation was a necessary but insufficient turning point in American politics. This Executive Order of President Lincoln was an insufficient legal means for securing fundamental citizenship rights for African people, given that under the original constitutional definition of "citizen," African people were not included.[10] Nevertheless, through the Emancipation Proclamation the executive branch of the federal government did formulate policy that created a positive climate for the necessary constitutional amendments. Consequently, the Thirteenth, Fourteenth, and Fifteenth Amendments to the Constitution were passed primarily to guarantee blacks the rights of national citizenship.

Even though the postwar amendments established the legal basis of substantive political rights, social progress for Blacks continued to be hampered by institutional racism. At the close of the nineteenth century, many of the substantive rights guaranteed to Blacks under the Fourteenth Amendment were eroded by U.S. Supreme Court decisions, most notably *Plessy* v. *Ferguson,* 163 U.S. 537 (1896), and its sucessors. By 1954, the effect of affirmative legal decisions had been dissipated completely as segregation or legalized discrimination received recognition as the supreme law of the land.

Black Intellectual Activism

Despite the erosion of substantive legal protections, black intellectuals affirmatively sought full civil and political rights for African people. In attempting to acquire the benefits of an education, many of these leaders forthrightly faced the stone wall of segregation in American higher education. Despite the legislative initiatives designed to advance educational opportunity for Blacks after the Civil War, most notably the Morrill Land Grant Acts of 1862 and 1890, the total number of black college graduates was only 2,500 by 1900. Thirty-two years later the number had increased to 23,000, of which 21,383 represented enrollments in traditionally black institutions.[11]

These black institutions constituted the only means by which the majority of Blacks could acquire advanced education, though much of this education was designed primarily to help Blacks become more self-reliant, particularly in the rural South. Booker T. Washington, a leading supporter of this idea, placed considerable emphasis on industrial training. He envisioned his Tuskegee Institute, founded in 1881, as playing a critical role in combating segregation. Washington was strongly committed to a philosophy of gradualism and held that Blacks would attain self-improvement through agricultural development, which would in turn cause whites to lend the black race greater respect.

Such scholars as W. E. B. DuBois developed a more comprehensive social and educational program for Blacks. In a period when the white majority ignored the legitimate aspirations of Blacks, DuBois struggled for intellectual clarity among black intellectuals. His perception of the Black condition in America derived from his involvement with Blacks on all levels of society. He not only interacted with the leading thinkers of his time, but also became directly involved with Blacks from the lowest economic stratum. While at Fisk University he wrote

of his experiences in the rural districts of Tennessee:
> It was an enthralling experience. I met new and intricate and unconscious discrimination. . . . All the appointments of my school were primitive: a windowless log cabin; hastily manufactured benches; no blackboard; almost no books; long, long distances to walk. And on the other hand, I heard the sorrow songs sing with primitive beauty and grandeur. I saw the hard, ugly drudgery of country life and the writhing of landless, ignorant peasants. I saw the race problem at nearly its lowest terms.[12]

The divergent approaches of Washington and DuBois produced varied results in terms of affirmative action. Both leaders served as catalysts for Black social change. Washington's activism received widespread support from white philanthropic organizations and individuals, most notably John D. Rockefeller and Andrew Carnegie, as a result of which Washington became, in the eyes of most whites, the undisputed leader of Black America. He was an adviser to presidents Theodore Roosevelt and William Taft and by the time of his death in 1915, he had firmly established Tuskegee Institute as a leading black institution. At the same time, however, Washington left unchallenged the racist social and political philosophies of the times, which sanctioned the relegation of Blacks to menial jobs and inferior schools.

DuBois, on the contrary, tackled these problems head on. DuBois's intellectual perspective was shaped by his experiences at Fisk and at Harvard University. Despite his education at Cambridge and Berlin, he could not get a position at a white institution: his first job was a one-year appointment teaching Latin and Greek at Wilberforce College. Unlike Washington, DuBois believed that black scholars should affirmatively challenge the inherent racism in American social and political institutions, especially in white colleges and universities. Rather than accept as valid the racist white scholarship pertaining to the status and condition of African-Americans, DuBois began to analyze the condition of his people from an Afrocentric perspective. Consequently, while an assistant instructor at the University of Pennsylvania, he conducted a comprehensive study of the pathological effects of poverty and urban life upon Blacks. His findings, summarized in *Philadelphia Negro* in 1898, led him to conclude that crime and other forms of so-called socially deviant behavior among black Philadelphians were functions of poverty and disease rather than of inherent criminal tendencies.

From DuBois's pioneering work in Philadelphia there sprang a new black intellectual movement which refused to compromise with racist philosophies that did not recognize the full human potential and worth of African people. During his approximately thirteen years at Atlanta University, DuBois continued to spearhead research into Black life and culture as well as to provide leadership for a black intellectual class that agitated for equal access in all areas of American life. The fruit of this affirmative activism was the birth, near the turn of the century, of the Niagara Movement and the National Association for the Advancement of Colored People (NAACP).

Finally, the affirmative action of Washington and DuBois led to the creation of black institutions whose primary purposes were to provide educational opportunity and affirmatively to alter the segregative nature of American society. During this early part of American history, affirmative action can be seen as a reaction to segregation and discrimination. Much of the responsibility for this action fell upon such Blacks as Washington, DuBois, William Monroe Trotter, and Marcus Garvey. During a period when Blacks were treated as less than full citizens, white industrial institutions failed to take affirmative action to include Blacks within the mainstream of economic life.

Regardless of the historical period, blacks found no open doors to employment opportunities. During the Great Depression many Blacks felt the sting of unemployment much more severely than whites, the proportion of Blacks unemployed during this period being 60 percent greater than that of whites.[13] Even with the onset of the Second World War and the resultant need for additional manpower, the unemployment situation for Blacks remained relatively unchanged as compared to that of the white population. Blacks continued to face discrimination from both employers and unions despite the national need for increased utilization of the workforce. This failure to utilize Blacks in industry was due in large part to the overtly racist policies of major unions, in particular the American Federation of Labor (AFL).

Affirmative action against these racist union practices was initiated primarily by A. Philip Randolph, president of the Brotherhood of Sleeping Car Porters, who often spoke out against the racist policies of the unions. For example, at the AFL's 1940 convention, Randolph charged that the unions were responsible for Blacks being locked out of job opportunities:

> The most conspicuous and consistent denial of employment of Negroes which can be attributed almost directly to union influence is found at

the Boeing Aircraft Corporation in Seattle, Washington. From the very beginning of the National defense program, the Boeing Company has given as its excuse for not employing Negroes the fact that it had a contract with the Aeronautical Mechanics Union, Local 751, International Association of Machinists, AFL, and that the union accepts white members only.[14]

Mr. Randolph, not only agitated at major conventions for full employment opportunities but also took his protest directly to the streets. This popular mobilization forced the federal government to move affirmatively to protect Blacks from discrimination in projects receiving federal contracts and assistance.

The Executive Response

The executive branch's first step to provide legal protection for black workers was a direct response to A. Philip Randolph's threat to lead a march on Washington. In order to avoid such an onslaught of people, President Franklin D. Roosevelt on 25 June 1941 issued Executive Order 8802, a federal administrative action that prohibited employers and unions from discriminating in the defense industries. The order also established a five-person Fair Employment Practices Committee (FEPC). Its only power was the investigation and facilitation of voluntary compliance.

On 27 May 1943, President Roosevelt expanded the jurisdiction of the FEPC through Executive Order 9346, which gave the civil rights agency the power to investigate complaints of discrimination in all industries affecting the national interest. Although initial governmental action was precipitated by popular agitation, increased concern on its part arose from the realization that racial conflict in industries affecting the war effort could seriously compromise the national interest.

In the eyes of government, the FEPC then did more than merely protect the rights of Blacks; it functioned to maintain tranquillity between the working classes. When the commission's conciliatory powers failed to bring about the desired goal of industrial peace during wartime, the federal government did not hesitate to exercise its broad powers under the National War Labor Board (NWLB). On 19 December 1943, for example, President Roosevelt signed Executive Order 9408, directing the secretary of state to take control of the Point Breeze, Maryland, plant of the Western Electric Company. In

February 1943 white workers at the plant voted to go on strike after the NWLB and FEPC voted to uphold the partial desegregation of plant facilities. The federal government retained control of the facility until 23 March 1944,[15] relinquishing it at about the same time that the FEPC was terminated. With the end of the war, the federal executive's commitment to equal rights diminished; it did not revive until 1965, when President Lyndon Johnson issued his Executive Order 11246.

There was very little progress in the federal administrative response to discrimination immediately following the demise of the FEPC. In the absence of popular agitation and a national emergency, the government had little incentive to act affirmatively in protecting the rights of Blacks. Between 1946 and 1951 there was no executive policy in respect to discrimination in projects receiving federal contracts. Not until 2 December 1951 did President Harry Truman issue Executive Order 10308, creating the President's Committee on Government Contract Compliance. This committee was largely ineffective and did little to protect Blacks from discrimination.[16] President Dwight Eisenhower issued Executive Order 10479 in 1953 and Executive Order 10557 in 1954, but both orders failed to enforce the executive policy against discrimination in projects funded by federal contracts. Vice-President Richard Nixon chaired the President's Committee on Government Contracts during this period, a circumstance that may explain the lack of policy implementation.

The Civil Rights Movement

The affirmative struggle of black people significantly altered the government's laissez-faire approach to civil rights issues. In the early 1950s the NAACP, led by attorney Thurgood Marshall, challenged Jim Crow in education. The end result of this affirmative challenge was the *Brown* decision of 1954, in which the U.S. Supreme Court held that segregated educational facilities were inherently unequal and violated the Fourteenth Amendment to the Constitution.

This decision represented a turning point in American civil rights law. Even though the Fourteenth Amendment originally had been passed with the intent of securing fundamental rights for Blacks, its full impact lay dormant for about fifty-eight years. The sole initial purpose of the Fourteenth Amendment was: "the freedom of the slave race, the security and firm establishment of that freedom and the protection of the newly-made freeman and citizen from the oppressions of those who had formerly exercised dominion over him."[17] By 1880, however, the Supreme Court had expanded the protections afforded by the Fourteenth Amendment to include Celtic Irishmen.[18] Subsequently, the protections guaranteeing equal protection under the law were extended to Chinese[19] and Austrian resident aliens.[20]

Although the legal protections under the Fourteenth Amendment had been significantly expanded to other races by the time of *Brown,* the decision nevertheless represented a fundamental change in the legal response to discrimination. This decision and the Civil Rights Movement created the climate for the passage of the Civil Rights Act of 1964 and other laws. The President's Committee on Equal Employment Opportunity had been created in 1961 by President John Kennedy, but its enforcement powers were limited and seldom exercised.[21] Title VII of the 1964 Civil Rights Act, however, prohibited discrimination against Blacks and others on the basis of race, color, sex, religion, and national origin. Through this act, protections that had been won by the struggles of black people were extended to women, aliens, and Jews. Therefore, affirmative action won by Blacks benefited other individuals as well.

In 1965 President Johnson issued his Executive Order 11246, providing protections for a host of minorities, including women. This order not only confirmed the essential equal opportunity protections that had been guaranteed by the Civil Rights Act, but went a step further in requiring affirmative action in addition to equal opportunity. Prior to this executive order, Blacks affirmatively sought to end racial segregation and discrimination in employment and other areas of American life. The executive order, however, sought to shift this responsibility directly to employers. No longer would equal opportunity suffice, but employers were required to take positive, result-oriented steps toward the elimination of discriminatory barriers. Through Executive Order 11246, civil rights enforcement finally came of age; the Office of Federal Contract Compliance was set up within the Department of Labor and given strong enforcement powers.

Compulsory Affirmative Action Plans

The most significant aspect of the order was its requirement that employers who receive at least $50,000 in federal contracts and employ at least fifty employees develop written affirmative action programs with appropriate goals and timetables. In order for companies to continue doing business with the federal government, these plans had to conform to the format outlined in Executive Order 11375, commonly referred to as "Revised Order Number 4." Failure to comply with the order can result in contracts being delayed, suspended, or terminated. As a minimum the affirmative action plans should include: (1) development of a personnel data base; (2) a statement of policy forbidding discrimination; (3) appointment of an individual in charge of an affirmative action program; (4) examination of the conditions of employment, including recruitment, hiring, promotion, salaries, and others; (5) identification of areas of underutilization and development of specific plans to overcome these areas; and (6) development of numerical goals and timetables.

These compulsory plans grew out of the government's need to address the legitimate demands raised in the Civil Rights Movement. Overnight, federal contractors and subcontractors had to begin analyzing their personnel policies and decisions in order to determine the extent to which Blacks, women, and other minorities were being utilized. In addition, appointments of affirmative action officers had to be made to develop, monitor, and implement the programs. Once appointed, these officers began to meet periodically and formed local, regional, and national associations. On the national level the American Association for Affirmative Action was formed in 1973 with an initial membership of well over three thousand individuals. The ultimate role and effectiveness of these professional organizations is still unclear. Some have been troubled by internal political rivalries and conflict between ethnic groups, for example, between Blacks and chicanos. In addition, many affirmative action officers are unsure of their role with respect to their ultimate allegiance to their employers as opposed to members of the "protected class."[22]

Affirmative Advocacy

Unlike most other jobs, the position of affirmative action officer grew out of the black struggle to achieve full status as human beings and, as such, more than any other position, it should be accountable to the black community. Affirmative action officers who consider themselves to be mere paper pushers and not advocates for the oppressed are ignorant of the nature of affirmative action and its driving force: social pressure. Without both internal and external pressure against the employer, institutional discrimination will continue to manifest itself. Affirmative action, therefore, must be viewed as another means of struggle against continuing racial discrimination and economic exploitation. If properly understood, affirmative action laws and regulations that have evolved in the last decade can have a positive impact upon the condition of Blacks.

Affirmative advocacy is critical because of the nonbenign nature of racism and economic exploitation. Discrimination is not a passive phenomenon, but is dynamic and serves continually to lock Blacks out of economic and social privilege in America. Under the Carter administration, the tone for affirmative advocacy was set by Weldon Rougeau, director, Office of Federal Contract Compliance Programs, and by Eleanor Holmes Norton, chairperson, Equal Employment Opportunity Commission.

Through Executive Order 12086, effective 8 October 1979, the Office of Federal Contract Compliance Programs (OFCCP) has sought affirmatively to enforce the affirmative action obligations as stipulated by Executive Order 11246. Rougeau has targeted such growth industries as coal, banking, and insurance for class scrutiny, a process facilitated by the streamlining of civil rights enforcement agencies under OFCCP.[23] Rougeau, an attorney, has warned employers that compliance is an obligation imposed by law through the contracting process and that companies that fail to comply will be severely penalized.

The OFCCP has carried through on its threats. It has debarred Uniroyal and Prudential corporations from federal contracts and has obtained back-pay settlements in a number of cases. For example, in a recent consent agreement signed between the Labor Department and Chase Manhattan Bank, Chase agreed to provide special job training, education, career counseling, and promotion "incentive" payments. Approximately $600,000 is to be paid in promotion incentive payments, $1 million for job training and counseling, and $450,000 for legal fees.

This affirmative enforcement has provoked a reaction from federal contractors. Most of the major employers filed a class action lawsuit against the OFCCP and other civil rights enforcement agencies, alleging that due to the contradictory nature of civil rights laws and regulations, compliance was virtually impossible, and that the court therefore should enjoin their use until the government eliminated the inconsistencies. At the heart of the challenge was the plaintiffs' contention that shifting government policies made it impossible for them to understand federal compliance requirements fully. For example, they argued that certain prior policies, such as veteran preferences, contradict the current policy initiatives with respect to affirmative action for women.

The lawsuit was eventually dismissed, but the argument of shifting governmental policies remains relevant. This type of civil rights enforcement manifests the commitment of the director of the OFCCP, himself a product of the Civil Rights Movement. The same vigorous enforcement has emanated from the EEOC, a direct result of the leadership of a strong black female attorney, Eleanor Holmes Norton. Under her leadership, the EEO promulgated the *Affirmative Action Guidelines,* which provide a defense against lawsuits that challenge affirmative action programs on the basis of reverse discrimination. Under the regulations, if a voluntary program is devised in conformity with the regulations and a reverse discrimination complaint is filed, the commission will enter a finding of "no reasonable cause" and dismiss the complaint. This procedure was designed to serve as an incentive for compliance. Under the Reagan administration these guidelines have been eliminated altogether.

In general, the Reagan administration demands less governmental entanglement with private industry, a stance that has a direct impact on the role of the affirmative action officer. When government threatens to enforce civil rights laws, companies at least take the minimum steps toward compliance and therefore hire affirmative action officers. In the absence of this threat, companies will, for the most part, eliminate the position.

Affirmative action officers should, therefore, ally with community groups, agencies, and individuals who support a strong governmental enforcement policy. Since affirmative action evolved as a direct consequence of black liberation struggles, its survival depends upon the same social forces. An affirmative action officer must be willing to take direct action against his or her employer when there is reasonable belief that the employer is engaged in discriminatory practices in violation of federal/state laws and regulations. An officer who engages in this kind of conflict with his or her employer of course risks being fired, though an important legal protection found in Title VII of the Civil Rights Act may provide some relief for an aggressive officer faced with termination. Section 704 (a) of Title VII states:

> It shall be an unlawful employment practice for an employer to discriminate against any of his employees or applicants for employment because he has opposed any practice made an unlawful employment practice by this subchapter, or because he has made a charge, testified, assisted, or participated in any manner in an investigation, proceeding, or hearing under this subchapter.

This protection against retaliation accrues to any individual. Most affirmative action officers are required by company policy to oppose discriminatory practices and it may be argued that affirmative action was designed for this very purpose. It would appear, therefore, that the officer would be opposing discriminatory practices by virtue of performing his or her employment responsibilities. If the officer opposed discriminatory practices in a vocal manner, he or she would be protected according to 704 (a).

A federal district court has considered this issue involving a non-officer in *Gee* v. *Boorstin,* 22 FEP Cases 1313 (1980). In *Gee* Sylvia H. Gee, a black female brought an action against Daniel J. Boorstin, chief executive officer, Library of Congress. In her complaint Ms. Gee alleged that she was discriminated against on the basis of race and sex, and was retaliated against when the defendant failed to promote her to a GS-10 supervisory position in 1975. Ms. Gee had been employed at the Library for approximately twenty-four years, and during that time actively protested against what she perceived to be discriminatory practices. In the 1970s she was a member and director of an organization called Black Employees of the Library of Congress (BELC). Under her leadership BELC was instrumental in lobbying Congress to include the Library of Congress under Title VII's protections, and in getting the American Library Association to conduct public hearings into alleged discriminatory practices at the Library.

After reviewing all the evidence, Judge Barrington Parker held that the Library of Congress had violated Title VII by failing to promote Ms. Gee to a GS-10 position. The judge said of her: "In general, it is fair to say that Ms. Gee was an outspoken employee, an irritant who stood up and presented unwelcomed challenges whenever she saw or suspected racial discrimination." The court ordered her immediate promotion, retroactive to 8 April 1976, the date of her complaint, as well as back pay and counsel fees. More important, the court enjoined the Library of Congress from "retaliating, discriminating against, or in any manner prejudicing or acting adversely against the Plaintiff or any other employee because of participation in this case."

The protection against retaliation has been significantly broadened under two U.S. Court of Appeals decisions. In *Sias* v. *City Demonstration Agency,* 18 FEP Cases 981, the Ninth Circuit (San Francisco) held that protection under the opposition clause to Section 704 (a) was afforded an individual who opposed an employment practice that was reasonably believed to be discriminatory. This sanction of the reasonableness test considerably expands the scope of protection afforded by the opposition clause. Prior lower court decisions had held that the protections under the opposition clause prevailed only if the opposed practices were in fact discriminatory. In rejecting the old test, the Ninth Circuit adopted the reasoning of a federal district judge in *Hearth* v. *Metropolitan Transit Commission,* 436 F. Supp. 685, 688, 18 FEP Cases 329, 331 (D. Minn. 1977):

> But this court believes that appropriate informal opposition to perceived discrimination must not be chilled by the fear of retaliatory action in the event the alleged wrong doing does not exist. . . . The elimination of discrimination in employment is the purpose behind Title VII and the Statute is entitled to a liberal interpretation. When an employee reasonably believes that discrimination exists, opposition thereto is opposition to an employment practice made unlawful by Title VII even if the employee turns out to be mistaken as to the facts.

In *Womack* v. *Munson,* 22 FEP Cases 1079, the Eighth Circuit (St. Louis) reversed a decision of a district court and awarded Thomas Womack back pay and reinstatement because of a retaliatory discharge. The court concluded that the prosecuting attorney for the Sixth Judicial District of Arkansas discriminated against Mr. Womack, a black investigator, for bringing a class action against the sheriff of the county. Mr. Womack was employed by the prosecuting attorney at the time of the suit and had served as deputy sheriff. Within twenty days from informing Mr. Munson of the suit, Mr. Womack was fired.

Although the protection against retaliation can serve as a useful tool in fighting discrimination in the workforce, an employee must guard against possible termination for other legitimate reasons. For example, in *Lowe* v. *WCAU-T.V.,* 21 FEP Cases 594, a district court held that an employer did not retaliate when it discharged an employee who filed a complaint with EEOC when he refused the superior's direct order to answer his telephone. In another case involving an affirmative action officer, a district court held in *Smith* v. *Singer Co.*, 19 FEP Cases 1509 (1979), that an employer did not violate Section 704 (a) when it discharged an affirmative action officer who filed a complaint with the EEOC but failed to inform his employer of such filing, in violation of his duties and responsibilities. One of his duties was to keep management informed about all aspects of affirmative action compliance, including complaints filed with outside enforcement agencies.

The Limits of Affirmative Action

The most obvious drawback to a legal challenge to discrimination is the cost involved. Lawyers are expensive and a lawsuit against a major corporation involves numerous depositions and court appearances for motions and hearing. Voluntary affirmative action, whether in response to federal compulsion or not, represents an acceptable response to a historical legacy of discrimination. However, *Regents of the University of California* v. *Bakke,* 98 S. Ct. 2733 (1978), placed limitations upon the extent to which competitive considerations of race could be used in admissions decisions, particularly in the public sector. At issue in *Bakke* was the constitutionality of a University of California at Davis Medical School policy that reserved sixteen of the one hundred first-year seats in the school for minority students. In a divided decision, the U.S. Supreme Court rejected the university's rationale for the development of the special admissions program. In an effort to justify the program under the Fourteenth Amendment and thus to demonstrate a "compelling state need" as required under constitutional law, the university argued that the special admissions program would serve the purposes of: (1) reducing the historical deficit of traditionally disfavored minorities in medical schools and the medical profession, (2) countering the effects of societal discrimination, (3) increasing the number of physicians who will practice in communities currently underserved, and (4) obtaining the educational benefits that flow from an ethnically diverse student body. In order for the program to withstand constitutional scrutiny the purposes had to be both "substantial" and "necessary." The Court rejected the first three arguments, upheld the fourth one, but concluded that the program in question was not "necessary" for the creation of a diverse student population.

The Court's rejection of societal discrimination as a legitimate rationale for the program placed considerable limitations upon public employers. The Court reasoned that a state has an interest in eliminating the effects of specific instances of racial discrimination, but that the university failed to show prior discrimination. If the Court had upheld societal discrimination as a legitimate basis for affirmative action in *Bakke*, considerable impetus would have been gained in the struggle for equal opportunity.

What *Bakke* prohibited for public employers, *Kaiser Aluminum and Chemical Corp.* v. *Weber*, 20 FEP Cases 1, sanctioned for private ones. Unlike *Bakke*, *Weber* approved the use of affirmative action programs that were designed to eliminate "traditional patterns of racial segregation." The program at issue in this case reserved for black employees 50 percent of the openings in craft-training programs at the Gramercy, Louisiana, plant. This decision marked an important milestone in that the Court explicitly sanctioned the use of history as a means of determining the legality of affirmative action programs. According to Justice William J. Brennan, Jr., who wrote the majority opinion, it would be ironic for a program designed to carry out the purposes of the Civil Rights Act to be in violation of said act. He explained that the Civil Rights Act sought to integrate Blacks into the American mainstream through full participation in the workforce.

In order to promote full utilization of Blacks in these crucial areas of American life, the Court reasoned that Title VII was intended to serve as a "catalyst to cause employers and unions to self-examine and to self-evaluate their employment practices and to endeavor to eliminate, so far as possible, the last vestiges of an unfortunate and ignominious page in this country's history." The Court upheld the affirmative action program because it was designed to eliminate "old patterns of racial segregation and hierarchy," an aim consistent with the intent of the Civil Rights Act. It would appear from *Weber* that affirmative action programs in employment, particularly in the private sector, will survive legal challenge if their purpose is to remedy racial exclusion and if they are properly constructed.

In this decision, the Court noted that Kaiser's affirmative action plan was temporary and intended to eliminate racial imbalance and not to promote racial balance. According to the Court, the preference would be lawful only until the percentage of black skilled craftworkers in the Gramercy plant approximated the percentage of Blacks in the local labor force. This qualification constitutes a significant limit on affirmative action: it sanctions certain programs only to the extent that they are designed to promote mirror percentages between the workforce and the community. Under the mirror percentage scheme an employer could justify only an affirmative action program that sought to have its black workforce profile equal the percentage of Blacks in the community. If a company is located in an area of little black population, it would have little justification for constructing a vigorous affirmative action program to benefit Blacks.

Redress for centuries of exclusion and exploitation cannot be adequately addressed through litigation and voluntary affirmative action programs. Justice would require that every black person in the United States receive compensation for past and continuing denials of human rights. Anything less than full compensation, access to jobs, education, and decent housing would appear mere pacification. The gains that have been made in affirmative action are the results of the continuing struggles of Black people. As Justice Thurgood Marshall argued in his dissent to *Bakke,* affirmative action programs to ameliorate the present effects of two hundred years of discrimination are lawful. If Blacks as a class have been systematically denied opportunity through individual and governmentally sanctioned discrimination/segregation, then Blacks as a class should receive some form of equitable redress.

One need only peruse the pages of history to ascertain the depravity and pervasiveness of this class discrimination. Unlike other individuals who voluntarily immigrated to this country, Blacks were brought here as chattel slaves. The chattel slave in America had no rights. He was regarded as property, as articles of commerce. In *Dred Scott v. Sanford,* 60 U.S.(19 How.) 393 (1857), the U.S. Supreme Court upheld the dehumanization of Black people, thus making this subordination constitutionally acceptable throughout the land.

The struggle for human dignity and equality under the law has demanded great personal sacrifice from both Blacks and whites. The Thirteenth, Fourteenth, and Fifteenth Amendments of the U.S. Constitution, born out of the bloodiest conflict between Americans, laid the foundation for new substantive rights for Black people. The

Supreme Court decision of *Brown* v. *Board of Education* put an end to legally supported segregation. Since *Brown* the right of Black people to equal treatment under the law has been affirmatively established by many other statutes and cases, the most notable being: the Civil Rights Act of 1964, the Voting Rights Act of 1965, and cases such as *Jones* v. *Alfred H. Mayer, Co.* (1968). Under *Jones* the U.S. Supreme Court recognized the power of Congress under the Thirteenth Amendment to abolish all "badges and incidences of slavery." According to the Court, Congress has the power to determine what the badges and incidences of slavery are, and then to enact an appropriate legislative remedy. The Congress has yet to pass legislation on affirmative action. Such legislation, derived from a legislative history of prior discrimination, would bring the day of full reparation much closer to African-Americans.

Given the repressive social climate in the United States, however, there is little likelihood that Congress will take such strides. Therefore, Black people's ultimate destiny must be decided by themselves. Reformist measures, such as affirmative action programs, are incapable of bringing full freedom to the mass population. Some progress will be made. Employers may be compelled to hire Blacks until their numbers inside the plant mirror their population in the community. While such measures may be necessary mechanisms for affording Blacks some of society's benefits, they are, without greater public commitment, insufficient.

It is precisely because this public commitment is not forthcoming that Blacks must recognize that their ultimate destiny is linked not with a world system that is rapidly failing, but with the progressive struggles of Third World peoples. Affirmative action creates the false impression that Black salvation and freedom can be obtained through integration. While Blacks struggle to integrate the jobs and schools of America, they must be ever on guard against the system's attempts to use them to fight against the legitimate aspirations of Third World people. If the effect of widening the doors of opportunity for African-Americans is that America can thereby use black CIA agents against the legitimate struggles of African people abroad, then affirmative action will have become a detriment rather than a benefit to Black people. The possibilities that this may occur are very real as increasing numbers of black students graduate from colleges and universities without a clear understanding of imperialism and its relationship to both Africa and the Black community in America. It is therefore incumbent upon Blacks to continue to agitate for full access to opportunities, but more important, it is critical that African people demand accountability from those individuals who are the beneficiaries of this agitation. Those who work in and benefit from affirmative action owe their wordly gains in no small measure to the struggles of Black people to achieve full human dignity. It is these struggles that will advance the cause of affirmative action beyond integration to the full liberation of all who are still victims of racial discrimination and economic exploitation.

Notes

1. W. E. B. DuBois, *The World and Africa*, (New York: International Publishers, 1946, 1972), p. 44.
2. Ibid., p. 46.
3. Ibid.
4. Ibid., p. 54.
5. Ibid., p. 65.
6. Ibid., p. 20.
7. Matthew T. Mellon, *Early American Views on Negro Slavery* (Boston: Meador Publishing Co., 1934), p. 73.
8. Augustin Cochin, *Results of Slavery* (Freeport: Books for Libraries Press, 1863, 1970), p. 100.
9. David Walker, *An Appeal to the Coloured Citizens of the World* (Boston, 1892), p. 70.
10. A. Leon Higginbotham, Jr., *In the Matter of Color, Race and the American Legal Process: The Colonial Period* (New York: Oxford University Press, 1978), pp. 6-7.
11. *Quarterly Review of Higher Education Among Negroes*, vo. 1, no. 1 (January, 1933): p. 29.
12. W. E. B. DuBois, *Dust Of Dawn: An Essay Toward an Autobiography of a Race Concept* (New York: Schocken Books, 1968), p. 31.
13. Herbert Hill, *Black Labor and the American Legal System* (Washington, D.C.: Bureau of National Affairs, Inc., 1977) p. 175.
14. Ibid., p. 178.
15. Ibid., p. 246.
16. Ibid., p. 379.
17. Slaughter-House Cases, 16 Wall. 36, 71 (1873).
18. Strander v. West Virginia, 100 U.S. 303, 308 (1880).
19. Yick Wo v. Hopkins, 188 U.S. 356 (1886).
20. Traux v. Raich, 239 U.S. 33, 41 (1915).
21. Hill, *Black Labor,* p. 380.

22. Protected "class" has been defined by federal civil rights agencies for affirmative action purposes as women, Blacks, Asian and Pacific Islanders, Hispanics, and American Indians.
23. Prior to consolidation under OFCCP, contract compliance authority was lodged in eleven federal agencies.
24. 22 FEP Cases 1315 (1980).

VI

Modernity and Other Directions in African and Caribbean Literature

Ju Ju Woman, Phillip L. Mason

CHAPTER 11

The Peopling of a Story: A New View of Characterization in African Literature

Daniel P. Kunene

We propose an approach to characterization in African literature which recognizes anonymity as a legitimate concept in the evaluation of the people in the story and their success (or lack thereof) in fulfilling the artistic functions assigned to them. Anonymity is conceived as a continuum that ranges from total anonymity at one extreme to total individuality at the other. In the process of examining this concept at work, we hope to address, at least in part, the problem of "flat" characterization which critics point to with such monotonous regularity in their discussions of this literature. One hopes also that it will become evident from this discussion that "flatness" is not necessarily bad, that it is indeed sometimes an inevitable consequence of the literary genre chosen by the author. In a new and methodologically adequate approach, the term "flat" and its derivatives should be replaced by a positive set of terms that recognize the legitimacy of anonymity.

One critic of African literature who has at least placed the problem of characterization in its correct perspective is Albert Gérard. He says:

> Clearly, the most important literary effect of European influence was the introduction of the novel and—in a later phase—of stage drama, new genres completely alien to traditional art. But both the novel and stage drama are the outcome of a particular form of civilization, the premises of which are entirely at variance with those of indigenous African cultures. They are the favorite medium of an individualistic society; they focus on the exploration of individual character; they feed on the analysis of private emotions and motivations of experiences. On the contrary, like most technologically underdeveloped, small-scale societies, whose survival can only be ensured by the closest group cohesion, African cultures are based on values that are primarily societal. The main functions of literature are: to preserve the religious myths of the group, to perpetuate the memory of its past in semilegendary chronicles

---

Daniel P. Kunene is a Professor in the Department of African Languages and Literature at the University of Wisconsin-Madison

and so to bolster its sense of collective identity and dignity, to record the wisdom pragmatically accumulated by generations of ancestors in proverbs and gnomic tales, and to celebrate the prowess of kings and warriors, whose mighty deeds have ensured the power and the glory of the group. This is why so many African novelists and playwrights have been unable—as has often been observed and deplored—to achieve convincing individual characterization. In many cases, they continue the folktale tradition of emphasis on anecdotal incidents or on allegorical morality. The absence of any native tradition in those genres also accounts for clumsiness in plot management and in the depiction of personal emotions: constant resorting to implausible coincidences and awkward handling of the love theme are illustrative of the difficulties that they will have to overcome.

The importance of Gérard's observations lies in his realization that an individual-oriented society makes rather different demands on the writer than does a communal-oriented society. If we accept this basic premise, we should conclude that the writer's style and his approach to characterization are just as much a response to his situation as are his choices of theme and plot. The critic's first duty, then, is to accept the legitimacy of the writer's response to these societal challenges. Plus or minus excellence must be defined within the general ambience of these circumstances. That is to say, we will, no doubt, always have good writers and mediocre ones, regardless of the environmental stimuli to which they are responding. But as critical readers, we must first correct or adjust our own perspective. If we need new methodological tools, we must get on with the job of forging them. Given this corrected perspective, we would have to say that plus or minus excellence constitutes a judgment that may be applied to any part of the anonymity-individuality continuum. In other words, there would, potentially, be good and bad characterization regardless of whether the characters were totally anonymous, partially anonymous, or totally individualized. But no point in the spectrum would be automatically assigned the label "good" or "bad."

In evaluating writers who operate, or have largely operated, in communal-oriented societies, it is easy to fall into the trap of assuming a mono-directional evolutionary process, especially if our own viewpoint is informed by a materialistic social order in which the technologically advanced civilizations are automatically assumed to set the standards and the pace for everything else. Gérard himself reflects this assumption in the latter part of the above passage, from the sentence beginning, "This is why so many novelists and playwrights have been unable," to the end of the passage. Statements such as: *"have been unable . . . to achieve convincing individual characterization"*; *"clumsiness in plot management and in the depiction of personal emotions"*; and *"awkward handling of the love theme"* inevitably lead Gérard to the conclusion: *"are illustrative of the difficulties that they* [the African writers] *will have to overcome"* (my emphasis). This conclusion could, quite legitimately, be considered highly paternalistic. The general argument of critics who make this assumption would seem to go something like this: If we are all moving, in our technological preoccupations, toward manufacturing the bomb, then we are automatically also moving, in our literary preoccupations, toward manufacturing individualized characters. The question is: Are we?

Another weakness in this perception is its suggestion that there is a certain ideal state to which all creation is moving, and that everything else is important only insofar as it brings us closer to that state. Viewed in this light, the literary effort of those African-language writers who produce characters that do not fit the description "round" would not be judged as legitimate or valid as a good in itself but only insofar as it leads to *the* good, namely, fully individualized characters.

It seems to me we ought to reject both premises because they are both false. First, in our spiritual values as Africans, we are not necessarily going in the same direction as the nuclear bomb swingers. If we find ourselves there, it will not be because we deliberately chose to go in that direction. Second, it seems to me that we cannot escape the axiom that what is, is. What is also helps to determine what shall be, but this fact does not make what is unimportant in its own sake, that is, as a value within the psychologically encompassable "present." If what *is* were unimportant, then life would be utterly impossible because it would be nothing more than a perpetual state of expectancy.

The conception and portrayal of character in most African-language literature and certain aspects of style are so intimately interrelated that the one often determines the nature of the other. In this regard, the concept of plus or minus anonymity has been found to be the most productive. Between the extremes of totally anonymous and totally individualized characters are characters of varying degrees and manifestations of partial anonymity. In total anonymity the author strives to blur the outlines of the characters so that they merge with the rest of the community. In oral narrative, which has played a major role in creating the tradition of the anonymous character that inevitably has been passed on to the written literature, these characters, when cast in minor roles (i.e., roles complementary to the major plot), are often called "the people" or referred to by some suitable pronoun. They act primarily as "watchers," who always make appropriate comments at suitable moments in the progression of the narrative, are always on the side of right and justice, and help to guide the story toward a successful resolution. This technique has been taken an important step further in written literature, where peripheral anonymous characters are often used to represent both the good and the bad elements in society.

One important feature of total anonymity is that the characters are not given any names. As in oral narrative, they are "the people," or (in the singular) "a certain person," "a certain man," "a certain woman," and so on. In some cases, indeed, all we have is a disembodied voice without any reference to its human source.

Though partially anonymous characters often have the distinction of having a name, namelessness is not ruled out, and many of them, though identified as individuals in other ways, share with the totally anonymous characters the distinction of not having a name. The concept of an anonymous character with a name appears to be a self-contradiction, but in fact, since anonymity in characterization involves much more than the mere presence or absence of a label, the contradiction is only apparent. Consider, for example, a writer who takes a vice or a virtue and gives it a name just as he would a human being. It seems to me that such a writer represents a whole slice of humanity in that one label. He gives it legs and arms, as well as a nervous system so that its five senses can operate. He gives it a voice. Yet its impulses are not individual impulses but those of a whole slice of humanity, and its words and actions are primarily moral statements for the edification of society.

Anonymous characters are, therefore, both part of the act and a commentary on the act. This is much more obvious where they are not the protagonists but are to varying degrees off-center. When "the people" are invoked, this technique bears some resemblance to the chorus of Greek tragedy—a resemblance that remains even when one recognizes both the changes the chorus underwent over time and the fact that, unlike the chorus, anonymous characterization is as yet free from formal structure.

The totally individualized character is, of course, the so-called rounded character. We not only know what he is saying or doing and observe his outward gestures, his bodily attitudes, and his facial expressions, but we also know what he is thinking. We know that while he has certain constant personality traits, he is neither entirely a saint nor entirely a devil, but is always somewhat selfish and somewhat public-minded. His most private thoughts are sometimes crude and socially unacceptable, and the narrator acts as a filter that refines them for our sensitive ears.

The major focus of this presentation is on anonymous characterization, not only because it has hitherto received no attention, but also because its elucidation inevitably broadens our perception of individual characterization. We will further restrict our inquiry in this essay to secondary, or what we have elsewhere referred to as "off-center" or "peripheral" characters, to the exclusion of the principal protagonists. The purpose is to make a clear distinction between action (performed by the protagonists) and reaction (a response from the "on-lookers," i.e., the story's off-center characters). This is an absolutely essential distinction because, even though the concept of anonymity is applicable to both groups of characters, the function of *commenting* on the plot and its progression is much more obviously a function of the "peripheral" characters, who form a kind of "audience within the drama," than of those in the heat of action.

In Thomas Mofolo's three works, *Moeti oa Bochabela, Pitseng,* and *Chaka,* we have excellent examples of anonymous characters who rally to expose and condemn socially unacceptable behavior. In *Moeti,* Fekisi, the hero of the story who has no peace in his soul because of the evil in his society and his restless search for the Creator, consults "certain men whom he trusted" and asks them to tell him about God. To illustrate man's evil nature and his ingratitude, they tell him the story of the All-Swallowing Monster, the Kgodumodumo, which one day appeared suddenly from the horizon and ate up all living things, with only one expectant woman escaping by a ruse. The child she bears shortly afterward is a precocious boy who instantly grows up into a young warrior and then insists on going to release the people from the stomach of the Monster. He succeeds in this difficult and dangerous task, and as a reward the people give him a lot of cattle and make him their king. But not long afterward, out of envy, they seek to destroy him, and ultimately succeed in doing so. These men also tell Fekisi that God once lived among the people, but that because of man's evil ways God withdrew to a place where man would find it very difficult to reach him, somewhere far on the other side of Ntswanatsatsi. They sympathize with Fekisi's convictions and ideals, and they share his outrage at the corruption of their society.

Another intervention by "the people" takes place in the scene where Phakoane, Fekisi's neighbor, a habitual drunkard and wife-beater, comes home from a drinking spree to find that his son has been killed by lightning. He is about to beat his wife for having failed to protect his child from the lightning, when "the people of the village" stop him.

In *Chaka,* Mofolo uses "the people" a great deal, especially in the earlier part of the book, to comment on Senzangakhona's ill-treatment of his own son, Chaka, and his wife, Nandi. "The women" in particular lash out with songs in which satire, sarcasm, and innuendo combine to expose Senzangakhona's cowardice and meanness. When Senzangakhona finally throws his son to his enemies with the shout, "Kill him!", "the women" sing mournfully:

[1] Hele-helele! Medimo, le re hopole,
Le tadime rona baa bolaelwang tjala lee siyong;
Hele-helele! Badimo, le dipaki tsa rona,
Le dipaki tsa mohl'a masimong.
Helele! Morena ha a na nnete,
Ha a na nnete, ke lempetje,
Hoja re mo tswaletse ngwana e motona,
Ngwana e motona, kgala-bahale.
Helele! Senzangakhona o tshaba lehala,
O mathela moratheng!

Alas! You gods, think of us,
Look upon us who are killed for a crime that is not there.
Alas! You spirits, you are our witnesses,
You are the witnesses of that day in the fields.
Alas! The king is without truth,
He is without truth, he is a chameleon,
Even after we have born for him a male child,

> A male child, conquerer of the mighty ones.
> Alas! Senzangakhona is afraid of his equals,
> And vents his rage upon the defenceless!

Not only does this song reflect communal concern over Senzangakhona's outrageous act, but it also reaffirms the solidarity of "the women" as a group who literally suffer with Nandi because, like her, they are wives and mothers and they feel that a part of them has suffered in the suffering of Nandi. It is a point of extreme cogency that they say, "we have born for him a male child," and not, "she has born for him a male child."

Likewise, when "the men" display cowardice and run away from a charging lion—an act aggravated by the fact that in their flight they desert their comrade who has been caught by the lion—"the women" and "the girls" chide them in song. At the same time, to "the men's" eternal shame, songs are composed praising the young Chaka who stood alone against the predator, killing it, though too late, alas, to rescue its victim. "The women's" song goes:

[2] Batho ba ile, ra sala le basele,
  Ra sala le di-ka-batho, e se bona!
  Chaka re tla mo re'ng e le ngwana?
  Basadi ba ha Ncube, hlollwang,
  Basadi ba ha Senzangakhona ha ba na thuso,
  Mosadi ke Nandi a le mong to,
  Hobane o tswetse ngwana e motona ka hohle.

> True men are gone, we remain with strange beings,
> We remain with men-like beings, who are not men!
> What can we do with Chaka, a mere child?
> O, you women of Ncube, see this wonder,
> The women of Senzangakhona are useless,
> Nandi alone is a woman,
> For she bore a male child in all respects.

The reference to Chaka as "a mere child" underscores the dilemma "the women" find themselves in, for, though Chaka's deed makes him the only *man* any woman would be proud of, he is to them no more than a child, and any amorous relationship with him would be tantamount to incest.

"The girls" too composed their own song which, the narrator tells us, they sang deliberately where there were crowds of people:

[3] Hae ha Ncube ha ho bahlankana,
Mohlankana o mong feela:
Hae ha Ncube ha ho banna,
Banna ke makwala kaofela,
Ba balehile ba siya wa mophato wa bona naheng,
Ba siya thak'a bona a tshwarane le sebata,
A betile tau ka ditlena!
Senzangakhona ha a na batho, o tla bolawa ba ile!
Senzangakhona, lata ngwana wa hao a orohe,
Ke ngwana e motona, letshola-thebe,
O tla o lwanela, a o hlolele dira.

Here at our home, at Ncube's, there are no young men,
There is but one young man of worth;
Here at our home, at Ncube's, there are no men,
For all the men here are cowards,
They ran away leaving their age-mate in the field,
Leaving their comrade wrestling with a wild beast,
Gripping a lion by its jaws!
Senzangakhona has no men, they will desert him, and he will be killed.
O, Senzangakhona, come fetch your child and take him home,
He is a male child, a shield-bearer,
He will fight for you and conquer your enemies.

In the scene where Chaka, having just fled from his enemies in the village, is mourned by all of creation, anonymous "people" congregate at the place where the fighting took place. They come as members of the community, both from the village where the tragic events occurred and from neighboring villages. They are there to share the grief of the grief-stricken. They were first alerted to the fact that something was wrong by the cry of despair from the girl who was caught by the hyena at night, followed by the girl's screams of joy and incredulity after Chaka rescued her, and later by the wailing of the mothers and sisters and lovers of the slain and the wounded in the fighting in which Chaka's enemies were after his head. Some were crying for Chaka himself, wondering how cruel was the sorcerer who had turned his father's heart against him.

In the above illustrations the anonymous characters are as close to the center of the action as possible. They do what they can to influence events to take a turn for the better. We will now examine situations where the anonymous characters remain in the background and merely comment on the action without in any way trying to influence it. Such comment either approves or disapproves of what is happening at center stage, and is in the nature of gossip. In Mofolo's *Pitseng*, on the very day Mr. Katse, the new preacher and teacher, arrives in Pitseng, news of his rescue of some men who were trapped in the snow on the mountainslopes flies with amazing speed through the villages of the valley of Pitseng. The rescue had taken place on the eve of Katse's arrival, while he and his family and the men escorting them were sheltered in a cave where they shared their food, their fire, and their blankets with the refugees. Mofolo carries this "good" gossip in a dialogue involving anonymus voices:

[4] Ditaba tsena tsa titima ka lebela lee kang la moya, tsa tlala hohle sekgutlong sena sa Pitseng, ke ho re tsa tsejwa ha Mofoka, ha Phoka, dikgohlong ha Mosia, ha Moeletsi le ha Tondini, Bathepung; tsa tsejwa hohle moo ka matsatsi a mabedi; mme ha batho ba bua, puo ya eba: "O kile wa utlwa, mmoleid o fihlili?"—"Ee, ke utlwile hore mmoledi o fihlile, mme o fihla ka ditaba tse kgolo."—"O fihlile ka ditaba tse kgolo, tsee hlomolang pelo, empa tsee monate, tsa kgotso."—"Ee, ke hobane o fihla a eteletswe pele ke lehlwa, pontsho ya hore pelo ya hae e tshweu, mme le ditaba tseo a tlang ka tsona di jwalo."

This news ran with the speed of the wind, and it filled this entire valley of Pitseng; that is to say that it came to be known at Mofoka's, at Phoka's, among the cliffs at Mosia's, at Moeletsi's, and at Tondini's among the Bathepu; it was known in that entire place in two days, and when the people spoke, all they said was: "Have you heard? The preacher has arrived."—"Yes, I have heard that the preacher has arrived, and he is accompanied by important happenings."—"He is accompanied by important happenings which touch one's heart, which are yet pleasing, and are things of peace."—"Yes, it is because he comes heralded by snow, an indication that his heart is white, and the affairs about which he has come are like that also."

"Evil" gossip is characterized by malice. Its main function is to maintain social cohesion among its practitioners, fortuitous and ephemeral though such relationships may be. In that sense, it could be considered amoral rather than "evil." It is endemic to society, and when conditions are right it latches onto its subject like a parasite attacking its host. It thrives on such crises as love triangles, murders, corruption among prayer women, seduction, drunken behavior, and sexual promiscuity; it can be activated by envy or simply by the sadistic pleasure of seeing a fellow human being suffer.

One of the best examples of this kind of gossip is found in R. R. R. Dhlomo's *Indelela yababi*. After the heroine, Delsie Moya (an ex-teacher), and the hero, Thomas Gwebu (an ex-priest), have absconded to Johannesburg from Amanzimtoti in Natal because of the scandal arising from Gwebu's extramarital impregnation of Moya, they frequent places of entertainment such as concerts and dances, behavior that is considered a sign of moral laxity. Dhlomo is convinced that people who have lived in Johannesburg for a long time and been corrupted by its ways are intent on corrupting others. He says "these people who live this kind of life in Johannesburg" have no other aim than that "you should be one of them." Gwebu is later murdered in a love-triangle rivalry and, at a subsequent court hearing to determine how he died, "all these people who have filled up this court" have come out of curiosity. They are eager to hear the outcome of the case so that they can have something to gossip about. Characterizing them as false friends, Dhlomo goes on to moralize about them, saying:

[5] Kulapho buphelela khona lobubuhlobo balababantu. Uthi omunye wabo angavelelwa ishwa, esikhundleni sokuba bamkhalele, bamsize, ubezwa sebeqhwebana izinqulu ngaye. Sebethi wayenzani wayethi ungcono kunathi. Yikho-ke bebuthene lapho. Bazozizwela okubi okungase kubaphe into yokuhlafunwa ngemilomo kuze kuvele elinye ishwa futhi.

That is the extent of the friendship of these people. When one of them is overtaken by misfortune, you hear them gossiping about him instead of sympathizing with him and helping him. They now ask what was he doing; he thought he was better than us. That is why they are assembled here. They have come to hear for themselves whatever ugly thing which may give them something to chew in their mouths until another misfortune strikes.

When, after the case, they peer into Delsie's eyes to see whether she is happy or sad at her boyfriend's death, they do so, the narrator tells us, so that they may have another juicy bit for their gossip. They are disappointed to observe sadness in her face because that means she cannot be suspected of having wished his death or at least of having found it "convenient."

Here we have an interesting hybrid form of narrative speech in which the narrator's reporting of events merges with the "voice" of the anonymous characters involved. In the first two sentences we hear the narrator's voice telling the reader *what usually happens* ("When one of them is overtaken by misfortune, you hear them gossiping about him . . ."). The third sentence is a true hybrid, beginning with the narrator's "they" and ending with the characters' "us" ("They now ask what was he doing; he thought he was better than us"). "They" is still within the *habitual past,* i.e., that is *what they usually say* under those circumstances. In the last two sentences, the narrative is picked up once more by the narrator's voice, but this time it narrates *what is actually happening* (That is why they are assembled here. They have come to hear for themselves . . .). Although this mixing of past narrative carried by the narrator's voice with a free indirect style is found quite regularly in Dhlomo's book, it is perhaps more striking here by reason of the fact that the words carried by the characters' "voice" are not in quotes. For our present purpose, the important thing is that we have here another manifestation of a group "voice" or the "voice" of an unidentified individual speaking for himself/herself and the rest of the group.

Another example is the scene in Guybon Sinxo's *UNomsa* where Sinxo tells how the young and beautiful female teacher Nomsa is fervently sought after as a lover by the prosperous-looking, handsome, church-going young Vel'esazi. But Nomsa instinctively recoils from him, feeling certain that Vel'esazi's outward appearance is a mere facade behind which lurks a man of evil designs. Seeing that Nomsa is serious about rejecting him, Vel'esazi resorts to threats of witchcraft which he carries out by sending his night-prowling witchcraft animals such as *Tsib'amanchwaba* (Grave-jumper) to bang on her window and jump on her roof. She is so frightened that she develops a fever and becomes delirious. The gossip-mongers are anxious to hear what "the lady teacher" says in her rantings and, despite the doctor's orders, pile into her room. But by this time Nomsa is so weak and mentally enfeebled that she is unable to talk properly; all she can say is, "Vel'esazi, 'thanda" (Vel'esazi, love). Everybody concludes from this that her illness is due to her unfulfilled love for Vel'esazi, a belief that Vel'esazi encourages.

[6] Bathi bakumxelele loo nto uVel'esazi *abantu,* wayigudisa wathi kudala uNomsa eyithetha into yokuba uyamthanda. Noko ke, yena Vel'esazi, uthe akayinanza ngani loo nto, ecinga okokuba uyaqhula lo mntwana (p. 49, my emphasis).

It happened, when *the people* told him this, Vel'esazi added his own frills to it, saying that Nomsa had long been telling him that she loved him. However he, Vel'esazi, had not taken that seriously, thinking that this child was merely teasing him.

As this last example shows, a central character is sometimes brought into verbal communication with peripheral anonymous characters, in this case Vel'esazi and "the people." Another excellent example occurs when Mrs. Adams, Nomsa's landlady, seeing her fever going down on the day of Vel'esazi's first visit since her illness, concludes that the two things are related, and then declares to everybody she meets:

[7] "Kanti umntu uphantse wafa na, wafa siyeke elona yeza uVel'esazi? Uthe akufiha uVel'esazi walala, ebengasali iveki yonke! Hayi, ngoku ndinethemba lokuba uya kuphila; litsho negqira. Kodwa uya kusuka athi ni ke, kuba akathandwa nguVel'esezi?"

Wayithunga ke ilali unina kaNongendi ngala mazwi, wahlebeka uNomsa (p. 50).

"Who could have guessed that this person was on the point of dying while we withheld the real medicine, Vel'esazi? The moment Vel'esazi came, she was able to sleep, something she had not done for a whole week! Well, now I am hopeful that she will recover; even the doctor says so. But what is she going to do since she is not loved by Vel'esazi?"

She wove the entire village with these words, the mother of Nongendi, and Nomsa became the object of gossip.

The disembodied voice is a constant feature of anonymous characterization. Hypothetical "dialogues" abstracted from prevailing communal sentiments are created by the author as in (4), where some voices (presumably two, but there could be more) talk about the new preacher's arrival and his "good Samaritan" deed in rescuing the travelers caught in the snow. Mofolo is here conveying to the reader a sentiment that reflects the gratitude of an entire community represented by these disembodied voices. Mackenzie Ntšala provides another good example in his *Sekhukhuni Se Bonoa Ke Sebatalali* when he describes the general buzz of activity on a morning in Leraha's village:

[8] Mantswe a batho ba baholo a a utlwala, motho o utlwa feela:
"Dumela moo Nnyeo!"
"Ee, dumela!"
"O sa phela?"
"O ya kae?"
"Ke ya masimong" (p. 13).
The voices of the older people are heard. All that one can hear is:
"Good day, So-and-So?"
"Yes, good day to you!"
"Are you well?"
"Where are you going?"
"I am going to the fields."

Here again we are given a general sense of what happens on a typical morning in a Sotho village: People go in different directions — to the fields, to the well, to take their animals to pasture, and so on. They meet and inquire after each other's health. That Ntšala suggests this is happening on a particular morning, namely the morning on which certain specific events in his story take place, does not alter the fact that it is a *typical* morning scene, a contextualization of the narrative rather than the narrative itself. The lack of individual identity in the voices speaking is thus reinforced by the *habitual* rather than *specific* time sense conveyed in the passage.

As already hinted in the preceding paragraph, the anonymity of a character is sometimes accentuated by a resort to the habitual past tense (as against the narrative past tense). The author tells what *used to happen* (habitual) and not what *actually happened* (narrative), thus adding a generalized past time to the nonspecificity of character. Sinxo does exactly this when he tells how newly arrived teachers *used to be* objects of malicious gossip among "the people" in whose place they had come to work.

[9] Abantu bakowethu bayihleba ititshala, okanye umfundisi le mini kanye afikayo: "Hayi, le ntwana ayinakufana nomfundisi wethu uNantsi, owayekho apha weenza oku noku!" (p. 18).

Our people gossip about a teacher or a minister on the very day he arrives: "O no, this little thing will never be like our minister So-and-So who was here and did this and that!"

Here everything has been reduced to a deliberate vagueness as evidenced by "So-and-So" instead of a specific name, and "this and that" instead of specific actions. As a result, the "voice" that speaks the quoted words is even more difficult to relate to any specific person.

It is a reasonable assumption that anonymous characters will be more likely to occur in certain types of compositional structures than in others. A writer who is concerned with extracting moral lessons from people's behavior is also interested in illustrating such lessons for the reader. Depending on the directness or subtlety of his approach, the story will be carried forward by means of episodes of varying degrees of starkness through which he tries to reach the reader's heart, but mostly succeeds in reaching his head. Each episode will, in turn, have an example as its core. Such examples differ in length and intensity. When they involve peripheral characters, the episodes are often so brief that the characters are like flitting shadows that are forgotten as soon as they have fulfilled their roles. In *Indlela yababi*, Dhlomo, quite early in the story, introduces John, the handsome, well-groomed young man who knocks on the door of Delsie Moya's parents' house one evening as soon as they have gone their different ways—the father to a meeting in Pietermaritzburg, and the mother to a women's prayer meeting—and Delsie is left alone. John's intention is, obviously, to engage in some amorous adventures with Delsie. Dhlomo has taken care to prepare the reader not only for this sort of eventuality but has, in none too subtle a manner, hinted at how the reader should react. He does this in a scene, set just before the parents' departure, in which they quarrel rather heatedly over Delsie's upbringing, the father complaining that his wife is too permissive and that Delsie will fall into evil ways. John's entry, then, is a fulfillment of this fear. The scene between him and Delsie does not last long, and John makes his exit as suddenly as his entry.

We see here another influence of oral tradition in which characters and other actors are created as needed and then put aside as soon as they have fulfilled their roles. John is simply conjured up into a temporary existence. Once the point is made, he is pushed into oblivion and the story goes on as if he had never existed. In his conversation with Delsie, we get to know that she arranged his visit that evening, presumably because she knew in advance that both her parents would be away. But the reader is not made privy to this knowledge in time to avoid the feeling that John's appearance is a kind of conjuring trick. It is of no little significance that Dhlomo does not give John a surname, in fact, it is surprising that he gives him a name at all.

A little later in the story, when Delsie is living away from home as a school teacher in Amanzimtoti, this illustration is carried to its tragic conclusion when the Reverend Thomas Gwebu impregnates her and, after a short visit home by Delsie, at which time her parents find out the truth, she and Gwebu abscond to Johannesburg. There is now no return for either of them, for Johannesburg is not only an impersonal city where fugitives merge like silent shadows with nameless crowds who do not know their backgrounds, but a city rife with opportunities for further corruption. It is, in the moral sense, a city of the damned. So Delsie Moya's and Thomas Gwebu's experiences in this city, the places of entertainment they go to, the company they keep, their failure to go to church, their promiscuous love affairs leading eventually to Gwebu's murder late one night after their return from a dance, and Delsie's wading deeper and deeper into sin—all are but an elaboration of the illustration of the wicked moving inexorably to their destruction. It is a fulfillment of a prophecy carried by the very title of the book: *Indlela yababi,* the way of the wicked. It is important to note here, however, that when Thomas Gwebu replaces John as Delsie's accomplice, we have two principal characters, and that is why this particular "illustration" is virtually the entire story.

The wandering hero is another kind of compositional design conducive to the use of anonymous characters. In stories of this type, the principal character is on a journey during which he or she is confronted with a variety of situations and people. This is what happens in S. E. K. Mqhayi's *UDon Jadu,* in which Dondolo (alias Don) is traveling on foot to his father's sister's place in the country. His experiences during this journey, which are recounted from the first person-direct observer point of view, include the following: He meets two policemen, one white, one black. They stop him and demand his pass. He observes that the black policeman is more aggressive and antagonistic than the white one. After this he is confronted by robbers as he walks through a forest, but they scatter in flight when they think that he is taking a pistol from his bag. Next he is stopped by two angry Boers on horseback who speak harshly to him, swearing and threatening to beat him up with their sjamboks. They are shortly joined by another, older Boer who turns out to be their father, and who is even more aggressive. Dondolo escapes by sheer luck. These and the other characters he meets fulfill their roles and are forgotten as soon as the particular crisis is resolved and the protagonist turns his back on them. As transitory examples, they need have no names. In fact the descriptive labels they are given—"policemen," "robbers," "Boers"—and terms such as "Herdboys" and "girl novitiates undergoing initiation," which are used to describe later groups, are more important than names, for they have a connotative significance that makes the sophisticated reader expect specific kinds of unpleasant confrontations between them and the protagonist. To reinforce this, the protagonist-cum-narrator concludes each episode with an Aesopian-style moral arising out of that episode.

Yet another feature of the anonymity concept is "group characterization," which always involves peripheral characters. Such groups are either amorphous, being temporarily mobilized around a transient topic of interest as in Dhlomo's courthouse scene, or identified by some special feature that they hold in common. Examples of the latter include the girls and the women in illustrations (1), (2), and (3), where peer group solidarity is the basis of their flocking together, and "the detectives" investigating Thomas Gwebu's death, who are held together by a common profession. These detectives, one may mention in passing, provide another variety of the disembodied voice as they speak to the government doctor who is examining the corpse. As "the detectives" ask the doctor the nature of Gwebu's stab wound, an abstracted "voice" speaks for the group as a whole. (Abaseshi babheke engosini yendlu befuna abakufunayo. Bese bebuzisisa kudotela wakwaHulumeni: "Inxeba linjani dotela elimbulele?" —The detectives searched in the far interior of the house looking for whatever they were looking for. Then they questioned the government doctor closely: "How is the wound that caused his death, doctor?" [p. 62]). That is to say, the narrator does not say, *One of the detectives said . . .;* he says, *The detectives said . . .,* and then quotes the words spoken.

Whether they are amorphous or in common-feature clusters, group characters may intervene in the action and attempt to change the course of events. We saw excellent examples of this in (1), (2), and (3), where Mofolo makes "the women" chastise Senzangakhona with their tongues and appeal to the gods for intervention, and "the women" and "the girls" chide the cowardly behavior of the men and praise Chaka's valor with their songs, following the episode of the lion. To do this, the group characters involved have to be close to the center of action. But group characters may be peripheral to the main action and comment on it from the sidelines, as we have seen in the examples from Dhlomo. Either way, group characters constitute what might be called a "participating audience" within the story. Their verdicts on what is going on in the center are varied, and so are their reactions. Except when they are close to the center and try to influence events from going in the wrong direction, we are not necessarily expected to take them as a cue that tells us how to react to the actions of the protagonists. When they engage in "evil" gossip, we are, in fact, expected to avoid emulating them.

Conclusion

I suppose one would have to concede that some African prose fiction writers *intend* to write European-style novels, and *intend* to create "rounded" or fully individualized characters. That is their choice, and one would have to regard them in the same light as African-language poets who experimented with rhyme and, to a lesser extent, with syllabic metrical rhythm. The experimentation of course always has a potential for success. But regardless of whether it succeeds or fails, it is always exciting to venture into those new, unexplored avenues. If, in the process of experimenting, certain traditional or indigenous techniques continue to interfere, then it means that those techniques are demanding our attention, and we cannot afford to ignore them.

We confront precisely this kind of situation in the matter of "characterization." I think the concept of "peopling" a story would seem to be in tune with what happens in the creative works we have quoted and numerous others as well. Failing to create fully individualized characters is not all failure, as shown above, but is accompanied by varying degrees of success in the application of the concept of anonymity, whether the writer is conscious of it or not, whether he is striving for something else or not. Also, as indicated above, anonymity in characterization does not mean failure to produce a good, inspiring, and convincing story. We need only look at Thomas Mofolo's *Chaka,* which has received international acclaim, to see the truth of this assertion. *Chaka* simply thrives on anonymous characters both central and peripheral. Nandi, for example, is a partially anonymous character, in spite of the centrality of her role. This is underscored by the fact that Mofolo gives her no part in dialogue throughout the book. The only time we hear her voice is during the episode of the killing of the cowards, very far into the narrative, when she intervenes and begs her son to stop the killing. Senzangakhona, Nandi's husband and Chaka's father, another very important protagonist, says just one word in the story—"Mmolayeng!" ("Kill him!")—as he hands Chaka over to his enemies. In addition, there are numerous anonymous and partially anonymous characters who appear either singly or in groups and are at various distances from the center of the stage. Yet Mofolo's book is an undisputed international success.

This subtle play with lights and shadows in illuminating or obscuring the story people, ordering them singly or in clusters, controlling their distance from center stage, and making them virtually an audience within the story, is a heritage that has come down from oral narrative art. It is informed by aesthetic principles in which group identity is of parmount importance.

There may be some virtue in the fact that the technique of anonymity in characterization has, so far, been used quite unconsciously by the writers concerned, since that way it has, so far, not been exposed to the danger of having a rigid formal structure. Nevertheless, it is my opinion that the gains to the literature are likely to outweigh the disadvantages if the writer masters the technique and consciously applies it in his writing. If we, as literary critics, give exposure to what the writers have been doing all along, and simply help in formulating it into principles of literary composition by discovering its underlying laws, we would be doing a tremendous service to the literature by acting as mirrors in which the literary artist sees more clearly what he has done, and can, hopefully, improve on it. I do not see such an act as an exercise in prescriptive authority.

Works Cited

Dhlomo, R. R. R. *Indlela Yababi* (Pietermaritzburg: Shuter and Shuter, 1946 [3d ed., 1970]). *Zulu.*
Mofolo, Thomas. *Chaka* (Morija, 1925, [repr., 1957]). *Sesotho.*
Mofolo, Thomas. *Moeti oa Bochabela* (Morija, 1907 [repr., 1957]). *Sesotho.*
Mqhayi, S. E. K. *UDon Jadu* (Lovedale, 1929). *Xhosa.*
Ntsala, Mackenzie. *Sekhukhuni Se Bonoa Ke Sebatalali* (Johannesburg: South African Institute of Race Relations, 1954). *Sesotho.*
Sinxo, Guybon. *UNomsa,* (Lovedale, 1922). *Xhosa.*

CHAPTER 12

As a Sounding Brass and a Tinkling Cymbal— Modernist Fallacies and the Responsibility of the Black Writer

Mike Thelwell

> Yea, even though I speak with the tongues of men and of angels, and have not compassion; I am become as a sounding brass and a tinkling cymbal. . . . I am nothing.   —First Corinthians 13.6.

> In America when I was younger the term black literature referred to only one country . . . America. Talking about black literature today one is really talking about the world . . . about Brazil, Nigeria. . . . We had been dealing with, controlled by really, a vocabulary coming out of an arbitrary invention called Europe, where the frame of reference has always and only been Europe itself. That frame of reference has shifted and a new vocabulary is needed.
>
>   —James Baldwin, *New York Times* Interview, 1979

> A writer dies inside when he betrays, like a paid spy, the rhythm of his race.   —Derek Walcott

    Responsibility, of any sort, is not a term having much currency in the fashionable gibberish of our age. It clearly is not a concept with which the modernist mood is comfortable in any context, save perhaps, where it finds expression in those tiresome and redundant formulations of bourgeois egotism, for example, "one's responsibility to one's self," "to one's inner being," "to one's private vision," *ad nauseum*. On these rare occasions of uncomfortable association we are almost certain to hear of the writer's paramount responsibility to his private *vision* and to his *Art,* quite as though both had, in splendid isolation, sprung full-grown from his fevered genius like Athena from the forehead of Zeus, untouched by human society, history, politics, or culture. "Art," in this usage, has a meaning not unlike God in another, somewhat older usage: at once mystical and transcendent, it

---

Michael Thelwell is a Professor at the W.E.B. DuBois Department of Afro-American Studies at the University of Massachusetts/Amherst

is all-demanding, all-consuming, the object of ultimate concern yet displaying a charmingly paradoxical democratic aspect in that it is quite willing to assume whatever arbitrary and eccentric form the peculiar needs and obsessions of its worshiper and creator may dictate.

The subject of this paper, however, is precisely responsibility—a responsibility neither private nor subjective which all Black writers share, whether they choose to recognize it or not. This responsibility seems to me so clear, so unambiguous, so historical, so self-evident, and so absolute that failure to recognize it would necessitate either willed blindness or egregious stupidity on the part of a writer who is black. In addition, such a failure of perception and consciousness calls into question not only the writer's intelligence and seriousness, but also causes us to doubt fundamentally the value of the entire literary undertaking. The question is inescapable: Why would any black person, representative by definition of an oppressed people, espouse the obsessively subjective and private reasons that modernists give as their motivation, aesthetic concerns, and literary preoccupations? And given these preoccupations and purposes, should anyone read the results, much less regard them seriously?

Surely, our increasingly narcissistic world abounds with ways and means of exorcising personal trauma short of writing them down and boring the public. "A little sincerity is a dangerous thing," said Oscar Wilde, "more bad poetry having been created out of sincere feeling than from any other source." I am a firm believer that if one suffers from guilt or insecurity one should undertake psychoanalysis; if haunted by ghosts and demons, see a priest; if beset with sexual inadequacies of any sort, consult the encouraging variety of therapists, professionals, and experts which now exists. If the problem is marital in origin, one can, depending on its seriousness, get a divorce, buy a whip, or establish separate bedrooms; for naked self-expression I am given to understand that a loud scream in the night is far more immediate and satisfying than scribbling endlessly; and if the problem is one of repressed aggressions, one can always either get drunk and wreck the bar or join the armed services, thereby with a single act improving both the nation's defenses and its literature.

I should make it clear that the following discussion is devoted specifically to the novel, although much of my argument has implications for drama, despite the marked differences in the material requirements, cultural ancestry, and potential of the two forms. Modernist poetry is not included, that phenomenon having advanced entirely too far into the upper reaches of arbitrary subjectivism, preciosity, and privatist aestheticism to be considered anything other than therapy. I am unable to perceive in that particular thicket much evidence of the shared conventions of meaning, form, purpose, communication, and intention which would make it accessible to rational and productive discussion. Undoubtedly the failing is mine, because a similar imaginative failure prohibits me from seeing anything but an ink blot in one of Rhorschach's cards. Yet, I am told that there are those people to whom these ink smears are profoundly and wonderfully meaningful. And, indeed, my aesthetically more advanced colleagues are able to fill volumes with eloquent and closely reasoned explications of the mysteries of modernist poetics. To my poor benighted mind, alas, these explications shed, not a dim or feeble light, but no light at all upon the explicated. Just as the latter seems beyond poetry so the criticism hovers on the outer fringes of prose, having passed into those rarified altitudes of semantics and sensibility where a poor, culturally deprived West Indian Negro such as I am quite incapable of following. Thus, I can offer no useful discussion of modernist poetry: the widespread practice of explaining the already sufficiently obscure by means of the more obscure is one that I gladly concede to my modernist colleagues. But, this is the only concession that I am prepared to make . . . willingly.

You may well be wondering exactly what all this has to do with the culture of the Black World and its novelists? Unfortunately, as I hope to show, a great deal too much, in far too many cases, for the health of our literature. But since it would be unseemly of me to commit here the very sins of self-indulgent assertion in the absence of evidence or history for which I have been berating the modernists, I had best turn first to some basic questions of definition and cultural history.

The movement in European culture (which my good friends on that excellent Pan-African journal *Okike* love to characterize as "Euro-modernists obscurantism") is the result of developments among elements of the European bourgeoisie between the wars. It is important to take some time to understand precisely what modernism was and was not in its origins because both cases are at some distance from the picture that is generally presented today. Modernism patently and emphatically was *not* a spontaneous response of mainstream European artists to a new historical reality. That is to say it was not some spontaneous and inevitable historical expression of Western cultural necessity, as claimed by its proponents, unless *all* of Western culture was more spiritually depleted, morally bankrupt, and creatively exhausted than can conceivably have been the case. It was and is an expression of bourgeois literary style and fashion: the capricious and arbitrary creation of a small, identifiable, and recondite element of the bourgeois avant-garde, whose neurotic egotism, distressing and unhealthy personal lives, and political conservatism it expressed. For example, quite apart from their work, one does not have to study at any length (I have not and have no interest in doing so) the biographies of T. S. Eliot, Ezra Pound, Marcel Proust, André Gide, Gertrude Stein, James Joyce, Sigmund Freud, Virginia Woolf, and Samuel Beckett (to name those luminaries of the modernist movement who come readily to mind) in order to conclude that collectively they were as self-obsessed, unpleasant, and eccentric a group of people as one could hope to avoid having to meet. So, even though, it seems to me, the modernist movement represents a capricious minority that became inordinately influential, its rise and its dominance over European art and letters suggest that there might indeed be some grounds for arguing that modernism was an expresson of some deep malaise in European bourgeois culture.

It is perhaps a simplification, but for our purposes a necessary simplification of a complex and ambiguous development, to say that the modernist revolt was essentially one of style, or more acurately, of content disguised as style—an open and unabashed call to an aesthetic elitism of bourgeois sensiblity. Its influence manifested itself in music, painting, and the theater, as well as in poetry and prose. While there were at times flurries of progressive and humanist expression—most usually in painting and theater—modernism was more characteristically the excuse and justification for a general retreat from the wide-ranging engagement with social and moral questions which had characterized the best of nineteenth-century European literature. In the novel, modernism generally rejected realism and the broad and humane social vision and moral concern that had characterized the great Russian, French, and English novelists of the previous century, in favor of formalist experimentation for its own sake, a celebration of aestheticism, the cult of the individual consciousness and sensibility, and the internalizaton of experience and concern. While it contributed a number of technical innovations—which when put to serious purpose could and did add to the arsenal of technical devices available to the novelist and thus to the flexibility and capability of the form—modernism was not in its essence either a progressive or regenerating development. It was a retreat into emptiness.

When the novel abandons realism—that is, the obligation to recreate, crystallize, sharpen, and illumine human experience in ways that are recognizable and realistic, against a setting of accurate social and political detail; the obligation to capture credible and convincing psychological and class motivation and responses in its characters—when it in effect abandons history and cultural reality, what is left it? It has but three avenues: (1) a turning inward to private fantasy and the exploration of the sores and lesions of the novelist's psyche; (2) experimentation with form, in which complexity of language and structure become their own ends and stylistic eccentricity is substituted for content; and (3) related to that, a literariness, the cannibalization of the past, the picking over of the corpses of earlier works. Instead of dealing with the world, the novel must turn to writing about writers and about writing—composing elaborate literary puzzles replete with allusions, references, borrowings from, and parodies of earlier works. "Art" becomes the subject of art.

All these developments represent a truly monstrous abandonment of the artist's responsibility as it had been conceived in the humanistic traditions of Western art. I would remind you that one central evidence of decadence in a literary tradition is the arrival of that historical moment at which the creation of new and vital formulations and interpretations of cultural reality becomes secondary to the parody and cannibalization of earlier works.

Marxists argue that these developments were the inevitable consequences of a backlash among a self-centered, morally bankrupt bourgeoisie that, politically threatened and traumatized by events in Russia, consciously turned away from any engagement with the irresolvable class contradiction and social injustice implicit in bourgeois privilege. That thesis may be a trifle too schematic; I am not sure. But what is absolutely clear is that the emergence and rise of modernism in Europe represented a rather abrupt turning away from what had been the first responsibility of the novelist—that of *communicating* generally shared and accessible truth and perceptions, which implicitly must mean socially and culturally derived insights and knowledge. In the celebration of the individual consciousness, communication became secondary to "self-expression," no matter how arcane, private, and neurotic in its inspiration. Similarly, the emphasis on literary allusion (cannibalism), elaborate structural invention, and private reference as ends in themselves is obviously not geared primarily to communication. James Joyce, a celebrated pioneer down these literary cul-de-sacs, is alleged to have boasted that only four people fully understood *Finnegan's Wake* and that two of them were dead. While the story may be apocryphal, the reverence in the voice of the teacher who told it to me was not—and that is significant. It was also said of Joyce, by no means the worst offender among the modernists, that it used to be that novelists were men of wide learning and broad interests in human events. What Joyce demonstrated was that all a novelist needed to know was himself. Regrettably, that lesson is *not* lost on many among my brothers and sisters.

Unfortunately the story does not end there; there is a related development that has had an even greater impact on the literatures and cultures we are interested in. Under well-deserved attack from a public that felt, with excellent reason, that it was being put upon, patronized, and ripped off by the self-centered and arrogant effusions of modernism, this movement generated a gang of critical fellow travelers—the priests and proselytizers for the new dispensation. These rascals developed—as priests will—an elaborate critical gospel in defense and explanation of the faith. Although these explanations made no more sense than the art they were intended to explain, significant elements of the doctrine and dogma invented by the clerisy lurk to this day in the dark crevices and corners of the academy, just waiting to pounce upon and infect the susceptible minds of the young. These are the influences that are infecting black modernists, for I suspect that most of them do not read the Torah; instead they only receive the commentaries.

These critical justifications are, however, much more insidious than the works themselves. They seek to render what should really be considered aberrations of false consciousness and egotism as necessary and inevitable expressions of "the modern condition" and "the state of the culture." The style and content of modernism, they argue, was appropriate to the times, for the conditions of realism could no longer express the alienated condition of man in modern society (they were too coherent and made too much sense). Nor could the traditional modes of realism any longer adequately express the fragmented, self-conflicted psyche of modern man, living as he does in a state of high anxiety, emotional isolation, and spiritual desolation. It is the peculiar arrogance of the bourgeois intelligentsia to generalize a universal from their own neurotic dysfunction: the ills of the bourgeoisie becoming, in their assertion, the very essence of the human condition. Thus, the basic issue became not the creative exhaustion of the avant-garde, not their intellectual arrogance and self-celebration, not their moral aberration and lack of artistic discipline and political vision—in a word, their decadence of mind and spirit. No, it was *human existence* itself that was blighted, suddenly inchoate, and void of value and meaning. Where once human beings had walked, robots, ciphers, and humanoids now rattled aimlessly around the mechanistic wasteland of an industrial mass society shrouded in gloomy and suffocating existentialist smog.

Thus, modernist art was *necessary*; all the artist was doing was struggling to escape the grasp of dead convention to create those necessary new forms, devices and structures by which this grim new reality might be apprehended and expressed. This has to be the most outrageous and transparently self-serving excrement ever served up in the interest of justifying decadence. And not only that, if one failed to recognize just how splendidly the modernist mode—through a triumph of the individual will, the anguished visions of alienated geniuses—had forged the language, forms, and modalities to reflect the disjointedness of the age, one had only one's own undeveloped sensibility to blame.

This aesthetic shell game traded on bourgeois insecurity. It was not any newer than the emporer's spring outfit, but it worked wondrously well at intimidating bourgeois audiences who demonstrated that they would endure any boredom, accept any insult to their intelligence rather than be found out of step with intellectual fashion, or be thought deficient in taste or sensibility.

The working classes were having none of it, however. They knew what they liked, and modernist excretia was not it; they stopped reading the stuff. There is evidence that the European working class once participated to a surprising degree in intellectual life, had actually read and been instructed by serious novels in the nineteenth century. (The London poor, for example, are said to have devoured the serialized novels of Charles Dickens, recognizing therein a faithful depiction of their lives and social circumstances.)

Over time, literary modernism—once shocking and controversial—became the orthodoxy of our time. Once "daring and experimental," it passed rapidly into cliché, then to doctrine and now into sacred dogma, so enshrined in the hearts and minds of the Western literary establishment that its tenets are not even critically examined anymore. It would be of little concern to me that modernist dogma lay over the West like a toxic cloud impoverishing the literature and reducing the phrase "critical thought" to a hollow mockery. The problem, however, is that, like other of the West's toxic wastes, it seeps out of Europe and America and poisons the wellsprings of the Black World—a most insidious form of cultural colonialism. As a result of modernism's effect, our literature is in danger of bypassing maturity and plunging directly from infancy to decadence.

First, let us attempt a description of literary modernism in its contemporary incarnation.

In the contemporary modernist novel the emphasis is on fragmentation rather than coherence. Elements of experience never coalesce into meaning, and the part is frequently greater than the whole. Its style runs to pastiche, collage, and willful and eccentric distortion rather than organic and intelligible meaning. The contemporary modernist novel is a function of shattered mirrors and refracted images, a mockery of purposeful intelligence and communication in favor of glib and easy effects. It is quite useless for the projection of political and moral vision or statement. Its tone is parodic and its impulses contemptuous—both of the reader and of observable reality. It essays contempt and succeeds only in being contemptible.

The mood of modernist fiction: gloomy, fashionably cynical, sneering at all save its own preoccupations with obscurity of allusion and gratutious structural complexity—all for no discernible artistic reason.

Its literary preoccupations: images of sickness and perversion; physical deformity and grotesquerie as emblems of moral deficiency. It lacks the passion to be erotic and is only pornographic; a pornography of the spirit. Where it occurs, sex is either mechanical, grim, and joyless, or violent, perverted, and exploitative.

The rendering of character: originality is much evoked, by which the authors seem to mean that a character who acts in ways previously consecrated by human behavior is insufficiently original. This view leads, ironically, to a predictable aberration: modernist characters must not obey any recognizable pattern of human motivation and response. Yet, it *is* possible to predict certain things about these modernist originals: there will be no discernible reason for their actions. Given a choice they will choose the sensationally perverse, the morally disgusting, the degrading, but these choices will be so arbitrary and eccentric as to have neither meaning or effect. But they will be *original*.

Another modernist value: inventiveness, a facility for creating new forms of perversity. To take some examples from recent Black American fiction: a mother douses her sleeping son with kerosene and roasts him; a woman bites off her lover's genitals. Even inventiveness has its conventions: thus, any young black woman in certain kinds of fiction must be sexually abused during adolescence by an older male relative. Inventiveness is shown by the choice of relative, the circumstances in which the act occurs, and the ingenuity with which the act is rendered as painful, humiliating, and traumatic as is humanly imaginable.

Now, let us turn to the processes by which modernism is diffused into the cultures of the African world, Black America, and the Caribbean. This diffusion takes place as a result of myth and institutions. Young Black writers frequently find themselves in Western institutions of higher education whose departments of literature have long been hotbeds of modernism. (An African or Caribbean university is a Western institution.) Here at the hands of the clerisy the young writer learns the catechism and, unless the student has a highly developed sense of literature and of his or her national cultural imperatives, that student emerges like the previous generation of colonized intellectuals: a zealous convert to the inevitability of Western literary fashion. The second institution is the bourgeois publishing establishment. Unless the young Black writer is from a country that has made a decisive break with the practices and traditions of its colonial past and also established a national publishing house or indigenous industry, he will find himself seeking publication in the West, as many of us are forced to. This is unhealthy because the Western publishing establishment is effectively in the hands of the disciples of modernism. These editors generally have no concept of the Black World, and see no reason why their own inclinations and preoccupations should not be perfectly adequate for expressing the experience of these countries. They are not inhibited by judgment, modesty, or humility from imposing their literary taste on the young Black's work, or at least trying to do so. Moreover, they have no political or economic interest in Black novelists who wish to address their own people. To them the Black novelist is to function as a kind of foreign correspondent for the West, their novels being nothing more than literary dispatches sent back to titillate the bourgeois audience and to reaffirm its preconceptions of the Black World. In their defense it should be said that these editors are only serving their own gods and cultural consituencies—their class interests, if you will. Too many Black writers refuse to see that these interests are not and cannot be the same as ours.

Closely allied to the publishers is the Western critical establishment, long since the captive and tool of the modernists. Literally all of the influential journals of literary opinion in the West are firmly in the control of some coterie, cult, or sect of the modernist dispensation. These organs tend to seek out and bring to prominence those writers of the non-European world who best demonstrate that they have ingested and can regurgitate modernist style and dogma in their work. Seeing this situation, young Black writers begin to think that the path to literary success lies in imitating those of their number who have won the accolades of the bourgeois press. Thus, the modernist movement—which at this point has exhausted any limited contributions it could make to literature—appears all-encompassing, authoritative, pervasive, and inevitable. It represents "high" literature. To some of us one is not a respectable and respected writer until the *New York Review of Books* and the two *Times*es (London and New York) have certified that fact. This attitude has consequences that are quite unhealthy for indigenous literary development. Consciously or otherwise, one responds to the pressure to address one's work to the critics of these organs, rather than to one's own people, unless one is very clear about one's purposes in writing and the responsibilities incurred in doing so.

Any Black writer who writes about black peoples, societies, and cultures but who addresses his work not to the people who are his subjects but to the Western literati is nothing but an exploiter of his own. Such a writer accepts and perpetuates the colonial mission in literature begun by the Kiplings and Conrads of the imperial age.

This phenomenon raises another very important and troublesome question. How is it that so many writers of the Black World—men and women who in their private and public discourse seem wondrously clear on questions of history and imperialism, who seem sophisticated and clear-eyed, even militant, in their nationalism, whose economic analyses are impeccable—seem to become totally recolonized when they sit down to write fiction? Why, in so many cases, do they either not see an alternative or not feel a need to avoid adopting Western modes, Western perspectives, even Western biases.

One can only conclude that the literary recolonization of Black writers—a colonization of style, purpose, implied audience, literary concern, and intention—is possible only to the extent that we do not subject Western literary myths and assumptions to the same searching scrutiny we give to their political motives, interests, actions, and rhetoric. Yet, in fact, the relationship between the two areas is close—even symbiotic—and certainly their ancestry is the same.

What, for example, are the fundamental cultural assumptions that lurk behind all the uncritical prattle about "the Artist" and "the Universal"—concepts that are among the most sacred of the cows in the herd of Western literary pieties. When we are told (as I was as an undergraduate by a charming Irish lady who taught "the humanities" in a black college) that all literature has the same audience—"the international community of educated men and women"—what assumptions are implicit in that apparently innocuous vocabulary? I doubt the good lady professor had any notion precisely how Europocentric, culturally chauvinist, and reductive that formulation really was.

When Black writers accept the mission consciously to act as "universal artists," as so many of them do ("I don't want to be merely a black writer, I want to be a writer"), what are they in fact agreeing to? Does the term "Universal" describe anything in reality? Who today dismisses Aeschylus or Sophocles as parochial and limited simply because they created only Greek characters, worked within a narrowly hellenistic cultural and religions frame of reference, and addressed only a Greek audience? Or Faulkner because his characters are all narrowly regional and from the backwaters of America?

But a black editor of that bumptiously avant-garde, Third World journal *Yardbird* asked Chinua Achebe to describe the nature of his interest in creating a particular character. Significantly, the editor seemed interested only in the one of Achebe's characters who had traveled to Europe. Achebe answered: "I am working on the notion that he [the character in question] becomes a mythic figure and a person who tests the limits, not only of a tribal person, or a person with a *national* identity, but in fact he becomes a kind of universal figure and tests *human* limits" (editors' emphasis).

Under the circumstances Achebe's restraint was exemplary, perhaps too much so. For, two pages later, apparently not satisfied that he had made himself clear, the brother returns to worry the issue: "But were you thinking of him as reflective of broad universal human characteristics? You didn't just aim this for a *Nigerian* audience?" (emphasis mine). Perhaps, I reflected upon reading this passage, the broadest, most universal human characteristic is stupidity.

Similarly, what exactly—especially in modernist parlance—is meant by "Artist"? Does the term still describe anything useful, and is it a description to which any self-respecting Black honorably can aspire? What was otherwise an extremely intelligent, articulate, and culturally informed review of *The Harder They Come* by a Black academic concludes with the following language: "Thelwell views himself as a political writer, a cultural nationalist, an activist. But what this novel admirably demonstrates is that he is first of all a consummate artist."[1] First of all? Hardly. Of course I think I know what was intended, but is the unexamined dichotomy really inevitable? Are the categories "artist" and "cultural nationalist," or "political writer," truly incompatible. To the modernist mind they clearly are. To my thinking, however, any Black novelist who is not consciously and purposefully a cultural nationalist is an aberration. If modernists insist on the dichotomy our choice is clear. As effective as are the institutions in literary colonization, that is, the universities, publishers, and critical journals, they would be ineffective if we ourselves were not so uncritical of certain fundamental assumptions about literature, culture, the role of the novel, and the purposes of the novelist which underlie the mythology.

Because, even if modernist perceptions of the state of western culture and the role of the novel therein were accurate, so far as the West is concerned (I suspect they are not and have succeeded only in rendering the novel quite irrelevant as a serious force in cultural and social life), they certainly do not describe the situation in the Black World. To accept them is to suggest that the West and the Black World are at the same historical point in cultural development. They are not. We are evolving, forming, and creating a vital cultural and literary tradition while similar traditions in the West are clearly degenerating.

The cultural and historical situation of the Black World demands entirely different aesthetic, artistic, and literary imperatives and purposes at this time. Among our people the novel has *not* exhausted its usefulness, has not run its course. In the nineteenth century when European nationalism was emerging, the great novelists of Europe played a signal role in defining national character and a shared sense of cultural and national identity. The Black novel has not yet given to our people those unifying images of their historical experience and identity. Their lives, their culture, their national experience and consciousness, the struggle and travail of their forefathers—they have yet to see these things clarified, distilled, crystallized, made available and accessible through serious, realistic, artistically responsible political novels. We owe that to our people and to history. If ever a generation of writers had a clear, inescapable historical responsibility, it has to be the generation of Black writers coming to maturity at this point in the Black struggle for cultural autonomy, national identity, and integrity in the world.

In an exchange with me, the good professor Irving Howe suggested that I oppose V. S. Naipaul's work because I want to see Black culture and experience produce political tracts rather than "honest novels."[2] I quote from my reply: first, an honest novel of Black life is addressed primarily to the Black World, for purposes and about issues that are serious and important in the context of their cultures. Such a novel does not distort the experience and consciousness of a people by imposing the now discredited and alien point of view which informs the colonial novels of the Carys, Kiplings, and Conrads of the imperial age, a tradition in which the Black World and its peoples are mere backdrops and ciphers onto which any nonsense can be forced. Such a novel must proceed organically and naturally out of the sensibilities, cultural traditions, and linguistic styles of the people who are its subject.

Such a novel cannot proceed out of a glib, fashionable modernist cynicism—an unearned despair in which everything is beyond human effort. Rather, it must be predicated on the assumptions that there is a future for which to struggle; that present conditions however grim are not beyond the reach of the people's decency, will, and intelligence; and that the writing and reading of such novels are not only testaments to that faith, but integral parts of that struggle.

An honest novel of the Black World seeks to contribute to the people's evolving sense of their historical and cultural identity and a shared sense of national purpose. To the extent that such novels succeed, they will in part create their audience. This is a challenge and an honor not given to Western novelists today. Any black writer who forgoes this gift of history in favor of catering to the Western bourgeoisie is condemned not by egotistic ambitions and vanity, but by a colossal stupidity.

Honest novels of the Black World seek to make a contribution to the evolving form, to the content and purposes of a vital, modern, and purposeful tradition of black literature. They do not seek to latch unto a moribund and thoroughly discredited colonial tradition that serves only to exploit, patronize, and mutilate our cultures for frivolous if not sinister reasons. And these are responsibilities; responsibilities not to our "Art" our "Visions" our "Genius," but to our people, our cultures—and most of all to our children.

Notes

1. *Richmond Times-Dispatch,* Prof. Daryle Dance, 7 July 1980.
2. Letter to *New York Times Book Review,* 24 June 1979.

VII
Pan-Africanism and Development in the African World

Africa Series II, David P. Bradford

CHAPTER 13

Pan-Africanism, A Contemporary Restatement: Fundamental Goals and Changing Strategies

W. Ofuatey-Kodjoe

Like socialism, Pan-Africanism is one of those terms which is much used and often little understood. There seems to be a great deal of confusion about the meaning of the term—confusion not only among lay people but also among scholars. For example, one commentator has defined it as an "organization, a system of beliefs, an ideology, a symbolic goal which is derived from the French Revolution, Marxism, Wilsonian idealism, Gandhism and Garveyism!"[1] This confusion exists even within the ranks of self-proclaimed Pan-Africanists.[2]

The Problem of Definition

Though the confusion about the concept of Pan-Africanism has led some observers to conclude it is impossible to define,[3] there are serious reasons why we must make an attempt. First, it is precisely this confusion that has been responsible for some of the most serious setbacks of the Pan-African movement.[4] Second, as many Pan-African conferences have demonstrated, no serious discussion of the concept can proceed without some agreement on its meaning.[5] What follows, therefore, is an attempt to restate as clearly as possible the nature and content of Pan-Africanism in the light of historical experience, and to suggest its implications for African peoples in their present circumstance.

Toward a Definition

Any definition is an imposition of conceptual categories on facts and, in that sense, all definitions are arbitrary. This situation need not cause any undue concern, however, once the definition provides us with the ability to differentiate the phenomenon it purports to define from other things.[6] If a definition is to accomplish this end, we must first identify the type of facts which we hope to encompass within its

---

Dr. W. Ofuatey-Kodjoe is the Director of the Africana Studies and Research Institute at Queens College (CUNY) in New York City

conceptual net. Therefore, in order to define Pan-Africanism it is necessary to make some statements about the type of data we are looking for.

First, Pan-Africanism is a body of *ideas* (beliefs, opinions, convictions, etc.), in much the same way that socialism and fascism are bodies of ideas. Obviously, Pan-Africanism may differ from these thought systems with respect to its precision, theoretical rigor, and so on, but like them it is a system of ideas.

The identification of Pan-Africanism as a body of ideas has crucial analytical significance, for it immediately directs our investigation to the writings of those who have presented these ideas—the Pan-Africanists. It may be argued, however, that identifying a Pan-Africanist is bound to be problematic until we know what Pan-Africanism is. To solve this problem, we might begin our analysis by looking at the organizational activities of self-proclaimed Pan-Africanists, hoping to establish the core of their objectives and their strategies. From this core of organizational objectives we can proceed to consider the more theoretical formulations that seem to constitute the basis of these objectives.

As an axiomatic point of departure, let us posit that a Pan-Africanist organization is formed for the purpose of propagating, disseminating, and attempting to actualize the ideas of Pan-Africanism. Let us say further that a Pan-African *movement* exists when several Pan-Africanist organizations are engaged in relatively frequent collaboration for the pursuit of their common objectives. To put it simply, Pan-Africanism is a body of ideas held by Pan-Africanists, some of whom are active in Pan-Africanist organizations, and many of these organizations maintain collaborative relationships with each other in what can be characterized as a Pan-African movement.[7] Thus, to define Pan-Africanism we must first identify the Pan-African movement and analyze the purpose and strategies that have characterized it.

The Pan-African Movement

The fascinating story of the origin and development of the Pan-African movement has been told elsewhere,[8] and we will attempt only a brief outline in order to highlight its fundamental goals, the ideas that underpin these goals, and the strategies that have been adopted for their achievement.

The birth of the Pan-African *movement* can be traced to the formation of the African Association in London in 1897, under the leadership of Henry Sylvester Williams.[9] This organization had two attributes that are relevant to the present discussion. First, it was made up of "several representative members of the [Black] race;"[10] second, its purpose was "to promote and protect the interests of all subjects claiming African descent, wholly or in part, in British colonies and other places, especially in Africa."[11] The first conference of this organization was called the Pan-African Conference, a name chosen to demonstrate two fundamental characteristics: that membership was open to all people of African descent, and that it was committed to all Africans whatever they may be. As Bishop Alexander Walters, the conference chairman described it: "For the first time in the history of the world, *Black men had gathered together from all over the world—with the object of discussing and improving the conditon of the Black race.*"[12]

Since the establishment of the African Association, many other Pan-Africanist organizations have been formed: Comité de Defence De La Race Negre, League of Coloured Peoples, the Universal Negro Improvement Association, the International African Service Bureau and the All-African Peoples' Organization, to name but a few. Some of these organizations have lasted longer than others, some have been more successful, and they have differed as to tactics and membership.[13] But all have accepted the *oneness* of all people of African descent and committed themselves to their betterment. This shared characteristic of Pan-African *membership* and Pan-African *commitment* defines all these organizations as Pan-Africanist. At any time, then, the Pan-African *movement* can be thought of as the collectivity of those Pan-Africanist organizations that recognize that they share this fundamental commitment and therefore maintain a more or less collaborative relationship with each other, sharing some (but not necessarily all) meetings, conferences, and other activities.

The Ideology of Pan-Africanism

To the extent that political action is purposeful, it must be predicated on some conscious link in the minds of political actors between their goals and their assessment of the situational context.[14] The programmatic activities of people organized in an association or a movement therefore imply the existence of a collective consciousness of goals as well as a shared perception of the historical-social context within which the organization has to operate. This group consciousness may be explicitly stated in major theoretical expositions, or pieced together from manifestos and declarations. In either case it provides the total intellectual world of the organization or movement, including its view of the world, its goals, and its prescribed strategies. This body of ideas—representing the cognitive, normative, and strategic thought of the movement—constitutes its ideology.[15] In this sense, then, we can say that Pan-Africanism is the ideology of the Pan-African movement—an ideology that expresses its world view, its fundamental goals, and its strategies as they have evolved over the years. On this basis, we can delineate the content of the ideology of Pan-Africanism by referring to the basic character and fundamental goals of the Pan-African movement, as well as to the discussions within the movement on both its operational environment and the alternative strategies available to it.

As we have already established, the Pan-African movement is basically a movement by which people of African descent have sought to advance their own welfare. On this basis, Pan-Africanism reveals itself as an ideology with a cognitive component that recognizes all African peoples, both in Africa and in the diaspora, as constituting one folk, or nation; an evaluative component that deplores the condition of this nation and is committed to enhancing its welfare and prestige; and a strategic component (or more accurately, several contending strategies) for the achievement of this goal.

Pan-Africanism is thus a *nationalist ideology,* since it incorporates within itself the two characteristics common to all nationalist ideologies, namely, the identification of a nationality and the commitment to the empowerment of that nationality.[16] In Pan-Africanism the relevant nationality is defined to include all Africans and peoples of African descent. It is this commitment to all peoples of African descent, regardless of the political boundaries that separate them, that makes it a pan-national ideology, similar to Pan-Slavism, Pan-Germanism, or Pan-Turanianism.[17] These two aspects of the Pan-Africanist ideology—the idea of an African nationality and the commitment to the empowerment of that nationality—demand closer scrutiny.

The African Nationality

Like advocates of other nationalisms,[18] Pan-Africanists believe that all peoples of African descent belong to the (pan) African nation on the basis of a shared cultural identity, a shared historical experience, and most important, an indivisible future destiny.

Common Identity

The Pan-Africanist assertion that all peoples of African descent share a common identity is based on the notion that they share to a significant extent a culture that separates them from non-Africans. The argument is not that all Black people are exactly alike. It is acknowledged that local conditions have imparted a peculiar local flavor to each Black community, thus making it possible to distinguish between West Indian, Afro-American, Afro-Brazilian, West African, and East African. Indeed, differences are recognized even within each of these large African communities: southerners and northerners in Afro-America; Trinidadians, Jamaicans, and others in the West Indies; Nigerians, Senegalese, and others in West Africa; and even smaller tribal communities within these groups. Pan-Africanists hold that a fundamental cultural unity transcends all these local differences in a way that has been significant for the history of these people.[19] This cultural unity is represented by a complex of values variously described as Blackness, Negritude,[20] Melamism,[21] or the African Personality,[22] and there is some debate as to its actual content. But regardless of the name they use, Pan-Africanists agree that it represents "the whole complex of civilized values—cultural, economic, social and political—which characterizes the black people, or, more precisely, the Negro-African world."[23]

Common Experience

The characteristics that a people select to represent their cultural identity and to differentiate themselves from others have varied widely. In some cases, a common language has been considered the badge of national identity; in other cases religion, and so on.[24] Whatever these characteristics have been, however, they have always been chosen because they are an important factor in the collective experience of the group. Thus, when a nationality has been persecuted or oppressed on the basis of its religion, as in Northern Ireland, that religion is cherished as a badge of identity. The Pan-

Africanist has chosen the skin color of the African as a symbol or badge to represent the cultural complex that defines his national identity, for skin color has been the identifying characteristic used to justify the exploitation, oppression, and dehumanization of African peoples everywhere.

As the Pan-Africanist sees it, wherever the African has been, whether in America, the Caribbean, or in Africa, his experience—the Black experience—has seen virtually the same exploitation, persecution, discrimination, and spiritual violation at the hands of non-Africans—all of these acts justified on the basis of an elaborate but specious ideological edifice that alleges the subhumanity, savagery, and inferiority of Black people. As Julius Nyerere put it:

> From the very beginnings of this movement, until now, men and women of Africa, and of African descent, have had one thing in common—an experience of discrimination and humiliation imposed upon them because of their African origins. Their color was made into both a badge, and a cause of their poverty, their humiliation and their oppression.[25]

Common Destiny

For the Pan-Africanist, the idea that all African peoples share a common destiny is simply a matter of projecting into the future what has occurred in the past. For the Pan-Africanist, an accurate view of the world emphasizes that the fact of his race has been an important factor in how the African has been dealt with by non-Africans. This is a fact of life. Whatever the achievements of an African, he is accorded essentially the same treatment that Africans generally receive. If the group as a whole is respected, so too are its members, even the loneliest one. If the group is despised, the most renowned member of that group faces the same contempt. For the Pan-Africanist, then, all Africans stand or fall together. For him, the freedom or enslavement, dignity or degradation, greatness or weakness of all African peoples is indivisible.[26] In sum, Pan-Africanists maintain that on the basis of a common identity, a shared heritage, and an indivisible destiny, all African peoples should properly be seen as being of one nation.

The Commitment to National Empowerment

Belief in the common nationality of all African peoples is not by itself sufficient to characterize one as Pan-Africanist, for many who share the belief do not have a commitment to that nation. For instance, it is clear that Leopold Senghor believes in the existence of a Negro-African nation, but his commitment is not to that nation but instead to its assimilation or subsumption into what he describes as a Civilization of the Universal.[27] Pan-Africanists are separated from other Africans by their commitment to this African nation, in the same way that American nationalists are committed to the United States, Nigerian nationalists to the Nigerian nation, and Ewes to the Ewe nation. That is to say that Pan-Africanists consider the African nation the unit with which they most intensely and unconditionally identify themselves. To be a Pan-Africanist is to be able to declare "I was born in East Africa, I am Kikuyu and Kenyan, but for me, the *most important* thing is that I am African."

The logic of the Pan-Africanist commitment to the African nation derives from the common destiny of all Africans and the indivisibility of their fate. On that basis, Pan-Africanists maintain that the only way to guarantee their own freedom, dignity, and welfare is to enhance the power and prestige of the entire African nation. Thus, the fundamental goal of Pan-Africanism is the empowerment of all African peoples.

Pan-Africanist Strategies

While all Pan-Africanists agree on the fundamental goal, there has been a great deal of polemical debate, not unlike the debates among socialists, about the appropriate strategies to be adopted in pursuit of the fundamental goal. Different Pan-Africanists have advocated such different strategies as African regeneration, the liberation of colonial territories, African unity, and African socialism—the choice of strategy depending on their perceptions of the situation and their estimates of the possibilities open to them and the resources available.

This debate has been responsible, in part, for the confusion among scholars about the meaning of Pan-Africanism. In some cases commentators have confused strategies for fundamental objectives and have defined Pan-Africanism in terms of the strategies. Examples of this error are Rayford Logan's definition of Pan-Africanism as "self-government or independence by African nations south of the Sahara,"[28] and Apter and Coleman's interpretation of Pan-Africanism as "the building of larger African political unities."[29]

It is important to understand that while independence and unity are important interim goals, they are not the ultimate objectives of Pan-Africanism, but merely strategies called forth by the logic of the ideology in particular phases of the African revolution. These strategies, therefore, gain their coherence, their meaning, and their justification in the context of the ideology of Pan-Africanism, the ultimate goal of which is the empowerment of all African peoples in relation to non-Africans. In order to fully demonstrate this point, let us explore more closely the relationship between the ideology of Pan-Africanism and the various strategies that have emanated from it.

Pan-Africanism and the Strategy of Protest

During the early phases of the Pan-African movement, most of the organizations saw themselves as protest groups.[30] As they saw it, the problems facing Black people were discrimination and Jim Crow in the West, backwardness in Africa, and European threats against the integrity of the then independent Black states. Therefore, their interim objectives were: the maintenance of the independence of Abyssinia, Liberia, and Haiti; the end of discrimination against "civilized" Negroes; and the protection and positive "development" of the African natives by the European imperial authorities.[31] The intellectuals and elitists who controlled the movement during this phase were basically integrationist and reformist. They believed in a sort of liberal internationalism and held that their objective—the *eventual* realization of equality for Blacks through integration and assimilation—could be achieved through the good will of well-informed Europeans.[32] They therefore adopted a strategy of protest, petition, and publicity. Their activities centered on seminars and conferences, such as the DuBois Congresses, where they attempted to dramatize the plight of African peoples and issued appeals for their amelioration.[33]

Pan-Africanism and the Strategy of Black Zionism

Marcus Garvey's idea of the redemption and regeneration of Africa was an alternative strategy to assimilation. As Garvey put it, "Let us work towards the one glorious end of a free, redeemed and *mighty* nation."[34] In his view, there are certain immutable historical laws that account for the growth, development, and downfall of nations and peoples. For Garvey the key to the greatness of a people is power.[35]

> If we must have justice, we must be strong.... Let us not waste time in breathless appeals to the strong while we are weak, but lend our time, energy and effort to the accumulation of strength among ourselves by which we will voluntarily [sic] attract the attention of others.[36]

In other words, if African peoples were going to achieve equality, they had to acquire power and to acquire power they had to organize.

> Organization is a great power in directing the affairs of a race or nation toward a given goal. To properly develop the desires that are uppermost, we must first concentrate through some system or method, and there is none better than organization. Hence, the Universal Negro Improvement Association appeals to each and every Negro to throw in his lot with those of us who, through organization, are working for the universal emancipation of our race and the redemption of our common country, Africa.[37]

This organization would seek to liberate Africa and to create there "a government, a nation of our own, strong enough to lend protection to the members of our race scattered all over the world, and to compel the respect of the nations and the races of the earth."[38] Contrary to DuBois, Garvey recognized that Africans could not expect assistance from Europeans in accomplishing their liberation. Indeed, he expected resistance and therefore saw the need for struggle—even armed struggle.[39] His method, therefore, was to avoid dealing with whites unless absolutely necessary,[40] and instead to concentrate on increasing pride and self-confidence among African peoples through the manipulation of symbols, to gain a foothold in Africa and use it as a nucleus for the reestablishment of a great West African state through the *selective repatriation of suitable Afro-Americans*[41] and their cooperation on an equal footing with the Africans.[42]

Pan-Africanism and the Strategy of Colonial Independence

The Fifth Pan-African Congress (1945) marked a significant shift toward a radicalization of the ideology of Pan-Africanism. Not only was there a shift from elitism toward mass participation, but, more important, there was a shift from integrationist reformism toward a strategy of colonial liberation. Furthermore, it was intended that the liberated territory would be reconstructed along the lines of democratic socialism and that the ex-colonies would eventually be unified.[43] In pursuit of independence, Pan-Africanists settled on the method of nonviolent, noncooperative political action, although they reserved the right to use force as a last resort.[44]

The decision to liberate the colonial territories was made in the face of the fact that the colonial territories were geographically separated and frequently administered by different colonial governments. For the Pan-Africanists, however, the independence of the colonial territories was never an end in itself. Independence was an instrumental objective: a *sine qua non* for national reconstruction and African unity. As George Padmore put it:

> The revolution taking place in Africa is threefold. First, there is the struggle for national independence. Second is the social revolution which follows the achievement of independence and self-determination. And thirdly, Africans are seeking some form of regional unity as the forerunner of the United States of Africa. However, until the first is achieved *the energies of the people cannot be mobilized for the attainment of the second and third stages which are even more difficult than the first.*[45]

For Pan-Africanists, then, the utility of a colonial territory's independence depends on the extent to which it can contribute to the reconstruction of African society[46] and African unity.[47] On this latter point, Nyerere has noted that "the African national state is an *instrument* for the unification of Africa, and not for dividing Africa: African nationalism is meaningless, is dangerous, is anachronistic, if it is not at the same time Pan-Africanism."[43]

It is important to note, however, that before any consideration of unity, the usefulness of the independence of a colonial territory could be measured by the extent to which it contributed to the total liberation of Africa. As Kwame Nkrumah noted on the eve of the independence of Ghana, "The independence of Ghana is meaningless unless it is linked with the total liberation of Africa."[49] The justification for this position is predicated on the assumption that the equality and dignity of African peoples are indivisible. As the argument runs, the European justification for the exploitation of Africans is that *Africans* (not Kenyans, Yorubas, or Central Africans) are inferior. This being the case, the problem of the African can be solved not by the independence of one African state but only through the collective acquisition of power.

Pan-Africanism and the Strategy of African Unity

Like colonial independence, African unity was a strategy for dealing with the realities of the African situation *at a particular time* in order to achieve the ultimate goals of the African revolution. Faced with the reality of a balkanized continent at the point of independence, Pan-Africanists saw African unity as a way of consolidating their newly found sovereign status and combating a neo-imperialist scramble for Africa.

> We know that even after our independence has been achieved, that African personality which we would build up will depend on the consolidation of our unity, not only in sentiment but in fact. We know that a balkanized Africa, however loudly it may proclaim to the world its independence and all that, will in fact be an easy prey to the forces of neo-imperialism.[50]

Beyond safeguarding the independence of the African states, political unity was considered important for a reason that is even more central to the fundamental Pan-Africanist objective of collective empowerment. First, from the Pan-Africanist viewpoint, it is logical to have *one* state represent, speak on behalf of, and articulate the collective will of the African nation. Second, the only way to increase the power of the African peoples is to increase the power of the one state that represents them. Simply put, in unity there is strength: "As long as Africa remains divided, not merely territorially but in such a way that there is prestigious rivalry, even hostility, between country and country, that continent will not have the *strength* and *importance* which its size and natural wealth ought to give it."[51] For Pan-Africanists, therefore, the logical solution to the problem of Africa is to combine the many mini-states into one super-state. The only debate among Pan-Africanists is over the best way to achieve a United States of Africa.[52]

Pan-Africanism and Reconstruction

For Pan-Africanists, the question of reconstruction after independence was directly relevant to the empowerment of African peoples.[53] Some thought was given to this question at the Fifth Pan-African Congress where a resolution was adopted favoring the reconstruction of liberated territories on the basis of "economic democracy as the only real democracy."[54] This statement marked a shift from Garvey's capitalist bourgeois nationalism toward the notion that the African masses should be the beneficiaries of the Pan-African revolution that was being advocated in their name.

Further thinking, in response to the need to develop models of reconstruction, made it clear that the question of reconstruction was directly tied to the issue of culture. First, national liberation (as opposed to assimilation) implied the repudiation of the ideology of the superiority of white culture which had been used as a justification for colonialism.[55] Indeed, the only legitimate justification for national liberation is the retrieval of the national culture from the foreign domination that stifles its development in order that "the Africans themselves [can] order and perfect their own lives."[56] As Franz Fanon eloquently put it: "If we want to turn Africa into a new Europe . . . then let us leave the destiny of *our* countries to Europeans. They will know how to do it better than the most gifted of us."[57]

Furthermore, if Africans are to avoid the negation of their liberation which is brought about by the continuation of the colonial institutions, then the Africans must, in the words of Edward Blyden, "advance by methods of [their] own."[58] And these methods cannot be truly African unless they have been authenticated in the culture of the African people. Thus, progress that is orderly and rational and that promises to enhance the power and dignity of Africans is possible only if the policies of reconstruction are based on the positive principles and values of African culture—the African personality.[59] These concerns motivated the 1958 Conference of the All-African Peoples Organization, called "to formulate and proclaim our African Personality based on the philosophy of Pan-African Socialism on the ideology of the African Non-violent Revolution."[60]

In the past few years, then, Pan-Africanists seem to have settled into the notion that African society should be reconstructed on the basis of the egalitarian and communalistic principles of political and economic organization that are embodied in African culture. Some attempts to apply this perspective can be found in such doctrines as *Ujamaa*,[61] *Melanism*,[62] and *Consciencism*.[63]

One of the developments that has accelerated the realization that the pursuit of the fundamental goal of *Pan-Africanism requires the establishment of socialism* in Africa has been the increasing entrenchment of neocolonialism. The argument is quite straightforward. The neocolonial states that have been established in most of Africa have robbed the African people of the power that presumably was promised to them at independence. Thus, if the fundamental Pan-Africanist objective of empowering African peoples is to be achieved, the neocolonial states must be destroyed.[64] And they cannot be destroyed unless their imperialist-capitalist base is replaced by socialism, through armed struggle.[65] As Cabral has noted:

> The Neo-colonial situation (in which the working classes and their allies struggle simultaneously against the imperialist bourgeoisie and the native ruling class) is not resolved by a nationalist solution: it demands the destruction of the capitalist structure implanted in the national territory by imperialism, and correctly postulates a socialist solution.[66]

Pan-Africanism and Non-alignment

If, as we have consistently argued, the fundamental objective of Pan-Africanism is the empowerment of African peoples, then it is a most significant issue of international politics. For if Africans make any genuine strides toward equality, they will have changed international society almost beyond recognition. As we have seen above, the motto of "independence and unity" was designed to give African peoples greater independence—not the narrow independence of overthrowing colonial rule but a greater political, economic, and ideological independence in the international political arena.[67] In the words of Kwame Nkrumah: "For too long in our history, Africa has spoken through the voice of others. Now, what I have called an *African Personality* in international affairs will have a chance of making a proper impact through the voices of Africa's own sons."[68]

In the formulations of the immediate post-independence period, Pan-Africanists urged that this African Personality be manifested in international affairs through policies of positive neutralism and nonalignment.[69] During the past few years, however, such developments as detente and the deteriorating economic status of the poor states have led to reassessments of the policies to be pursued by Africans in their quest for power. In the ensuing and still unresolved debate, several approaches have been suggested, including an alliance with other third world countries[70] and African participation in a worldwide struggle against imperialism and neocolonialism.[71]

Pan-Africanism—A Restatement

We have attempted to demonstrate that Pan-Africanism is an ideology based on the idea that all African peoples share an indivisible destiny and a commitment to enhance the power of this African nationality. We have also tried to show that in the pursuit of this fundamental objective, Pan-Africanists have advocated a variety of interim goals and strategies, based on their perceptions of the immediate situation and the resources available to them. Thus, at different times Pan-Africanists have proclaimed such instrumental goals as independence, African unity, African reconstruction along the lines of traditional socialism, and nonalignment. This constant evolution of instrumental goals stems from the fact that each of these strategies is fraught with contradictions in relation to the fundamental objective of Pan-Africanism, contradictions that have driven Pan-Africanists to reexamine their prescriptions.

The strategy of national liberation was a logical response to the contradictions inherent in the integrationist strategies of the early Pan-Africanists—strategies that were supportive of the notion of Black inferiority which had been used to justify colonialism.[72] Soon after many of the African states achieved independence, however, it became clear that independence itself had certain built-in contradictions. In one African country after another, the negotiated independence produced a neocolonial state in which power was left in the hands of a comprador elite that was socialized to be receptive to the capitalist mode of production and assimilationist attitudes.[73] For these elites independence was a mechanism that gave them the opportunity to imitate the West and continue its "civilizing mission."[74] Instead of real independence, then, we have a farcical semblance of independence in which Africans are coopted by European interests to aid in the exploitation of the African masses.[75] Characteristically, most of these states have shown little interest in the total liberation of Africa.[76] Nor have they shown any understanding, sympathy, or support for the struggles of peoples of African descent in the diaspora.

Under these circumstances, it should not be surprising that the kind of "unity" that has evolved in Africa has also contradicted the fundamental goal of Pan-Africanism. After independence there was widespread hope that unity would follow. There was hardly an

African political leader who had not at one time or another, and always with considerable enthusiasm, maligned the Europeans for the "balkanization" of the continent and lamented the pernicious effect of such fragmentation. Their statements led many observers to conclude that nearly all African leaders favored unity, and were determined to bring it about.[77] Yet the connection between *independence* and *unity* proved more difficult than had been anticipated. It soon became clear that one African leader's interpretation of unity was not the same as another's, and that some of them were not interested in African unity at all. Whereas the few Pan-Africanists saw unity as a means to consolidate the power of Africa and to strengthen the struggle against colonialism and neocolonialism, the majority of African leaders deemed unity to be useful only if it could be used to maintain the neocolonialist status quo. The paradox inherent in this situation is manifested in Kwame Nkrumah's statements admonishing the leaders of neocolonialist countries to create a United States of Africa, the chief purpose of which was to fight neocolonialism.[78]

Pan-Africanists have debated the most feasible way to create a union of African states. In 1965, for example, Nkrumah advocated a total unification of all African states, while Nyerere seemed to think that a series of regional unifications—a prelude to total unification—would be more feasible and more lasting. This in-house debate is not to be confused with the fundamental disagreement between Pan-Africanists and the "micro-nationalists," however. It is important to emphasize that the African unity of the Pan-Africanists involved the political union of the African states, and was therefore not consistent with the kind of international organization represented in the Organization of African Unity. From the outset, some Pan-Africanists viewed the formation of the OAU with alarm. For instance, Sam Ikoku noted that "The OAU as it is presently constituted will never allow us to achieve African political union. And because it cannot evolve in this direction, the OAU will tend to degenerate into an organism protecting the existing regimes in various African countries."[79]

It was clear to the Pan-Africanists that many kinds of unity were antithetical to their purposes. For example, to argue that the kind of unity advocated by Cecil Rhodes is consistent with Pan-Africanism is, in their view, patently absurd. Similarly, the OAU was considered antithetical to Pan-Africanism and dangerous to the true interests of the African peoples. In the words of Felix Moumie, "That would be confusion which will profit only Neo-colonialism and imperialism and which will induce African leaders to relegate to the background the fundamental problem of the struggle against Neo-colonialism in order to amuse themselves with economic and social hocus-pocus."[80]

The crisis of Pan-Africanism is that it is caught up in the contradictions of the strategies that have led to the present condition of African peoples. The integrationist reformism of the early DuBois-style Pan-Africanists gave way to the strategy of national liberation by consitutional decolonization. However this new strategy produced neocolonial states — states that retain virtually the same machinery of imperial domination and the same economic relationships that originally brought them to a position of dependency in the world capitalist economic system. In addition, the attempt to unify the continent politically has also produced paradoxical results. Instead of a form of unity which can lead to the collective empowerment of African peoples, the OAU has emerged as a sort of trade-union of bourgeois, neocolonialist governments dedicated to the maintenance of the status quo.[81] Finally, the internal policies of these countries have kept power out of the hands of the African peoples on whose behalf the nationalist revolutions were ostensibly carried out, and their foreign policies have not appreciably increased their power in the contemporary international system. As a result of these contradictions, the Pan-African movement seems to have stalled, and Africans are caught powerless in an international system characterized by super-efficient techniques of collective imperialism.

Toward New Directions In Strategy

Under these circumstances, the strategy that Pan-Africanists adopt must avoid the dissipation of precious effort and concentrate on goals that they have both the *capacity* and the *opportunity* to implement. They must avoid the confusion between the fundamental goal of Pan-Africanism and certain intermediate strategies that were advocated by some of their ideological forefathers. For example, mass emigration from the diaspora to Africa or the federation of Africa, both of which were advocated as means of establishing a great African state, are only strategies and not the ultimate goals of Pan-Africanism. While both may have been appropriate at some point, and may be appropriate again under different conditions, they are at this time both unlikely and probably illogical.[82]

In other words, Pan-Africanists must evolve strategies that are more consistent with their present operational environment. In order to accomplish this aim, they must first analyze objectively the present conditions of African peoples throughout the world, attempting to determine which strategies have the best potential for realizing their ultimate goal—the empowerment of all African peoples. Whatever strategy they adopt must be based on three premises:

1. The fundamental Pan-Africanist concept of the indivisibility of the African people.
2. The acceptance of the limitation of economic and military resources and therefore of present political capability.
3. The crucial importance of the weapon of ideological clarity.

This last premise is particularly crucial, because as I have argued, ideology speaks to consciousness, self-interest, and long-term goals. A people who understands who it is and how it is to progress is not likely to submit to someone else's definition of goals and methods. On the basis of these premises it will be possible for Pan-Africanists to develop a multifaceted strategy of "coordinated differentiation" which will attempt to achieve the following goals:

1. The liberation and empowerment of all African peoples both in Africa and in the diaspora.
2. The organization of liberated African societies on the basis of socialism so as to safeguard their independence by eliminating the threat of neocolonialism.
3. The political unification of the African states into one powerful state by the cooperation of the African masses.
4. The formation of strategic alliances with all the enemies of imperialism.

These goals have two specific implications. First, by destroying the neocolonial state as a power separate from the masses and replacing it with the power of the masses, the socialist revolution will create a new and different society in Africa.[83] Second, Afro-Americans in the United States will use their economic and ideological resources to maximize Black political power and thereby neutralize Western intervention in revolutionary developments in Africa.

In sum, Pan-Africanists must carry out the political functions of traditional electoral politics: attempting to gain access to positions of power in the structure of government, pressuring the foreign policymaking machinery, mobilizing politically conscious constituencies (and expanding that category by education and politicization), carrying out tactically rational political violence, and giving direct aid to Africa in crisis situations, carefully monitoring whatever instrumental gains might accrue. But the area in which untiring efforts must be invested is in the *education* of the next generation of Black leaders, the inculcation of the meaning of Black identity and purpose and commitment to the entire African world.

The Need for Organization

The existence of a coherent, realistic, ideology does not by itself guarantee the success of the programs that emanate from it. As Marcus Garvey noted long ago, ideology like religion needs disseminators and propagators; it needs proselytizers and disciples, and disciples need organization. In short, an ideology, no matter how appropriate, can be effective only in connection with a movement. Unfortunately, Pan-Africanism is essentially an ideology in search of a movement, and unless it finds a movement it might as well be dead. Therefore, in order to achieve the goals outlined above, it is imperative that we revive the Pan-African movement. This time the movement cannot be limited to America, where it started, or to Africa. This time it must have not only a headquarters and a secretariat, but it must also be taken to the grassroots, wherever Black people live, be it in Detroit, or Nairobi, in Lagos, London, or Kingston. We need a dynamic global movement, one that will be the advocate of all African peoples and propagate the Pan-African ideology. It must be responsible for the following functions:

1. Advocacy of the rights of African peoples in all the decision-making centers of the world including the halls of the African governments, the OAU, and the United Nations.
2. Provision of a clearinghouse for information about all African peoples to each other.
3. Provision of reciprocal support from one African community to another in struggle.
4. And most important, the ideological training of the young cadres.

The Pan-African movement has produced many past heroes, including Blyden, Garvey, Padmore, and Nkrumah. As they have always pointed out, the struggle promises to be a long one, but they left us the legacy of the ideology for our survival and eventual victory. It is our responsiblity to educate those who will come after us. Therefore, we must recover from our ideological confusion. We must take up the struggle and advance it toward a keener awareness and a tighter organization, from which will come the cadres with the will, the capacity and, most of all, the ideological clarity that the struggle demands.

Notes

1. Charles F. Andrain, "The Pan-African Movement: The Search for Organization and Community," *Phylon*, 23, no. 1 (Spring 1962): 10-14. For other examples of confusion about the meaning of Pan-Africanism see George Shepperson, "Pan-Africanism and 'Pan-Africanism' Some Historical Notes," *Phylon*, 23, no. 2 (Winter 1962): 346-357, and St. Clair Drake, "Pan-Africanism, Negritude, and the African Personality," *Boston University Graduate Journal*, 10 (1961): pp. 38-51.
2. For instance, while Ben Rogers describes both DuBois and Garvey as Pan-Africanists, George Padmore claims that DuBois is "the father of Pan-Africanism, the rival political ideology to Garvey's Black Zionism." See Ben F. Rogers, "William E. B. DuBois, Marcus Garvey and Pan-Africa," *Toward a Negro History*, 40 (April 1955): 158; and George Padmore, *Pan-Africanism or Communism?* (New York: Roy Publishers, 1956), p. 89.
3. Samuel W. Allen, "Introduction," in American Society of African Culture, ed., *Pan-Africanism Reconsidered* (Berkeley: University of California Press, 1962), p. 12. Also Imanuel Geiss, *The Pan-African Movement* (New York: African Publishing Co., 1974), p. 3.
4. For a full discussion of this point, see W. Ofuatey-Kodjoe, 'Pan-Africanism in Crisis." in W. Ofuatey-Kodjoe, ed., *Pan-Africanism: New Directions in Strategy*. (Washington, D.C.: University Press of America, 1982, forthcoming).
5. Note the discussion between Rayford Logan and Anthony Enahoro on the definition of Pan-Africanism in American Society of African Culture, ed., *Pan-Africanism Reconsidered*, pp. 37-52, 69-74.
6. For a discussion of definitions, see Abraham Kaplan, *The Conduct of Inquiry* (San Francisco; Chandler Publishing Co., 1964), chap. 2.
7. The corollary of this formulation is that not all Pan-Africanists are active in organizations, while some may be members of several Pan-Africanist organizations at the same time. Furthermore, collaboration and cooperation between various Pan-Africanist organizations need not be automatic, in spite of shared fundamental objectives.
8. Of the innumerable works on the Pan-African movement, perhaps the most comprehensive is Imanuel Geiss, *The Pan-African Movement*.
9. Geiss, *The Pan-African Movement*, p. 177. See also Alexander Walters, *My Life and Work* (New York, 1917), p. 253.
10. *Report of the Pan-African Conference held on the 23rd, 24th and 25th July, 1900, at Westminster Town Hall, Westminster S. W., London* (n.d.-ca. 1900), p. 1.

11. Ibid., p. 18.
12. *The Times,* 24 July 1900, p. 7. Italics are mine.
13. See Ofuatey-Kodjoe, ed., *Pan-Africanism: New Directions in Strategy.*
14. Harold Sprout and Margaret Sprout, *The Ecological Perspective in Human Affairs* (Princeton: Princeton University Press, 1965), pp. 11-15.
15. See Willard A. Mullins, "On the Concept of Ideology in Political Science," *APSR,* 65, no. 2. (June 1972): 503.
16. For a discussion of the nature and elements of nationalism, see Rupert Emerson, *From Empire to Nation* (Cambridge: Harvard University Press, 1960), pp. 89-187, Also, Hans Kohn, *The Idea of Nationalism* (New York: Macmillan Co., 1945).
17. For an analysis of pan-movements, see Hans Kohn, "Pan-Movements," *Encyclopedia of the Social Sciences,* ed. E. R. A. Seligman (New York: Macmillan, 1937-), II: 544-553.
18. See for instance, Carlton J. H. Hayes, *The Historical Evolution of Modern Nationalism* (New York: Macmillan, 1937).
19. See Chukwulozie K. Anyanwu, *The Nature of Black Cultural Reality* (Washington, D.C.: University Press of America, 1976), pp. 327-328; 337, and passim.
20. Leopold Sedar Senghor, *On African Socialism* (New York: Praeger, 1964).
21. Stanislav Adotevi, "The Strategy of Culture," *The Black Scholar,* 1, no. 1 (Nov. 1969): 28-35.
22. W. E. Abraham defines the African Personality as "that complex of ideas and attitudes which is both identical and significant in otherwise different African cultures." *The Mind of Africa* (Chicago: University of Chicago Press, 1962), p. 39.
23. Quoted in Paul Signumd Jr. ed., *The Ideologies of Developing Nations* (New York: Praeger, 1963), p. 248.
24. Emerson, *From Empire to Nation,* pp. 89-187.
25. Keynote Address to the Sixth Pan-African Conference, held at the University of Dar es Salaam, 1974, quoted in *Africa Report,* (Sept.-Oct. 1974), p. 3.
26. See Ali Mazrui, *Towards a Pax Africana* (Chicago: University of Chicago Press, 1967), pp. 60ff, 177ff.
27. Senghor, *On African Socialism,* p. 35.
28. Rayford W. Logan. "The Historical Aspects of Pan-Africanism," in *Pan-Africanism Reconsidered,* p. 37.
29. David E. Apter and James S. Coleman, "Pan-Africanism or Nationalism in Africa," ibid., p. 81.
30. Immanuel Wallerstein, "Pan-Africanism as Protest," in Morton Kaplan, ed., *The Revolution in World Politics* (New York: Wiley, 1962), pp. 138-139.
31. Geiss, *The Pan-African Movement,* pp. 229-262; Padmore, *Pan-Africanism or Communism?* pp. 105-136.

32. This idea was expressed in the following words by Harold Moody, then president of the League of Coloured Peoples: "We are under a democratic government and that government is acting as trustees for us until we can stand on our feet under the strenuous conditions of modern times. We must believe that they want the best for their wards." Imanuel Geiss, *The Pan-African Movement*, p. 344.
33. See for instance the famous appeal "To the Nations of the World," delivered by DuBois at the 1900 First Pan-African Conference, in Walters, *My Life and Work*, pp. 257-260.
34. Amy Jacques Garvey, ed., *Philosophy and Opinions of Marcus Garvey*, vol. I (New York: Universal Publishing House, 1923), p. 5 (italics are mine).
35. Quoted in Okon Edet Uya, *Black Brotherhood: Afro-Americans and Africa*, (Lexington, Mass.: D.C. Heath and Co., 1971), p. 183.
36. Amy Jacques Garvey, ed., *Philosophy and Opinions of Marcus Garvey*, vol. 2 (New York: Universal Publishing House, 1926), p. 12.
37. David E. Cronon, *Black Moses* (Madison: University of Wisconsin Press, 1962), p. 120.
38. Quoted in Uya, *Black Brotherhood*, p. 184.
39. Garvey, ed., *Philosophy and Opinions*, vol. 1, p. 11.
40. Uya, *Black Brotherhood*, p. 187.
41. Ibid.
42. Ibid., p. 718.
43. Padmore, *Pan-Africanism or Communism?* p. 170. See also Kwame Nkrumah, *Ghana: An Autobiography of Kwame Nkrumah* (New York: Praeger, 1957), p. 38.
44. Padmore, *Pan-Africanism or Communism?* p. 170.
45. George Padmore, *A Guide to Pan-African Socialism: A Program for Africa*. (Accra: Guinea Press, 1957), p. 18 (italics are mine).
46. Abraham, *The Mind of Africa*, p. 36.
47. Kwame Nkrumah, *I Speak of Freedom* (New York: Praeger, 1961), p. 164.
48. Quoted in Colin Legum, *Pan Africanism: A Short Political Guide*, (New York: Praeger, 1962), p. 126.
49. Nkrumah, *I Speak of Freedom*, p. 107.
50. Statement by Julius Nyerere to the Second Conference of Independent African States, 1961. Quoted in Legum, *Pan-Africanism*, p. 111.
51. Abraham, *The Mind of Africa*, p. 304. Italics are mine.
52. See for instance, *Pan-Africanism Reconsidered*, p. 107.
53. Abraham, *The Mind of Africa*, p. 115.
54. Padmore, *Pan-Africanism or Communism?* p. 170.
55. Thomas Hodgkin, *Nationalism in Colonial Africa* (New York: New York University Press, 1960), p. 179.
56. Alex Quaison-Sackey, *Africa Unbound* (New York: Praeger, 1963), p. 33.
57. Quoted in Sam Anderson, "Revolutionary Black Nationalism in Pan-

African," *The Black Scholar*, vol. 2, no. 7 (March 1971): 22.
58. Quoted in Legum, *Pan-Africanism*, p. 263.
59. Abraham, *The Mind of Africa*, p. 38.
60. St. Clair Drake, "Pan-Africanism, Negritude, and the African Personality," p. 534.
61. Julius Nyerere, *Uhuru na Ujamaa* (Dar es Salaam: Oxford University Press, 1968).
62. Stanislav Adotevi, "The Strategy of Culture," pp. 28-35.
63. Kwame Nkrumah, *Consciencism* (New York: Monthly Review Press, 1970).
64. Azinna Nwafor, "Liberation and Pan-Africanism" *Monthly Review*, 25, no. 6 (Nov. 1973): 18.
65. Amilcar Cabral, *Revolution in Guinea* (London: Stage 1 Books, 1969), p. 86.
66. Ibid., p. 106.
67. See Julius Nyerere's comment in *Africa Digest* (London, October 1961); also Quaison-Sackey, *Africa Unbound*, p. 34.
68. Kwame Nkrumah, *I Speak of Freedom*, p. 125.
69. Quaison-Sackey, *Africa Unbound*, pp. 35-58.
70. In his speech to the Sixth Pan-African Conference, Nyerere argued that Pan-Africanism cannot achieve its goal of equality for African peoples "if it caused Africa and the Caribbean to try to isolate themselves from the rest of the Third World." *Africa Report* (Sept.-Oct. 1974).
71. Azinna Nwafor, "Liberation and Pan-Africanism," p. 28.
72. Padmore, *Pan-Africanism or Communism?* p. 131.
73. Abraham, *The Mind of Africa*, p. 139.
74. Ibid., p. 142.
75. Nyerere, *Uhuru na Ujamaa*, p. 90.
76. An analysis of contributions to the OAU Committee on Liberation and other bodies, shows that apart from the very few Pan-Africanist-oriented states such as Tanzania, most of the Africans have paid no more than lip-service to the cause of national liberation in southern Africa.
77. For a full discussion of this, see W. Ofuatey-Kodjoe, *Pan-Africanism and African Unity: The Role of Ideology in the Politics of African Unity* (Columbia University: Institute of African Studies, 1968).
78. Nwafor, "Liberation and Pan-Africanism," p. 25.
79. *L'Enticelle*, 20 January 1966.
80. UPC "African Unity or Neocolonialism," 30 May 1962, quoted in Immanuel Wallerstein, *Africa: The Politics of Unity* (New York: Random House, 1967), p. 108.
81. Azinna Nwafor, "Liberation and Pan-Africanism," p. 24-25.
82. Ibid., p. 25.
83. Ibid., p. 19.

MALCOLM
(May 19, 1925—February 21, 1965)

Malcolm had a way of drawing a circle around where you might be standing and asking you if you were going to just keep standing there. He always pointed out the choice to move, the fact that you empower yourself. His community still stares at the circle around Harlem, around New York City, Black America, and Black South Africa. Twenty years after his death the struggle for empowerment in this city and change in Africa are part of his complex legacy.

CHAPTER 14

Pan-Africanism: From National Liberation to National Reconstruction

Ronald W. Walters

Sensitive to the fact that several definitions of the Pan-African phenomenon exist, we should say at the outset that we understand the term to describe that essential range of human relations among peoples of African descent which exemplifies the integrity of African civilization.[1] Structurally, our perspective focuses upon the relations between Africans in the United States and their relations with the states and peoples of the African continent.

Such a definition assists us in formulating the thesis that if one understands the historical sweep of these relations, then the periodic "awakening" of the Pan-African response, especially in the so-called Diaspora, has a fundamental rationale.[2] Particularly when one examines Diaspora-continental African relations, similar to the relations between child and parent, one sees that they have been marked by the attempt of Diaspora Africans to remove the barriers that prevent them from reestablishing viable linkages with the motherland. To this extent, the linkage has been constant, but the form of the response has had much to do with dynamics in America, in Africa, or in world affairs.

This definition is easily applied to twentieth-century Pan-Africanism if one considers, for example: (1) U.S. factors (the Garvey Movement, the DuBois conferences, the Civil Rights Movement, and the Black Power Movement); (2) African continental factors (colonialism, the independence movement, wars of national liberation); and (3) world factors (World Wars I and II, imperialism, the rise of the Third World). The central thesis of this paper, however, is that the future manifestations of Pan-Africanism in the Diaspora will be controlled by the African continent's transition from the struggle for national liberation to the struggle for the national reconstruction of formerly

---

Dr. Ronald Walters is a Professor in the Political Science Department at Howard University in Washington, D.C.

colonized states, nearly all of which have won their liberation only recently.

With the recent independence of Zimbabwe, the national liberation struggle in Southern Africa has progressed to the point that the last territories where Africans remain to be liberated from the oppression of white settler colonialists are Namibia and South Africa. The focus upon South Africa has been important because, just as in other cases, opposition to colonialism by Africans has provided the strongest cement for Pan-African relations between the Africans and their brothers and sisters in the Diaspora. This focus upon South Africa has been long and consistent, playing a particularly important role in the history of Pan-Africanism.

At the 1923 Pan-African Conference, for example, W. E. B. DuBois referred to the barbarism of Jan Smuts, leader of South Africa, in a resolution that condemned him for sending South African soldiers to massacre hundreds of defenseless Africans in Namibia (formerly South West Africa).[3] In 1941, Alphaeus Hunton, working with DuBois and Paul Robeson in the Council on African Affairs in New York City, organized a rally of five thousand Blacks at Abyssinia Baptist Church in Harlem to donate food to striking South African miners who were being starved by their white bosses. Again, in 1945, a resolution of the Fifth Pan-African Congress said:

> This Congress pledges itself to work unceasingly with and on behalf of its non-European brothers in South Africa until they achieve the status of freedom and human dignity. This Congress regards the struggle of our brothers in South Africa as an integral part of the common struggle for national liberation throughout Africa.[4]

In pursuit of this struggle, George Padmore, who had written the history of the Fifth Pan-African Congress, suggested that Africans had to confront another group of "Pan-Africanists" headed by Jan Smuts. "The Pan-African movement which he represents is a union of the white rulers of Kenya, Rhodesia, and Union of South Africa to rule the African continent in the interest of its white investors and exploiters."[5] Padmore said this scheme matured at first as the concept of a "greater South Africa," by which South African whites acquired a mandate to South West Africa and attempted to annex Bechuanaland, Basutoland, and Swaziland, which became British protectorates. But it continued in the functional cooperation among the British East African territories, the Portuguese territories, the South Africans, and their allies in the West—cooperation that led to the increased integration of the Southern African region into the world political economy.

Over the last fifteen years, this functional unity of white "Pan-Africanists" who have controlled Southern Africa has been successfully challenged by an authentic Pan-African movement. This movement has been basically the work of committed revolutionary African nationalists in the territories of Guinea-Bissau, Angola, Mozambique, and Zimbabwe, supported most immediately by states in these regions. These revolutionaries, however, have been supported by interracial and interdemoninational political organizations and churches, as well as by committed Pan-Africanists in the African Diaspora. This work has included the provision of funds, medical supplies and clothing, political education for the masses, educational and survival support for refugees, and the development of strategies to influence government policy. These efforts have been acknowledged in various ways, including the recent statements of Prime Minister Robert Mugabe of Zimbabwe at Howard University and in Harlem, where he evoked themes of racial responsibility and solidarity to jubilant black audiences on 27 and 28 August 1980.

Despite the intensity of the current feelings and actions being directed toward the South African regime by national liberation support groups in the U.S. African community, it is still possible to discern the outlines of a completed struggle and the achievement of African political objectives in that region. The closing of the Namibian and South African chapters will mark a watershed in the history of the continent's total struggle for liberation from at least the formal manifestations of colonial rule. This transformation in political power relationships will establish a new basis of social relations which will in turn affect the nature of the Pan-African movement elsewhere. The question is thus what form that transformation will take and what it portends with respect to the objectives of the Pan-Africanists and their movement activities.

The New Challenges: The New Basis

One of the most intractable problems is the tension between national ideology and the establishment of a progressive environment for human development, because the political and economic mediating factors are still largely conditioned by forces outside the newly independent states themselves. Generally speaking, the new ideology of those who come to power during the change from dependence to independence develops from a concern for the way in which the colonial system for centuries denied people the opportunity for human development. It has been stated with clarity by astute African leaders and thinkers that the transformation from subject status to independence and freedom is meant to create the possibility that the masses, through the exercise of enlightened and legitimate leadership, will be able to manage the resources of their territorial and cultural (including material culture) endowment so as to construct a vision of their own destiny and then fulfill that vision by their works. Given that colonialism has prevented Africans from accumulating capital in any significantly modern forms, the leaders of the newly independent states have set about realizing their social living requirements through a program of socialism designed to spread the meager wealth equitably among the masses.

These social requirements are real, for the social needs of the people were long subordinated to the colonialists' need to exploit the raw materials of these areas and the labor of Africans.[6] This vicious exploitation resulted in illiteracy, disease, high rates of mortality, and inefficient social structures. It is worth recalling the experience of Kwame Nkrumah, who said: "When I sat down with my party colleagues after independence to examine our urgent priorities, we framed a short list. We must abolish poverty, ignorance, illiteracy and improve our health services. These were direct and simple objectives not exactly amenable to legislation."[7] But then, he went on to say why he reached the conclusion that these social requirements must be met by socialist government.

> I have already made it clear that colonial rule precluded that accumulation of capital among our citizens which would have assisted thorough-going private investment in industrial construction. It has, therefore, been left to government, as the holder of the means, to play the role of main entrepreneur in laying the basis of the national economic and social advancement. If we turned over to private interests the going concerns capitalized out of national funds and national effort, as some of our critics would like to see us do, we should be betraying the trust of the great masses of our people for the greedy interests of a small coterie of individuals, probably in alliance with foreign capitalists. Production for private profit deprives a large section of the people of the goods and services produced. If, therefore, we are to fulfill our pledge to

the people and achieve the programme set out above, socialism is our only alternative.[8]

The "short list" that Nkrumah and his colleagues drew up is indeed, by his own further elaboration, a massive agenda of the human needs faced by every newly independent state in Africa and throughout the Third World. Since the time of Ghanian independence, we have seen that the "short list" can be further extended by the way in which independence is achieved. For example, the recent war in Zimbabwe has affected not only that area, but the surrounding states as well, and the same has been true in Angola, Guinea-Bissau, and Mozambique. To the existing deprivation caused by colonialism one must therefore add the impact of evolution upon the people, which although it has the positive effect of weakening colonialism also results in broken family units, injury, disease, thousands of fatalities, and the creation of vast numbers of refugees and other displaced people, not to mention serious destruction to whatever material goods had existed. Social tensions are produced by such deprivation as well.

Nkrumah also mentioned the government's crucial role in satisfying the social requirements of the people, but it is also worth noting that in both the Ghana of 1957 and the Zimbabwe of 1980, even though independence was achieved through political agitation, violence, and full-scale war (in the case of Zimbabwe), the British government succeeded in structuring the post-liberation governments in ways that rendered impossible the unfettered use of the newly acquired political power. In both cases, British paternalism dictated constitutional clauses that "protected the minority population," which was also a political opposition.[9] Although British paternal policy also appeared to protect the rights of the African majority in white settler states, it protected a bourgeois African minority in Ghana and a white minority population in Zimbabwe. The institutionalization of these forces in opposition to the government that represents the will of the people has complicated the government's task of establishing programs in direct accord with the people's wishes.

We can gain some perspective on the economic objectives of these governments by consulting the studies that suggest that a per capita Gross National Product of $505 would be necessary "to meet the basic needs of all individuals [in black Africa] both with and without income redistribution." But in mid-1975, such countries had only $230 per year of per capita GNP.[10] In the early 1960s the prescription for a rate of growth sufficient to meet development needs was the massive infusion of foreign capital in the form of loans, grants, commodity transfers, in-kind technical assistance, and personnel training programs. This program required that developed countries reach a foreign assistance goal of at least 0.7 percent of GNP, a level that, unfortunately, has not been achieved in either the 1960s or the 1970s.

Meanwhile, Third World countries, including African countries (represented in the U.N. by the "group of 77") have asserted that the piecemeal approach to the problem of development is grossly unsatisfactory because the severe imbalance in world material resources perpetuates the inherent problems of development, especially where economic competition is allowed in the marketplace. They recognize that the transfer of material (including human) resources enabled Europe and America to reach their present level of development. This awareness has led them to demand a New International Economic Order, a term that sums up the series of proposals by which less developed countries would achieve relative parity of economic status through growth fostered by special concessional arrangements. These demands recognize fully the need for easier loan and grant conditions—a need that stems from the fragile nature of African economies and their extreme susceptibility to fluctuations in such things as the price of energy, which is currently staggering even many developed nations. In addition, these demands are a response to the inflexibility of many international lending agencies, including the International Monetary Fund, whose loan conditions imply the adoption of the capitalist economic model—a condition that is impossible for such nations as Tanzania and Jamaica, which have already rejected capitalism.[11] Moreover, the existence of regional African economic consortia, such as the Economic Community of West African States and the Lome II Convention, has not yet mitigated the problem of achieving sufficient capital and favorable trading arrangements.

World Bank economists agree that

> the international policies required to achieve such an increase (of foreign exchange availability to poor countries) include substantial trade liberalization, particularly in the products that can be exported by the poorer countries, and an increase of some 20 percent in concessional lending to the poor countries. Although this increase would

imply a rise in the share of GNP devoted to official development assistance (ODA) by the OECD countries from the present level of 0.35 percent, it would be substantially less than the international target of 0.70 percent if it could be concentrated in the poorest countries.[12]

But the substantial pull of national political and economic interests keeps the developed countries from meeting their target of 0.7 percent of GNP in economic assistance to LDCs or concentrating it toward the poorest countries. In most cases, the reversal of exploitative patterns of trade and the increase of economic assistance would prevent the developed countries from exercising significant control over the resources of the poor countries through multinational corporations. In other cases, altruism, rather than hard economic or political considerations, could be the basis for a reversal of economic relations—but such altruism has not been the "stuff" of international relations; rather, developed states have exploited their comparative advantages.

One example of this exploitative pattern is Zaire's long-term debt of $3.5 billion, which may be accounted for by its substantial dependence upon external financial agencies. By mid-1979 the World Bank had approved $523.6 million in loans; development assistance mainly from France, Belgium, West Germany, and the United States had topped $500 million by 1977; the U.S. Export-Import Bank had advanced credit and loans totaling $550 million in 1979; and the Government of Zaire, now in arrears amounting to $1.3 billion on the debt is even more heavily dependent than ever.[13] Of course, the largess of the developed nations is a function of their participation in the mineral extraction industry in Shaba province, where the United States and other European countries (but also the Soviet Union and China) are purchasing the 60 percent of the world cobalt supply and other minerals that are located there. A recent Congressional report indicates:

> Further U.S. influence should be directed toward a more favorable Zairian investment code, to establish incentives for international mining companies to sink venture capital and technical know-how into Zairian mineral resources. Third, the United States should encourage Mobutu to expand programmatic and market-oriented regional economic dealings based on nonexclusive principles. The subcommittee takes the position that undertaking these goals as a part of U.S. policy would improve the availability of minerals to the West, and thus reduce at least

in part the risks involved in U.S. dependence on foreign mineral supplies.[14]

This situation in Zaire indicates that developed countries are indeed willing to expand the range of their economic and technical assistance provided the pay-off is substantially related to their economic, political, or security interest. Still, it must be pointed out that at $130 per annum, the per-capita GNP of Zaire is one of the lowest in Africa, and thus for all the economic activity generated by the minerals industry, the people scarcely benefit.

One of the factors that has increasingly hardened the attitude of developed nations is the condition of their own economies, weakened recently by high oil prices together with increased global economic competition in such basic industries as steel, textiles, and automobiles. This situation has resulted in the pursuit of aggressive policies designed, for example, to correct the $9 billion (1980) unfavorable balance of U.S. trade with Nigeria, largely accounted for by petroleum sales from Nigeria to the United States. In August 1979, a presidential trade delegation, headed by Ambassador Andrew Young, succeeded in doing an estimated $1.5 billion worth of business for private U.S. firms on one trip. These desperate efforts to gain trade parity advantage are made even though Nigeria has deliberately reduced its $1.1 billion (1980) in imports from the United States in an effort to stimulate its own industrial production—in other words, to break the cycle of dependence upon the foreign supply of goods.

The Nigerian strategy is the right approach to the transfer of technology, provided its tough investment code also includes an investment strategy that not only involves Nigerians in management (affirmative action style), but that also demands that productive capacity be located in the country and eventually placed under indigenous management. The demand of LDCs for the "transfer of technology" should not be viewed as exotic or irregular, for it is the principal strategy through which the West already has helped South Africa to gain self-sufficiency in many industrial commodities since World War II. In fact, so complete has been the transfer of technology in some industries such as automobile production, that U.S. divestment would probably mean that while American managers closed their offices and came home, South African white managers would continue to produce vehicles in those same plants.[15] Why then has it been so difficult to transfer technology from Europe and America to black and brown people in the Third World and Africa? Perhaps the factor of international racism should be added to the other difficulties of political and economic exploitation we address.

Thus, the difficulties of fulfilling the social requirements of African peoples through the traditional strategies of political economy are many and growing more vexatious as the gap between them and the developed states widens. The resulting tensions are reflected by official corruption, military coups, territorial rivalries, and the exacerbation of the existing problems represented by Nkrumah's "short list." The situation is critical, as illustrated by even the briefest look at the problem of health. World Health Organization figures show an average of about 200 doctors per country in Africa, with an average of 150 inpatient care facilities of all kinds and a ratio of 1.9 beds for every 1,000 persons. There is also a crippling shortage of medical and allied health care personnel of all kinds, as well as of usable equipment and supplies. Thus, more than 50 percent of the population of the African region does not have ready access to health establishments, and the quality of those that exist is far from satisfactory.[16]

These are the problems that provide the basis for the new relations with Africa by Pan-Africanists, and we will next examine what roles they can play to supplement those who are in charge of the African governments.

The Place of Pan-Africanists

In the new stage of African liberation, Pan-Africanists conceivably have at least three roles to play: (1) to provide resources and technology *directly* to African groups and states, (2) to provide the *financial and other resources* with which the selected country or organization can acquire other resources, and (3) to provide "leveraging" in the process of *influencing U.S. policy* to deliver financial resources and technology.

To begin with, countries in Africa such as Nigeria are devising projects to acquire their own technologists by sending them to be trained in other countries, including the United States. Recently, one of the five hundred Nigerian students who had been sent to the United States asked me, "Why is it not possible for you, our brothers and sisters, who have skills and resources, to come to Africa and help us, rather than for us to come here so far from home?" The answer to this question is that while it is an indispensable national goal for Nigeria to have its own trained manpower, African-Americans nevertheless do have a role to play. One example of this role is the Pan-African Skills Program sponsored by the Inter-religious Foundation for Community Organization of the National Council of Churches of the U.S. This program grew out of the perception that there was a need to provide skilled black manpower directly to African countries and proved to be a useful idea and operation. It was poorly funded, narrowly focused, and not vigorously received by the recipient governments, however. Still, one can claim that this program, which operated in the late 1960s and early 1970s, is an appropriate model, with the major modification that such programs should be supported by the full apparatus of the beneficiary country's national policy and be managed by that government. This modification means that if, as many African governments have said, Blacks with skills are needed to assist them in the development process, this factor should play a serious part in *national development planning* and be dealt with through inter-facing administrative structures in the African country and the Diaspora.

Second, the model for providing funds with which a country can acquire its own technology has also already been developed by Pan-Africanists as a part of the liberation movement. And although there are often problems with regard to the utilization of such funds, there is also strong evidence that the funds provided have been utilized for productive purposes. A substantial amount of such funds have come from the religious community and from Pan-African activists organizations, but the major donors in the liberation-development have of course been other nations and international organizations. One example of a financial assistance effort by Pan-Africanists was that headed by Robert Van Lierop, working with the Mozambique government's O Povo Organizado (the people organized), which raised nearly $50,000 from small donors in the United States to build a hospital in Mozambique. This effort, which succeeded in a relatively short time in 1975, was closely attuned to the policy and priorities of the government it served, which is making the transition from liberation to nation-building activities. Yet another effort has been carved out by the Southern African Support Committee, headed by

Sylvia Hill in Washington, D.C. This project, which initiated Zimbabwe Week, has been very successful in raising funds, clothes, and medical supplies for Zimbabwe, with the funds alone totaling over $35,000 annually for 1977-1979. This project too has focused on the health and welfare field. Other organizations such as the Southern African Relief Fund have in the past helped to alert the African-American community to the importance of refugee problems, and there are many other such efforts in other U.S. cities. Given the expense of resources needed for development, such projects must be placed on a more consistent and fully institutionalized basis. The myth must be laid to rest that the American black community does not have financial resources, for in fact it has a $104 billion GNP, the ninth largest in the world, larger than that of Canada. Blacks do not yet possess the institutional machinery to capture and divert this resource to their own use, however, either for domestic or international purposes.

Third, the act of "leveraging" within governmental institutions is directed toward mobilizing a constituency to influence policy decisions and resources where Africa is concerned. One aspect of the present conservative mood in Congress, a focus for such mobilizing activity, is an almost hysterical attention to America's growing dependence on the mineral resources of Africa. This situation is acknowledged by many—including Congressman James Santini, chairman, Subcommittee on Mines and Mining (House), military leaders such as Secretary of State Alexander Haig, former Commander of U.S. forces in NATO, representatives from such corporate interests as U.S. Steel, Texas Instruments, and Rockwell, and intellectuals such as Daniel Fine (MIT) and Roger Fountaine (Georgetown University). At the same time, however, these men exhibit no such unanimity on the question of increased economic assistance to Africa, and some have even supported interests opposed to the development of Black majority rule, especially in Southern Africa.[17]

Nevertheless, Blacks have exercised some leverage in legislative affairs relating to Africa. For example, before Congressman Parren Mitchell's bill passed in 1975, the United States had never contributed to the African Development Fund, but his bill established an initial three-year appropriation of $25 million which has now grown to $50 million.[18] Similarly, Congressman Charles Diggs, Jr., had an impact in the development of a long-term program of economic assistance to the drought-ridden Sahel region, which resulted in an appropriation of $200 million over a ten-year period. He was also instrumental in seeing that a program of $100 million for regional economic assistance in Southern Africa, initially proposed by former Secretary of State Henry Kissinger for white settlers in Zimbabwe, was reprogrammed to provide development assistance to all black states in the region in 1976-1977. One could cite other examples from experience, but the point is that there is growing attention to this problem on the part of Black legislators at the national level. At the state level, the progressive legislator Senator Jack Vaughn of Michigan was instrumental in passing a law that prohibited the state from doing business with corporations heavily involved in South Africa.

While it is recognized that the maximization of such "leveraging" capability is related to the efficacy of Black-voter influence in American electoral politics, there is a concomitant recognition that many Pan-Africanists are often strongly alienated from electoral politics. This situation has bred an ambiguity with respect to legislative influence participation. One instance of this ambiguity surfaced in the 1972 African Liberation Day demonstration, which attracted 50,000 African-Americans in Washington, D.C. At the same time, there was a proposal that the leadership of the program carry out a lobbying activity, since the vote on lifting the ban on U.S. participation in Rhodesian sanctions was coming up the next week in the House of Representatives. This proposal, which might have prevented the subsequent House vote to lift the ban and allow the United States to trade with Rhodesia (in violation of U.N. sanctions), was rejected by the leadership. Fortunately, there is now a black lobby organization, TransAfrica, which is performing the lobbying function in a systematic way and enjoying some notable success.

The above discussion has focused on the Congress, but in the Executive branch the problem is also profound, for it is there that the resources are actually spent. And, in this regard, Pan-Africanists have almost no practical effect, as an entire coterie of Black consultants and technical assistance organizations have, for some time, competed daily for contracts to perform services to various African countries in the development field. While white organizations, including many universities, have benefited from this activity financially far more than black ones, the values and motivations of those Blacks who are involved warrant serious consideration. Illustrative of this problem is the study on Zimbabwe financed in 1976 by the Agency for International Development, but channeled through the African American Scholars Council, a black organization in Washington, D.C., which formerly made grants for scholarly studies on Africa. This study, headed by former Director of the AID/Africa Bureau, Samuel Adams, was set within the framework of the State Department's concern with the nature of the "transition to majority rule" in Zimbabwe, and the attendant "programming requirements" for AID. The mission was to develop pertinent information and recommendations concerning the political and economic situation in the two territories of Zimbabwe and Namibia, formulating explicit options for the exercise of U.S. economic assistance policy through the transition period and upon independence.

The problem with such a study, of course, is that in meeting the requirements of AID, it also fit into the economic and political intelligence needs and policy framework of Henry Kissinger's effort to achieve a settlement compatible with the interests of such powerful economic forces as Lohnro Ltd. (England) and Union Carbide, Allegheny Ludlum, and other U.S. corporations. These interests necessitated the careful orchestration of a "peaceful settlement" to preserve the important mining infrastructure of Zimbabwe for Western exploitation. This project was attacked in the United States and by the liberation movements (ZANU/ZAPU), on the grounds that the struggle for self-determination itself means that, upon independence, the people should have the freedom to determine the shape of their own economic and political systems. Nevertheless, in defense of this project, spokespersons for the AASC suggested that "Black Americans should make up their minds whether or not they will be engaged in such activities."[19] An additional irony of this project was that while it was headed by a black man, two white scholars, Robert Rotberg of MIT and Eliot Berg of Michigan State University, shared substantially in the $340,000 contract for their work on the project reports.

It is possible to argue that the real question is whether Blacks should be involved in such projects at all, and, if so, on what basis, with what *values* underlying their participation. Here, the Pan-Africanists encounter value conflict not only with other Blacks but often with the leaders of African governments or ministries as well. The latter's values are shaped by different realities and include a certain reluctance, given their fragile political base, to refuse U.S. governmental assistance of any kind or to risk alienating the big power in any way. This Pan-African "catch-22" might be amenable to common approaches—or even an agreed-upon divergent approach—if there were a facility and an opportunity for reaching a general consensus.

Thus, a fundamental problem of the old "liberation" basis of Pan-African relationships repeats itself, largely because it has not yet been reconciled in the new "reconstructionist" phase, to the question of who speaks legitimately for the African community in the United States where the interests of continental Africa are concerned. There are many continental African leaders who, seeing life through an official state lens, would automatically accord such legitimacy to the highest Black elected official or group of elected officials. But the Pan-Africanist often naively assumes that because he or she has strongly, courageously, and consistently fought for the freedom of Africans for many years while the official Blacks may have done less, Pan-Africanists have an implied right of legitimacy which Africa and Africans are bound to respect. Many African leaders identify with this activist element of the U.S. African community, but they always find a tension between the overriding question of international relations and relations based purely on the ideals of Pan-Africanism and often give priority to the former. As a result, the African leaders often accord priority to the Black who increasingly represents either private interest or the narrow national interest of the United States rather than the broader and more human-oriented interest of African peoples in both the United States and Africa.

One problem of this sort centers on the symbolism of former ambassador to the United Nations, Andrew Young. As a symbol of African-Americans, Young made a contribution to diplomacy which did much to show that Blacks were both competent, possessed of different values, and interested in their well-being as African peoples. To many Africans, therefore, he seemed to fulfill the role of a Pan-Africanist in official clothes. But it became clear that his instructions from the U.S. government, especially as they concerned the solution of black majority rule in South Africa, were not compatible with those of African peoples on the continent or among many in the United States itself. This fact was sharply illustrated at the Maputo Conference in Mozambique, sponsored by the U.N., where Young's view—that

American civil rights tactics and negotiation rather than armed struggle were relevant to the African experience—was strongly resented by most of the delegates from Africa, as well as by the delegation of Blacks from the United States.[20]

Nevertheless, even where nonofficial, civil rights "black leaders" (such as Rev. Leon Sullivan, Rev. Jesse Jackson, Vernon Jordan, and others) who have traveled to South Africa are concerned, one sees that their position, the position of the U.S. government, and that of the U.S. corporate structure are often virtually the same. Having easy access to Africa and considerable "visibility," these individuals have been able to take the initiative, the result being that, more often than not, the "legitimate" voices on Africa, from the perspective of both the U.S. government and African heads of state, are individuals who are, in fact, closest to the state and benefit from its largess.

The Pan-Africanist, therefore, has a difficult agenda that must encompass: (1) support for progressive policy initiatives such as the repeal of the Byrd Amendment or the retention of the Clark Amendment (prohibiting CIA operations in Angola), (2) opposition to reactionary policies within government and to those who support them, be they black or white, and (3) organization to establish a legitimate base for direct contacts with African governments, so that an alternative channel is created for the authentic expression of the views of ordinary Africans residing in the United States.

The Problem of Viable Linkages: Beyond Settlement

From all that has been discussed relative to the potential of Pan-African activity within the context of the contemporary situation, it is obvious that the ad hoc nature of Pan-Africanism in both theory and practice *must be ended* and a serious attempt made to develop common institutions where dialogue, planning, and program development can take place. I suggest, then, that the basic design drafted by the Sixth Pan-African Conference, which called for the establishment of such institutions as the Pan-African Center for Science and Technology, was a correct approach, but one that was perhaps, on the one hand, premature because it was undertaken before continuous dialogue had produced a consensus about the intent of such institutions.[21] On the other hand, ideological conflict also played a role in destroying this idea, but it is clear that politics eventually must yield to the need to improve the quality of human life. However, the

Pan-Africanist must seriously address the problem of making progressive values compatible with the utilization of modern technology.

Periodic conferences such as the FESTAC of 1977 in Nigeria, though useful, should not be considered the primary instrument we need, both because they meet too infrequently and because they are structured basically to be forums for formal dialogue among the mixture of official and unofficial representatives from African communities throughout the Diaspora. It has been four years since the FESTAC in Nigeria and seven years since the Sixth Pan-African Conference in Dar es Salaam, Tanzania, and there is no firm commitment to holding either another FESTAC or a Seventh Pan-African Conference. Perhaps the meetings referred to above should be only occasional affairs, leaving the more meaningful interactions to nongovernmental institutions that are free from governmental instruction. Still, the lack of a secretariat that could foster such interinstitutional contacts means that such cooperation might not occur at all were it not for the government funds granted to private institutions. Nevertheless, a proposal for a Seventh Pan-African Conference has been in existence since 1979, initiated by the leader of the Organization of African Trade Union Unity, Dennis Akumu.[22] The model here, however, is for an extensive period of intercontinental consultation, planning, and program proposal development before the Conference, so that when the meeting takes place its basic purpose will be to highlight and affirm areas of consensus relating to concrete programs. A Pan-African secretariat should be established on the African continent with representatives from the Diaspora, and it should seek to encourage and facilitate the development of common programs of action among African peoples. A new Congress of African Peoples should be called in the various regions of the Diaspora to set in motion a process leading to the establishment of proposals for common action with African governments and private organizations both in the United States and in each region. There are signs of the reinvigoration of the mass movement in the United States, and the question of legitimate and substantive relations with Africa should be an aspect of the new state of mobilization in which problems on the African continent are being addressed.

Conclusion

Now, much of what we have said is predicated upon Nkrumah's

original dilemma or the nature of the transition from colonialism to independence—on whether or not it is revolutionary in character, and the possibility of the transfer of revolutionary values to the independent status. For example, many Pan-Africanists, preferring revolutionary nationalist states, have not maintained contacts with the government of Kenya because of their conviction that the country's leaders have repudiated their revolutionary origins. In contrast, Guinea, confronting great obstacles in its lack of resources, has attempted for over a decade to maintain a consistently revolutionary state in the liberation period. We therefore see the importance of the transition between the struggle to achieve independence and the attainment of independence itself. When this matter was put to Bishop Abel Muzorewa in the summer of 1978,[23] the then leader of Rhodesia responded that there was no relationship between the two but he could not see (or he might have seen very clearly) that his own attempt to protect the interests of the white settlers in the transition period would have meant no essential change in the nature of the most vital power relationships between the whites and the black majority in the period of political independence.

Our view is supported by Amilcar Cabral, who in 1964 was looking forward to the nature of the state even as he was immersed in struggle. At a seminar in the Frantz Fanon Center in Treviglio, Milan, from 1 to 3 May, he was considering this question, suggesting that the moment the stage of liberation was reached and the petite bourgeoisie took power, the oppressed reentered his own history, and powerful external contradictions conditioned the internal contradictions in a new way. Nevertheless, he continued, "For a revolution to take place depends on the nature of the party (and its size), the character of the struggle which led up to liberation, whether there was an armed struggle, what the nature of this armed struggle was and how it developed and, of course, on the nature of the state."[24] In the series of steps suggested by Cabral, it would appear that "the nature of the armed struggle and how it was developed" constitutes the more important stage for an examination of the transition, because in the development of revolutionary struggle there appears an ideology, new behaviors, and new institutions as instruments of change. Thus, Cabral's further thought that "whether or not socialism can be established immediately after the liberation . . . depends upon the instruments to effect the transition to socialism" is related to whether or not the struggle itself was imbued with socialist ideology, socialist practices, or socialist institutions.[25] The relationship among these factions is firmest in the case of Guinea-Bissau both before and after independence, and in a few other states as well.

The most important implication of Cabral's discussion for us, however, is the view that *revolutionary values* are a necessary part of the transition and affect the character of the state. Here, in discussing the post-liberation role of the petite bourgeoisie, the class that would most immediately inherit the instruments of the state, he said: "I think one thing that can be said is this: the revolutionary petty bourgeoisie is *honest;* i.e., in spite of all the hostile conditions, it remains *identified with the fundamental interests of the popular masses"*[26] (my emphasis). This is, of course, what Fanon meant by "class suicide," and it constitutes a standard of values which could condition the ideology and behavior of Diaspora Pan-Africanists in their approach to the types of activity previously suggested, such as the direct provision of various services and resources to African states, the provision of financial support to states and organization, and influencing U.S. policy toward Africa.

At the same time, it is necessary to note that it is often difficult to detect these values because a revolution suggests no subsequent ideology, and the concept of the transition stage also implies a *consolidation* of whatever revolutionary experience there has been (or lack of one). Although revolutionary states have often chosen socialism as the model for their development, states take different routes to socialism, because (as we have seen in Mozambique, for example) the masses may be unevenly involved in the revolutionary process—in their participation in the revolutionary institutions, in their understanding of the revolutionary ideology and tactical objectives, and consequently, in their level of national consciousness. Also, external contradictions such as Mozambique's dependence upon South Africa economically condition the nature of the transition and make a pure ideological consolidation of the revolution impossible.

Pan-Africanists in America were initially somewhat impatient with the slow pace of revolutionary change in Zimbabwe, an impatience that resulted from their presumption that the masses entered the new history all at the same pace, and that they therefore possessed a national consciousness. But Frantz Fanon has implied that the building of national consciousness in the consolidation stage requires more than ideology. It also requires the establishment of a party base in the institutions of government, the acquisition of fundamental knowledge of the state (knowledge kept from those involved in revolutionary struggle by the colonialist white settlers), and the development of a rudimentary strategy for proceeding to the next stage by minimizing the disruption to those resources that have already been consolidated. A rational period of grace—which implies trust—then, also becomes a necessary value in the period of the consolidation of the gains from revolutionary struggle and the transition to new stage.

In a basic sense, however, we have been concerned with the challenges that have emerged in the new stage of independence and with the changes in Pan-African responsibilities and activities which are needed to conform to these stages in African development. And just as Cabral has stated that the nature of the stage will depend upon the instruments utilized to achieve its objective, he also says that "after liberation there will be people controlling the police, the prisons, the army and so on, and a great deal depends on who they are and what they try to do with these instruments."[27] We make this same analysis of Pan-Africanists who would support nation-building activity in Africa, and in so doing raise the problem of the contradiction of the progressive/reactionary conflict among Pan-Africanists on the one hand, and the need for an inclusive ethic on the other.

In many places in Africa, both rural and urban, this writer has witnessed African-Americans performing valuable tasks as teachers, physicians, entrepreneurs, and the like. While many of them manifest the values of a person born to comfort, privilege, and the material advantages that mark a Western socialization, others (that is to say, those without an evident and refined ideology) are making extremely important contributions on *African* terms. What, then, is the place of a highly refined ideology in the development stage of Pan-African activity? Some Pan-Africanists have shaped their own ideology so that, like the All-African Peoples' Revolutionary Party in the United States, they can identify as closely as possible with the political ideology of individual leaders, who in this case is Kwame Nkrumah. But the attendant polarization problem is illustrated by the strong identification of some Pan-Africanists with either the MPLA or the UNITA in Angola in 1975 when the civil war broke out, creating tension and a "civil war" of sorts within the African community in America.[28] It appears, then, that in the new stage of Pan-African activity, a highly defined ideology remains the instrument by which "progressive" and "reactionary" practice is identified. The primary criteria will be based on the activities engaged in, the interests served, and the intended ultimate objectives.

However, as we have seen in the cases of the Sixth Pan-African Congress, in the reverberations of the Angola crisis in the American Black community, and in other cases, these divisive problems are polarizing because they are essentially arguments among partisans of one side or another. It should be recognized that the great majority of African peoples, some of whom would make excellent contributions to the growth of Pan-Africanism, are seldom touched by such debates, indeed are often confused by them. Such debates are the inside currency of those in Africa and in the Diaspora who struggle to shape the direction of the future growth of Pan-Africanism, and such interactions of many varieties among peoples of African ancestry will surely grow due to worldwide improvements in communications, transport, and in a general understanding of each other. But these interactions are likely not to grow, as in the past, as part of a fervent ideological movement, but instead as a natural process of the rediscovery of one's identity and the expansion of the human potential of all African peoples. With such possibilities, it would be disastrous to abort such growth of Pan-Africanism by erecting a rigid ideological standard for participation in Pan-African activities. In fact, one of the most serious challenges Pan-Africanists must face is the removal of the mystique and exoticism from this concept and practice: it must be taken from the realm of elitist debate among political activists and allowed to generalize its potential among millions of African peoples throughout the world.

Although we have not previously defined the identity of a "Pan-Africanist," we should suggest that we view such a person as someone who places a value on a concrete identification and relationship with the peoples and the land of his or her African ancestry within the framework of our meaning of "development."

This intentionally broad definition should not obscure the fact that Pan-Africanists are indeed a very small part of the population of African peoples all over the world. Nevertheless, we have attempted to argue that they have a responsibility to recognize that there is indeed a shift in the basis of relations between the African Diaspora and the continent of Africa from the process of national liberation (which overcame colonialism and established political independence) to the process of national reconstruction (in fact, part of the continuation of the process of national liberation of peoples based on the quest for progressive human development).

Second, we have with equal vigor posited that in the transition, the values of Pan-Africanists are important because in their support for the initial processes of political independence they developed certain values that are also relevant to the eventual process of achieving human development and the satisfaction of social needs. These values were evident not only in their ideology but also in their supportive work projects and activities.

Third, while we recognize that ideology is important as a guide to Pan-African activity in the new phase of national liberation—the reconstruction period—we question how close a "fit" there must be between the ideology of the Pan-Africanists in the Diaspora and those on the African continent, because of the difference in material conditions and divergent histories and culture. What appears to be necessary is that there are created new forms of Pan-African cooperation through new practices and institutions by those who clearly understand the stakes and the problem and who accept the responsibility of leadership.

Finally, we have concluded that it is most important to demystify Pan-Africanism and to make it functional in an effort to generalize its potential among African peoples as the surest method of supporting the integrity of African Civilization in the world.

Notes

1. Ali Mazrui, for example, has isolated at least five dimensions of Pan-Africanism: Sub-Saharan, trans-Saharan, trans-Atlantic, West Hemispheric, and Global. *Africa's International Relations: The Diplomacy of Dependency and Change* (Boulder: Westview Press, 1977), p. 68.
2. Vincent Bakpetu Thompson, *Africa and Unity: The Evolution of Pan-Africanism* (London: Longman, 1969); Ras Makonnen, *Pan-Africanism from Within* (London: Oxford, 1973); Owen Mathurin, *Henry Sylvester Williams and the Origin of the Pan-African Movement* (Westport: Grennwood Press, 1976); Herschelle Challenor, "The Influence of Black Americans on U.S. Foreign Policy Toward Africa," in Abdul Aziz Said, ed., *Ethnicity and U.S. Foreign Policy* (New York: Praeger, 1977), pp. 139-174; Ronald Walters, "Pan-African Organization in America: A Brief Review of Forms," in Lennox S. Yearwood, ed., *Black Organizations:*

Issues on Survival Techniques (Lanham: University Press of America, 1980), pp. 89-102.
3. Philip Foner, ed., *W. E. B. DuBois Speaks* (New York: Pathfinder Press, 1970), p. 274.
4. George Padmore, ed., *History of the Pan-African Congress* (Manchester: African Federation, 1945), p. 58.
5. Ibid., p. 26.
6. See the classic study by Walter Rodney, *How Europe Underdeveloped Africa* (London: Bogle-L'Overture Publications, 1972).
7. Kwame Nkrumah, *Africa Must Unite,* (New York: International Publishers, 1963), p. 118.
8. Ibid., p. 119.
9. See ibid., pp. 72-86; also the Lancaster House Constitution Document proposals, London Press Service, 3 October 1979.
10. J. P. Cole, *Geography of World Affairs* (Baltimore: Penguin, 1979), p. 287.
11. "Storm Over Jamaica," *Black Enterprise Magazine,* October 1980, pp. 53-56.
12. "Growth and Poverty in Developing Countries," *World Bank Staff Working Paper,* no. 309, The World Bank, 1978, p. 37.
13. "Sub-Sahara Africa: Its Role In Critical Minerals Needs of the Western World," Report, Subcommittee on Mines and Mining of the Committee on Interior and Insular Affairs, U.S. House of Representatives, 96th, July 1980, p. 4.
14. Ibid., p. 14.
15. A typical assessment is that "most analysts are convinced that a total American withdrawal would prompt officials in Pretoria to back repatriation of U.S. assets and to order local firms to take over existing facilities." Crucial Stakes for U.S. Firms in South Africa," *U. S. News and World Report,* December 1979, p. 43.
16. Annual Statistical Summary, World Health Organization, African Regional, 1976.
17. Most of the individuals mentioned have written chapters in a newly released publication, "The Resource War in 3-D, Dependency, Diplomacy and Defense," World Affairs Council of Pittsburgh, Pittsburgh, Pa., 1980.
18. Consult the report, *Legislation on Foreign Relations Through 1979,* vol. 2, U.S. House of Representatives and the U.S. Senate, March 1980, p. 352, for details.
19. See James Turner and Sean Gervasi, "The Economic Future in Southern Africa: An Analysis of the AID Study on Zimbabwe and Namibia," Corporate Information Center, National Council of Churches, New York, September 1977.
20. Speech of Ambassador Andrew Young, 19 May 1977 (impromptu remarks, not the prepared text), United Nations International Conference in Support of the Peoples of Zimbabwe and Namibia, Maputo,

Mozambique, 16-21 May 1977.
21. See *Black World,* March 1974, p. 8; also Resolutions and Speeches from the Sixth Pan-African Congress, Tanzania Publishing House, 1976, pp. 200-214.
22. Declaration on Pan-African Responsibility, (Delegation of African peoples attending the Jamaica Conference on Apartheid, sponsored by the United Nations), Kingston, Jamaica, May 1978.
23. Interview, writer with Bishop Abel Muzorewa, tape recording, 19 July 1978.
24. Amilcar Cabral, *Revolution in Guinea* (London: Love and Malcomson, 1969), p. 57.
25. Ibid., p. 59.
26. Ibid.
27. Ibid.
28. This tension crystallized in a conference on U.S. involvement in Angola, 6-8 Feb. 1976, Howard University, which was attended and sponsored by Pan-African activists.
29. The "Appeal" for attendance at the Sixth Pan-African Conference in July of 1972 was made in the name of the person "who has a commitment to the liberation of Africa and African people; . . . with capabilities and resources which should be put to use for our people instead of against them; . . . who sees clear need for a rekindling of political understanding and cooperation among African people; . . . realize[s] the urgency for 'recreating a climate of hostility to imperialism in Africa.' " *Black World,* March 1974, p. 9.

VIII
Political Economy of the Black World

Storm Warning, Phillip L. Mason

CHAPTER 15

Africanization of Management

Willard R. Johnson

Introduction

To those who believe that the "development" of a society means acquiring the power to affect the economic and social well-being of its people under the normal conditions of hardship and poverty which exist in the developing world, it is clear that African development requires the Africanization of the principal decision-making structures of the business sector.

Africans seem to believe that the person in the driver's seat is the driver. But it is becoming clear that in the newly independent African states, those who sit in the seats of political command are like a driver at the rear of a hook and ladder firetruck who can help the vehicle round the corners more neatly and affect the general manner of its progress, who can make it zig or zag, but who cannot change its general direction. Those who direct the flow of business investment, who lead the large foreign enterprises, who organize the world markets for tropical products—it is they who sit in the real driver's seat. Often it is they who have laid out the road itself.

The African states have taken diverse approaches to the goal of taking over business command posts in order to steer their societies more in directions of their own choosing. Some, like Tanzania, Nigeria, and Zambia, have nationalized ownership of the major business and industrial enterprises. Others, like Kenya and Cameroon, merely take a minority equity position in the ownership structure of such enterprises. All of them have adopted, to one degree or another, planning programs that are designed to orient and sometimes to constrain the business sector. So far, however, there has been little progress in actually Africanizing the decision-making positions that govern the day-to-day operations of the larger business firms, and

---

Willard R. Johnson is a Professor in the Political Science Department at the Massachusetts Institute of Technology in Cambridge, Massachusetts

even less in positions that command the allocation of company resources.

Contradictory Perspectives about Collaborative Approaches

The nature, extent, and cause of the lack of progress in Africanization of management is perceived differently by Africans and expatriates. Let's examine these differences, in terms of perspectives on race, place, and pace.

Perspectives on Race. There are different perceptions as to whom Africanization is intended to serve, and these differences stem from different perspectives about race. The anticolonial campaign left a peculiar legacy. On the official record Africans often feel called upon to deny that they oppose, on the basis of race, Europeans having the top positions in government and industry. They affirm that they aim only to "nationalize" these positions, that is, to employ nationals (citizens) of the country. Europeans who take out local citizenship presumably would be accepted in high positions.

Official propaganda, whether from the governments or from the private companies, differs from privately expressed opinions about the question, however. The company spokesmen (expatriates) believe that the Africans are really interested in advancing Blacks into the higher positions and that the professed commitment to "multiracialism" among the citizenry of the newly independent countries is really superficial. Many Africans privately agree. The prevailing opinion is that the real objective being pursued is the transfer of higher posts or black Africans. After experiencing the color bar and racially based domination in their traditional homelands, Africans are prone to want to see all the "outsiders" (Asian as well as European) outside. Students of Africanization, such as Tore Rose, have stated that "to suppress the color bar aspect is a disservice to a frank discussion of the problem."[1]

Particular attention has been drawn to the role played in East Africa by Asians, especially East Indians, who occupied a middle position between Africans and white settlers in terms of economic status during colonial times. They dominated petty commerce and some of the wholesale trade. After independence the Indians were pressured by Kenya, Tanzania, and Uganda to leave these countries. They were required to take out local citizenship and obtain work permits, but most of them refused to apply for local citizenship, preferring to retain their British citizenship, though this ceased to be sufficient to secure admission to Britain, which barred their immigration in 1968. Apparently few wanted to go to India, a country in which many of them have relatives, but which most have never seen. Some of those who did opt for citizenship in the East African countries have found it difficult to obtain work permits, and thus continue to be under pressure to leave.

The development of a fairly large group of people in East Africa who are pressured to leave, but have no place they wish to go that will take them in, has brought a significant amount of critical attention to bear on Kenya and Uganda. Western news media have gloated over what they proclaim to be black racism. In response to such criticism, the late Minister of Economic Development and Planning Tom Mboya stated:

> The first thing we did [after independence] was to allow all non-Africans a period of two years in which to decide to register as Kenyan citizens, or to stay in the country as aliens. That period ended in December 1965. Those who remained in Kenya as aliens must have understood, right from the start, that the country, in its development would, at some stage or another, have to introduce policies that would promote development for the citizens of the country. And what happened is that we have introduced legislation which requires that employers in the future, and this is four years after independence, would employ non-Kenyans only if they had a work permit.[2]

As for those who chose to leave, even in cases where they took with them skills Kenya needs in her development efforts, Mboya stated:

> As Minister for Planning and Development, I can state categorically that the Asians who have left Kenya can be regarded by all of us as "good riddance." In fact, the sooner they leave, the better. We need here men who are committed, men who feel identified to the cause and aspirations of the country. Not those who are going to resist and block our programs for development.

It is important to realize that outside Uganda, East Africa still falls short of replacing Asians and other non-Africans with its own indigenous people in business and even government. The top leadership has been surprisingly insistent, especially in Tanzania which has a more thoroughgoing ideological stance of "self-reliance" and self-help, on permitting non-African citizens to occupy prominent positions. One of the top ministers in President Nyerere's cabinet has been an Asian, and another is a European. In mid-1971, the head of the National Bank and the National Insurance Company told me that "the managers who are not African are mainly there because they have the knowledge, and they are, after all, Tanzanians. You can't do anything about this. The financial manager, for instance, is a Tanzanian (of Asian extraction) so we are not going to localize this job. He is going to be there."[3]

Multiracialist policies, adopted in response to the direct and personalized racism that marked the colonial days, have combined with a dire need for skilled manpower to cause Eastern and Southern African black states to continue to utilize expatriate personnel in quite sensitive positions. Some of these posts affect the program of Africanization itself, because the development corporations need highly trained, technically qualified professionals. Using expatriates in these positions can reintroduce racist perspectives of more complex and ambiguous form, however. A strand of personal prejudice about the capability and potential of Africans generally interweaves with two other European attitudes toward the Africans to create a complex but potent obstacle to the enthusiastic pursuit of Africanization. One of these attitudes concerns the general level of education among the local population; the other concerns the role of the "work ethic" in African culture.

Unfortunately, we find those who hold this mixture of negative perspectives in the very institutions that the African states have created to promote local business development or to serve as the vehicles for local partnership with foreign enterprise. The person in charge of management development for the Tanzania National Development Corporation, for example, told me in the summer of 1971 that this job was very difficult because he lacked the raw material with which to work. He was complaining, in part legitimately, that the base of educated Tanzanians was very small, but he saw fit to default on the task of training local people in management by leaving this responsibility to the expatriate companies themselves. In doing so, he and others like him have left the job of preparing for Africanization to the people whom it will displace. Asked whether one could use training programs to counter the problem of Africans who had been groomed over a long period to take over a specific expatriate post, only to accept a position elsewhere at the last minute, a high-ranking official of the Uganda Development Finance Corporation responded in a manner that questioned whether the local culture, in terms of its attitudes toward the work ethic and more general moral commitments, was at fault:

> You tell me how you develop a sense of obligation. I don't know. This is the one big problem—how do you develop in anyone a sense of obligation, if that moral obligation is just not inherent in his makeup.... You've got an entirely different situation on the continent [Europe]. People do have an obligation to their work. This is not inherited naturally; it's something that's been built up for many years, because there has been a shortage of work and work is so important to them, if they wish to live, that it pays them to be loyal to their employer. Here, in this community, if you're a good man there are a thousand channels open to you.[4]

The local Ugandans, however, didn't seem so impressed with these "thousand channels," and wondered why they could not get more of the top management positions still held by expatriates.

Perspectives on Place. What place in the hierarchy of command will nationals, whether African or others, occupy? Will they fill important command posts or intermediate, token positions designed mostly for show?

There is widespread use of tokenism, with companies employing the bare minimum of Blacks, often placing them in positions of prominence, which have little effective power. In a large European-owned firm, the first position to be Africanized is usually that of public-relations director, and one or two Africans are often put on the board of directors among a dozen Europeans.

It is not clear that Africanizing the highest management and control positions of the larger enterprises was a primary objective of the African countries in the aftermath of independence. Their concern with rapid economic development, their lack of a large manpower pool or trained management and business talent, and competition from governmental administration and education for the limited number of better educated Africans, all made it reasonable for the African states to continue to rely on the expatriate staffs of the international companies. Only as more direct control of these enterprises is deemed necessary to influence the economic, political, and social life of the country will control of these positions become a matter of the highest priority.

Thus, even where foreign enterprises have been nationalized, as with the financial and insurance institutions, and the major manufacturing firms and importing establishments of Tanzania, Africanization of top decision-making positions proceeded very slowly. Perhaps one of the most suggestive cases of nationalization of ownership of enterprises without the transfer of the command positions is that of the Zambian copper companies. The holdings of the Anglo-American group of companies and of the Roan Selection Trust were nationalized in 1969. After repeated failures in discussions that dated from the time of independence in 1964, the Zambian government reached agreement with these companies whereby the mineral properties were nationalized, and the companies that were exploiting them were reorganized so that the Zambian government held 51 percent of the equity shares. No Zambians were prepared to run these companies, however, and the government therefore had to sign a ten-year management contract with them.

The initial Zambianization plan, running through 1975, failed to project African control in any of the seventy top command positions. The highest Africans could rise would be "mining engineer." Dissatisfaction over this and several other features of the 1969 buy-out arrangements led President Kaunda to pay off the bonds and attempt to abrogate the management contracts. After protracted resistance by the minority shareholding MNCs, Kaunda announced in February 1974 that new articles of association had been agreed to by company managers, who would ask their stockholders for ratification. Kaunda also announced his choices for the first African managing directors of the two mining complexes—Wilson Chakulya, the former minister of labour, and David Phiri, who had served as a director of Anglo-American.

Elevating Africans up the ladders of income, benefits, and power is the objective of Africanization programs from the African point of view. Sometimes, however, the companies instead elevate the job title and fatten job descriptions in the annual reports, without substantially changing the tasks or the functional importance of the employee. It is a tactic reminiscent of the South African approach. In independent, as well as in white-dominated Africa, foreign firms are learning that by simply reclassifying jobs held by Africans, they can beguile many outsiders who claim to be interested in promoting equal pay for equal work between white and black. Sometimes this procedure permits them to create the illusion of job advancement.

Another familiar ruse is to elevate the whole command structure in terms of formal job descriptions, job requirements, and advancement criteria, so that expatriates doing the same work as before may be elevated in title and prestige. This tactic may have the effect of creating whole job categories that are made to appear beyond the qualifications of Africans. D. Nzomo, a research associate of the Institute of Development Studies of the University of Nairobi, noted:

> Enterprises have been known to place people in this [professional] category on blown-up job titles, job elements and remuneration to avert the pressure to Kenyanize.... Establishments may have discovered that they can avert the pressure from the Government by raising the qualifications required for the post and then arguing successfully that qualified nationals are not available.[5]

From the African perspective, much of the "advancement" they have achieved in the few programs conducted thus far has been illusory. Africans are often put into positions for training in management functions without ever being allowed to manage anything. The Kenyan minister of labour has noted, for example, that a number of enterprises indulged in a kind of "window dressing by appointing a handful of them (Kenyans) to posts with high sounding titles, but which, in fact, carry little responsibility."[6] They may be brought into non-jobs, given a desk outside the expatriate's door, and told to learn by watching. This practice is decried by P. K. Kinyanjui, the general manager of the Kenya National Trading Corporation:

> Many companies have employed delaying tactics by wrongly overemphasizing experience. We all know that experience is vitally important, especially in the senior positions. But it must be realized that one will not gain experience in managerial skills until one is appointed a manager.[7]

In Nigeria, despite legal requirements to train Africans for higher posts, many companies that did so are reported to have preferred to release Africans, whose training they had supported, from contracts that would have required them to work for the company for a given period of time, rather than appoint them to the higher command positions.[8]

Expatriate technical assistants who are given the tasks of training someone to take over their jobs, as is legally required in all East African countries, sometimes claim that this is an ineffective way to promote localization. They complain of being expected to perform their full range of normal functions and then to carry out the training functions as well. Somewhat hypocritically, however, they decry the obligation not only in terms of efficiency, but also in terms of their distaste for "sitting next to Nellie," as they call it. At least one African, J. K. Geçau, the personnel manager of the British American Tobacco Company in Kenya, has expressed some sympathy for this attitude. He has stated, "this, with all the goodwill in the world, as a training procedure, leaves much to be desired."[9] He felt that those most capable of performing the job functions might honestly not be very good at the training. Hiring someone specifically to train the local counterparts may be preferable to using technical experts but has its own problems in terms of effective training. In any case, such training staff is not available.

It seems the expatriates' lack of commitment to displacing themselves is equally as important as their lack of training skills. John C. Shearer is reported to have found in his study of localization efforts in Latin America that job protection on the part of the expatriates was inherent in the structure of most companies.[10] Training was often neglected so that when vacancies did develop the expatriates could not find qualified nationals to fill them. Rose concluded that "in some cases it is undoubtedly true that the African is indeed being unfairly held back, usually because of conscious or unconscious job protection by his expatriate superior." One might suppose that the expatriates need not take special precautions to protect their jobs since so much wider a range of alternatives is available to them, at least in comparison to those available to the Africans who are their potential successors. But this may not be the case. Many of the expatriates in high positions in Africa actually are "second stringers" within their firms who have found their access to the top blocked. They are willing to take posts far from the home seat of power, and thus to jeopardize their further advancement even more, because these positions offer material amenities and an opportunity to exercise a wider range of authority than they might soon enjoy at home. Rose cites the frequency of this situation as a reason to localize management.

In a striking parallel to the Black American experience, black Africans often find that the first position that opens up to them in the larger white-managed firms is that of vice-president for public relations, or of personnel manager. One expatriate personnel manager has stated, "I don't know of a single instance where an African is the top man in control of expatriate capital."[11]

Africans, therefore, remain very far from the control of company policy or of decisions affecting the basic allocation of resources. Increasingly, companies are including Africans on their boards of directors, but this advance still leaves them short of effective power, as their number seldom surpasses two out of a dozen or so. The absence of real change, despite the presence of African directors, may have other causes as well, as Nzomo notes:

> Once one is on the inside, one won't cause any waves for one is constantly kept aware of one's immediate personal interests. From where then, will the pressure to Kenyanize come? Once those who are supposed to implement the policy decisions become part and parcel of the establishment, they aid in the discovery of ways and means of averting the pressure. After all, they are not so enthusiastic to see their colleagues become their equals in terms of socio-economic class, for they might surpass them, especially if they seem to "have what it takes."[12]

On the other hand, token membership on the board of directors of the larger expatriate firms may at least provide Africans a monitoring device, and a progressive influence over the company's recruitment and manpower development programs. Strong personalities, or persons having exceptionally good connections with the government, may achieve influence out of proportion to their vote. In any case, there are not very many Africans who have achieved even the token position of member of the board of directors. In Kenya, for example, there were only four black Kenyans and a couple of Ugandans among the top fifty directors of the more substantial enterprises in 1968.[13] Many Europeans held multiple directorships at that time. Lord Inchcope of the Mackenzie-Dalgety Group of firms, for example, once held thirty-six seats on Kenyan boards of directors, although he was resident in London. Local resident H. Travis held forty-three Kenyan directorships. Occasionally, an African has held multiple seats, as in the case of S. Nyanzi, but that is because as the director of the Uganda Development Corporation (UDC), which had substantial investments in them, he was a director of each affiliated company.

Governmental regulation through legislation and other general legal controls are the main instruments of localizing control of company policies. With respect to Africanization, such instruments entail the requirement of work permits that can be of quite limited duration, or that explicitly require the expatriate to train a local successor.[14] The means that Nigeria uses to control such matters have been quite extensive—including not only a license to do business, but also residency permits, and requirements that governmental approval be secured in order to import new equipment or personnel, or to expand a plant.

It is not clear how much the use of theoretically "non-renewable" and short-term work permits has actually sped Africanization, however. In Kenya, the report "Who Controls Industry in Kenya?" did find that by the middle of 1968 the number of Kenyans in managerial positions in all areas of national life was steadily increasing. The report even warned of the emergence of a managerial class. Kenya undoubtedly has a long way to go before it has a middle class proportionate in size to that of Nigeria, however, and in Nigeria the number of expatriates continued to increase until it peaked in 1970. In 1964, when immigration permits were required of the expatriates, 1,167 were awarded. Nigerian economist R. O. Ekundare has concluded that Nigeria found it more difficult to enforce Nigerianization of management than of the public sector.[15] The need for professional and technical talent may be so great throughout the newly independent states that work permits may be renewed despite failure to train an African counterpart.

Governmental, or in some cases private, indigenous partnership with expatriate capital may be a way of making token African representation on a board of directors effective. Although the Obote government sought to place an increasing share of industry and commerce under local control, or in partnership, the Uganda Development Corporation then generally took only a minority share of the stock of a company. Nonetheless, it exercised considerable power because if the firms were not responsive in their plans for Africanization (in terms of recruitment, training, and promotion), they were sometimes denied entrance. Once the companies had gained entrance, the UDC's power was reduced. The leadership of the UDC has also indicated that it moved slowly with respect to the Ugandanization of some companies, such as the Industrial Chemicals and Fertilizers Company, because of a lack of technically competent Africans. "We have got our eyes on some people working there . . . with the purpose of grooming one of them to take over the management in the future," the general manager stated, "but sometimes even where the UDC is a partial owner we have had trouble getting our way about Ugandan advancement, because sometimes shareholding is not very big and the other party was very set against us."[16]

It is important to understand that these divergent African/foreign perspectives on the place Africans are to occupy in the management hierarchy of expatriate firms reflect differences in objectives. The Africans are interested in acquiring power to influence the direction of the companies concerned, and through them to influence the direction of the national economy. Often this is a prerequisite to the success of their efforts to chart new directions in political and social development. The expatriate firms see the Africanization problem primarily in terms of public relations interests, an entrance requirement to do business, and protection against the loss of their assets. Occasionally the expatriate firms point out that African personnel cost them less and thus may enhance the viability of the firm economically, although this approach is usually more than counterbalanced by their almost invariable image of Africans as less productive than expatriate personnel.

Expatriate arguments against Africanization reveal a good deal about the nature and some of the ambiguities of the motives involved. Rose summarizes these attitudes:

> The main argument [against Africanization] revolves around the question of loyalty to the company and the possible character weaknesses of human beings.... Another argument is that the home office can better deal with Americans since they talk the same business language and may know each other from working in the United States. To Africanize would mean confusion and inefficiency from the communications standpoint. The solution to this problem would also overcome another objection that the nationals do not have enough experience; that is, they have not been exposed to the whole operation, particularly at the American end.... These objections are clearly related to the question of control, which is of great concern to the company. The last expatriate bastion to fall has nearly always been the position of controller—except for the most senior managerial position, which has not yet fallen at all. The worry is that expense accounts will run riot, brothers-in-law will draw fat salaries for non-existent jobs and so on.[17]

Perspectives on Pace. Given the divergent perspectives on the race and place of Africanization, the differences between expatriate and African satisfaction with the pace of this process should come as no surprise. Everyone can perhaps agree that the pace is slow, but they will differ as to whether or not it is too slow.

Writing in the immediate post-independence period for most of Africa, and prior to the independence of most of the East African countries, Guy Hunter pointed out that only 15 to 25 percent of the managerial-level positions had been Africanized in West Africa, and perhaps only half that number in East Africa. Since these figures also included Africans in publicly owned enterprises, the level of Africanization in the private sector must have been considerably lower.[18]

Writing several years later, Rose reported that, accepting whatever definition of management the companies used, some of the large European companies in English-speaking Africa had reached the point that they projected an image of being highly Africanized. He cited the Shell Oil Company's operations in Nigeria, which had 7 percent of its management positions filled by Africans in 1957 and increased this figure to 55 percent by 1965. A large U.S. oil company, on the contrary, had only two Africans out of its twenty managers in Nigeria, and none at all in its operations in other African countries. Two large internationally owned raw material concerns, one with more than 20,000 African employees, had only one African manager each. Some firms reported making efforts to recruit Africans from U.S. universities, but by 1966 only one of the recruits had reached the first step of the management ladder.[19] Some of the more recent American companies seemed to have made more rapid progress.

Nzomo's 1971 study of American firms operating in Kenya (see Table 1) did not find Africanization to have proceeded to any significant degree. Indigenous Kenyans (black Africans for the most part) occupied slightly less than one-quarter of the "managerial/executive" positions. The largest single nationality group among the American firms were British nationals, who numbered nearly 41 percent.

Only 15 percent were American, although these had the highest salaries, the highest levels of education, and presumably the highest posts. Most of these firms had been operating in Kenya for eight years or more, many (46 percent) since before June 1960. Less than 2 percent had been there for under two years. These firms, therefore, had plenty of time to settle in and develop African personnel.

From the standpoint of advancement up the scale of remuneration, which may reflect the extent of one's responsibility as well, Africans lagged far behind (see Table 2). Nearly two-thirds of the British,

Americans, and other Europeans reporting their income (and a third of the Americans did not report it) were found to be receiving over 3,000 pounds a year, but only about one-quarter of the reporting indigenous Kenyans did so. This situation existed despite the fact that these Kenyans had *higher* levels of education than the British nationals who were involved. The largest single block of managers is grouped into the salary range 3,000-4,000 pounds a year, and one-fifth of the indigenous Kenyans were at that level. Most of the other groups had a slightly larger proportion of their people at that level, but it was the base for them, whereas the great bulk of Kenyans, indigenous and naturalized, fell below. Called managers, the Africans were nonetheless usually performing only as foremen or in similar positions.

Circumstances of Compelled Change

Change Controlled by African Initiative. Uganda provides examples of two quite different approaches to the radical change of fully Africanizing the management of the business sector. Milton Obote attempted to achieve a quick but orderly change, implemented with the forced help of the companies involved. Idi Amin carried out a convulsive expulsion of the entire non-African commercial, technical, and managerial class.

Uganda had attempted to stimulate African entry into business in the early 1950s.[22] Concern for attracting foreign investment and skilled manpower moderated the pursuit of this objective, however, as the desire for the retention of such factors moderated the Mugabe policies during the early period of his government in Zimbabwe. In its early years the Obote government emphasized guarantees against nationalization of foreign investment,[23] but few of its efforts to promote African business development proved successful. The National Trading Corporation, which, in a government effort to assist Africans to compete with Asian traders, took over the wholesale trade in items handled by the petty-traders, produced major scandals, particularly in connection with credit schemes.

In a switch, President Obote published the "Common Man's Charter" in 1969. This document signaled a major change in the economic and Africanization policies of the Ugandan government, and was characterized as a move "to the left"—a move meaning "that political and economic power must be vested in the majority." The new platform made Africanization of business, trading, and management a key objective.

A Committee on Africanization of Commerce and Industry was appointed and claimed that "The Minister [must be] ruthless in his actions to bring Africans into business." In connection with the committee's report, one member of Parliament asserted: "We want black faces occupying senior posts."[24] The committee's concern had been fired by the evident lack of headway, despite the longstanding efforts to elevate Blacks into these senior positions. This failure is reflected in Table 3, which is based on the committee's findings.[25]

The committee was especially concerned about the role of the banks and what it thought to be their particular resistance to Africanization. The banks are reported to have insisted that it required a minimum of twenty-five years to produce general and assistant general managers and local directors, and a minimum of fifteen years to produce managers and assistant managers. The committee felt that this was not the pattern of preparation for Europeans, and asserted that, in any case, it did not intend to wait until the twenty-first century to take over the top positions. The committee thereupon recommended that all foreign firms and "parastatal organizations" (owned by the state) replace all noncitizens with Africans within five years. The chairman of the committee also demanded nationalization of the banks and institutions of finance, as had been carried out in Tanzania.

The government rejected both the five-year proposal and nationalization of the banks, but did ask banks and insurance companies to incorporate in Uganda, which was taken as a signal of the government's intention to nationalize.[26] These firms were also asked to deposit L20 million locally, and to enter into partnership with the government. Negotiations began with some firms in late 1969 about offers of shareholding to the government. In May 1971, however, Obote stepped up the pace considerably by ruling that all import and export business would be done through parastatal bodies, and that 60 percent ownership in the banks and financial institutions would be acquired by the government. Compensation for these shares was to come out of future profits, unlike the situation with the nationalized copper companies in Zambia, where the state was obliged to pay the fixed rates of compensation irrespective of the firms' profitability. The government later compromised its position under pressure from the companies, the British Government, the International Monetary Fund, and the World Bank and accepted the Zambian copper model. A new scheme required a 10 percent down payment to Shell-British Petroleum, with the remainder converted to a loan at 7.5 percent interest, payable within five years irrespective of the profitability of the firms. A management contract was also signed at a fee cost of 1 percent of net profits. With respect to the banks, especially the largest, Grinleys, a new bank was to be created, 60 percent of which would be owned by the Uganda government and to which the expatriates would turn over their local operations. They were permitted to shift much of their operations into their Kenyan subsidiaries, however.

Other companies apparently accepted the new policies with more grace. Some seemed to be relieved to have the uncertainties cleared away and a local partner interested in the success of their interests. The rationale of such an approach was summarized by *The Economist*:

> It will be a tragedy if potential investors in Africa are mistakenly led to believe that there is no longer a place for them there. Although doing business in independent Africa now calls for a high degree of political acumen, the opportunities available to those who possess it are good. The risks are greater than in more settled parts of the world, but so are the returns.... The shrewdest businessmen ... have argued ... that 49 percent stake in a business whose success is underwritten by government participation may be more valuable than 100 percent of a concern exposed to all the political winds that blow.[27]

Such pressures then eased and the policies for the expatriate companies were put into limbo, when, on 25 January 1971, the former boxer Field Marshall Idi Amin, in a move that was not apparently motivated specifically by economic policies, overthrew the Obote government. He did not officially scrap the Africanization policies, but clearly indicated that they would be pursued slowly. Amin sought to cultivate the cooperation of the Asians and the expatriate communities. The program of nationalization was formally dropped in May, except in the few cases where agreement had already been reached with the companies, and even there he invited them to review the agreements. The banks, insurance companies, the East African Steel Corporation, and two locally owned sugar companies were required to sell to the government, not 60 but 49 percent of equity shares. No one demanded black faces in the senior posts.

But, in August 1972, in one of his characteristic reversals, President Amin gave noncitizen Asians ninety days to leave the country. The twenty-three thousand Asians who were already Ugandan citizens later were included as well, then exempted. Professionals were initially exempted from, then included in the order to quit. Amin announced he had launched an economic war. Kampala businessmen predicted the general collapse of the Ugandan economy.

Most Asians left the country whether included in or exempted from the orders. In one blow the petty commercial class and much of middle management were eliminated. The government established a commission to survey business holdings and to supervise their sale to Ugandans, but this commission was subsequently rusticated and the army began to distribute the Kampala assets of the departed Asian community. Most of the larger enterprises, such as the Madhvani industrial complex, were turned over to the UDC, long directed by a highly reputed professional economist from Acholi.

The economy soon revealed the severe ravages of Amin's war.[28] The 1974-1975 budget message delivered by the minister of finance carried the news that the gross national product had declined from its 1969 growth rate of 11 percent to 3.1 percent in 1971 and 1972, and the negative rate of 1.2 percent in 1973. Although many European businessmen, especially the British, remained, production in the industries they normally dominated fell off sharply. Copper production was down in 1973 by 29 percent, mining and quarrying by 26 percent, and manufacturing by 5 percent. The balance of international payments was in deficit, as was the government itself. In June 1978, after seven years of Amin's destructive rule, nothing was functioning well, and the general populace was preoccupied with surviving. Most of the country's production was marketed illegally. The minister of finance admitted that the economy had been in decline ever since the army had come to power, although he felt a return to economic growth could finally be discerned. The government would still be Shs. 2,600m in deficit, however, despite booming prices for coffee. What had once been among the most efficient civil services in Africa had been devastated. Administration was so poorly conducted that the government had failed to collect Shs. 68m owed it by the tenants of the so-called Departed Asians' Property Custodian Board. The new government that came to power after the fall of Amin in April 1979 would have to start from scratch. It was possible, reported *Africa* magazine in May 1979, to pick up from the files which were scattered across the floor of Amin's residence one marked "Budget," only to find it filled with a report from the State Research Bureau about an assassination attempt.

The conditions that prevailed in Amin's Uganda hardly provide an appropriate framework within which to assess the viability of any approach to Africanizing management, whether through carefully planned and staged programs or through forced crash programs. But the experience of the new Ugandan government, after it was determined that neither Mr. Binaisa nor General Ojok but rather the returned Milton Obote was the head of it, and once life returned to normal, may well show whether the directly productive sector can be adequately handled by African managers. In the summer of 1980 there were rumors, however, that Uganda officials were appealing to Asian businessmen to return.

Change Controlled by Expatriates. Mozambique offers an example of radical change in the composition of the managerial, commercial, and technical class which resulted from the convulsive self-removal of the expatriates who had monopolized such functions. The demise of metropolitan Portuguese rule, officially recognized in September 1974 with the inauguration of a transitional government, was followed by the demise of the last-minute effort by an element of the Portuguese settler community to implement its own U.D.I. (unilateral declaraton of independence), in the style of the Rhodesian settlers. During the period of the transitional government, that is, until 25 June 1975, about twenty thousand Portuguese, mostly small shopkeepers but including many more substantial businessmen and technicians, fled the country. In the aftermath of independence itself, over one hundred thousand more emigrated. One analyst believed they were frightened by the government's rush to implement socialist policies and "prevent the emergence of a bourgeoisie";[29] it is also probable that they were not prepared to accept black rule.

Although many of the Portuguese settlers were themselves uneducated or poorly educated and lacked high-level technical and commercial or managerial skills, the fleeing settlers eliminated most of what trained manpower there was in Mozambique. There had been virtually no Africanization after five hundred years of often harsh

Portuguese rule. At the time of independence there were only 636 Africans attending secondary school in the entire country, and only four Africans in university studies. Over 85 percent of the population was illiterate and only about 15 percent even spoke Portuguese.

The few experienced and dedicated administrators available after independence were strained to the limit. There followed a crisis in the availability of essential goods and the state itself took over wholesale and even entered into retail operations. *Africa* magazine (May 1980, p. 15) reports that "by 1976, there were over 200 stores—known as people's shops—that were under the direct superintendence of the State." Abandoned housing units were also taken over and run by the state in what became a rather large bureaucracy whose members sometimes benefited personally from its favors.

Initially, nationalization actions were directed at abandoned businesses. In 1978 this process was extended to some of the major business operations of continuing residents, who were charged with "economic sabotage," including the deliberate run-down of production and the illegal export of foreign exchange.[30] Three of the largest companies in the country, in heavy industry, mining, and sugar, were nationalized. The coal mining company was charged with deliberately extracting too little coal. The sugar company suffered a decline in production from 173,000 tons in 1973 to about 45,000 in 1978, and had laid off over 7,000 workers. Nationalization was a way of saving it from liquidation. But in none of these instances would the takeover by the state solve the problems of management disloyalty to the goals of the revolutionary government, or the problems of management inefficiency. In fact, the inefficiency problem may have worsened. A company that makes marble objects and that had been nationalized after its owner fled abroad reported in 1978 that it had not been able to obtain essential raw materials because the state, its new owner, had not granted the necessary import licenses since 1975. Similarly, a shortage of sweaters was blamed on the fact that knitwear maufacturers had not been granted licenses to import acrylic yarn.

There has been gross inefficiency and neglect in the operations of many of the enterprises owned or controlled by the state. The sugar plant and estates mentioned above went for forty-eight months without harvesting their crop, losing 5,000 hectares of sugar productivity for a period. The state takeover of the factory was basically a subsidization. Other operations were affected by neglect of fundamental operational procedures. Vital documents were often left to molder in drawers, while vital goods rotted on the docks. One report noted that "industrial production was estimated to have fallen by 50 percent between independence and mid-1976."[31] Even by the most optimistic projections, agricultural production would not return to pre-1974 levels until 1981. Balance of payments deficits continued to be severe, totalling $280 million in 1978. Per capita income had fallen from its estimated level of about $250 at independence to about $125 in 1978.

Of course, the economic problems that Mozambique had to face did not all stem from managerial inexperience or ineptitude. Independence was followed by the oil crisis, recession in the country's export markets, a fall in sugar prices, even drought and flooding. The loss of the technical class, small and inept as it was, coupled with the sabotage carried out by many persons before they left and by some who stayed, was also compounded by the increasingly burdensome support that Mozambique gave to the Zimbabwean liberation struggle, including the loss of up to $130m a year from the closing of her ports and railways to Rhodesian shipping. Jobs for 86,000 people were lost as a result. Also contributing to economic difficulties were the demise of South African and other tourism, and finally, the destruction of important border area infrastructure. It is a wonder that Mozambique survived at all.

Foreign technicians have been crucial to her survival. Scores of Soviet experts have worked there, and over six hundred Cuban technicians were expected to arrive at the end of 1978 under the terms of a new cooperation agreement with Cuba. Mozambique also entered into an agreement with East Germany for technicians and for the expansion and reorganization of the metallurgical and metal works sectors. The country even relied on South African technicians to run important functions in its railways and ports.

The problem of management corruption, sabotage, and inefficiency became a policy issue of increasing importance to the government, until in March 1978 President Machel declared a new war—on "the enemy within." He promised a large role for private enterprise, especially for the smaller companies that provided services to the people. The state bureaucracy would have to be purged and reorganized. The state would not continue to be involved in small businesses (trading, restaurants, and the like), but rather with large development projects, as well as the major social sectors of education, health, housing, and justice. Machel asserted that "the state should not sell matches."

Conclusion

Where international capital is concerned, African societies have not yet solved the problem of transferring the technology of effective business and organizational management to local people and institutions, nor have they created an effective mix of competence, incentive, control, and freedom for the development of indigenous enterprises. The ability to do so in the future may determine Africa's chances of surviving the 1980s, a decade in which the convergence of a rapidly growing population, enormous debt, runaway energy costs, uncertain and weak export markets, barriers to industrial exports, falling food production, and failure to diversify economies may pose overwhelming problems.

One fundamental reason for this failure to Africanize management has been the lack of a real commitment to this objective by most of the expatriate staffs and the international investors to whom the process has been entrusted. This situation has a special relevance for Afro-Americans, who have increasingly frequent opportunities to participate in African development, not only as individual technicians or staff, but even as investors, either independently or in partnership with local businessmen and government institutions. For their part, Afro-Americans can at least demonstrate understanding of and sympathy for the African desire to be in charge of their own show. There is also an increasing Afro-American familiarity with Africans which makes it possible for Black Americans and Africans to enter into business partnerships, where trust is an important ingredient to success. When they come as individual technical or managerial experts, Afro-Americans can be expected to carry a commitment to assist their African counterparts in acquiring the *personal* skills and attitudes necessary to build up successful technical operations, the first step in the successful transfer of the technology of management.

There is a second fundamental element in this process which would not offer any advantage to Afro-Americans, however—that of developing a distinct and complete local "organizational competence" for an enterprise or organization. This involves the achievement of a smooth overall performance of a unit as a whole. Only when this is achieved by local people working together and, ultimately, on their own, will such a competence be a truly indigenous phenomenon. Subsidiaries and partnerships of international firms, even if Afro-American-owned, find it most difficult to accomplish this task, for structural and not just for personal reasons. But even where international capital and corporate structure is not involved, local governments must allow local operations sufficient latitude in decision making, and strong enough material incentives to produce full effort and to promote the learning by doing and by mistake that is the only teacher of genuine "organizational competence."

A third fundamental element of the process is the hardest of all to accomplish, but Afro-Americans do have some advantage in making a success of it: the development of a genuinely local expression of the organizational competence that is peculiar to an exogenous international firm. This goal requires substantial change in the way international firms currently operate abroad. Ultimately, the aim is a truly global firm with no distinctive national character at its core. Taking the process to its logical extension we can envision that such a firm will have people in the highest ranks who come from a variety of cultural and geographical backgrounds, yet preserve their own cultural orientations, or at least the capability to return to them. They must insist on a degree of adaptability and sensitivity at headquarters which enables the firm, when viewed from the perspective of the localities, to fit in. Afro-Americans can play an important instructional and sensitizing role because their education and cultural endowments enable them to be effective with the current leadership of American firms that operate abroad. At the same time, their commitment to assist Africans not only to take charge of operations in their home territories, but also to get into the power structures of these firms even here in the United States, can play a significant role in attaining this goal.

In the final analysis, however, the real test of management development in Africa is for Africans to build up their own institutions in their own way, with their own technical processes that utilize their own resources. To avoid technological isolation and unnecessary duplication, Africans must have access to technological information and education. They will need political assistance in gaining access to markets and centers of training and information in the industrial world. And they will need greater latitude of action and experimentation at home.

So far, none of these fundamental processes has been carried very far in Africa. Future economic development there, and the political peace and development that are based on it, will require a much greater measure of success than we have seen to date.

Notes

1. Tore Rose, "The Problem of Africanization," in Jerome W. Blood, *Management Looks at Africa* (New York: American Management Assoc., 1966), p. 138.
2. Tom Mboya, on Mike Wallace (narrator) CBS News Special on Black America, 16 July 1968.
3. Nsekela, General Manager, Tanzania National Bank, interview with authors, Dar-es-Salaam, August 1971.
4. Interview with the author, Kampala, Uganda, August 1971.
5. D. Nzomo, "Occupational Kenyanization in the Private Sector," Institute of Development Studies, University of Nairobi, Staff Paper No. 108, August 1971, p. 14.
6. Minister of Labour, Government of Kenya, Report of Speech to Careers Conference of 28-30 March 1968, p. 30.
7. P. K. Kinyanjui, "Lecture on Problems Faced in the Africanization of Staff," East African Seminar on Labour Problems in Economic Development, 2-28 April 1967. International Institute for Labour Studies, Geneva, 1967.
8. R. O. Ekundare, "The Political Economy of Private Investment in Nigeria," *Journal of Modern African Studies*, 10, no. 1 (May 1972): 46.
9. J. K. Geeau, "Lecture on Personnel Training and Development in East African Industries," East African Seminar of Labour Problems in Economic Development, 2-28 April 1967. International Institute for Labour Studies, Geneva.
10. Rose, "The Problem of Africanization," p. 149.
11. Ibid.
12. Nzomo, "Occupational Kenyanization," p. 15.
13. "Who Controls Industry in Kenya?" Working Party of the Department of Christian Education and Training, 1968, pp. 144-145.
14. Samuel Suckow, *Nigerian Law and Foreign Investment* (The Hague, 1966).
15. R. O. Ekundare, "Political Economy of Private Investment in Nigeria," p. 46.
16. Angoma, acting general manager, Uganda Development Corporation, interview with the author, Kampala, August 1971.
17. Rose, "The Problem of Africanization," p. 141.

18. Guy Hunter, *The New Societies of Tropical Africa* (New York, 1972), p. 226.
19. Rose, "The Problem of Africanization," p. 150.
20. Nzomo, from data in "Occupational Kenyanization," p. 17.
21. Ibid., p. 17.
22. The Small Industries Development Fund was established in 1952, and an African Trade Development Section of the Ministry of Commerce and Industry was established as well. In 1963, African Business Promotions was created as a subsidiary of the Uganda Development Corporation, which itself had been founded in 1951.
23. Selwyn Ryan, "Economic Nationalism in Uganda and Ghana," Makerere University, revised version of paper presented to Canadian Association of African Studies, 6 February 1970 (mimeo), p. 3.
24. Ibid., p. 13.
25. From figures reported in Ryan, "Economic Nationalism," p. 16.
26. The following discussion is based on Ryan, "Economic Nationalism," pp. 17-19.
27. *The Economist*, 23 August 1969, p. 56, quoted in Ibid, p. 22.
28. *African Research Bulletin: Economic, Financial and Technical Series*, Africa Research Ltd., Exeter, England, May 15-June 14 1974, p. 3140.
29. Roger Mann, "Mozambique's Stalled Revolution," *The New Leader*, 16 August 1976, pp. 5-6.
30. *Africa Contemporay Record*, 1978/79, B341 ff. Most of the following is based on this source.
31. T. Hodges, "Mozambique," in G. Carter and P. O'Meara, eds., *Southern Africa in Crisis* (Bloomington, Ind., 1978), p. 65.

CHAPTER 16

The Political Economy of the Black World—Origins of the Present Crisis

Bernard Magubane

> Each generation must write its own world history. And in what period has that been more necessary than in the present?   —Goethe

The Black world is in the throes of a profound, pervasive crisis. So much everyone agrees. But what kind of crisis? How can it be explained? And how can it be solved? To consider the economic state of the Black world today is at the same time to confront a baffling paradox. The Black world is supposedly free politically. In the United States Black political representation at the local, state, and national level is at an all-time high, and a number of major cities boast Black mayors. In Africa and the Caribbean, black governments are in power. The Black community in the United States is potentially powerful economically and politically, if only this power can be mobilized, and the situation is similar for Blacks in the Caribbean, Latin America, and Africa. Africa is already a major producer of minerals, accounting for 80 percent of the world's annual gold production, 75 percent of the diamonds, and 30 percent of the vanadium, the antimony, the chrome, and manganese, as well as significant quantities of copper, uranium, and petroleum. The continent also has vast unexploited deposits of iron ore, bauxite, phosphates, uranium, platinum, copper, nickel, tin, and fluorspar. In addition, it has a vast agricultural potential. The Caribbean, though fragmented geographically, is not without economic potential, if only a proper political framework can be found. Yet despite these possibilities, the economic situation of the Black world is bleak. Poverty, malnutrition, and disease are taking a heavy toll of the present generation and threaten the next generations.

Bernard Magubane is a Professor in the Anthropology Department at the University of Connecticut in Storrs, Connecticut

Is Africa and the rest of the Black world condemned to eternal suffering and poverty? Condemned by whom? Is God or Nature to blame? Is it the oppressive climate, racial inferiority? Religion, customs? Or may not its plight be a product of history, made by human beings, and so capable of being changed by human beings? What does a glance back to the past teach us about our predicament? History has different meanings depending on one's position in the modern world. At the risk of being called a brooder, let me see what the history of the last four hundred years has meant for the Black world and how its lessons can be used to explain our present dilemma.

History's great tradition, writes William Appleman Williams (1973: 8), is to help us understand ourselves and our world so that each of us, individually and in conjunction with our fellow men and women, can formulate relevant and reasoned alternatives and become meaningful actors in making history. He goes on to say that the historical experience is not one of staying in the present and looking back. Rather, it is one of going back into the past and returning to the present with a wider and more intense consciousness of the restrictions of our former outlook. "We return with a broader awareness of the alternatives open to us and armed with a sharper perceptiveness with which to make our choices. In this manner it is possible to loosen the clutch of the dead hand of the past and transform it into a living tool for the present and the future." Barrington Moore, Jr. (1967: 508) concurs about the purpose of studying history when he writes: "But if the men of the future are ever to break the chains of the present, they will have to understand the forces that forged them."

In a classic study with a frightening title—*Open Veins of Latin America: Five Centuries of Pillage of a Continent*—Eduardo Galiano, a Peruvian writer, tells us about the attitude toward the past among those to whom the current world order gives great privileges. He writes that veneration for the past always seemed reactionary to him. "The right chooses to talk about the past because it prefers dead people: a quiet world, a quiet time. The powerful who legitimize their privileges by heredity cultivate nostalgia. History is studied as if we were visiting a museum, but this collection of mummies is a swindle. They lie to us about the past as they lie to us about the present: they mask the face of reality. They force the oppressed victims to absorb an alien, dessicated, sterile mummy fabricated by the oppressor as if it were the only one possible" (1973: 288).

These remarks by Williams, Moore, and Galiano are apposite to the theme of this paper. Black people cannot be nostalgic about the past nor can they look at the past as if it were composed of dead mummies. Indeed, our past cannot be frozen into dead images. What happened to our forebears constitutes a living reality that, if forgotten, can only deepen our present tragedy The theme of this seminar is "Consolidating Africana Studies: Bonding African Linkages." What does this theme mean in terms of the political economy of the Black world today?

One of the distinctive facts about the Black world and its problem is that it is part of contemporary history. Black people were not always poor or backward. Black poverty, I would like to suggest, cannot be understood unless we are prepared to adopt a worldwide perspective, that is, not merely to brood about what happened to us in the past, but to see how the cumulative development of the past continues to influence the present situation.

For most white peoples the past four hundred years are an era of pride, its excesses perhaps to be regretted but its achievements far surpassing them. It brought prosperity to the largest numbers of Europeans and their descendants wherever they happened to settle in the modern world. Thus, for the white world the recent past has been a story of victory and power. For the Black world, however, the colonial and imperial era is a cause for shame, the source of all the problems we face in the modern world. It is an era that distorted human relations, assailed and devastated our humanity. In short, the past has been a record of defeats and humiliation.

The economic plight of the Black world is historically rooted in the exploitation that resulted from the expansion of the world capitalist system. The African slave trade not only integrated the Black world into the world capitalist economy, but was also the major source of primitive accumulation for European and American capitalists. The ideological consequences of slavery, that is, the association of a black skin and genetic inferiority, persist in the modern world. Thus, any discussion of the current economic plight of the Black world must recognize the fact that Black economic distress is not a fact of nature, but a consequence of our integration in the world capitalist economy in the last four hundred years.

In the middle of the nineteenth century, studying the development of the capitalist mode of production, Karl Marx already understood the important role that the exploitation of Blacks played in the development of the world capitalist economy. In a letter to P. V. Annenkov (1846) he explained that:

> Direct slavery is just as much the pivot of bourgeois industry as machinery, credits, etc. Without slavery you have no cotton; without cotton you have no modern industry. It is slavery that has given the colonies their value; it is the colonies that have created world trade, and it is world trade that is the pre-condition of large-scale industry. Thus slavery is an economic category of the greatest importance.
>
> Without slavery North America, the most progressive of countries, would be transformed into a patriarchal country. Wipe out North America from the map of the world, and you will have anarchy—the complete decay of modern commerce and civilisation. Cause slavery to disappear and you will have wiped America off the map of nations.
>
> Thus slavery, because it is an economic category, has always existed among the institutions of the peoples. Modern nations have been able only to disguise slavery in their own countries, but they have imposed it without disguise upon the New World. [Marx, 1971, 94-95]

In chapter 31 of the first volume of *Das Kapital,* Marx again returned to the role of Africa and the slave trade as a source of primitive accumulation.

> The discovery of gold and silver in America, the extirpation, enslavement and entombment in the mines of the aboriginal population, the beginning of conquest and looting of the East Indies, the turning of Africa into a Warren for the commercial hunting of black skins, signalized the rosy dawn of the era of capitalist production. These idyllic proceedings are the chief momenta of primitive accumulation. [1977: 915]

The forced integration of the Black world into the capitalist world economy has proved both durable and continuous. Indeed, the prosperity of Western civilization has grown through the continuous negation of the Black world in both Africa and the Diaspora. Every step forward in modern history has been at the same time a step backward in the position of the oppressed and exploited Black majority. Whatever benefits a few enjoyed have necessitated suffering for the many. Indeed, when we look at the constellation of factors that currently contributes to Black poverty and suffering, we in fact are witnessing the cumulative impact of the fundamental moments in the growth of the capitalist world economy and its impact on the Black world. As a result of capitalist development, Africa and its peoples suffered first the agony of slavery and second, as a consequence of this, the horror of colonization. The cumulative impact of these interlocked experiences needs to be examined very thoroughly, for there is no way to understand the nature of our predicament except by confronting black experience in the various stages of the evolution of the capitalist world economy.

The African people, unlike any other people, were scattered across the developing capitalist world as involuntary servants, forced to work for nothing. This international dispersion made the African the first true international proletariat, and in a sense made the fortunes of capitalism inseparable from the misfortune of Blacks. Marx could have been thinking about Black experience when he spoke of "a class with *radical* claims, a class in civil society that was not a class of civil society, a class which was the dissolution of all classes, a sphere of society which had a universal character because of its universal suffering and which claimed no particular right because no particular wrong but simply general wrong was perpetrated on it, which could no longer invoke a *historical* but only a human title, which did not one-sidedly oppose the consequences but totally opposed the premises of [world capitalist economy]—a sphere, finally, which could not emancipate itself without emancipating all other spheres of society, a sphere, in short, that was the complete loss of humanity and could redeem itself only through the complete redemption of society. This dissolution of society as a particular class was the proletariat" (1956: 70).

The capitalist world used Africa and its peoples for all the benefits of which the human mind can conceive. In time a belief took root that Africa and its people were forever destined for exploitation by the capitalist world.

The Impact of Slavery Defined

Let us start with the first Black experience under capitalism: the slave trade and its legacy for the Black experience in the capitalist world. The capture and enslavement of black labor for the enrichment of European and American capitalists has been dealt with by many Black writers, including W. E. B. DuBois, Eric Williams, and Walter Rodney. They have shown in a way that cannot be disputed how the traffic in human cargo provided opportunities for European and American capitalists to accumulate the primitive capital that in time led to the prodigious wealth of Western Europe and North America. This is not to say that Black people were the only source of primitive accumulation under capitalism or that their experience was unique. On the contrary, we were one part of the vast humanity that was despoiled by capitalism. Even as we talk about Black experience, then, we should never lose sight of our commonality with what DuBois (1964: 15-16) called "that dark and vast sea of human labor in China and India, the South Seas and all Africa; in the West Indies and Central America and the United States—that great majority of mankind, on whose bent and broken backs rest today the founding stones of modern industry—[we] share a common destiny; [we] are despised and rejected by race and color, paid a wage below the level of decent living."

Yet the Black experience, though sharing much with that of other colonized peoples, was at the same time unique, and that uniqueness is a fundamental issue. The Black experience under capitalism has been but one tragic experience after another. Indeed, it is the sheer cruelty of that experience which made Black people, in the words of one anthropologist, the outcast from human evolution itself. And whenever the capitalist world experienced a crisis of accumulation, the burden was shifted to the shoulders of black labor and African resources were used to rescue Europe from its difficulty.

Through all that has been and will yet be written about the various aspects of the African slave trade, one fact remains indisputable—the slave trade has been inseparable from the underdevelopment and impoverishment of the Black world. Since the era of what Marx called the "rosy dawn," Africa and the African, whether at home or abroad, have been held hostages to capitalist accumulation. For the developing capitalist world economy, the captive African was the proverbial goose who lays the golden egg. For the slave trader, the African was an ideal commodity and source of wealth; for the planter, the slave was not only an instrument of production, but also capital par excellence. As Marx (III) put it, "the price paid for a slave is nothing but the anticipated and capitalized surplus-value or profit to be wrung out of the slave" (1962: 788). The African, either as a commodity for the trader or as a slave forced to work for the planter, became the original stock of capital which, if not a necessary, was a sufficient condition for the primitive accumulation of capital. Africa and its peoples are thus the most durable source of primitive accumulation that the capitalist world ever created. Lest I be accused of exaggeration, look at who is responsible not only for maintaining, but also for benefiting from the horrors of apartheid in South Africa. Thus slavery was crucial to Black experience under capitalism and it has determined the whole of our subsequent history in the modern world.

Slavery shattered the fabric of African society. The immediate effect was a dramatic quickening of Africa's decline and subsequent penetration by foreign elements. In a sense, as has been pointed out, the slave trade was the beginning of the underdevelopment of Africa, and the African slave was the first proletarian to suffer the full weight of capitalist exploitation and dehumanization. In the words of DuBois:

> The sinister traffic, on which the British Empire and the American Republic were largely built, cost black Africa no less than 100 million souls, the wreckage of its political and social life, and left the continent in precisely that state of helplessness which invites aggression and exploitation. "Color" became, in the world's thought, synonymous with inferiority. "Negro" lost its capitalization, and Africa was another name for bestiality and barbarism. [1978: 17]

The most enduring legacy of slavery is of course the racist ideology, which was called into existence and is still sustained by the exploitative policies of the capitalist classes in Europe and North America. The seemingly autonomous development of contemporary racism should not be allowed to obscure the fact that this need to exploit and dehumanize black labor remains the dominant stimulus in the development of the new forms of racism espoused by, among others, William Shockley and Arthur Jensen. Until our view of the economic plight of the Black world is grounded in an understanding of its past, we will lack the basis for any clear understanding both of our present predicament and of the contradictory possibilities that can yield a strategy for overcoming both our exploitation and racism.

The Legacy of Colonial Imperialism

The abolition of slavery in the early nineteenth century led to the colonization of Africa, thus continuing the process of primitive capitalist accumulation at the expense of Africa and the African wherever he was. Whereas the African slave was transported across the ocean to provide labor power in the distant plantation economies of the Caribbean and North America, the indigenous populations of colonized Africa not only saw their land conquered and subdivided among European powers, but were themselves made an organic accessory of those lands, thus becoming one of the conditions of production in the plantations and mines that European capital exploited. Thus, while the advent of mercantile capitalism in the fifteenth century saw the exploitation of African labor power outside Africa, the advent of colonial imperialism saw the exploitation of African resources with African labor—again for the benefit of Europe's ruling classes. From the nineteenth century, Africa's resources and its people became one of the foundation stones for further capitalist accumulation. W. E. B. DuBois, who lived at the height of Euro-American hegemony and witnessed first hand Africa's partition among the European powers, wrote in 1915:

> Most persons have accepted the tacit but clear modern philosophy which assigns to the white race alone the hegemony of the world and assumes that other races, and particularly the Negro race, will either be content to serve the interests of whites or die out before the all-conquering march. This philosophy is the child of the African slave trade and the expansion of Europe during the nineteenth century. [1970: 139-140]

In examining the record of the part played by Black labor in the evolution of the capitalist world economy, one is stuck by the extent to which the attitudes of European and American capitalists influenced the fortunes of Afro-Americans in the second half of the nineteenth and the twentieth century. In America, assumptions about black inferiority almost always stemmed from the tendency to associate the Black with the backwardness of Africa, whose people were not supposed to have evolved to the level of Europeans. A tenuous logic held that Blacks in America had inherited certain genetic defects. The African's own lack of independence—the direct result of colonization—was translated into the denigration of Black folks and their exclusion from the U.S. constitutional process even after the Civil War had supposedly freed them. As they were reduced to so many units of labor power in the plantations and ghettos of America, the Blacks became all but invisible. In the second half of the last century and the first half of the present, the capitalist world, viewing all things from an imperialist perspective, could not acknowledge the humanity of the Black world. How could they? Even today the master-race syndrome leads many white people in Europe and America to identify with the status quo in South Africa and to regard an African revolution there as an ultimate horror.

With the rise of colonial imperialism, the European bourgeoisie proposed (or hoped to create) a system of exploitation applying to all Blacks, wherever they might be. As long as white capitalist hegemony was a fact of life in Africa and elsewhere, the equality of black and white in America was a contradiction that imperialism could not accept. Indeed, the political exclusion of Blacks and their reduction to second-class citizenship after the war of emancipation can be explained only as an accommodation by U.S. ruling circles to the demands inherent in the general phenomenon of white hegemony over the so-called non-white world. In 1919 DuBois (1920, 1969: 50) observed that instead of standing as a great example of the success of democracy and the possibility of human brotherhood, America had taken her place as an awful example of its pitfalls and failures, so far as black and brown and yellow peoples were concerned (1920, 1969: 50).

The legacy of slavery and imperialism divided humanity into two races: the superior and the inferior. The latter toiled for the superior and the superior were real human beings; the inferior were either half-human or less. True, among what DuBois called the white lords of creation, there were lower classes, whose existence in many respects resembled that of Blacks. Where possible, the loyalty of the poor whites was bought by giving them preferential treatment at the expense of Blacks. In this world of white capitalist hegemony, equality between black and white was unthinkable; the very thought was a crime against the laws of nature. By an almost common consent, the white capitalist world was determined to hold Blacks everywhere in a servile status. DuBois, whose perceptive commentary on this period has already been referred to, remarked that the history of the last two decades of the nineteenth and the early part of the twentieth centuries were:

> epitomized in one word—Empire, the domination of White Europe over Black Africa and Yellow Asia, through political power built on the economic control of labor, income and ideas. The echo of this industrial imperialism in America was the expulsion of the Black men from the

American democracy, their subjection to caste control and wage slavery. [DuBois, 1965: 10]

Colonialism has been defined as a system of rule which assumes the right of one people to impose its will upon another. This situation leads inevitably to a situation of dominance and dependency. Once African societies lost their national autonomy, Africans everywhere became objects rather than subjects of history. In America, the Blacks became simply the *negro* problem, and in Africa the African became a *native* problem. Once so designated, Blacks everywhere were banished from the history of humanity. Jean-Paul Sartre writes that

> everyone has felt the contempt implicit in the term "native" used to designate the inhabitants of a colonized country. The banker, the manufacturer, even the professor in the home country, are not natives of any country: they are not natives at all. The oppressed person, on the other hand, feels himself to be a native; each single event in his life repeats to him that he has not the right to exist. [1968: 215]

With a few modifications what Sartre says about native applies to anybody called a *negro* in the United States and elsewhere. We can see, then, that the major impact of imperialism was on the historical place of Black people: throughout the Black world colonial imperialism produced doubt, paralysis, stagnation, and in some cases, regression.

At the Berlin Congress in 1885, the European powers divided Africa and its resources among themselves; in that single act Africa's independent historical development was abrogated. The violent usurpation and incorporation of Africa's productive forces into the world capitalist economy meant that the African had been denied the sole means of independent development. Amilcar Cabral writes that "both in colonialism and in neo-colonialism, the essential characteristic of imperialist domination remains the same: the negation of the historical process of the dominated people by means of violent usurpation of the freedom of development of the national productive forces" (1969: 82). The monopolization of Africa's means of subsistence negatively affected Blacks all over the world. Indeed, as long as colonialization predominated, the history of Africa and its peoples was in serious danger of sinking into oblivion. Even before the formal institutionalization of colonialism, those who controlled information sought to justify slavery through the continual assertion that history was a European monopoly. The impact of slavery on European thought is nowhere better exemplified than in Hegel's introduction to the *Philosophy of History*:

> The peculiarly African character is difficult to comprehend, for the very reason that in reference to it, we must quite give up the principle which naturally accompanies all *our* ideas—the category of Universality. In Negro life the characteristic point is the fact that consciousness has not yet attained to the realization of any substantial objective existence—as for example, God, or Law—in which the interest of man's volition is involved and in which he realizes his own being. This distinction between himself as an individual and the universality of his essential being, the African in the uniform, undeveloped oneness of his existence has not yet attained; so that the Knowledge of an absolute Being, an Other and a Higher than his individual self, is entirely wanting. The Negro ... exhibits the natural man in his completely wild and untamed state. We must lay aside all thought of reverence and morality—all that we call feeling—if we would rightly comprehend him; there is nothing harmonious with humanity to be found in this type of character. The copious and circumstantial accounts of Missionaries completely confirm this, and Mohammedanism appears to be the only thing which in any way brings the Negroes within the range of culture. [1956: 93]

Having thus maligned the African, Hegel concluded that:

> Another characteristic fact in reference to the Negroes is Slavery. Negroes are enslaved by Europeans and sold to America. Bad as this may be, their lot in their own land is even worse, since there a slavery quite as absolute exists; for it is the essential principle of slavery, that man has not yet attained a consciousness of his freedom, and consequently sinks down to a mere Thing—an object of no value. Among the Negroes moral sentiments are quite weak, or more strictly speaking, non-existent. [1956: 96]

As a consequence of such deliberate distortions, Africans, whether at home or in the Diaspora, could not escape a humiliation and impoverishment that was not only economic but also spiritual and cultural. Though they worked and created the wealth on which modern capitalist society was built, they were not integrated into the societies that held them captive. Divested of authority over their own history, wealth, and culture, the Africans found themselves plunged into distorted and spurious forms of existence. As Frantz Fanon put it:

> Colonial domination, because it is total and tends to over-simplify, very soon manages to disrupt in spectacular fashion the culture life of a conquered people. This cultural obliteration is made possible by the

negation of national reality, by new legal relations introduced by the occupying power, by the banishment of the natives and their customs to outlying districts by colonial society, by expropriation, and by the systematic enslavement of men and women. [1963: 190]

In the period from 1875 to 1950, the capitalist world not only exploited Africa and its peoples; it made a huge intellectual and emotional investment in racism. Working from racist assumptions, philosophy, literature, sociology, biology, psychology, and so on all joined in an effort to degrade the Black to a mere caricature of the human. The aim was not only to justify black exploitation, but also to convince the oppressed themselves that their condition was the unfortunate result of their natural inferiority. It was believed that the constant repetition of this message would break the Black's power of resistance. Thus the world came to believe that everything good and honorable was "white" and that everything bad and dishonorable—including the devil—was "black."

It is a tragic paradox of the Black situation today that racist ideas and assumptions are on the ascendancy once again. It thus seems that recent efforts by Blacks to emancipate themselves have turned into nothing. The Black petite bourgeoisie have become accessory to the enslavement of their own masses by accepting the economic status quo as legitimate. The emancipation of the Black world and the rest of the oppressed is inconceivable without breaking and melting down the chains of economic bondage and our reified historical consciousness. An adequate form of historical consciousness, in place of a mystifying false consciousness, is vital to any radical demystification of the prevailing structures of domination. For us, the task of developing an adequate historical consciousness should be a major tool for both economic and cultural decolonization.

As we have seen, the various justifications for our subjugation emanated from an adroit manipulation of our past to serve the interests of the exploitative world capitalist order. Understandably, therefore, there is a profound need to study the political economy of capitalism and its role in the crisis that has confronted the Black world and the other peoples capitalism has victimized. A proper historical consciousness will be an integral part in the struggle for genuine emancipation. The importance of books such as *The World and Africa* by W. E. B. DuBois, *Capitalism and Slavery* by Eric Williams, *The Black Jacobins,* by C. L. L. James, *Discourse on*

Colonialism, by Aime Césaire, *The Wretched of the Earth,* by Frantz Fanon, *How Europe Underdeveloped Africa,* by Walter Rodney, and *The Shaping of Black America,* by Lerone Bennett, Jr., to mention just a few, cannot be overemphasized. After reading these books, one can no longer give a respectful hearing to those whose activities perpetuate our plight. Familiarity with such writings makes it extremely difficult to defend Blacks who equate the interests of Blacks with those of capitalism, as some Black spokesmen have recently tried to do.

Whether we like it or not, the Black world is still caught up in the capitalist world economy and its exploitative structures. Our greatest problem at the moment is that the concepts that shape and guide our struggles are distorted by a lack of clarity about the nature and source of our poverty. During and after World War I, the Black masses began slowly to diagnose the historical nature of their condemnation to poverty. Leaders and organizations emerged in various parts of the Black world which began to mobilize politically to fight for equality and emancipation. The spread of the Pan-African movement and the Garvey movement throughout the Black world expressed, among other things, the fact that Black people were first and foremost an international proletariat. The leaders of these movements recognized that Black poverty was not our fault but our misfortune, resulting from Africa's loss of self-determination.

In the interwar years, the Black world learned many painful but necessary lessons about the nature of western civilization and the world capitalist economy. Hitler and Mussolini may not have been the crowning jewels of western civilization, but their rise to power was itself a great lesson to the people who were told that they were discriminated against because they were backward and ignorant. The Great Depression also proved to all that economic difficulties and racial discrimination were inextricably intertwined. Racism was used to make some white people rich and all black folks poor.

This same period saw the gradual disappearance of the faith, still cherished by some Black intellectuals, that progress was possible in a world dominated by white capital. This agonizing disillusionment necessitated a major reevaluation of the role of the Black world in modern society. The Black world and its organizations were never able to formulate what it would take to achieve true Black emancipation, however. A moral critique of white domination—a critique dissociated from revolutionary struggle—proved hopelessly inadequate. Today, we seem not to have learned anything from the lessons of the past.

The Black world, though oppressed, exploited, and discriminated against, wholeheartedly supported the struggle against fascism, hoping that after the war the position of Blacks in the United States would be improved and that European colonies would be freed. As far as the Black world is concerned, World War II marked the transition to the beginning of a new, qualitatively higher historical phase. The war destroyed once and for all the myth of white supremacy. It also spelled the end of the concession-begging tendencies that hitherto had dominated the politics of the Black world. The war registered fundamental changes in the development of the Black struggle for liberation.

The defeat of fascist imperialism in World War II created a situation that enhanced anticolonial and antifascist struggles. Thanks in part to the strengthening of the world socialist system, the imperialist powers' attempt to regain their lost ground was thwarted, as was the attempt to put the so-called nigger back in his place. The Fifth Pan-African Congress that was held in Manchester in 1945 strengthened the bond between the national liberation movement in Africa and the Afro-American struggle for equality. From 1945 to the present, racists and imperialists have found themselves on the defensive.

The thirty-five years since the end of World War II have seen important changes in the political situation of the Black world. The limited and imperfect political independence achieved in Africa since the late 1950s and the achievements of the U.S. Civil Rights Movement have created conditions in which the masses of the Black world are better able to understand the nature of their economic situation. For this reason alone, we should not underestimate the significance of political sovereignty and the achievement of legal equality by Black folks in the United States; both are essential if the Black world is to advance toward the ultimate goal of complete emancipation.

Looking back at the situation of the Black world from the vantage point of the early 1980s, it is increasingly evident that the predominate issues of our epoch, which are the consequences of colonialism and imperialism, are coming to a head. The question that occupies the center of the world stage today is that of the so-called *Have* and

Have-Not peoples. Among the *Have-Nots,* the Blacks are the worst off. What does it mean *Not to Have* or to be described as a *Have-Not?* According to Marx,

> Not to Have is not a mere category, it is a most disconsolate reality; today the man who has nothing is nothing, for he is cut from existence in general and still more from a human existence; for the condition of having nothing is the condition of complete separation of man from his objectivity. Not to Have is the most desperate spiritualism, a complete unreality of the human, a complete reality of the dehumanized, a very positive to have, a having of hunger, of cold, of disease, of crime, of debasement, of all inhumanity and monstrosity. [1956: 59]

Conclusions

It would be hard to deny that political emancipation was a major breakthrough for all the colonized people of the world. But it also would be hard to deny that in the recent years since the heady days of civil-rights marches and independence celebrations the majority of Black people have been disappointed in the workings of their governments. In the United States, as well as in Africa and the Caribbean, Black folks have a theoretical right to elect legislatures at the various levels of government, yet the governments that rule them seem to lack the authority to make the decisions that would improve the quality of their lives. The economic emancipation of the Black world seems to be as far off today as it was fifty years ago.

The question that now faces us all is: why after the achievement of political emancipation is the situation of the majority of our people so bad? Today, as in the days when imperialism flourished, the Black world remains in the grip of poverty, illiteracy, disease, and hunger. Even though they are no longer subjected to the humiliation of institutional racism and colonial rule, little has changed for the Black masses. Frustrated by the unfulfilled promises of political emancipation, the Black world yearns for a new era. This condition of the majority of Black folks demands that we reexamine the last thirty years in an attempt to explain the current malaise.

First and foremost among the reasons for this malaise is that those who led the struggle for political emancipation in the post-World War II era had no vision of the power structure that rules the modern world or lacked a clear idea of what constitutes true emancipation. As Cabral explained, "the ideological deficiency, not to say the total lack of ideology—constitutes one of the greatest weaknesses of our struggle—if not the greatest weakness" (1969: 92-93). Mesmerized by electoral politics, the Black leadership failed to realize that substituting Black officeholders and leaving the structure of the world economy intact was doomed from the outset. Quite early in his life, DuBois (1969: 290) had understood that "the solution of letting a few of our capitalists share with whites in the exploitation of our masses, would never be a solution of our problem, but the forging of eternal chains."

Black elected officials have been unable to realize the radical social transformations that are needed to fulfill the economic aspirations of the masses of the Black world. Their failure has two sources. Objectively, Black elected officials are circumscribed and neutralized by the immense aggregate power preserved by those who control and direct the world economy. Subjectively, and this factor is far more important, those who claim to speak for the Black masses have been contained ideologically; that is, they are committed to the economic status quo as defined by the capitalist mode of production. By accepting the status quo as the limiting framework for reforms, these spokespeople for the Black world have relinquished the will to transform society and find themselves unable to articulate a vision of a new world order. Elected Black officials have thus gained not real power, but the permission to operate the status quo on behalf of their narrow, petit-bourgeois interests. They remain tied to the apron strings of the colonial heritage and as a result, dependency is the ever-present reality, curbing even their own limited aspirations.

Genuine independence for Black masses means nothing if it does not bring with it the negation of the historical forces that were originally responsible for the process we call underdevelopment. Again Cabral (ibid., 83) is informative when he writes, "The national liberation of people is the regaining of the historical personality of that people, its return to history through the destruction of the imperialist domination to which it is subjected."

The violent usurpation of the Black world's productive forces and its freedom of development constituted the principal and permanent characteristics of our domination and quite obviously, genuine freedom can come about only when the productive forces of the Black world have been completely freed from every kind of foreign domination. In short, recovery of the resources that have always been usurped is simultaneously the recovery of our destiny. Today, there is a painful recognition that, like formal equality before the law, formal political independence cannot by itself solve the Black world's acute social and economic problems.

For centuries the Black world has been deprived of the responsibilities of its own destiny. The slave was aware that this total deprivation was unmediated, and the same was true during the colonial and imperial era: the colonizer ruled and the colonized obeyed. Formal independence was granted under neocolonialism, but our people were made to accept rulers and politicians who would defer major economic decisions to the exploiters of yesterday. Today, Blacks everywhere continue to abdicate control over basic areas of their national life, and are unwilling to come to grips with the reality of Black impoverishment. We are ruled by a camprador bourgeoisie that voluntarily chooses capitalist solutions to problems of poverty—partly because it is intellectually conditioned to believe in such solutions and partly because of personal expediency, for any other solutions would mean mass involvement—a situation that these leaders have come to fear. The objective poverty of the masses of the Black world stares us in the face but we either ignore it or gloss over it. As a result Black politics have become a way of life which is completely divorced from reality.

References

Cabral, Amilcar. *Revolution in Guinea, An African People's Struggle*, 1969, London, Stage I.

DuBois, W. E. B. *On the Importance of Africa in World History*, 1978, New York, Black Liberation Press.

DuBois, W. E. B. *The Negro,* 1970, New York, Oxford University Press.

DuBois, W. E. B. *The Autobiography of W. E. B. DuBois,* 1969, New York, International.

DuBois, W. E. B. *Dark Water: Voices from within the Veil,* 1969, New York, Shocken Books.

DuBois, W. E. B. *Black Reconstruction in America, 1860-1880,* 1964, New York, Meriden Books.

Fanon, Frantz. *The Wretched of the Earth,* 1963, New York, Grove Press.

Galeano, Eduardo. *Open Veins in Latin America; Five Centuries of the Pillage of a Continent,* 1973, New York, Monthly Review Press.

Hegel, Georg W. F. *The Philosophy of History,* 1956, New York, Dover Publications.

Marx, Karl. *Capital*, vol. 1., introduced by Ernest Mandel and translated by Ben Fawkes, 1977, New York, Vintage Books.

Marx, Karl. *Capital,* vol. 3, 1962, Moscow, Foreign Languages Publishing House.

Marx, Karl and F. Engels. *The Holy Family or Critique of Critical Critique,* 1956, Moscow, Foreign Languages.

Marx, Karl. *The Poverty of Philosophy,* 1971, New York, International Publishers.

Moore, Jr., Barrington. *Social Origins of Dictatorship and Democracy,* 1967, Boston, Beacon Press.

Sartre, J. P. "Materialism and Revolution," in *Literary and Philosophical Essay,* trans. A. Michelson, 1968, London, Hutchinson.

Williams, William Appleman. *History as a Way of Learning,* 1973, New York, Franklin Watts, Inc.

SELF-DETERMINATION

Our destiny is largely in our own hands. If we find, we shall have to seek. If we succeed in the race of life it must be by our own energies, and our own exertions. Others may clear the road, but we must go forward, or be left behind in the race of life.

If we remain poor and dependent, the riches of other men will not avail us. If we are ignorant, the intelligence of other men will do but little for us. If we are foolish, the wisdom of other men will not guide us. If we are wasteful of time and money, the economy of other men will only make our destitution the more disgraceful and hurtful.

—Frederick Douglass

How Long? The answer is: As long as we permit it. I say that Negro action can be decisive. I say that we ourselves have the power to end the terror and to win for ourselves peace and security throughout the land.

—Paul Robeson

Black men, you were once great; you shall be great again. Lose not courage, lose not faith, go forward.

—Marcus Garvey

CHAPTER 17

The Political Economy Approach in African Studies

Nzongola-Ntalaja

The relevance of Marxism to the study of Africa was denied for a very long time by the vast majority of Africanists. Since 1960, however, the number of Africanist publications written from a Marxist perspective has steadily increased to the point that it challenges the hitherto dominant body of academic literature on Africa by bourgeois social scientists. If the Marxist presence in African Studies today is part of the worldwide Marxist revival that followed de-Stalinization, it is basically a function of the historical development of the struggle of the African peoples against imperialist domination and exploitation.

This essay seeks to show how the development of a political economy approach that is essentially radical and of Marxist inspiration is intimately related to the national liberation struggle in Africa, a struggle that has been waged against both colonialism and neocolonialism. This aim is realized through a critique of African Studies as a Western-dominated field of research which has either ignored or distorted Marxism as a scientific method of inquiry.

Marxism as a Scientific Approach

Marxism or historical materialism is a living science, and not the ideas of some dead thinker or thinkers. It is a revolutionary world outlook developed by Karl Marx, Friedrich Engels, V. I. Lenin, and their followers to provide adequate solutions to the concrete problems facing the working and exploited classes in their struggle for emancipation. As such, it is "the concrete analysis of concrete conditions" guided by a revolutionary theory which seeks to understand the world in order to change it.[1]

Nzongola-Ntalaja is a Professor in the African Studies and Research Program at Howard University in Washington, D.C.

Marxism is not the only radical ideology of those who seek to change the world. In all historical epochs oppressed peoples throughout the world have resisted their exploited and oppressed conditions by upholding visions of a brighter future of equality, justice, and material prosperity. This ideological resistance of the oppressed as well as their egalitarian ideal, or what Alain Badiou and Francois Balmès call "the communist invariants" of the revolted masses,[2] has found expression in the radical ideologies of a variety of protest movements.

What distinguishes Marxism-Leninism from the religious myths and utopian theories that preceded it in expressing the aspirations of the oppressed is the fact that it is a materialistically and historically grounded scientific theory. Its major attributes are: (1) the rejection of both idealism and crude or mechanistic materialism, (2) the affirmation of the dialectical character of reality, both natural and social, and the dialectical relation between circumstances and human activity, (3) the emphasis on the material conditions of production as the cornerstone of social activity and historical change, (4) the assertion of the primacy of society over the individual, and (5) the insistence on the unity of theory and practice.

As a scientific approach, Marxism consists of two united but distinct disciplines, *dialectical materialism,* the Marxist philosophy and theory of science, and *historical materialism,* the Marxist science of society and history. The notion of the dialectic refers to both an objective activity involving tensions and oppositions between interacting forces and elements (the dialectic as a natural or historical process) and the critical investigation of this activity (the dialectic as a scientific method). The dialectic as a scientific method is distinct but inseparable from the dialectic as historical activity. Their unity, which expresses the unity of theory and practice in Marxism, defines the scientific character of dialectical materialism as a discipline that seeks to know the world as it *really is* through practical involvement in its affairs, and not as it *appears* through passive contemplation.[3]

This dialectical approach is the basis of Marxism's conviction that scientific knowledge cannot be divorced from the material and historical conditions of its production, that it is closely linked with politics. Marxism thus rejects the positivist view of a value-free science as a bourgeois ideological position,[4] for what passes for neutral or "objective" analysis in the academic social sciences is usually supportive of the interests of the dominant classes and/or the preservation of the established order.[5] In this regard, dialectical materialism is a revolutionary science whose purpose is to depict the class position of the proletariat and other exploited classes in a truthful representation of the real world, as opposed to the distorted and illusory picture presented by the bourgeoisie and its agents.

As a method of inquiry, dialectical materialism seeks to apprehend all reality in its movement and tendencies, in the complex unity of its different aspects and contradictions. Since the whole and its interdependent and interacting parts are inseparable, no phenomenon can be fully understood in isolation. In studying a concrete object as a synthesis of multiple determinations, as a unity of opposites, dialectical materialism aims to grasp it at its roots and thereby to reveal the underlying factors and processes that determine it. As a dialectical theory and a theory of change, Marxism is necessarily a theory of processes and, accordingly, a theory of contradictions.[6] As a method of inquiry for which change is a central part of its particular object, it requires a historical perspective.

Dialectical materialism provides the epistemological foundation for historical materialism, a science that studies how historically specific systems of social production originate, function, and change. The fundamental concepts of historical materialism are *mode of production,* the form that forces and relations of production take as an organic totality of economic, political, and ideological practices, and *social formation,* a concrete society at a given point in time as characterized by the predominate mode of production.[7]

"Mode of production" is an abstract concept, one that does not exist at the level of concrete reality. A theoretical construct with the help of which concrete societies may be studied. it is rooted in both the dialectical conception of reality and the materialist conception of society and history. The first theoretical basis of this concept has to do with Marx's concept of labor as the fundamental human activity. Products of the creative activity of nature, human beings do in turn transform nature through their labor to produce and reproduce their social existence. And it is the primordial character of this activity which is expressed through the second theoretical basis, the idea that the way a society creates and maintains its material conditions of existence not only takes precedence over all other aspects of human life but also determines in the last instance its politics, culture, and development.

The analysis of a mode of production or of a matrix of modes of production specific to a social formation must therefore begin with an examination of the production relations in their totality as productive forces, or the way in which individuals relate to nature through their labor,[8] and as class relations. The latter aspect refers to the way in which individuals interact with each other as social groupings determined by their relationship to the productive process and their opposition to each other with respect to the appropriation of the surplus product—the difference between total production and the producers' necessary consumption. Class relations do exist wherever this surplus is appropriated by those who do not produce. These relations are, in other words, an expression of the fundamental contradiction and the antagonistic relationship implicit in any mode of production based on surplus appropriation by nonproducers. The contradictory and antagonistic relations thus created constitute the basis for class struggle, and it is the struggle of the fundamental classes of the dominant mode of production which determines the historical development of a social formation.[9]

It is with reference to the fundamental reality that class relations constitute in modern society and to the class struggle as the dynamic factor of historical change that Marxism seeks to apprehend historical reality through class analysis. And it seeks to do so from a revolutionary perspective—from the standpoint of the interests of the exploited class or classes. The purpose of such an analysis is to provide the exploited classes an adequate interpretation of the concrete problems facing them, thereby enabling them to carry out a successful revolution. This is the meaning of Marx's eleventh thesis on Feuerbach—"The philosophers have simply interpreted the world, in various ways; the point is to change it."[10] It is also the meaning of the life and work of all the great Marxists, beginning with Marx and Engels.[11] The realization of the unity of scientific theory and revolutionary practice by Marxists is best exemplified by V. I. Lenin, a revolutionary leader whose intellectual output consists of 55 volumes of completed works, all of them attempting to answer a single question: "What is to be done?"

Given the objective place of intellectuals in modern society as a petite bourgeoisie, their scientific practice cannot be neutral. It must be oriented toward either the interests of the bourgeoisie and its allies or those of the exploited masses. In this regard, the message of the eleventh thesis, as well as that drawn from the exemplary lives of Marx, Engels, and Lenin, concerns those intellectuals who have developed a "communist consciousness,"[12] who have deserted the ruling class or alliance,[13] and who are determined to commit "class suicide"[14] in order to become revolutionary workers. These intellectuals have as their essential task the systematization of the revolutionary ideas, notions, and representations of the proletariat and other exploited classes into a scientific and revolutionary program of social transformation, on the one hand, and the organization of these classes in the revolutionary struggle, on the other.

As a living theory, Marxism never ceases to develop itself, for it is constantly sharpening its analytical tools and applying its scientific method to new realities or to those hitherto forgotten.[15] It is a science that needs to be developed further; it does not need to be revised in a fundamental way, as social democrats and advocates of "Eurocommunism" contend, nor does it need to be superseded by a qualitatively new form of theoretical framework, as implied by the term "neo-Marxism."[16] These and other proposed cures for "orthodoxy," "dogma," or "rigidity" are clearly the wares of imaginary doctors, since the illness whose symptoms these critics claim to detect doest not exist. Marxism stands against all apriorism and all dogma. Georges Gurvitch, one of the most eminent academic sociologists or our time, wrote that Marx was the least dogmatic of all the founders of sociology.[17] A scientific approach based on the belief that it is people who make their own history, Marxism is guided only by dialectical materialism, class analysis, and revolutionary practice.

A Periodization of African Studies

Is the Marxist problematic relevant to the study of Africa? This is the question that this essay attempts to answer in the affirmative. To prove its greater usefulness as a truthful scientific reflection of the realities being faced by the African masses and as their best guide to revolutionary action, historical materialism must meet the criterion of scientificity proposed by Antonio Gramsci for any problematic that seeks to replace others. "A new science," Gramsci writes, "proves its efficacy and vitality when it demonstrates that it is capable of confronting the great champions of the tendencies opposed to it and when it either resolves by its own means the vital questions which they have posed or demonstrates, in peremptory fashion, that these questions are false problems."[18]

Who are the great champions of the anti-Marxist tendencies in African Studies and under what conditions have they dominated the field? To answer this question adequately we must first periodize African Studies and examine the role that historical materialism has played, or failed to play, in their evolution within the advanced capitalist countries of Western Europe and North America, as well as in colonial and neocolonial Africa.

The periodization that follows draws heavily on Jean Copans's excellent essay on the history and sociology of African Studies.[19] Though it differs from Copans's periodization in some respects, it is based on the political and epistemological grounds that he has stated so well and that are consistent with historical materialism in its scientific rather than its vulgar form. Since every practice produces a theory, Copans is correct in maintaining that any periodization must confront the ideological and theoretical configuration of concepts to the specific historical and social contexts of scientific practice.[20] In this way, the development of African Studies is to be analyzed in terms of the connection between Western capitalist imperialism and Africa, a connection whose changing forms determine the nature of scientific practice, which in turn justifies, conceals, or calls into question the connection itself.[21] From this perspective, the entire history of African Studies can be seen as a succession of conflicting paradigms or problematics, those which lend themselves to justifying or concealing the true nature of this connection on the one hand, and those which reveal it and reject it on the other. The history of the field, like that of the underlying reality it reflects, can be divided into five periods: 1500-1885, the era of primitive accumulation and "exploration"; 1885-1920, the period of colonial conquest; 1920-1945, the high colonial period; 1945-1960, the period of nationalism and decolonization; and since 1960, the period of neocolonialism.

Primitive Accumulation, Adventure, and Exoticism

The first and longest period in the history of African Studies is also the one for which little if anything can be said about Marxism, which itself arose toward the end of the period, in 1845.[22] The period begins around 1500, with the establishment of trade relations between the African continent and the emerging, and Europe-based, capitalist world economy. During the nearly four hundred years that followed the creation of this connection between capitalism and Africa, Afro-European relations were dominated first by the slave trade, which constituted the primary method of primitive accumulation in Africa, and then by the trade in the raw materials needed for industrial production in Europe.[23] The writings of the European merchants and adventurers who traveled in Africa during this period were directly or indirectly related to these two factors.

The first detailed descriptions of African social formations and states were written by African and Arab Muslim scholars like Al Bakri, Yakut, Ibn Battuta, Makrisi, Al Hassan Ibn Muhammad (Leo Africanus), and Es Sadi.[24] Until the nineteenth century, when scientific interest in the exploration of Africa won official sanction in Europe, African writings by Europeans consisted chiefly of travel narratives by merchants and/or official representatives of European interests in Africa. One such author is Archibald Dalzel, who was for four years governor of the British fort at Whydah, in the Kingdom of Dahomey, and subsequently governor at Cape Coast, during the eighteenth century. His book, *The History of Dahomey, An Inland Kingdom of Africa* (London, 1793), is a sophisticated apology for the slave trade.[25] A second example is provided by the writings of Duarte Barboza, Duarte Lopez, John Dos Santos, Andrew Battell, and Antonio Gamitto, all of whom were involved in the Luso-African trading frontier in Central and Southern Africa. Two Scots, Mungo Park and James Bruce, were perhaps the only travelers to have gone to Africa for mainly scientific reasons before 1800.[26]

The activities of geographical societies, Christian missions, the press, and other ideological apparatuses that had provided a forum for the expression of anti-slavery opinions in Europe became practicable only after the abolition of the slave trade.[27] The slave-trade lobby had made it very difficult if not impossible "to organize from Europe any other kind of contact with Africa."[28] The establishment of new and different kinds of contact after the abolition cannot, however, be attributed simply to a "decisive victory" by the anti-slave movement, as Roland Oliver and J. D. Fage suggest.[29] The slave trade lost its *raison d'etre* when it became a fetter on the expanded reproduction of capital, which then required the extraction of African raw materials for European industries. The abolition of the slave trade was therefore necessary to eliminate its disruptive impact on this extraction (or "legitimate commerce," as it was called), as well as to maximize the productivity of African labor power by exploiting it locally.[30].

This is the context in which to place the exaltation of "Christianity and commerce" in the narratives of the great nineteenth-century travelers, men like Hugh Clapperton, Dixon Denham, René Caillé, Heinrich Barth, Richard Burton, John Speke, David Livingstone, and Henry Morton Stanley. In the characteristically bourgeois approach of studying social reality from the perspective of the ruling classes, their writings consisted for the most part of descriptions of the courts of kings and emperors and of royal activities. These adventurers placed so much emphasis on the exoticism of African social and political life, on the spectacular and the unusual, that "they missed much of the basic reality."[31] In spite of their limitations, these narratives have a historical significance in that they fed the insatiable desire for territorial acquisition among the European ruling classes and thus constituted the first detailed and essential intelligence on the basis of which Africa was eventually conquered.[32]

The development and worldwide expansion of capitalism was an integral part of Marx's analysis of the capitalist mode of production. The founders of historical materialism were therefore interested in the rise of imperialism and colonialism, and saw the latter as laying the basis—and only the basis—of social transformation and capitalist development in the conquered territories.[33] Although Marx and Engels did not undertake a systematic study of colonialist exploitation, they were convinced of the superiority of the capitalist mode of production vis-à-vis all precapitalist modes and of the ability of capitalism to destroy the noncapitalist economies of the colonized areas. If Marx seems to be overwhelmingly enthusiastic in predicting such an outcome in his writings on Asia, he is nevertheless careful to distinguish between the subjective motivations of the imperialists and the objective historical results of their deeds.[34]

In addition to the limitations of their general theoretical position on the role of capitalism in history, Marx and Engels knew very little about Africa.[35] Except for a few isolated remarks on Africa in their writings, they paid little attention to the continent. As a result of all these factors, historical materialism was unable to challenge the image of Africa portrayed in Europe by the representatives of European colonial interests.[36]

The Colonial Conquest and its Justification

The period of colonial conquest and occupation presents the best example of the fact, already underlined by Copans, that the five periods overlap one another.[37] And they do so in terms of both historical evolution and its reflection in the literature of African Studies. Even before the scramble for Africa at the end of the nineteenth century, a number of African territories had already been subjected to European control. The Portuguese had established a colonial presence in the coastal regions of Angola and Mozambique in the late fifteenth century. South Africa had been occupied by European settlers since 1652, although the total conquest of African societies did not come about until after the so-called Kaffir Wars, between 1835 and 1879. Algeria had fallen to the French in 1830, and European rule had been established in a number of West African coastal regions before 1879.[38]

These colonial territories represented less than 10 percent of the African continent in 1879. By 1901, however, all but a tiny fraction of it (namely, Ethiopia and Liberia) was being ruled by Europeans.[39] What happened during these two decades is known as the "scramble for Africa," a process that took place in two distinct phases: the partition of Africa on paper, 1879-1891, and the partition of Africa on the ground, 1891-1901.[40] Effective occupation, the criterion for legitimate territorial claim adopted at the Berlin Conference of 1884-1885, was never a reality in many a hinterland until after World War I.

The war interrupted the establishment of effective control in some areas, but it also helped the colonialists to develop the armies with which they eventually ended the last resistance to colonial conquest and occupation. Moreover, it resulted in Germany's loss of its colonies to Britain, France, Belgium, and South Africa.[41] The importance of the Berlin Conference as a culminating point in the partition of Africa and the significance of the political consequences of World War I for the colonial order in Africa explain the delimitation of this second period.

Essential themes in the diplomatic history of this period, partition and effective occupation were also the main preoccupation of the intellectual defenders of colonialism in the metropolitan countries. Representatives of the repressive and ideological apparatuses of these countries, the army and the bureaucracy on the one hand, and the Christian missions, the press, and learned societies on the other, these intellectuals dealt mostly with the immediate tasks of colonization: "pacification," or the establishment of effective control, and, as in the last phase of the previous period, "Christianity and commerce."

The dominant discipline was ethnography, or descriptive anthropology, which was practiced not by professional anthropologists, but by missionaries and colonial administrators striving to understand the languages and customs of the peoples with whom they came into contact. On the positive side, this work laid the foundation for a more rigorous study of African linguistics, history, and geography. On the negative side, the evolutionist and racist problematic in which it was conceived distorted African realities, giving rise to myths and sterotypes of all kinds, and reduced scholarly practice in African Studies to an undisguised apology for colonialism.

Whatever their scholarly value might be, the works of soldier-administrators and empire-builders like Louis Faidherbe, Maurice Delafosse, Frederick Lugard, and Harry Johnston served the purpose of legitimizing the colonial enterprise as a "civilizing mission." This ideology was also central to the advocacy of Christian missions in need of financial support for their work in Africa, and to the pro-imperialist lobby's effort to justify colonial exploitation to the metropolitan population, whose intelligentsia and working classes were being exposed to anticolonial ideas.[42]

Unlike the previous period, in which anticolonial voices were few or nonexistent, the years after the scramble saw the emergence of critical analysis of imperialism and colonialism. The analysis itself took several forms, from the basically journalistic writings of the humanitarian critics of the atrocities committed by a particular colonial power or administration against Africans to the scientific analysis of the structure and contradictions of the world capitalist system. The best example of the first kind of critique is provided by the successful campaign of Edmund D. Morel and his Congo reform movement against King Leopold's brutal rule in the Congo Free State.[43] Directed primarily against the abuses of colonial exploitation, this kind of critique does not call into question the colonial system itself.

The Marxist position, which represents the other and more radical form of critique, is best exemplified by Lenin's *Imperialism, The Highest Stage of Capitalism* (1917), his most important theoretical work.[44] The difference between the Marxist approach and other critiques of imperialism is very well stated in Lenin's brief remark on J. A. Hobson's book *Imperialism* (1902). Having made considerable use of Hobson's work for his own analysis, because of the "excellent and comprehensive description of the principal economic and political characteristics of imperialism" given by the English economist, Lenin finds that the author "adopts the point of view of bourgeois social reformism and pacifism."[45]

The point of view of historical materialism consists in revolutionary opposition to imperialism and its effects on the dependent territories, which must undergo a process of national liberation in order to develop economically.[46] Less significant than Lenin's *Imperialism* in terms of their impact on Marxist analysis of the development of capitalism in the periphery and the anti-imperialist struggle are Lenin's *The Development of Capitalism in Russia* (1899) and Rosa Luxemburg's *The Accumulation of Capital* (1913). These important books did not initially receive the attention they deserved from Marxist critics of imperialism and colonialism, and it is only today that they are being recognized as basic references for Marxist analysis of dependence and underdevelopment.[47] Luxemburg's work was the first detailed Marxist study of the role of the periphery in the process of capital accumulation at the center and of the effect of imperialism on the colonized areas. In her discussion of the social transformations which followed colonial conquest in Algeria, Egypt, and South Africa, she presents some excellent descriptions of primitive accumulation.

Anthropology and the Political Economy of Colonialism

The high colonial period, or the period of colonial consolidation, is characterized by the final realization of effective control and territorial occupation by European powers in their African colonies. In the field of African Studies, the period from 1920 to 1945 marked the transition from a dominance by amateurs to a dominance by professional researchers.[48] As Copans rightly puts it, effective occupation and control made scientific research possible by freeing the latter of "the constraints of maintaining order and *its own security*."[49]

Thus, with the repressive apparatus of the colonial state in control, acting through violence and the intermediacy of African rulers or chiefs, a new and specialized apparatus was needed to generate more knowledge about the colonized people and their milieu as well as to help formulate public policy. Since colonial policy revolved around economic exploitation, the colonialists needed to know how they could best use their African intermediaries to maximize cash-crop production, taxation, and labor recruitment. Ethnology or cultural anthropology was the discipline that met this requirement, and it became the colonial science *par excellence*.[50] Colonial governments not only employed anthropologists, but also encouraged colonial officers to undertake anthropological research. And the training courses for colonial administrators included anthropology.[51]

The dominant position of anthropology in African Studies was reflected in its privileged status within the new ideological apparatus of the colonial state—an apparatus that included governmental agencies and semiofficial bodies engaged in policy-oriented research. These research organizations and institutes included: for Britain, the International African Institute (IAI), founded in 1926 by, among others, Lord Lugard, the former governor-general of Nigeria and author of the doctrine of indirect rule, the Rhodes-Livingstone Institute, established in 1937 in Northern Rhodesia, and London University's School of Oriental and African Studies;[52] for France, the Institute of Ethnology of the University of Paris, established in 1926 and financed by the Ministry of Overseas France, the Société des Africanistes, created in 1931, and the Institut Français de l'Afrique Noire (IFAN), founded in 1938 at Dakar; for Belgium, the Tervuren Museum, established in 1897, the Colonial University at Antwerp, founded in 1920, the Institut Royal Colonial Belge (later Académie Royale des Sciences Coloniales), and the Académie Royale des Sciences d'Outre-Mer (ARSOM); and for Portugal, the Instituto Superior de Estudos Ultramarinos, originally established in 1927 as the Escola Superior Colonial by the Ministry of Colonies.[53] The research departments of colonial affairs ministries managed the organization and funding of research. Privately funded research was insignificant, except for the historical societies of various British colonies.[54]

Theoretically and methodologically, anthropological research was characterized by two major tendencies, one represented by the

British and one by the French. Given their empiricism and pragmatism, the British sought to understand the institutions, customs, and functional relations of the African social systems under their control, and they built their applied anthropology on the field-work method of investigation, which involved "the systematic and exhaustive collection of social data by trained observers working on the spot."[55] Informed by the theories of Bronislaw Malinowski, A. R. Radcliffe-Brown, and E. E. Evans-Pritchard, their analysis was basically functionalist and dealt primarily with concrete economic, political, and cultural problems.[56]

The French, on the contrary, were so marked by their rationalist philosophical tradition that until Marcel Griaule's Dakar-to-Djibouti field trip of 1931-1933, their anthropological work was done by armchair theorists relying on data collected by others.[57] In a basically Hegelian fashion, Griaule and his followers sought the principles of social life not in the economic and political institutions of African societies, but in the minds of Africans.[58] Like their English counterparts, they had little or no recourse to history, and they neglected to analyze the effect of colonialism on African societies. Like all defenders of the colonial system, they held and propagated the ideological view that colonialism was beneficial to Africans.[59]

Unfortunately, and in spite of the October Revolution and its worldwide impact, there were no Marxists who could challenge this view effectively in the metropolitan countries. Western Marxists were too preoccupied with the class struggle and the rise of fascism in Europe, or too stifled by Stalinist orthodoxy, to worry about the colonies. Moreover, colonial exploitation had allowed the advanced capitalist countries to improve the material conditions of their working classes, thereby contributing to the rise of a labor aristocracy marked by "social chauvinism" and to the renunciation of proletarian internationalism by the social-democratic parties that represented this class stratum and its petit-bourgeois allies.[60] Consequently, antiimperialist forces were very weak, and anticolonial writers within the Marxist tradition or close to it had little influence.

Since the field of African Studies had no use for them, the progressive critics of imperialism and colonialism during this period were not widely known and have remained obscure. Two outstanding exceptions are W. E. B. DuBois, the father of Pan-Africanism and a pioneer of radical Africana in the United States,[61] and Lord Olivier, a

British Labor party peer and Fabian Socialist, who wrote an explicitly materialist critique of the colonial-settler system in South Africa which anticipates most of the Marxist theses on the political economy of apartheid today.[62]

The Analysis of Social Change and Decolonization

During the next period of African Studies (1945-1960), the impact of the October Revolution and socialism was manifested in the Western response to the rise of the national liberation movement in the colonial and dependent territories—a movement that was seen as a threat to the survival of the capitalist system. Fearing the further enlargement of the socialist camp in the wake of revolutionary outbreaks in China, Vietnam, and Eastern Europe, the imperialist powers resolved to do all they could in order to cut their losses. Under U.S. pressure, they devised a decolonization strategy, one that limited the gains of the national liberation movement to political independence. Preparations for the latter varied considerably among the colonial powers, but it invariably included the granting of economic and social benefits to the African petite bourgeoisie in order to win this class to the anticommunist camp.

This process of social change and decolonization was reflected in African Studies. The economic and political struggles of this period as well as the major issues of nationalism and independence required a change of methodology and theoretical perspective. Since anthropology was clearly incapable of providing the analytical tools needed for the study of these problems, it was replaced by sociology as the dominant discipline in a field of study in which history and political science also became relevant.

Just as in the case of anthropology, there were considerable differences in the sociological research of the two major schools of African Studies before 1960: it was functionalist and synchronic in the British school, materialistic and historical—but not Marxist—in the French school. Unlike the French, the British sociologists did not effect a complete break with the previous period. Their major innovation was a more liberal outlook, as already evidenced in the critical analysis of migrant labor by Godfrey Wilson, the first director of the Rhodes-Livingstone Institute,[63] and a shift from emphasis on the study of traditional societies to an emphasis on the study of social change, particularly the impact of urbanization and industrialization on proletarianized and semi-proletarianized Africans.

The Rhodes-Livingstone Institute is perhaps the best representative of continuity and change in British social research, as it was involved in both anthropological and sociological investigations. The anthropologist Max Gluckman, the institute's director until 1947, defined its role as involving the study of "both tribes and urban situations in British Central Africa."[64] Acculturation, adaptation to the urban milieu, and the role of tribalism in these processes were some of the major areas of research. Undoubtedly, these were themes that colonial administrators and company managers were keenly interested in for purposes of controlling the pace of social change. Useful in terms of the descriptive data it produced, the work of the institute lacked a radical perspective, and it was therefore of limited value for understanding the dynamics of change in Central and Southern Africa.

The postwar social and political transformations were better reflected in the new French sociology. Under the leadership of Georges Balandier, the French school of African Studies went beyond both idealism and empiricism to produce a dynamic sociology of colonial exploitation, underdevelopment, and social change. This new sociology takes into account the real history of the African peoples, moves from an emphasis on small groups to a study of national groupings, and substitutes a materialistic and historical explanation for the Griaulian idealism that ignores the realities of colonialism.[65] Politically radical, the new problematic calls into question the colonial situation itself through a sympathetic study of anticolonial movements, from primary resistance to modern political parties, and promotes the study of African history. In addition to Balandier, Paul Mercier, Jacques Lombard, and Yves Person are among the scholars who were influential in this respect.[66]

Theoretically, Balandier's approach was close to Marxism but still reflected the influence of Marcel Mauss and Georges Gurvitch. Instead of the Marxist dialectic, Balandier uses Mauss's "total social phenomenon," a conception of reality which, as Copans suggests, contains "a large dose of Hegelian idealism."[67] And Gurvitch's "dialectical sociology" has a tendency toward formalism.[68] The application of a strictly Marxist problematic to African realities was the work of few researchers on the fringe of this school. Jean Suret-Canale, a member of the French Communist Party (PCF), is the outstanding representative of the Marxist tendency in African Studies during this period.[69]

In addition to the French school of African sociology, the most prominent European supporters of African nationalism and independence in the field of African Studies were four British scholars and activists: Thomas Hodgkin, Basil Davidson, George Shepperson, and Jack Woddis.[70] Hodgkin and Davidson are rightly recognized as "the founding fathers of radical Africanism in Britain."[71] Marxist in their overall ideological perspective, they are less so in their analytical and explanatory schemes. Their eclectic orientation is related to the antitheoretical tendency of British intellectual life on the one hand, and to the specific circumstances that affected their respective careers, on the other.[72] A member of the British Communist Party, Woddis is consistently Marxist in his writings, whereas Shepperson's work reflects a liberal perspective.

In tiny Belgium, scholarly support for decolonization came from an unexpected quarter. A. A. J. van Bilsen, a professor at the Colonial University at Antwerp, published in 1956 a "Thirty-Year Plan for the Political Emancipation of Belgian Africa."[73] This timid proposal, which was attacked in Belgium as a dangerous revolutionary document, had a positive impact in the Belgian Congo, where it stimulated the entry of the Congolese (now Zairian) petite bourgeoisie into the debate over independence.[74]

In the United States, a liberal tradition had been established in African Studies by Melville J. Herskovits's pioneering work in African history and anthropology.[75] This tradition was evident in the work that Rupert Emerson, James S. Coleman, and other Africanists did on African nationalism.[76] Like van Bilsen, Emerson took a rather positive view of colonialism as "a school for democracy," his overall perspective being somehow consistent with the neocolonialist goals of the most enlightened elements within the U.S. foreign policy establishment. Coleman, on the other hand, went beyond the paternalism of colonial officialdom to seek a clearer understanding of the nationalist movement from the standpoint of the class that assumed the leadership of the independence struggle, the African petite bourgeoisie.

Finally, a major characteristic of this period is that for the first time a large number of writings are published by Africans, both continental and Diaspora Africans, within as well as outside the field of African

Studies. Scholarly or polemical, the new writings were an expression of the rise to self-assertion of the peoples of Africa and of their desire to determine their own destiny. The Africans wrote from a variety of perspectives: (1) as students of the African past and its cultural heritage: Cheik Anta Diop, K. O. Dike, Aimé Césaire, Leopold Sedar Senghor, and the *Présence Africaine* group; (2) as analysts of their own societies under the colonial situation: K. A. Busia, Jomo Kenyatta; and (3) as spokespersons for nationalism, indepedence, and Pan-Africanism: Obafemi Awolowo, Nnamdi Azikiwe, DuBois, Gamal Abdel Nasser, Kwame Nkrumah, George Padmore, Ahmed Sekou Touré, Richard Wright.[76]

Most of these writers were radical in their ideological perspective. Except for Diop's Afrocentric reading of history, the historical and sociological studies were for the most part within the mainstream of liberal historiography and functionalism, respectively. Given their immediate objective, the political writings were basically pragmatic. They did, however, succeed in calling into question the colonial system, and in defending the right of African peoples to self-determination and independence.

Independence, Neocolonialism, and Modernization Theory

With the independence of the African states, new problems arose for the field of African Studies. Instead of dealing primarily with the relationship between Europe and Africa, it had to broaden its scope to include the study of relations between African social groups and between Africa and the world. Critical to both sets of relations was the fact that the African petite bourgeoisie had assumed political power in an essentially unaltered socioeconomic framework, thereby creating a situation with serious consequences for the struggle that African peasants and workers were waging for a better life. This section of the essay looks at the bourgeois analysis of this new situation; the following section examines the Marxist analysis.

The American school of African Studies possessed the best ideological and material means with which to assume a leading role in the study of Africa after 1960. Three interrelated factors help to explain this development. First, the neocolonialist strategy of the United States allowed liberal officials and academics to pose as true friends of Africa, as ardent supporters of decolonization and independence. From the American viewpoint, a carefully planned decolonization process was desirable, for it would not only prevent the enlargement of the socialist camp, but also open up new sources of raw materials, new markets, and new fields of investment for U.S. corporations.[78] This is the principal reason why the New Frontier liberals, whose "sophisticated anticommunism" and neocolonialist objectives were exposed in their handling of the Congo (Zaire) crisis,[79] did not hesitate at the outset to adopt as their own the Pan-Africanist slogan, "Africa for the Africans."[80]

The second and third factors were the desire on the part of U.S. authorities and corporations to know more about Africa and, as a consequence, the comparatively greater availability of research funds for African Studies in the United States. American scholars were invited to advise their government and to help formulate policy toward the countries on which they specialized. Graduate students in African Studies were encouraged, if not required, to conduct field research in Africa for their doctoral dissertations, and government and foundation grants were made available for this purpose. In addition, thousands of African students were admitted to U.S. colleges and universities in the early 1960s.

Given these highly favorable political, ideological, and material conditions, large numbers of Americans went to Africa as researchers. With their characteristic enthusiasm and energy, they produced an abundant literature on the continent. Political studies occupy a dominant position in this literature, due to (1) the dominant role of the political in bourgeois ideology, its "effect of isolation" vis-à-vis economic practice for purposes of masking class domination,[81] (2) the closely affinity between political science and the principal ideological themes of the first "development decade"—"nation-building," "national integration," "stability," and so on, and (3) the favorable disposition of liberal political scientists toward African nationalism. Theoretically, these studies were grounded in what became known as "modernization theory," a synthesis of the theories of social change and economic growth developed by academic sociologists and economists after World War II. This theory became the underlying paradigm of the "developmental approach" in comparative politics,[82] the subfield in which the study of Africa is located.

It would make little sense to show the specific deficiencies of modernization theory in African Studies without making reference to its general characteristics. In the pages that follow, these characteristics are briefly described in an attempt to show that the theory's inability to elucidate and explain African realities is simply a reflection of its general character as bourgeois ideology. This is not to say that modernization theory is merely an apology for bourgeois interests or a simple expression of the immediate interests of the dominant class.[83] It may in fact often be these things, but the important point here is that the "theory" represents a world view corresponding to the class interests of the bourgeoisie.

Philosophically, modernization theory is built on empiricism and formalism, and on the integration model of society, whose major analytical approach in contemporary social science is structural-functionalism.[84] If empiricism and formalism are epistemological obstacles to knowledge of the real as a synthesis of multiple determinations, structural-functionalism is too preoccupied with system maintenance and adaptation to provide adequate tools with which to understand conflict and radical change. A major reason for this conservative bias in comparative politics is suggested by J. M. Barbalet, who writes that "American political science, unlike its European counterpart, developed without questioning the fundamental basis of the society in which its polity operates; and, therefore, is both pragmatic—concerned with the day-to-day affairs of particular and diverse fractional interests, and empirical—focused on visible, computational variables."[85] It is consequently incapable of dealing with the more complex issues of inequality, exploitation, and the class struggle.

The faulty assumptions of modernization theory have already been exposed by Paul Baran, André Gunder Frank, and other critics.[86] They have shown that modernization theory is ahistorical, astructural, and ethnocentric. In the first place, it is ahistorical in its assumption of an original state of underdevelopment. It fails to see underdevelopment as a historical process involving the subjugation of the productive forces of the technologically backward areas of the world to the process of capital accumulation in the economically developed areas. It is therefore unable to establish a historical connection between development and underdevelopment, between the exploitation of the colonial and postcolonial territories of Asia, Africa, and South America on the one hand, and the development of capitalism in Western Europe and North America, on the other.

In the second place, modernization theory is astructural because it attributes underdevelopment to the absence or shortage of some critical factor (capital, entrepreneurship, achievement motivation, etc.), the introduction or improvement of which is likely to bring about development, to the satisfaction of all. By locating all the "causes" of underdevelopment in the poor countries themselves, modernization theory takes the effects for the causes, and through its specific factor analysis deals with isolated parts of the whole without looking at the entire structure of the world capitalist system and its role in creating and perpetuating underdevelopment. By confusing economic growth with economic development, it fails to see that development is a political rather than a purely technical problem, and that it involves contradictions between developed and underdeveloped countries, and between various social classes within the latter.[87]

Finally, modernization theory assumes that development means to become more like the West. Third World countries are depicted as being in desperate need not only of Western capital, technology, and skills, but also of Western values, in order for them to overcome serious and internally specific "obstacles" to development.[88] The conviction that these countries are to be remade in the Western image was strongest among American scholars, for whom the United States was the model of development—the "first new nation," as Seymour Martin Lipset put it [89]—and the terminal station of the train to modernity.[90]

Like intellectuals everywhere, American social scientists are influenced by political developments within their country. Donal Cruise O'Brien has shown that there was a significant shift of emphasis in the modernization studies of American political science from 1960 to 1970: from the advocacy of a democratic ideal during the first half of the decade, to a preoccupation with institutional order during the second half.[91] This shift was related to political developments and their repercussion on the domestic and foreign policies of the United States. These developments—ghetto rebellions, the Vietnam War, and other liberation struggles in the Third World—resulted in the substitution of force and repression for economic and social reforms as primary means of dealing with popular discontent at home and abroad. In the social science literature of this period, this shift is reflected in an interest in the development of Western-style political institutions in the Third World during the first phase, and in a concern with the establishment of any stable institutions capable of maintaining the neocolonial order during the second phase.

In the field of African Studies, these two moments manifested themselves in the optimistic forecasts concerning the "prospects for democracy" in postcolonial Africa on the one hand, and pessimistic warnings on the pervasiveness of political instability and disorder, on the other. The first position is represented by students of decolonization like David Apter, who dealt with the process of "institutional transfer" marking the transition from colonialism to neocolonialism.[92] The second position is best exemplified by Aristide Zolberg's book *Creating Political Order*, published in 1966.[93] Influenced by the conservative ideological positions of the Social Science Research Council's Committee on Comparative Politics,[94] Zolberg sees Africa as suffering from too little rather than too much authority, and advocates the creation of political machines of the American kind as means of maintaining stability.

From the advocacy of democracy to that of order, Africanist political science dealt mostly with the surface manifestations of African political life. Like the functionalist anthropology and sociology on which it built its theories of the political system and its development,[95] it was unable to come to grips with the essential reality of postcolonial Africa, which resides in imperialist exploitation through neocolonialism. Rather than being related to the structure of exploitation and the state that nurtures it, political conflicts and crises were depicted as resulting from one or a combination of the following factors: "primordial loyalties" or "tribalism," inadequate preparation for independence, personality conflicts, and excessive mass political mobilization and expectations.

The party of democracy had taken at its face value the declared commitment of the "Westernized" or "modernizing" elites to meet the challenge of the "revolution of rising expectations" in a positive way, and counted on economic and social development programs to reduce the ever-widening "elite-mass gap" in Africa. More realistic with regard to the ability of the new states to satisfy mass needs, the party of order feared the development of a revolutionary consciousness among the dissatisfied masses. It therefore deemed it essential to demobilize and depoliticize them in order to ensure stability and the maintenance of the system. State-building and nation-building had to take precedence over mass participation and a more equitable distribution of the surplus product.⁹⁶

Thus, in both its liberal and conservative expressions, modernization theory was basically elitist and antisocialist. It served the interests of imperialism and those of the new ruling classes of Africa, who were expected to maintain the neocolonialist connection either through the institutions of bourgeois democracy imported from the West or, failing that, through efficacious repressive structures. A bourgeois ideology, its role was to defend the established, capitalist order.

The Marxist Problematic

In spite of their overwhelming majority in the citadels of academic learning in the West and in Africa, the champions of this antisocialist tendency in the social sciences failed to stem the tide of the Marxist revival. Overshadowed by the modernization orthodoxy during the 1960s, Marxist political economy succeeded in establishing itself as a contending paradigm in African studies in the 1970s. In fact, it had already become the dominant tendency in France,⁹⁷ with the work of Jean Suret-Canale, Claude Meillassoux, Emmanuel Terray, Maurice Godelier, Catherine Coquery-Vidrovitch, Pierre-Philippe Rey, Pierre Fougeyrollas, Gerard Althabe, Jean Copans, and others.⁹⁸ Copans advances three reasons to explain the adoption of an explicitly Marxist perspective in French African Studies after 1960: the political support given to African independence and liberation movements, the close affinity between Balandier's approach and Marxism, and the particular characteristics of neocolonialism, which led to research on "the *economic* roots of exploitation and the *political* and *revolutionary* solutions for the overthrow of exploitation."⁹⁹ The first and last factors are interrelated, and they are applicable to the emergence of a Marxist tendency in African Studies in general.

What major problems have been raised and how has Marxism attempted to solve them? The elaboration of a Marxist problematic, as Copans rightly shows, covers the entire field of social and political studies, from the analysis of traditional social structure in Marxist terms (modes of production, social inequality, political and ideological superstructures, etc.) to the study of colonialism and neocolonialism as forms of imperialist exploitation.¹⁰⁰ According to Copans, this Marxist problematic is heterogeneous in nature, for "the theoretical divergences between Marxists are as numerous as those between Marxists and non-Marxists."[101] This last point is less valid if one excludes from the former group all those "people who call themselves Marxists without having read Marx"[102] or the Marxist classics, people who simply use a Marxist terminology without incorporating a Marxist perspective in their analyses, and vulgar Marxists.[103]

Theoretical divergences with regard to the Marxist perspective proper do exist, and they are a function of differences in political line, the lack of theoretical clarity, or both. Important as they are, political and ideological differences have consequences that are less significant than might be expected for the theoretical status of the Marxist tendency in African Studies today. This situation is a result of the relative infancy of this tendency and the fact that the majority of Marxist publications on Africa are produced outside the continent, and are thus removed from the actual political struggles taking place there.

More important in terms of the ability of the Marxist perspective to claim superiority of analytical power and greater explanatory value vis-à-vis bourgeois analyses is the lack of theoretical clarity. This theoretical confusion stems from a more fundamental weakness in Marxist studies of Africa today, and particularly in the English-speaking world, namely, their tendency toward eclecticism. Whatever its origin, whether in the appearance of a number of competing and partially interrelated approaches—Marxism, "neo-Marxism," dependency theory, underdevelopment theory—or in the relative respectability of academic Marxism, eclecticism has had the effect of sacrificing conceptual and scientific rigor to a disturbing confusion of Marxist and liberal categories of analysis.

John Saul's *The State and Revolution in Eastern Africa* is a particularly good example of this confusion, which reveals itself in his discussion of ethnicity, class, and the state.[104] Instead of elaborating a coherent theoretical framework with the help of interrelated concepts derived from the rich conceptual structure of historical materialism, Saul proceeds with a "theorization" typical of academic political science, taking up interesting hints from a number of writers who deal with unrelated topics. In so doing, he merely reproduces the vulgar sociologism and formalism of academic social science, where exercises in definition are often taken as serious efforts at explanation.

I do not wish to imply that Marxists cannot learn from bourgeois social scientists, for the latter can—and indeed do—succeed in providing adequate analyses of certain issues. My point is that their conceptual and explanatory schemes cannot be incorporated in a Marxist analytical framework without doing severe damage to the dialectical, historical, and revolutionary perspectives of the latter. A new science, Marxist political economy has as its immediate task the demonstration that bourgeois analyses are unable to explain African realities. And it must do so not by pointing to contrary empirical evidence—for is this not the way bourgeois scholars deal with one another?—but by attacking their amorphous concepts with parallel and richer concepts situated in a different problematic.[105]

In spite of the progress that has already been made in this regard,[106] the Marxist tendency in African Studies is still characterized by serious weaknesses in the manner in which concepts are formed and/or utilized. These weaknesses are especially evident in the discussion of the key concept of social class. What, for example, is meant by notions like "class-in-formation," "unformed classes," "fully formed classes," and so on? Are social classes biological phenomena, like flowers, which must grow and blossom? Many Marxists justify the use of such notions on the ground that European class categories cannot be applied mechanically to Africa, where classes are said to be "in the process of formation." At the same time, they hold that "classes do not and cannot exist only in their 'pure' form; there are a variety of transitional forms."[107] What, then, is the "pure" form of which the African variety "in the process of formation" is only a "transitional" form? Can it be anything other than the European ideal type?

These and other evolutionist conceptions are totally alien to Marxism. Unless Africans are somehow endowed with a special magic that excludes them from the general pattern of class formation which obtains in contemporary society, all the proposed qualifications of this nature are simply a convenient way of begging a number of theoretical questions. Class formation, understood as the appearance of distinct classes in a social formation as a result of the articulation of its various modes of production under the dominance of one of these classes, is a historical process. The characteristics of the class structure of *any* social formation are specific moments within this historical process and thus they are never static, nor can they be derived mechanically from the outside. They are determined by the specific articulation of the modes of production and its reflection at the political and ideological levels with the social formation.

Thus, if it is correct to say, for example, that social classes in underdeveloped countries do have characteristics different from those of classes in advanced capitalist countries, it would be a historicist fallacy to maintain that they are consequently "transitional" forms in the process of becoming more like the classes found in the latter countries. The nature and number of social classes in a formation cannot be determined in *a priori* fashion; they can only be established through a concrete historical analysis. What is pertinent for the analyst is to determine the conditions under which an effective class exists, as well as those conditions in which class fractions, strata, social categories, and social movements assume an autonomous political significance as social forces whose struggles are related to class contradictions without being reducible to the latter.

In this light, Marxist class analysis is applicable to Africa in each of its three epochs: ancient, colonial, and postcolonial. In Africa, as in all human societies, social classes are groupings of individuals determined by the fundamental character of the production process and the development of productive forces, and opposed to each other with respect to the distribution of the surplus product. The existence of this surplus, or the difference between the total social product and the necessary consumption by the producers, is a necessary condition of class formation. The sufficient condition is the appropriation of the surplus by nonproducers, who thereby exploit the producers. The imperial and royal states of ancient Africa, like the colonial and neocolonial states that succeeded them, served the purpose of insuring class exploitation and domination. And it is by raising and solving the question of social classes and the class struggle in all the formations under the control of these states that one can hope to understand and explain African social realities.[108]

It is now possible to give a brief outline of the major problems raised in the application of Marxist class analysis to Africa, with reference to five principal issue areas in contemporary African Studies: traditional societies, colonialism, the struggle for independence, the nature of the state in postcolonial Africa, and neocolonialism.

As pointed out above, the study of traditional societies from a

Marxist perspective is fairly well established in France, where it was influenced by the structuralist anthropology of Claude Lévi-Strauss and Balandier's writings on political anthropology.[109] In general, this issue area is characterized by an inconclusive debate over the applicability to Africa of Marx's concept of the "Asiatic mode of production,"[110] and over the other concepts proposed to replace it: Coquery-Vidrovitch's "African mode of production,"[111] Meillassoux's "lineage mode of production,"[112] and Samir Amin's "tribute-paying mode of production."[113] More useful in terms of understanding the connection between Europe and Africa and the role that African rulers played in its establishment and maintenance are the historical studies of Walter Rodney, Meillassoux, A. G. Hopkins, and others.[114]

With regard to colonialism, Balandier's concept of the "colonial situation" and Frantz Fanon's analysis of colonialism as a system of institutionalized violence gave Marxist students of Africa some fruitful elements for analyses.[115] But it was Suret-Canale who contributed the most systematic Marxist analysis of colonialism as a system of economic exploitation, political and administrative oppression, and cultural oppression.[116] The colonial-settler system, which constituted the most vicious form of colonial oppression, has been ably studied by Giovanni Arrighi, Bernard Magubane, Martin Legassick, Harold Wolpe, and others.[117]

As for the impact of colonialism on Africa, there is a high degree of agreement concerning its ill effects on the development of productive forces and the well-being of the peoples of Africa. Walter Rodney's *How Europe Underdeveloped Africa* is the best statement of this majority position.[118] The major dissenting view on the relationship between colonialism and underdevelopment is that of Geoffrey Kay, who sees underdevelopment as resulting from too little rather than too much exploitation.[119] This view, which borders on economism,[120] is rarely discussed in the literature.[121] Whatever the emphasis one chooses, the end result is more or less the same: the development of the periphery was contrary to the logic of imperialism and colonialism.

A factor contributing to the emergence of the Marxist problematic in African Studies, the struggle for independence has been dealt with successfully from the Marxist perspective. Frantz Fanon is to be credited for having opened the debate on this issue from a class perspective, and Amilcar Cabral for having provided the theoretical clarity required for elucidating the nature and objectives of the national liberation struggle.¹²² As a concept, national liberation refers to a reality that goes beyond decolonization and majority rule to include postcolonial struggles against imperialism and the various methods and forms of state through which it continues to operate in the Third World.

Just as the ability of Marxists to analyze the problem of national liberation in a satisfactory manner is a function of the higher level of theoretical clarity they have achieved on this subject, so their inability to achieve a similar result with respect to political dynamics in neocolonial Africa is a function of several factors, one of which is the relative infancy of this issue area as a field of inquiry from the Marxist perspective. Since the pioneering essay by Fanon on the African national bourgeoisie, many of the attempts to build on his great insights have revolved around his notion of a "bourgeoisie of the civil service"¹²³ in a kind of terminological gymnastics characteristic of the journalistic tendency of academic social sciences. Following this tendency, whose popularizers often take the ability to coin a new term or to draw a clever analogy as a substitute for analysis, scholars competed among themselves for the honor of finding the most appropriate term with which to define the governing class in postcolonial Africa.¹²⁴

More serious attempts to arrive at a meaningful definition of this class by correctly locating its place and purpose in the overall structure of a social formation and in the class struggle have also been made, however, but not without some degree of confusion and a number of theoretical errors. Samir Amin, Jean-Pierre Olivier, Mahmoud Hussein, Mahmood Mamdani, Issa Shivji, Colin Leys, and John Saul are among those Marxist students of Africa who have made a contribution in this regard.¹²⁵ The issue of the class nature of the postcolonial state, which I have discussed elsewhere,¹²⁶ occupies center stage in the literature, either explicitly, as in the works of most of the scholars mentioned here, or by implication. In the final analysis, no political economy is intelligible without the analysis of the crucial role the state plays in the economy. Recent developments in the Marxist theory of the state, in particular the outstanding contribution made by Nicos Poulantzas and Charles Bettelheim,¹²⁷ have influenced Marxist analyses of the state in Africa.

The politically relevant study of neocolonialism, like the study of the national liberation movement, is dialectically related to the establishment of a Marxist problematic in African Studies. What is neocolonialism, and how does it operate in Africa today? What is the African response to neocolonialism, and what are the implications of this response for the peoples of Africa? These are some of the questions which need to be answered, and they are related to the question of the nature of the state. To address these questions in a comprehensive manner, Marxists must begin to make a serious effort to study the various forms of capitalist and dependent states in Africa, with a view to determining the prospects for socialism on the continent. The liberation of Mozambique, Angola, Guinea-Bissau, and Zimbabwe has created the conditions for such a study. So far, however, polemical analyses based on sectarian positions have been more prominent than scientifically sound analyses.[128] This is an unfortunate situation, because it affects the ability of Marxists to provide the African masses the tools with which to organize their struggle against imperialism and neocolonialism.

Conclusion

If Marxist political economy has progressively established itself as a more useful paradigm than modernization theory in the study of Africa, it is still characterized by eclecticism and the lack of theoretical clarity. These deficiencies are reflected in all the major issue areas in the political economy literature of African Studies, particularly the portion dealing with postcolonial Africa, and this situation shows why the search for theoretical clarity must be considered the most important task within the Marxist tendency in African Studies today. Theoretical clarity and development cannot be sought for their own sakes, however, for Marxism is above all a practical science, one in which theory and practice are interrelated. In the present historical context, Marxists have the duty to provide African workers and peasants, as well as the liberation movements and workers' parties that guide their struggles, with the tools needed to fight imperialism, colonialism, and neocolonialism. Only with these tools can these forces build a free, just, and more humane society.

Notes

1. V. I. Lenin, *Collected Works* (Moscow, 1950), vol 30, p. 143, cited in Mao Tse-Tung, *Selected Military Writings of Mao Tse-Tung* (Peking: Foreign Languages Press, 1967), pp. 93-94.
2. Alain Badiou and François Balmès, *De l'idéologie* (Paris: Francois Maspero, 1976), p. 67.
3. See Mao Tse-Tung, "On Practices," in *Selected Readings from the Works of Mao Tse-Tung* (Peking: Foreign Languages Press, 1971), pp. 65-84; John Hoffman, *Marxism and the Theory of Praxis* (New York: International Publishers, 1975), chap. 5: "Consciousness as Reflection of Reality," pp. 71-108.
4. There are, of course, bourgeois social scientists who reject this viewpoint. See, for example, Maurice Duverger, *Sociologie politique* (Paris: Presses Universitaires de France, 1968), pp. 11-12.
5. See Manuel Castells and Emilio de lpola, "Epistemological Practice and the Social Sciences," *Economy and Society*, 5, no.2 (1976), 111-114. Martin Shaw, *Marxism and Social Science* (London: Pluto Press, 1975) esp. chap. 4: "Ideology: The Role of Sociology in Bourgeois Thought," pp. 62-89.
6. Badiou and Balmès, *De l'idéologie*, p. 36. For a succinct outline of this view of Marxism as a dialectical theory of historical processes, contradictions, and revolution, see Marx's *Afterword to the Second German Edition of Capital* (1873).
7. These and related concepts are defined in Nicos Poulantzas, *Political Power and Social Classes* (London: New Left Books, 1973), pp. 37-119, and in Samir Amin, *Unequal Development: An Essay on the Social Formations of Peripheral Capitalism* (New York: Monthly Review Press, 1976), pp. 13-30.
8. As a specific type of social relations of production which vary according to the level of development of productive forces, class relations do not occur in every form of society.
9. If Amilcar Cabral is correct in holding that in the colonial territories the struggle involves the colonized people as a whole "against the ruling class of the imperialist countries," he is mistaken in stating that in these territories "it is the colonial state which commands history." For he thus attributes historical change to institutions rather than to the class forces and relations that they reflect. See Cabral, *Revolution in Guinea* (New York: Monthly Review Press, 1972), pp. 68-69.
10. Karl Marx, *Theses on Feuerbach* (1845), Thesis 11.
11. These include V. I. Lenin, Rosa Luxemburg, Antonio Gramsci, Mao Tse-Tung, and Ho Chi Minh. Although he never called himself a Marxist, Amilcar Cabral will be remembered as a revolutionary leader within the Marxist tradition. His lucid class analysis, his commitment to "class suicide" and the formation of a revolutionary workers' party after independence, and the unity of revolutionary theory and practice that he

exemplified in his leadership of the national liberation struggle in Guinea-Bissau made him a true Marxist intellectual and revolutionary leader.
12. Karl Marx and Frederick Engels, *The German Ideology,* Part 1 (New York: International Publishers, 1970), pp. 94-95.
13. Karl Marx and Frederick Engels, *Manifesto of the Communist Party* (New York: International Publishers, 1962).
14. Cabral, *Revolution in Guinea,* p. 110.
15. Henri Lefebvre, *Pour connâitre la pensée de Karl Marx* (Paris: Bordas, 1966), pp. 273-274.
16. Whereas Eurocommunism is a revisionist tendency that reflects the problems and strategies of Communist parties in the West, neo-Marxism is a revisionist tendency of academic Marxists in search of more widely acceptable paradigms for social analysis. On the more important tendency, or Eurocommunism, see Santiago Carrillo, *Eurocommunism and the State* (Westport, Conn.: Lawrence Hill, 1978); Annie Kriegel, *Eurocommunism: A New Kind of Communism?* (Stanford: Hoover Institution Press, 1978); David Childs, ed. *The Changing Face of Western Communism* (New York: St. Martin's Press, 1980); Wolfgang Leonhard, *Eurocommunism: Challenge for East and West* (New York: Holt, Rinehart, and Winston, 1978).
17. Georges Gurvitch, *La Vocation actuelle de la sociologie,* vol. 2 (Paris: Presses Universitaires de France, 1963), chap. 12: "La Sociologie de Karl Marx," pp. 220-322.
18. Antonio Gramsci, *Selections from the Prison Notebooks of Antonio Gramsci,* edited and translated by Quintin Hoare and Geoffrey Nowell Smith (New York: International Publishers, 1971), p. 433.
19. Jean Copans, "Pour une histoire et une sociologie des études africaines," *Cahiers d'Etudes Africaines,* no. 43, 11:3 (1971), 422-447. A shorter version of this article, but one with some poorly translated passages, is published as "African Studies: A Periodization," in Peter C. W. Gutkind and Peter Waterman, eds., *African Social Studies* (New York: Monthly Review Press, 1977), pp. 19-31. All the references below are from the French version, hereafter referred to as Copans, 1971.
20. Copans, 1971, p. 429.
21. This formulation allows for the coexistence of conflicting paradigms, and is thus different from Copans's, for whom scientific practice "justifies, *then* conceals, and *finally* calls into question" the Europe-Africa connection. Copans, 1971, p. 431. Emphasis added.
22. See Louis Althusser, *For Marx* (London: New Left Books, 1977; Verso Edition, 1979), pp. 37-38.
23. Primitive accumulation is the process by which great masses of people are forcibly divorced from their means of subsistence so their labor power can be exploited by their conquerors and/or rulers to acquire more wealth. Africa's role in the crucial phase of capitalist development involving primitive accumulation was noted by Karl Marx in *Capital,* vol.

1 (New York: International Publishers, 1967), p. 751: "The discovery of gold and silver in America, the extirpation, enslavement, and entombment in mines of the aboriginal population, the beginning of the conquest and looting of the East Indies, the turning of Africa into a warren for the commercial hunting of black-skins, signalised the rosy dawn of the era of capitalist production. These idyllic proceedings are the chief momenta of primitive accumulation."

24. See Roland Oliver and Caroline Oliver, eds., *Africa in the Days of Exploration* (Englewood Cliffs: Prentice-Hall, 1965), pp. 8-26, 67-71. For accounts by classical writers, mainly on North Africa and the Horn, see Joseph E. Harris, ed., *Africa and Africans as Seen by Classical Writers*, the William Leo Hansberry African History Notebook, vol. 2 (Washington, D.C.: Howard University Press, 1977). In addition to Oliver and Oliver, the best anthologies of European travel narratives include Charles H. Jones, *Africa: The History of Exploration and Adventure* (New York: Holt and Co., 1875; Westport: Negro Universities Press, 1970); Margery Perham and J. Simmons, *African Discovery: An Anthology of Exploration* (Evanston: Northwestern University Press, 1963).

25. L. K. Waldman, "An Unnoticed Aspect of Archibald Dalzel's 'The History of Dahomey,'" *Journal of African History*, 6, no. 2 (1965): 185-192; Georges Nzongola, *Essai sur le Dahomey* (Brussels: Centre d'Etudes et de Documentation Africaines, 1971), Cahiers du CEDAF 5/71, p. 13.

26. It is difficult to see how Oliver and Oliver, *Africa in the Days of Exploration*, p. 59, can find Mungo Park's observations on African slavery to be "a sympathetic and objective account of slavery from the inside" when Park distorts reality in such statements as: "The slaves in Africa, I suppose, are nearly in the proportion of three to one to the freemen."

27. Roland Oliver and J. D. Fage, *A Short History of Africa*, (New York: New York University Press, 1963), 1968 ed., p. 135.

28. Ibid., p. 135.

29. Ibid., pp. 135-136.

30. Endre Sik, *The History of Black Africa*, 4 vols. (Budapest: Akademiao Kiado, 1970). Oliver and Fage agree with this position, in spite of their emphasis on the lobbying efforts of the antislavery movement: "Nothing better illustrates the exclusive character of the slave trade than the fact that having once abandoned it, Britain immediately proceeded to attack its continued practice by other nations. This was not done out of pure philanthropy or even self-righteousness, but for sound commercial reasons. Since the trade in slaves was so much easier and more profitable than any other African trade, it had to be internationally suppressed before legitimate commerce between Africa and Europe could develop." *A Short History of Africa*, p. 136.

31. Oliver and Oliver, *Africa in the Days of Exploration*, p. 2. This applies to all the writings of this period.

32. Although most journeys were financed by geographical and missionary societies, some, like the 1858-64 Zambezi expedition led by David Livingstone, were undertaken with the encouragement and support of the home government in Europe. In his account of this expedition, Jones writes that "Livingstone was made consul, which gave his undertaking a semi-national character; and the most liberal provision was made for him in the way of supplies, including a small steam launch, the *Ma Robert.*" *Africa,* p. 335.
33. See Karl Marx, "The Future Results of British Rule in India," *The New York Daily Tribune,* 8 August 1853, in Shlomo Avineri, ed., *Karl Marx on Colonialism and Modernization* (Garden City, N.Y.: Doubleday, 1968).
34. Gabriel Palma, "Dependency: A Formal Theory of Underdevelopment or a Methodology for the Analysis of Concrete Situations of Underdevelopment?" *World Development,* 6 (1978): 887.
35. Marx's concept of the Asiatic mode of production is in contradiction not only with the very ontological foundation of dialectical and historical materialism, but also with what we do know of the dynamics of precolonial Afro-Asian societies. According to Eric Hobsbawm, the historical knowledge of Marx and Engels on Africa was "virtually nonexistent." Karl Marx, *Pre-Capitalist Economic Formations,* edited and with an Introduction by E. J. Hobsbawm (New York: International Publishers, 1965), p. 26.
36. In fact, Marx and Engels used the same racist epithets that most Europeans employed to describe Afro-Asian peoples and societies. See Okello Oculi, "On Marx's Attitude to Colonialism," *The African Review* (Dar es Salaam), 4, no. 3 (1974): 459-471.
37. Copans, 1971, p. 431.
38. The best-known colonial settlements in West Africa were French Senegal and British Gold Coast, Sierra Leone, Gambia, and Lagos.
39. Roland Oiver and Anthony Atmore, *Africa Since 1800* (Cambridge: Cambridge University Press, 1967; 2d ed., 1972), p. 105; Oliver and Fage, *A Short History of Africa,* pp. 181-182. Liberia, of course, was a colonial-settler state where Americo-Liberian settlers oppressed the indigenous majority.
40. As Oliver and Atmore, *Africa Since 1800,* p. 103, point out, the partition of Africa is called "the Scramble for Africa" because of the hasty manner in which it was done, the European powers acting "like players in a rough game."
41. These colonies became mandates of the League of Nations. But as mandates of the C type, they were administered as any other colony by the mandatory power. Namibia (South West Africa), for example, virtually became South Africa's fifth province.
42. A prominent member of this lobby and a great publicist for the colonial cause was the American journalist Henry Morton Stanley, King Leopold's chief agent in what was to become the Congo Free State, from 1879 to

1884. According to L. H. Gann and Peter Duignan, *The Rulers of Belgian Africa 1884-1914* (Princeton: Princeton University Press, 1979), p. 191: "Stanley wrote copiously and well. His works, which were translated into French by Gérard Henry, played an important part in shaping procolonial attitudes in Belgium."
43. Morel wrote two major pieces against the Leopoldian system of primitive accumulation, *King Leopold's Rule in Africa* (London, 1904) and *Red Rubber: The Story of the Rubber Slave Trade Flourishing in the Congo* (London, 1906). For more information on Morel and the work of his Congo Reform Association, see E. D. Morel, *History of the Congo Reform Movement*, edited by William Roger Louis and Jean Stengers (Oxford: Clarendon Press, 1968).
44. Palma, 1978, p. 890.
45. V. I. Lenin, *Imperialism, The Highest Stage of Capitalism* (New York: International Publishers, 1939), p. 15.
46. Ibid., pp. 81-86. "National liberation" here implies overcoming dependence vis-à-vis international finance capital; it is not limited to political independence.
47. Palma, 1978, pp. 889-893.
48. Scholar-administrators did exist, and a number of them produced some interesting studies of colonialism, e.g., Lord Hailey (William Malcolm Hailey), Robert Delavignette, Hubert Jules Deschamps.
49. Copans, 1971, p. 432. Emphasis in original.
50. Kathleen Gough, "World Revolution and the Science of Man," in Theodore Roszak, ed., *The Dissenting Academy* (New York: Random House, 1967), pp. 135-158.
51. See Peter Duignan and L. H. Gann, "Introduction: Colonial Research on Africa," in Duignan and Gann, *Colonialism in Africa 1870-1960*, vol. 5: "A Bibliographical Guide to Colonialism in Sub-Saharan Africa." (Cambridge: Cambridge University Press, 1973), pp. 1-32.
52. Originally founded as the School of Oriental Studies in 1916, it was given its present name in 1938.
53. For the institutions of the other colonial powers, see Duignan and Gann, *Colonialism in Africa*, vol. 5, pp. 1-32.
54. Ibid., p. 21-22.
55. Raymond Leslie Buell, *The Native Problem in Africa*, 2 vols. (New York: Macmillan, 1928); Melville J. Herskovits, *Dahomey: An Ancient West African Kingdom*, 2 vols. (New York: J. J. Augustin, 1938).
56. Copans, 1971, pp. 434-435.
57. Ibid., p. 434.
58. Ibid., p. 435.
59. Ibid., p. 436.
60. Lenin, *Imperialism*, pp. 7-8, 109-122; Eric J. Hobsbawm, "Lenin and the 'Aristocracy of Labour,'" in Hobsbawm, *Revolutionaries: Contemporary Essays* (New York: Pantheon, 1973), pp. 121-129.
61. William Edward Burghardt DuBois, *The World and Africa: An Inquiry*

into the Part which Africa has Played in World History (New York: Viking Press, 1947), *The Selected Writings of W. E. B. DuBois,* edited by Walter Wilson (New York: New American Library, 1970).

62. Lord Olivier, *The Anatomy of African Misery* (London: Leonard and Virginia Woolf, 1927; New York: Negro Universities Press, 1969).
63. Godfrey Wilson, *An Essay on the Economics of Detribalisation,* 2 vols. (Livingstone: Rhodes-Livingstone Institute, 1941).
64. Max Gluckman, "Tribalism in Modern British Central Africa," *Cahiers d'Etudes Africaines,* 1 (1960): 55.
65. Copans, 1971, p. 436.
66. Balandier's major work, which was produced during this period, is *Sociologie actuelle de l'Afrique noire* (Paris: Presses Universitaires de France, 1955), translated in English as The Sociology of Black Africa (New York: Pantheon, 1970). The major works of Mercier, Lombard, and Person were published after 1960; their pre-1960 writings can be found in journals like the *Bulletin de l'IFAN* and *Etudes Dahoméennes.*
67. Copans, 1971, p. 435.
68. For a Marxist critique of empiricism and formalism, see Castells and de Ipola, 1976.
69. Jean Suret-Canale, *Afrique noire occidentale et centrale,* 2 vols. (Paris: Editions Sociales, vol. 1, 1961, vol. 2, 1964). Volume 2 is published in English as *French Colonialism in Tropical Africa* (New York: Pica Press, 1971).
70. Thomas Hodgkin, *Nationalism in Colonial Africa* (New York: New York University Press, 1957); Basil Davidson, *The African Awakening* (London: Jonathan Cape, 1955); George Shepperson, "External Factors in the Development of African Nationalism, with Particular Reference to British Central Africa," *Phylon,* 22, no. 3 (Fall 1961): 207-225, "Notes on Negro American Influences on the Emergence of African Nationalism," *Journal of African History,* 1, no. 2 (1960): 299-312; Jack Woddis, *Africa: The Roots of Revolt* (London: Lawrence and Wishart, 1960), *Africa: The Lion Awakes* (London: Lawrence and Wishart, 1961).
71. Peter Waterman, "On Radicalism in African Studies," in Gutkind and Waterman, *African Social Studies,* p. 5.
72. Ibid., p. 5.
73. A. A. J. van Bilsen, *Un plan de trente ans pour l'emancipation politique de l'Afrique belge* (Antwerp, 1955). See also his *Vers l'indépendance du Congo Belge et du Ruanda-Urundi: Réflexions sur les devoirs et l'avenir de la Belgique en Afrique centrale* (Kraainem, 1958).
74. On the role played by this class in the struggle for independence, see Georges N. Nzongola, "The Bourgeoisie and Revolution in the Congo," *Journal of Modern African Studies,* 8, no. 4 (December 1970): 511-530.
75. In addition to his work on Dahomey, cited in note 55 above, see *The Human Factor in a Changing Africa* (New York: Knopf, 1962).
76. Rupert Emerson, *From Empire to Nation: The Rise to Self-Assertion of*

Asian and African Peoples (Cambridge: Harvard University Press, 1960); James S. Coleman, *Nigeria: Background to Nationalism* (Berkeley: University of California Press, 1958).

77. See Martin L. Kilson and Rupert Emerson, eds., *The Political Awakening of Africa* (Englewood Cliffs: Prentice-Hall, 1965). The *Présence Africaine* group was established in 1947 in Paris by prominent French-speaking African intellectuals. The group publishes a journal, *Présence Africaine: Revue Culturelle du Monde Noir,* as well as books and pamphlets. During the 1950s, contributors included the foremost African nationalist intellectuals.
78. Cheikh Anta Diop, *Nations nègres et culture* (Paris: Presence Africaine, 1955), *The African Origin of Civilization: Myth or Reality,* edited and translated by Mercer Cook (Westport: Lawrence Hill, 1974).
79. On the neocolonialist strategy of the United States in Africa, see Stewart Smith, *U.S. Neocolonialism in Africa* (New York: International Publishers, 1974); E. A. Tarabrin, *The New Scramble for Africa* (Moscow Progress Publishers, 1974); Kwame Nkrumah, *Neo-Colonialism: The Last Stage of Imperialism* (New York: International Publishers, 1965).
80. The notion of "sophisticated anti-Communism and the way it informed U.S. actions during the Congo crisis are discussed in Stephen R. Weissman, *American Foreign Policy in the Congo 1960-1964* (Ithaca: Cornell University Press, 1974), pp. 113-254.
81. Poulantzas, *Political Power and Social Classes,* p. 213.
82. Gabriel Almond and G. Bingham Powell, *Comparative Politics: A Developmental Approach* (Boston: Little, Brown, 1965).
83. Martin Shaw, "The Coming Crisis of Radical Sociology," in Robin Blackburn, ed., *Ideology in Social Science* (Glasgow: Fontana/Collins, 1972), pp. 32-44; Shaw, *Marxism and Social Science,* p. 64, makes a persuasive case against such a "reductionist conception of ideology."
84. Ralf Darhendorf, *Class and Class Conflict in Industrial Society* (Stanford: Stanford University Press, 1959), distinguishes between the integration and the conflict theories of society as two basic philosophical models of social science analysis.
85. J. M. Barbalet, "Political Science, the State and Marx," *Politics: Australasian Political Studies Association Journal,* 9, no. 1 (May 1974): p. 70.
86. Paul Baran, *The Political Economy of Growth* (New York: Monthly Review Press, 1957); James D. Cockcroft, André Gunder Frank, and Dale L. Johnson, *Dependence and Underdevelopment: Latin America's Political Economy* (New York: Doubleday, 1972); Henry Bernstein, "Modernization Theory and the Sociological Study of Development," *Journal of Development Studies,* 7, no. 2 (January 1971); Donal B. Cruise O'Brien, "Modernization, Order, and the Erosion of a Democratic Ideal: American Political Science 1960-70," *Journal of Development Studies,* 8, no. 4 (July 1972): 351-378; Aidan Foster-Carter, "From Rostow to Gunder Frank: Conflicting Paradigms in the Analysis of Underdevelopment,"

World Development, 4, no. 3 (1976): 167-180.
87. Economic development and economic growth are not synonymous. Development means an amelioration in the material conditions of existence (food, shelter, clothing, security) of the population. These are what Denis Goulet, *The Cruel Choice: A New Concept in the Theory of Development,* 2d ed. (New York: Atheneum, 1977), p. 241, calls "needs of the first order." For Dudley Seers, "What are we Trying to Measure?" *Journal of Development Studies,* 8, no. 3 (April 1972): 21-36, development means the realization of human personality by overcoming poverty, unemployment, and inequality. Development thus implies a redistribution of a country's wealth in a way compatible with satisfying the basic needs of the population and eliminating poverty. As such, it is primarily a political problem.
88. André Gunder Frank, "Sociology of Development and Underdevelopment of Sociology," in Cockcroft et al., *Dependence and Underdevelopment,* pp. 321-397, makes a devastating critique of the theoreticians of "obstacles to development."
89. Seymour Martin Lipset, *The First New Nation: The United States in Historical and Comparative Perspective* (New York: Basic Books, 1963).
90. Cruise O'Brien, 1972, pp. 355-356.
91. Ibid. This is the theme of the article as a whole.
92. David Apter, *The Gold Coast in Transition* (Princeton: Princeton University Press, 1955), revised as *Ghana in Transition* (New York: Atheneum, 1963).
93. Aristide R. Zolberg, *Creating Political Order: The Party-States of West Africa* (Chicago: Rand McNally, 1966).
94. According to Cruise O'Brien, 1972, p. 353: "The committee was established in 1954. The academic members in 1971 were as follows: Gabriel Almond (from 1954, Chairman 1954-63); Leonard Binder (1962-); Philip Converse (1967-); Samuel Huntington (1967-); Joseph La Palombara (1958-); Lucian Pye (1954-, chairman 1963-); Sidney Verba (1962-); Robert Ward (1958-); Myron Weiner (1962-); Aristide Zolberg (1967-)."
95. See esp. Gabriel A. Almond, "Introduction: A Functional Approach to Comparative Politics," in Gabriel A. Almond and James S. Coleman, eds., *The Politics of the Developing Areas* (Princeton: Princeton University Press, 1960), pp. 3-64; Almond and Powell, *Comparative Politics;* and Gabriel A. Almond, *Political Development: Essays in Heuristic Theory* (Boston: Little, Brown, 1970).
96. In a major volume of the SSRC series on political development, Leonard Binder, James S. Coleman, Joseph La Palombara, Lucien W. Pye, Sidney Verba, and Myron Weiner, *Crises and Sequences of Political Development* (Princeton: Princeton University Press, 1971), see political development as the successive resolution of a series of crises known as identity, legitimacy, participation, distribution, and penetration. For the

party of order, there is no doubt that the "penetration crisis" ought to be assigned top priority in the newly independent countries.
97. If Marxists are not in the majority within the Africanist community in France, their work is clearly dominant in that it is the best known and most influential French literature on Africa.
98. See Copans, 1971, pp. 441-442, and Catherine Coquery-Vidrovitch, ed., *Connaissance du tiers monde: Approche pluridisciplinaire* (Paris: Union Générale d'Edition, 1978).
99. Copans, 1971, p. 439. Emphasis in original.
100. Ibid., p. 441.
101. Ibid., p. 441.
102. Ibid., p. 441.
103. A word of caution about reading Marx and the Marxist classics. Since Marxism is a living science rather than a dogma, such a reading ought to be encouraged, not for the sake of the sterile, scholastic kind of exegesis and polemic, but for the purpose of allowing the committed reader to discover the revolutionary kernel that must be developed further in theory and practice.
104. See Nzongola-Ntalaja, "Marxism and the Political Economy of Africa," *Omenana*, 1, no. 3 (Fall 1979): 141-159, for a critique of John Saul's book and other Marxist analyses of postcolonial Africa.
105. On the general epistemological question involved, see Nicos Poulantzas, "The Problem of the Capitalist State," *New Left Reviews*, 58 (November-December 1969): 69-70.
106. Notably in Marxist analyses of precapitalist social formations and of the struggle for independence in Africa.
107. U. Patnaik, cited in Hashim Gibrill, "Class and Class Struggle in Africa: A Discussion," Unpublished manuscript.
108. Pierre Fougeyrollas, "La question des classes dans les sociétés africaines," in Coquery-Vidrovitch, *Connaissance du tiers monde*, pp. 307-329.
109. Claude Lévi-Strauss, *Anthropologie structurelle* (Paris: Plon, 1974); George Balandier, *Anthropologie politique* (Paris: Presses Universitaires de France, 1969), English edition: *Political Anthropology* (London: Allen Lane, 1970).
110. Centre d'Etudes et de Recherches Marxists, *Sur le mode de production asiatique* (Paris: Editions Sociales, 1969).
111. Catherine Coquery-Vidrovitch, "Recherches sur un mode de production africain," *La Pensée*, 144 (April 1969): 61-78, English trans.: "Research on an African Mode of Production," in G. W. Johnson and M. Klein, eds., *Perspectives on the African Past* (Boston: Little, Brown, 1972), pp. 33-51.
112. Claude Meillassoux, "Le phénomène économique dans les sociétés d'autosubsistence," *Cahiers d'Etudes Africaines*, 4 (1960): 38-67, and *Anthropologie économique des Gouro de Côte d'Ivoire* (Paris: Mouton, 1964).

113. Amin, *Unequal Development*, pp. 13-58.
114. Walter Rodney, *How Europe Underdeveloped Africa* (Dar es Salaam: Tanzania Publishing House, 1972; Washington, D.C.: Howard University Press, 1974), *A History of the Upper Guinea Coast 1545-1800* (London: Oxford University Press, 1970; New York: Monthly Review Press, 1980); Claude Meillassoux, *The Development of Indigenous Trade and Markets in West Africa* (London: Oxford University Press, 1971); A. G. Hopkins, *An Economic History of West Africa* (London: Longman, 1973); Clive Dewey and A. G. Hopkins, eds., *The Imperial Impact: Studies in the Economic History of Africa and India* (London: Athlone Press for the Institute of Commonwealth Studies, University of London, 1978). Although the last two works are not Marxist, they contain a rich array of data on the Europe-Africa connection.
115. Balandier, *The Sociology of Black Africa*, chap. 1; Frantz Fanon, *The Wretched of the Earth* (New York: Grove Press, 1963).
116. Suret-Canale, *French Colonialism in Tropical Africa*.
117. Giovanni Arrighi, *The Political Economy of Rhodesia* (The Hague: Mouton, 1967); Bernard M. Magubane, *The Political Economy of Race and Class in South Africa* (New York: Monthly Review Press, 1979); Martin Legassick, "South Africa: Capital Accumulation and Violence," *Economy and Society*, 3, no. 3 (1974): 253-291; Harold Wolpe, "Capitalism and Cheap Labour-power in South Africa: From Segregation to Apartheid," *Economy and Society*, 1, no. 4 (1972): 425-456.
118. Hashim Gibrill, "Europe and Africa," *Monthly Review*, 35, no. 5 (October 1980): 51-56. This is a review of the book, published as a tribute to Rodney following his assassination on 13 June 1980.
119. Geoffrey Kay, *Development and Underdevelopment: A Marxist Analysis* (London: Macmillan, 1975).
120. Economism is the tendency of reducing all other aspects of social existence to epiphenomena of the economy and of tracing every historical event to some economic cause. Politically, it results in too much focus on short-term economic gains instead of long-run political objectives.
121. On Kay's book, see Henry Bernstein, "Underdevelopment and the Law of Value: A Critique of Kay," *Review of African Political Economy*, 6 (1976): 51-64.
122. Fanon, *The Wretched of the Earth*; Cabral, *Revolution in Guinea*, and *Return to the Source* (New York: Africa Information Service, 1973).
123. Fanon, *The Wretched of the Earth*, p. 179.
124. This competition was joined by non-Marxist scholars like Richard L. Sklar and Irving Leonard Markowitz, who coined the terms "managerial bourgeoisie" and "organizational bourgeoisie," respectively. Sklar, *Corporate Power in an African State: The Political Impact of Multinational Mining Companies in Zambia* (Berkeley: University of California Press, 1975), p. 199; Markovitz, *Power and Class in Africa* (Englewood Cliffs: Prentice-Hall, 1977), p. 208.

125. Samir Amin, "Le développement du capitalisme en Afrique noire," *L'Homme et la Société*, 6 (October-November 1967): 107-119; Jean-Pierre Olivier, "Afrique: Qui exploite qui?" *Les Temps Modernes* (1975), 346 (May): 1506-1551, and 347 (June): 1744-1775; Mahmoud Hussein, *Class Conflict in Egypt 1945-1970* (New York: Monthly Review Press, 1973); Mahmood Mamdani, *Politics and Class Formation in Uganda* (New York: Monthly Review Press, 1976); Issa G. Shivji, *Class Struggles in Tanzania* (Dar es Salaam: Tanzania Publishing House, New York: Monthly Review Press, 1976); Colin Leys, *Underdevelopment in Kenya: The Political Economy of Neo-Colonialism* (Berkeley: University of California Press, 1974); Saul, *The State and Revolution in Eastern Africa*.
126. Nzongola, 1979.
127. Nicos Poulantzas, *State, Power, Socialism* (New York: New Left Books/Schocken, 1979), *Political Power and Social Classes, Fascism and Dictatorship* (London: New Left Books, 1974), and *The Crisis of the Dictatorships* (London: New Left Books, 1976); Paul M. Sweezy and Charles Bettelheim, *On the Transition to Socialism*, 2d ed. enlarged (New York: Monthly Review Press, 1972).
128. See, for example, the debate on Angola in the *Review of African Political Economy*, 14 (1970): 107-110, and 15/16 (1979): 148-153.

www.ingramcontent.com/pod-product-compliance
Lightning Source LLC
Chambersburg PA
CBHW071146070526
44584CB00019B/2683